Liberty, A Better Husband

Liberty, A Better Husband

Single Women in America:
The Generations of 1780–1840

LEE VIRGINIA CHAMBERS-SCHILLER

Yale University Press
New Haven and London

Published with the assistance from the foundation established in memory of Philip Hamilton McMillan of the Class of 1894, Yale College.

Designed by Nancy Ovedovitz and set in Goudy Old Style type. Printed in the United States of America by Vail-Ballou Press, Binghamton, New York.

Library of Congress Cataloging in Publication Data

Chambers-Schiller, Lee Virginia, 1948–
    Liberty, a better husband.
    Bibliography: p.
    Includes index.
    1. Single women—United States—History.   3. United States—Social life and customs—1783–1865.   I. Title.
HQ800.2.C43   1984   305.4'890652   84-3524
ISBN 0-300-03164-5

The paper in this book meets the guidelines for permanence and durability of the Committee on Production Guidelines for Book Longevity of the Council on Library Resources.

1 3 5 7 9 10 8 6 4 2

To the memory of
Katherine Totman Bell
and to
Winona Hyland Chambers

Contents

Acknowledgments

The women in this study held a vision of liberty which encompassed three things: economic independence, a room of their own, and the expansion of the mind in congenial company. These remain the necessities for today's woman scholar. To my enormous gratitude, all were provided me by Radcliffe College in the shape of a postgraduate fellowship at the Mary Bunting Institute from 1978–80. The Lilly Endowment, Inc. generously funded these two years of research and study at libraries and archives in London and throughout the Northeast. The Institute provided not only a well-equipped office, an enthusiastic and professional staff, and the unparalleled resources of the Schlesinger Library, but also an environment rich in the stimulating conversation of other scholars at work on the subject of women in American society. Under the aegis of the Institute, as provided for by the Lilly Endowment, women's historians Nancy Cott, Anne F. Scott, and Ellen DuBois read this manuscript and made valuable suggestions to strengthen it. I thank them for their time, enthusiasm, learned commentary, and deep insight.

The resources of many fine libraries contributed to the research for this book. I extend my appreciation to the staffs of the American Antiquarian Society, the American Philosophical Society Library, the George Arents Research Library of Syracuse University, Butler Library of Columbia University, the Clements Library of the University of Michigan, the Colorado Historical Society, the Connecticut Historical Society, the Eleutherian Mills Historical Library, the Essex Institute, the Friends Historical Library, the Houghton Library, the Huntington Library, the Library of Congress, the Manchester Historical Association, the Massachusetts Historical Society, the John M. Olin Library of Cornell University, the Painter Library, the Pennsylvania Historical Society, the New York Historical Society, the Schlesinger Library, the Sophia Smith Collection of the Smith College Library, the Vermont Historical Association, and Dr. Williams Library, London. A special debt of gratitude is owed to Mrs. Charles R. (Sarah Fussell) Macaulay, who generously provided me with the letters of the Lewis family of Media, Pennsylvania.

No work of scholarship emerges from the private reveries of a single

mind. It is therefore with great pleasure that I acknowledge my intellectual debts to the following individuals. Harold C. Livesay, a master crafts-
man, taught me the art and skill of historical research and writing. I hope
that this book will in some small measure give him pride and repay his
effort, faith, and generous support. The 1980 University of Colorado
Faculty Seminar on Feminist Theory offered criticism of early versions of
chapters 8 and 9. Nancy Mann gave me of her exceptional editing skills
and Hardy Long Frank inspired me with the precision and elegance of her
own prose. Marcia Westkott and Barbara Engel both read this manuscript
in various states and shared with me perspectives from their own research.
All scholars and friends should enjoy the intellectual stimulation and
personal support that these two have provided me.

Many personal debts accumulate over the years. The fun of writing
acknowledgments for a first book is in recognizing the less tangible contributions of those persons who make one's life and work so meaningful. Jane
Curry's wit and wisdom have buoyed me since our days of trial and grace
at the University of Michigan. Marjorie Bell Chambers and William Hyland Chambers have served as models of intellectual commitment. They
have long given their children the freedom and resources to explore and
develop their different talents. We siblings have enjoyed the comfort and
strength of shared experience, laughter, combat, and love. I treasure Ken
for our common values and struggles, Bill for his vision and gentle
strength, Leslie for her courage and perception—all for themselves and
their companionship. Most importantly, I thank Lanning Stephen and
Devon Leith Schiller. This book gestated and grew with my son, whose
resilience and affection uplift me. Two such vibrant children require much
parenting—I could not have given as much to either without Lanning's
love and labor. His contributions to this completed work are too numerous to list but are reflected on every page.

Finally, I would like to thank Mary Kelley, editor of *Woman's Being,
Woman's Place: Female Identity and Vocation in American History* and the
editorial collective of *Frontiers, A Journal of Women Studies* for their permission to use portions of previously published work. My thanks also to
Dean Everley Fleischer of the College of Arts and Sciences at the University of Colorado, Boulder, who provided funds for manuscript typing.

[The article I wrote] was about old maids. "Happy Women" was the title, and I put in my list all the busy, useful, independent spinsters I know, for liberty is a better husband than love to many of us.

—*Diary of Louisa May Alcott,*
February 14, 1868

Introduction

This book is about liberty. It is about independence. It is about the search for autonomy among women in the waning years of the eighteenth and the first half of the nineteenth centuries. It is a study of those "busy, useful, independent spinsters" of whom Louisa May Alcott was one, and about whom she wrote, "for liberty is a better husband than love to many of us."[1] Beginning in about 1780, women of the middle and upper classes, the cradle of bourgeois individualism, manifested a dramatic new form of female independence. In increasing numbers, the daughters of northeastern manufacturers, merchants, farmers, and "poor professionals" rejected the "tie that binds." I will argue that this act was rooted in the desire to pursue autonomy, to explore the self, to expand intellectual and personal horizons, and to serve God and the community through the development and application of individual talents and abilities. In this way, American women internalized the individualistic ethic that grew from changes in the structure and values of the early modern family. In this way, too, they enacted the ideas and values of the European Enlightenment and American Revolution.

In the course of the eighteenth century, the values of individual liberty, personal autonomy, and equality of persons were not articulated solely in terms of the relationship between the individual and the state. Changing family relations also reflected the application of such values to the private sphere. Historians have documented the rebellions of sons against fathers over political authority and intellectual prominence, and the transfer of family property from one generation to the next. They have noted changes in the behavior and meaning surrounding sexual intercourse. They have remarked on shifts in the locus of authority for and the process of mate selection.[2] Considerably less attention, however, has been paid to the impact of such changes on women, whose lives and intellectual horizons did not expand as fully as did men's during this period.[3] Nevertheless, the efforts of women to evade, resist, or surmount the constraints on their personal development, their individual autonomy, and their social experience—and their all too frequent failure to do so—are central to our understanding of the eighteenth and nineteenth centuries in America.

1

In the late eighteenth century, and particularly after the revolutionary war, women searched for a new definition of their proper relationship to the state. This they ultimately found in the role of Republican Motherhood. Even before the war, however, the family served as the arena in which women asserted their individuality and desire for independence. Women gave considerable attention to marital relations. They demanded a new mutuality, a new respect, and authority in family decision-making.[4] Women also began to delay marriage. The average age of women at marriage crept upward while that of men remained fairly stable. A growing number of women never married.[5]

The reasons why women do not marry are complex. They involve both social and cultural factors which influence the rate of marriage in a particular society and period, and also those vagaries peculiar to individual character or family circumstance. In some periods, the marriage market acts to inhibit marriage and to augment singlehood. Perhaps the ratio of men to women in the population is high or low. The costs of supporting a family and the structure of the domestic economy may shape such choices. Society's needs with regard to population have some influence, as do attitudes toward children and child-rearing. The economic and social opportunities available to spinsters and bachelors affect their numbers, as does the social stigma (or lack thereof) attached to singlehood.[6]

In the late eighteenth and early nineteenth centuries, women voiced a number of reasons for never marrying, some of which were fairly traditional. As oldest daughters or last remaining unmarried daughters, some were consigned to family caretaking on the death of mother, sister, or sister-in-law.[7] Others labored as needed contributors to the family income in an increasingly wage-oriented, money economy.[8] Particular individuals deemed themselves unmarriageable and neither sought nor accepted suitors.[9] Yet other women so shied away from sexual intercourse or feared the dangers of pregnancy and childbirth that they avoided marriage.[10] Many rejected individual suitors without articulating any summary judgment about marriage itself.

Of interest to me are the select women in postrevolutionary America who suggested new, more modern reasons for rejecting marriage. For these, the decision not to marry followed from a rigorous assessment of the marital institution that found it wanting and in conflict with female autonomy, self-development, and achievement. Among these were women who internalized a beau ideal or rejected the thought of binding themselves legally, sexually, or intellectually to lesser men. Some expressed a desire for a greater intellectual life than was possible given the confines of marriage.[11] Others felt called to a vocation that could not be realized within the structure and duties of marriage or motherhood.[12]

Many consciously rejected the self-abnegation inherent in domesticity and spoke of their desire for self-actualization.

This book describes one path toward female autonomy and assertion in America—the path of singlehood. It is a path that varying numbers of women have chosen over the course of time, but which has particular significance with regard to the generations of women born between 1780 and 1840. On the one hand, these women represent the beginning of a demographic phenomenon which, until the last decade, uniquely characterized the nineteenth century in America. The number of spinsters in the colonial population was very low—never more than a few percent. The percent began to rise in the last decades of the eighteenth century and continued through the nineteenth: 7.3 percent for women born between 1835–38, 8.0 percent for those born between 1845–49, 8.9 percent for 1855–59. At its height, the trend represented some 11 percent of American women, those born between 1865 and 1875.[13] Although this demographic change occurred over the course of the century, the significance of early nineteenth-century spinsterhood does not rest solely with the numbers.

It has to do with the ways in which certain cultural concepts such as self-improvement, ambition, service, achievement, vocation, duty, and independence were shaped by the structure of gender in America. The women in this book articulated the value of female independence. They talked about the cultivation of the self—the female self. They exhibited a drive toward personal autonomy and expressed it in their single status, in their search for meaningful work, and in their thirst for education. The meaning of "single blessedness" in the antebellum Northeast was directly related to the nature of marriage and domesticity.

This book is based on the lives and writings of more than one hundred northeastern spinsters. By no means a random sample, these women were the daughters of the middle and upper classes, women who had the time, education, and inclination to write diaries or books, or who had books written about them. All these women were white, and with few exceptions were native-born and Protestant. Many were ambitious women in search of achievement, even recognition. It might be said that the sample is weighted in terms of such women because the documents available to the historian are largely those of accomplished or notable women. Those who eked out an existence doing wage labor or living at home caring for aged parents are perhaps underrepresented here, but they are by no means absent from these pages.

The problem of representativeness is always a difficult one for the historian, particularly she who records the lives of an elite or pioneering group. Some crucial points should be kept in mind by the reader. The majority of women who provide the sample for this study have identifiable vocations. While this may seem to set them apart from the majority of women at the time, it should be noted that such vocations rarely provided a living for the unwed woman and should not be seen as careers. Such callings were self-defined and had more significance in terms of personal identity and growth than of economic independence or professional life. Most spinsters, including these, lived at home with parents or siblings and moved between the domestic, vocational, and occupational realms according to the dint of family and economic pressure. Many taught school, for example. Teaching was one of a limited number of occupations open to women. It paid poorly and provided little job security. Teaching was often viewed by both employers and employees as temporary work. Few found in this their life's work or vocational identity, though they often resorted to it as a job, a way of making a living. Teaching made extraordinary demands on physical and emotional strength and only occasionally provided intellectual challenge or spiritual stimulation.

Furthermore, the drive for self-expression, autonomy, and achievement existed in the minds of those teachers who slaved away for little pay or satisfaction as well as those who accomplished something of moment. It touched not only the notable educators Catharine Beecher, Mary Lyon, or Elizabeth Peabody but also the more obscure teachers Laura Lovell, Caroline Weston, and Mary Gilpin. These values characterized many a family caretaker and domestic daughter (such as Carrie Rowland or Guilelma Breed) in addition to the seemingly more independent and public-oriented feminists Susan B. Anthony, Elizabeth Blackwell, or Frances Willard.

Even the achievements of those women who accomplished something of note must not be taken for granted. It cannot be assumed that women in all times pursue achievement as we understand it. The "notable" eighteenth-century woman, for example, was recognized for her housekeeping. Nor can it be assumed that independence is a constant value in human life. The appearance of independent, assertive, achievement-oriented women at the turn of the nineteenth century is a phenomenon that requires explanation.

This study does not exhaust the existing sources on northeastern spinsters in the antebellum period. The difficulty of identifying women by marital status no doubt excluded some from my vision, as did the choice not to pursue more of the famous. It does, however, provide a picture of the single experience from which one can form some generalizations and base future investigation upon. Although relatively few in number, these women comprised a highly visible and articulate minority. They were pioneers who blazed a trail that later generations of American women would follow under rather different circumstances in somewhat altered cultural contexts.

Given that research on Southern and Western women lags behind that of the Northeast, it may be foolhardy to speculate on the degree to which the experience of others resembled that of the women in this study. Nevertheless, I would hazard a few thoughts on the regional specificity of this work. Spinsters characterized the New England population far more than those elsewhere in the country throughout the nineteenth century. To the best of our knowledge, the percent of native-born unwed women in Massachusetts was virtually double that of American spinsters in general: 14.6 in Massachusetts as compared to 7.3 percent nationally in the 1830s, 16.9 to 7.7 percent in 1850, 22.6 to 10.9 in 1870.[14] Yet Massachusetts women were not alone in their drive for expanded horizons and personal autonomy, nor unique in choosing singlehood as their route. I venture to suggest that the same pattern emerged in the South and West as is seen here in the Northeast, but later in the century. It began in the South among women born in the 1840s and 1850s and became prominent there, as elsewhere, among women born after the Civil War.

The proliferation of the discourse on marriage which characterized the antebellum Northeast occurred in more straitened circumstances in the South. Historians of Southern womanhood have suggested that the institution of slavery had a powerful and highly complex impact on that of upper- and middle-class white marriage. The rebellion or independence of white women could no more be tolerated than that of black slaves, for any chink in the hierarchical structure of authority diminished it and carried the threat of demolition.[15] One intriguing story, published by Southern author Susan Petigrue King in 1854, suggests that some women saw in companionate marriage a desirable, but essentially foreign model.

The story follows seven young women who vow to meet again in ten years' time to compare notes on their marital experiences. After a decade, only one remains unmarried—the beautiful and accomplished Caroline Bloomfield, heiress of Oak Forrest. At age twenty-eight, she contemplates a proposal. Before accepting Edward Allingham, her dashing suitor, she reads the letters sent to her by her friends in fulfillment of their promise. The letters provide a grim view of husbands as either profligates or misers, as narrow-minded and authoritarian. Marriage has left these Southern belles burdened with child care and domestic responsibility and suffering from social and personal isolation. Having given up family and female friends in order to marry, they found no consolation or companionship in their spouses, who generally pursued their own interests, sometimes at considerable distance from their wives. Wrote one, "Perhaps you have chosen the wisest course in remaining single. I am very little my own mistress now, with so many claims upon my attention." Although Bloomfield does take a husband, she does so at the instigation of her sister-in-law, a Northerner. Dora Bloomfield criticizes Southern marriage and

Southern women, who "have such a trick of losing their own individuality in the imposing grandeur of the 'he' and 'him' who is the arbitor of their destiny." This ex–New Yorker challenges Caroline to undertake marriage in a spirit of mutuality, urging her to be neither tyrant nor slave, but to be moved only by compromise, compassion, and the ability to "bear and forbear."[16] It is ironic but not surprising to find in an ideal, the mutual respect of companionate marriage, an inducement to a higher rate of singlehood and greater independence among women.

Southern women born in the decades immediately following this study came to adulthood at the end of the Civil War. They faced a transformed society which held for them new opportunity as old barriers to female education and employment fell. Traditional concepts of patriarchal authority in the family and the idealization of the submissive, adaptable, servile Southern lady crumbled with the institution of slavery. The sex ratio (which had been inordinately high in the South) equalized in 1840 and fell below 100 thereafter. The sex ratio is given as the number of men per 100 women, hence a figure above 100 indicates more men than women in a population, and one below indicates more women than men.[17] Women of the middle and upper classes, therefore, faced new expectations with regard to the potential pool of marital partners. In the light of these social changes—the accumulating discontent with and critique of marriage, new social and economic opportunities, and a new constraint in the pool of potential spouses—Southern women began to articulate the same values of independence and achievement that emerged in the Northeast among women of earlier generations. Athough there had been no primary role for unmarried daughters before the war, afterward such women increasingly pursued a vocation or their own advanced education.[18]

Laura Clay (1849–1941) was the daughter of Cassius Clay of Kentucky, whose infidelities marred her childhood home. She lived with her divorced mother, Mary Jane Warfield of Maryland, until her death in 1900. Wrote Clay, "my own unhappy domestic life has left my eyes unblinded to the unjust relations between men and women, and the unworthy position of women." She ran a successful farm and devoted herself to female suffrage. In 1887, she told the Association for the Advancement of Women that, "there is no true liberty when one is dependent upon the will of others for the means of subsistence," and deplored those marriages rooted in economic necessity.[19] Clare de Graffenried (1849–1921) agreed. One of the Labor Bureau's first social investigators, this spinster from Georgia wrote that "the ability to maintain herself honorably whenever she chooses is essential to [woman's] dignity and freedom," whether married or single. Elizabeth Grimball of South Carolina had begun a teaching career during the war. Afterward, she rejected her parents' demands that she come home to live. "I have made up my mind to one thing. I will hereafter act upon my own judgment . . . I will not be a dependent old maid at home with an allowance doled out to me when I could be made comfortable by my own exertions."[20] Eliza Frances Andrews (1840–1931) of Georgia vowed never to marry in 1865, but rather "to pursue the career I have marked out for myself." She wanted to write, and did, although she is remembered for her work in women's education.[21]

As for the West, factors which simply did not exist in the East encouraged female autonomy there. While it may be said that some women exerted a certain independence (through geographical mobility) in coming west, nevertheless, the conditions of survival, the nature of migration, and the scarcity of women encouraged marriage. Among the numbers of single women missionaries and teachers who journeyed west before the Civil War, most married and became pioneer settlers. One estimate suggests a marriage rate (perhaps high) of 80 percent for those six hundred Northeastern spinster teachers sent west between 1848 and 1854 and sponsored by the National Board of Education (founded by Catharine E. Beecher, among others). A variety of occupations, both reputable and disreputable, were open to the woman who remained unwed. For example, the 1850 census for Comanche, Iowa, listed two teachers and two prostitutes—the only unmarried women in town. A study of Virginia City, Nevada, in 1875 revealed that among the adult female population, 68.5 percent were married and living with their husbands; 4.1 percent were widowed; 3 percent were adult daughters living at home; 0.6 percent were teachers; another 0.6 percent were nuns; 5 percent were "fallen" women of no listed occupation other than housekeepers for men with whom they lived; and 8.2 percent were prostitutes. In addition, there were a number of servants, a few seamstresses, laundresses, milliners, merchants, hairdressers, and telegraph operators, many of whom were surely married.[22]

It was the availability of cheap or free land, however, that encouraged single women to come west and enabled them to remain unwed. The Oregon Land Donation Act of 1850 granted claims to both men and women. The law was envisioned as an attraction for women who would provide wives for male homesteaders, and at first the change in law was primarily used to double a couple's holdings. Reforms in the Homestead Act of 1862, however, encouraged women to file for themselves. Olive Johnson White decided at eighteen that she would never marry. In 1866, she came west with her family to Nebraska, in search of a home of her own.[23]

By the 1880s, women were moving west in growing numbers. New research suggests that these were not the reluctant pioneers we have come to expect. Approximately 10 percent of land patents filed in two eastern

Colorado counties in the years prior to 1900 were claimed by single women. This rose to 18 percent after the turn of the century. Significantly, 55 percent of these women proved up their land (a process by which the entrant filed a claim, made improvements such as building a well or a house or plowing acreage, and provided proof of residency over a period of time). Their rate was roughly equivalent to that of male entrants.[24] Some claimed land in order to increase family holdings. As dutiful daughters, they filed on adjoining acreage with the intent of expanding the family plot. Also significantly, they received compensation for their claim, and many sold their land or its produce to advance their own purposes. Edith Kohl observed that a surprising number of women homesteading in South Dakota "had a purpose in being there. With the proceeds of a homestead they could finish their education or go into business."[25] Others filed alone, or in groups of women. In the mid-1880s, Clarissa Griswold of Minnesota heard about young women who had taken adjoining claims in Nebraska. They had built a house which covered a corner of each plot, thereby living and working together during the period necessary to establish ownership. She took a claim near Valentine, Nebraska, and proved up alone.[26]

"Bachelor Bess" Corey and Laura Crews may have been unusual, but they were not unique among homesteading women. Elizabeth Corey homesteaded near Pierre, South Dakota, in 1909 because "there wasn't room for all of us in the house, and I could make out better than any of the others." Frequently subject to proposals of marriage, Corey refused to ally herself with "those long-legged, evil-eyed monsters called men." She wished that there were a law requiring that proposals be verbal because these could be stopped before uttered; written proposals required an answer. Enthusiastic about her work and her property, Bess made a successful homesteader.[27] Laura Crews was the youngest of seven children of a widow who had homesteaded in Kansas and Iowa. She joined the land race in 1893 when the Cherokee Strip was opened in Oklahoma. Cherokee land was to be sold for $1.50 to $2.50 an acre to the first homesteaders to stake their claims. She raced a saddle horse seventeen miles in fifty-nine minutes to locate a good piece of bottomland near a creek. She worked the claim herself for years, living fairly hand-to-mouth before oil was discovered on her property.[28]

I do not wish to romanticize the West as the land of the free. Current research is contradictory on the subject of whether or not the western experience encouraged female independence.[29] The demographics and survival requirements of frontier life tended to encourage both marriage and varied sex roles for women. Whether these provided more independence or merely different constraints is difficult to judge. Nevertheless, the availability of land and the relative freedom from social proscription may have supported a degree of female autonomy by the late nineteenth and early twentieth centuries.

Regional differences are important in understanding family and social developments. I have speculated on the above in order to place this particular study in some regional context. The analyses of the Southern and Western experiences of spinsterhood are subjects for future research. Meanwhile, I believe that the Northeastern women described in this study set the pace and articulated the issues to be played out over the nineteenth century in America.

One final note regarding the relationship of this historical study to contemporary issues in women's studies. Recent literature has addressed the twin issues of autonomy and affiliation. Nancy Chodorow, Jean Baker Miller, and Carol Gilligan have explored the struggle of contemporary American women to achieve autonomy within the context of their relationships with others.[30] It is not a new struggle. This study of the lives of single women in the antebellum period illustrates both continuity and discontinuity in women's search for autonomy. On the one hand, the spinsters of the late eighteenth and early nineteenth centuries were pioneers. Their challenge to traditional female roles broke ground for their descendants and opened new possibilities for thinking about the nature of womanhood. On the other hand, their challenge fostered a reaction at the turn of the twentieth century, an antifeminist reaction that has rendered the present struggle rather different than that of the past. To understand the search for autonomy through singlehood pursued by these early nineteenth-century women is to reflect on the ways in which the idea of autonomy and the context, definition, meaning, and texture of female relationships have changed during the past two hundred years.

1

"Single Blessedness, Blessed Singleness"

The Cult of Single Blessedness

The view of spinsterhood as a fate worse than death is thought not only to represent the attitudes of the nineteenth century, but also the experience of antebellum women. In the absence of serious inquiry into the status, lives, work, and role of single women in America, the assumption remains that the spinster or old maid was a woman of low social status and self-esteem, lacking a positive identity or a viable social role, the object of opprobrium and ridicule. We think of these women as alone and lonely.

So deeply engrained in our historical awareness are such characterizations, that a recently published and acclaimed biography of author Louisa May Alcott presumes that, "in remaining single, Louisa had aligned herself with a group of women who were ridiculed and condescended to. She was tolerated as eccentric, regarded as pitiful and incomplete, probably disagreeable, and as a faded woman, incompetent to attract a man, fit only for the fringes of family and social life."[1] What, then, are we to make of Alcott's own words, written in 1868 as advice to young women, that "the loss of liberty, happiness, and self-respect is poorly repaid by the barren honor of being called 'Mrs.' instead of 'Miss.' " Spinsters, she assured her readers, were as a class "composed of superior women . . . remaining as faithful to and as happy in their choice as married women with husbands and homes."[2] Alcott herself rejected the stereotype of faded hopes and useless lives.

Women's history scholarship has, in the past decade, revealed much about the glorification of marriage and motherhood which emerged in the early nineteenth century as the Cult of Domesticity.[3] We have assumed that a belief in marriage as woman's best and proper destiny necessarily denigrated singlehood as an unnatural state to be avoided at all costs.[4] While some urged "any marriage better than none," nineteenth-century Americans held a variety of attitudes toward singlehood. A character in Charles Burdett's 1858 novel, *Blonde and Brunette*, for example, expressed the sentiment that, "Old Maidhood is a wretched, pitiable condition, to which the most unhappy marriage would be vastly preferable, as life, though wretched, is better than annihilation." Burdett married off his heroine Xanthine Blake in the course of the novel, but left her expressing quite a different view of her lost maidenhood. On her wedding night, Blake recited a poem, "The Convict Cell:"

> Yet like the criminal, who full well doth know
>   His own cursed treason wrought his coming fate,
> Mine heart must reap the harvest he did sow,
>   Whose wicked suasion made me change my state.
>
> But that's the sharpness of the traitor's grief,
> And makes my Willful error past relief.[5]

Xanthine Blake's submission to marriage brought her the sorrow and self-condemnation of one who felt that she had betrayed her better self. The two characters in Burdett's novel thus express contrasting views on the relative merits of marriage and singlehood. Both sentiments found broad adherence.

These conflicting attitudes toward singlehood and single women emerged gradually. Generally speaking, from British settlement to the Civil War, America viewed spinsters as first sinful, then supercilious, and finally singly blessed. Seventeenth-century New England deemed single-hood a sinful state, an evil to be exorcised from community life because solitary women menaced the social order.[6] Rather than allow women at liberty, most communities required the unmarried to live in licensed families headed by respectable, property-holding, church-affiliated men. Family supervision ensured virtue and orderliness, and prevented licentiousness and sin.[7] Single women over twenty-three wore the label "spinster." Those still unwed at twenty-six were dubbed "thornbacks" after an ugly sea skate with sharp spines on back and tail.[8] Although unmarried men also faced temptation in their solitary lives, they suffered no similar obloquy. Believed to be innately more susceptible to evil influences, women bore the brunt of social suspicion and experienced greater condemnation. John Dunton, a Boston bookseller, observed in 1686 that "an old (or Superannuated) Maid, in Boston, is thought such a curse as nothing can exceed it, and look'd on as a dismal Spectacle." Some puritans described old maids as fit only to lead apes in Hell.[9]

By the eighteenth century, the view of the unwed woman had ameliorated somewhat. To be unmarried was disgraceful, a reproach rather than a sin. Society regarded the spinster with more scorn than fear. Satirical literature belittled the old maid as an odd maid, a woman with peculiar personality defects and particular character foibles.[10] In these portraits, spinsters possessed unsurpassed curiosity, childlike credulity, absurd affectations, and spiteful natures. "Ruined health, soured temper, blighted youth" marked the maid abandoned and humiliated by a fickle suitor. Those past their prime exhibited "intolerable peevishness, envy of the young, aversion to the old, an insatiable avidity of conquest, and hopeless aspirations after matrimony."[11]

After the revolutionary war, however, some Americans dramatically changed their attitudes toward marriage and singlehood. At first tentatively, and then with greater assurance, they questioned whether marriage and motherhood comprised women's only true destiny. No longer considered sin or reproach, singlehood came to be held in regard as an expression of "self-reverence." Popular culture lauded women who held high standards for prospective husbands and who vowed to stay single unless they found a mate equal to themselves in morality, integrity, courage, and learning.[12]

Culturally prominent metaphors provided powerful imagery with which to honor such a course. The most popular image to arise in the last decades of the eighteenth and first years of the nineteenth century sprang from the republican ideals of the revolutionary war. In the spirit of the period, a Massachusetts poet referred to herself in 1794 as a "republic." Abhorring tyranny, she allied herself with freedom by remaining single.

> No ties shall perplex, no fetters shall bind,
> That innocent freedom that dwells in my mind.
> At liberty's spring such droughts I've imbibed,
> That I hate all the doctrines by wedlock prescrib'd.
>
> [R]ound freedom's fair standard I've rallied and paid,
> A Vow of Allegiance to die an old maid.[13]

As late as 1865, Mary A. Dodge used this metaphor in a similar way. Journalist, raconteur, political gadfly, and spinster, Dodge criticized the public dismay that accompanied a young woman's rejection of a "desirable offer" of matrimony. "That a woman should not avail herself of an opportunity to become the wife of a man who is well-educated, well-mannered, 'well-off,' seems to be an inexplicable fact," wrote Dodge. "He is her equal in fortune, position, character. Commentators 'cannot see any reason why she should not marry him.' " For Dodge, the important question was not why a woman should not marry but, rather, why she should. In true republican spirit, Dodge insisted that in amplitude of being most women exceeded any particular man; therefore, while "he may be 'just as good as she,' he might not be good enough for her." It not being democratic for a majority to yield to a minority, Dodge urged women to reject such proposals.[14]

While republican imagery dominated around the turn of the century, other popular motifs of female independence pervaded discussions of love and marriage, and equally conveyed society's changing attitudes. In a commercial vein, rich with the mercantile metaphors of a newly emerging market economy, *The Young Ladies Counsellor* urged women to say that,

> [Love] is
> The invaluable diamond, which I give
> Freely away, or else, forever hid,
> Must bury—like the noble-hearted merchant,
> Who unmoved by the Rialto's gold
> Or king's displeasure, to the mighty sea
> Gave back his pearl—too proud to part with it
> Below its price.[15]

Lucy Larcom undertook a variety of occupations: mill girl, teacher, poet, magazine editor, and author of a major autobiography as well as a series of inspirational works. Larcom's poem, "A Loyal Woman's No," contains a principled rejection of a politically and morally reprehensible suitor. Written in the labored imagery of the mid-century's romantic love of nature, it became an abolitionist rallying cry.

> Not yours,—because you are not man enough
>   To grasp your country's measure of a man.
> If such as you, when Freedom's ways are rough,
>   Cannot walk in them, learn that women can!
>
> Whether man's thought can find too lofty steeps
>   For woman's scaling, care not I to know;
> But when he falters by her side, or creeps,
>   She must not clog her soul with him to go.[16]

Such metaphors challenged the view of marriage as woman's sole, best course in life.

The transformation in American views toward singlehood appeared throughout antebellum culture: in the most private expressions of young women talking to one another, to their God, or to their kin; in the journals where they recorded their thoughts about marriage and confirmed their decisions to remain single; and in the didactic and prescriptive literature of the day, the marriage and advice manuals which urged the young woman to remain single rather than to risk her character, eternal soul, and earthly well-being in the lottery of marriage.

The words of women themselves provide the most startling evidence of a cultural reassessment of singlehood. Prior to the American Revolution, for example, one young New Yorker reflected on "the many Disadvantages that Accrues to our Sex from an Alliance with the other." But she could not reconcile her feelings about marriage with "the thought of being D[o]omed to live alone," and believed that few women in 1762 would voluntarily accept "the appellation of Old Made." The heart-rending diary of Rebecca Dickinson, a Hatfield, Massachusetts, seamstress, showed her obsession with her single status. Night after night, she returned home in loneliness, grief, and despair. She cried herself sick, "that others and all in the world was in Possession of Children and friends and a hous[e] and homes while I was so od[d] as to sit here alone."[17]

In the postrevolutionary era, however, young women began to talk about "the honourable appellation of old maid." They acknowledged that spinsterhood was "a situation that may be supported with great dignity." A Pennsylvania Quaker asserted that, "It is not marriage or celibacy, gives merit or demerit to a person, but a life ordered in the fear of the Lord." In more secular terms, a Massachusetts woman declared that as far as she and her single sisters were concerned, "we are as well of[f] as a grate many that is marr[i]ed. There is none without thar troubles as I Se[e] Marr[i]ed or not marr[i]ed."[18]

Some of these women chose to postpone or to forgo marriage. One New England maid told a close friend in 1782 that she would keep her maiden name. "I think it is a good one and am determined not to change it without a prospect of some great Advantage." This woman, to whom was attributed a "Love of Independence," married only late in life. A New Jersey spinster rejected "many offers" of marriage. Seemingly a most desirable mate, this "sensible and engaging," even "very superior," young woman determined to retain her freedom by never marrying.[19]

With the dawn of the nineteenth century, young women discussed the import of the marital decision. They evaluated the limitations and benefits of marriage and singlehood in terms that their grandmothers could not have imagined. Many agreed with well-known editorializers and advice-givers like Jason Whitman, Charles Butler, or Artemus B. Muzzey, who maintained that, "A single life is not without its advantages while a married one which fails . . . is the acme of earthly wretchedness."[20]

Both Eliza Southgate of Maine and Eliza Chaplin of Massachusetts eventually married, but as adolescents they debated with intimate friends the virtues and limitations of marriage and singlehood. Southgate wrote to her semisophisticated urban cousin, Moses Porter in 1800 that, "I do not esteem marriage absolutely essential to happiness, and that it does not always bring happiness we must every day witness in our acquaintances." She agreed that the single life was often considered a reproach to a woman but asked, "Which is the most despicable—she who married a man she scarcely thinks well of—to avoid the reputation of an old maid—or she, who with more delicacy . . . preferred to live single all her life?" In the summer of 1820, Eliza Chaplin wrote to her good friend Laura Lovell that she and her sisters had engaged in a similar conversation. Chaplin abhorred the disgust and contempt in which so many of the married couples she knew held one another. Although they "submit to the chains of hymen, and verbally acknowledge them silken . . . their conduct tells another tale," she wrote. Rather than endure the "unhappiness, that exists where minds are 'fettered to different mold'—and rather than be subject to the 'eternal strife' which in such cases prevails," Chaplin preferred "ever [to] remain in 'single blessedness,' and deem it felicity thus to live."[21]

Many undertook similar discussions with friends and family and came to similar conclusions. The beautiful Philadelphia philanthropist Rebecca Gratz (who may have served Sir Walter Scott as a model for Rebecca in *Ivanhoe*) wrote that she did "not know why married life affords so few examples [of happiness], it must surely be their own faults who choose their destiny when it is otherwise." Clementina Smith, daughter of a Brandywine Valley manufacturer, embraced her reputation as a member of the society of "old maids," and assured her friends that she was "safe against all invasions," and that her "territory" was "proof against every attack." She would be "*always* the same C. B. S." Samantha Vail, on the occasion of a family marriage, reminded her cousin, Susan B. Anthony, that she had always said she "*would* live an old maid" and she still said so. "I know I shall enjoy myself better." Mary Barton warned her sister Clara that she was "to[o] independent to marry any one." She suggested that together they keep "Old Maids Hall."[22]

Challenges to traditional attitudes about women's role and women's destiny became so widespread in the antebellum period that the Young Ladies Association of Oberlin College conducted debates in the 1840s and 1850s on such questions as "Is married life more conducive to a woman's happiness than single?" and "Is the marriage relation . . . essential to the happiness of mankind?"[23] Previously, women had not deemed these subjects debatable. Marriage was a fact of life. From marriage flowed all else of importance—a woman's social role, her status, any economic security she might have, and her identity in the family and community, in the church and body politic.

---------◄◉►--------

In comparing singlehood and marriage, antebellum women's literature (that literature both didactic and fanciful, written for women, and much—but not all of it—by women) favored marriage as that state in which women's character would be most fully developed and in which men and society would be best served. Yet few authors went so far as to suggest that marriage was the only true life for women or that any marriage was better than none.[24] Indeed, most took a balanced view in which they qualified their approval of marriage and acknowledged the potential benefits of the single life.

Women's literature limited its support of marriage in three ways. First, it recognized marriage as the best life *only* where the marriage was "true"—that is, where it was characterized by mutuality rather than male dominance. Spinster Ellen Maitland believed "that a married life is the happiest condition on earth, *when* the husband and wife are bound together by an undying, changeless affection—*when* they are mutual helpers in each other's trials—*when* they voluntarily bear each other's burdens." Mary A. Dodge, also known as author Gail Hamilton, found in the commonly used phrase *kind husband* proof of the relations deemed "proper" but not "true" in marriage:

Compared with a cruel husband, I suppose a kind husband is the more tolerable; but compared with a true husband, there is no such thing as a kind husband. You are kind to animals, to beggars, to the beetle that you step out of your path to avoid treading on. One may be kind to people who have no claims upon him, but he is not kind to his wife. . . . His wife is not his inferior, to be condescended to, but his treasure to be cherished, his friend to be loved, his advisor to be deferred to.

She heatedly objected to those who believed that such an attitude denigrated marriage. Dodge insisted that, on the contrary, she valued marriage and would not have it desecrated with so patronizing and oppressive an attitude as "kindness." She deemed marriage sanctified only when undertaken by equals and when based on mutual respect.[25]

Second, women's literature qualified its support of marriage by acknowledging that such ideal marriages were the exception rather than the rule. The heroine of "The Happy Bride" felt that "the unfortunate experience of several of her married friends, had given her a distaste for matrimony, and though she believed it an institution calculated to give the greatest amount of benefit to the largest class of the community, she doubted its utility with regard to her own individual experience." Alice Cary's novel *Married, not Mated* detailed the marital histories of numerous couples tragically flawed because the partners had chosen poorly and had held false ideas of marriage.[26]

Finally, women's literature confirmed the potential happiness of the single life. Catharine M. Sedgwick in her novel *Married or Single?* contended, "that there might be golden harvests reaped in the fields of single life, that it was not a condition to be dreaded, scorned, or pitied, but infinitely preferable to the bankruptcies of married life." Ellen Maitland assured her classmates that "A single life has its own happiness too, different in its kind from marriage yet differing little in its degree." Aunt "S.," the primary character in Louisa Tuthill's *The Young Ladies Home*, advised her niece, "You will think me prejudiced perhaps, in favor of my own condition, because I seem to you so happy." She felt that her niece, having idolized her, had prematurely rejected the idea of marriage. In attempting to give a more balanced picture of the single life, Aunt "S." admitted sadness at not holding the first place in any heart. Yet her niece believed her to be loved by everyone and followed her into "single blessedness." Mrs. Carvill, narrator of "An Old Maid," admonished a male companion that while she believed "the happiness and respectibility of a woman is most permanently secured by a good marriage," she recognized in the spinster Miss Atherton her "beau ideal of female excellence"—a description with which he agreed.[27]

Yet however qualified these authors were in their view of marriage, and however much they acknowledged the possibility of fulfillment in singlehood, they ultimately esteemed marriage more highly, even when speaking as single women. Susan Jewett recorded in the *Ladies' Repository* that she had never heard her maiden aunt say, "in view of all she had seen of the checkered lot of conjugal partners in the world, that she was thankful she had escaped their peculiar trials." Despite her recognition of the "golden harvests of singlehood," Catharine M. Sedgwick gave her heroine Grace Herbert "a happier fate" and married her off at the end of the novel. Even the critical Gertrude became the "happy bride." Ultimately, then, the didactic literature of this period presented an ambiguous portrait of marriage as an institution. It contained both a carefully constructed criticism of marriage (with the hope of institutional change) and a recognition of the potential richness of single life (without an unqualified affirmation of singlehood).[28]

The most striking attitude expressed in antebellum women's literature, however, was the commonly expressed view that it was better to remain single than to suffer the miseries of a bad marriage or to compromise one's integrity in order to gain a husband or a competency. From 1800 to 1860 this attitude found widespread currency in newspapers, periodicals, fiction, and advice books. In 1804, Charles Brockton Brown published an article entitled "Is Marriage or Celibacy Most Eligible, or Is the Matron or the Old Maid the Best Member of Society?" He argued that most women whose sole concern was to find a husband would succeed. By rejecting such a compromise, the old maid "conducted herself with the most perfect propriety, and [acted] a much more virtuous and honorable part in society." Benedict, "The Married Man," agreed in 1817 that "the female who carefully weighs her future state in the balance of good sense . . . may be wooed and not be won; she may be long . . . before she meets those important requisites in the wedded life, without which she prefers all the scorn an unthinking world would heap upon her." *The Ladies' Literary Cabinet* concluded that "A single lady, though advanced in life,/Is much more happy than an ill-match'd wife." Throughout the antebellum period, didactic writers such as Lanfear, Whitman, and Butler supposed that, "if she be agreeably situated as a single woman [let her] rest contented in a state of celibacy, which, though it may lack some pleasures, is far prefer-able to an imprudent or ill-assorted marriage." Artemus B. Muzzey told his readers that, "there is no such thing as an unconditional obligation to marry. . . . On the contrary, [a woman] is solemnly bound still to remain single, to wait until providence indicates to her a prospect of so changing her situation, as to enhance her usefulness and happiness."[29] The frequent repetition of this concept, "better single than miserably married," marked it as a cultural convention.

The significance of such a convention in a period known for its celebra-tion of marriage and domesticity is open to interpretation. Did it serve to affirm or even promote female singlehood, or to strengthen marriage by establishing guidelines for the careful selection of a marital partner? When viewed in the context of women's own thoughts on the matter and the qualified assessments of marriage found in women's literature, the broad dissemination of such a convention suggests a reevaluation of the costs of marriage and the benefits of singlehood in antebellum America. This critique of marriage provided a stimulus to and was an inherent factor in the proliferating discourse on marriage which historians have called the Cult of Domesticity. One aspect of this discourse focused on the process of selecting a life partner and emphasized the gravity, and hence the personal and social significance, of marriage.[30] The convention "better single than miserably married" underscored this message, and in so doing encouraged women to remain single in the face of any but the strongest impetus to marry. Reflected Mary A. Dodge, "the burden of proof lies upon motion not rest, upon [she] who changes, not upon [she] who retains a posi-tion."[31] In true dialectical fashion, the underside of the Cult of Domestic-ity was a Cult of Single Blessedness.

------◆------

The Cult of Single Blessedness upheld the single life as both a socially and personally valuable state. It offered a positive vision of singlehood rooted in Protestant religion and the concepts of woman's particular nature and special sphere. It promoted singlehood as at least as holy, and perhaps more pure, a state than marriage. As developed from 1810 to 1860, the central tenet of single blessedness noted the transitory nature of "domestic bliss" and encouraged the search for eternal happiness through the adoption of a "higher calling" than marriage. Whether moral or intellectual in na-ture, such a vocation was considered "thrice blessed":[32] blessed to the individual because it guarded the integrity of her soul; blessed of God because through it she committed her life to His work; and blessed to those for whom her efforts ensured a better life.

The Cult of Single Blessedness rested on the same idea as that which sparked early nineteenth-century Perfectionism and inspired much of the moral reform of the antebellum period—the radical Protestant belief that the true Christian lives according to the dictates of God's laws rather than man's social and institutional forms.[33] While most people in antebellum society viewed marriage as ordained of God, others saw it as far too humanly a social institution, subject to change and, indeed, in need of reform. Some argued that, whether ordained of God or not, no true Christian should regard marriage as either a primary or a sole goal in life. Through marriage one might serve God's will, but marriage was in and of itself neither everyone's calling nor anyone's salvation.

New England religious tradition acknowledged the primacy of the individual soul. A woman could not expect to receive God's grace through the sanctification of husband or children because God accepted no spiritual surrogates. On judgment day, she would stand before her maker alone, a separate soul. Her religious identity and spiritual state were her own and she alone was responsible for them. One consequence of this emphasis on individual salvation was that it undermined both the cohesion and the sanctity of marriage. Having no guarantee that her husband was saved, a wife had to remain sufficiently detached from him to ensure her own sanctity. Individuation upon death underscored the individual's existential singularity in life.[34]

A woman's task was to determine God's design for her life, open her heart to His plan, accept His grace, and submit to His will. The Great Awakening of religious fervor in early-eighteenth-century America produced an amelioration of the orthodox view that an individual's award of saving grace was God's work alone and granted by His will to a waiting petitioner. By the early nineteenth century, the individual might undertake good works in an effort to "complement God's will" and thus obtain grace.[35] Conversion—the acknowledgment of past sin, the acceptance of God's grace, and the assumption of God's direction over one's future life—was thought to prepare women for marriage. It came to actually preclude marriage. Some women found that God's will destined them for another calling and required of them duties other than wife and motherhood.

For "getting married" did not answer "life's great end," according to the anonymous author of the 1853 book *Single Blessedness*. He reminded his audience of their duty and destiny as immortal beings and urged them to fill their hearts with high and holy aspirations:

> Life has import more inspiring
> than the fancies of thy youth.
> It has hopes as high as Heaven.
> It has labor, it has truth.
>
> It has wrongs that may be righted.
> Noble deeds that may be done;

> Its great battles are unfought,
>   Its great triumphs are unwon.
>
> There are crushed and broken spirits
>   that electric thoughts may thrill:
> Lofty dreams to be embodied
>   By the might of one strong will.[36]

A 1852 short story, "The True Object of Life," urged women to determine their individual course in life and to define their appropriate sphere in accordance with the talents and gifts God had given them. The author depicted the lives of two young women endowed with intellect, social grace, and moral faculty. One studied to be a scientist and the other a moral philosopher. "Whatever motives others may attribute to us," they said, "we have followed that course which would best promote our own eternal happiness, and every one may be allowed to choose that pathway which [she] loves, provided it will enable [her] to attain the true object of this mortal life, that is, a preparation for heaven."[37]

Antebellum culture correlated goodness with usefulness, and usefulness with happiness. Everyone gave lip service to the aphorisms that "diligence is indissolubly bound to virtue" and "labor is worship." In *A Woman's Thoughts about Women*, an advice book for the young, Dinah Mulock posited that the single woman's time was her competency, and the purpose to which she put that time, her long-term investment. Women, she said, "hear that with men 'time is money'; but it never strikes them that the same commodity, equally theirs, is to them not money, perhaps, but *life*—life in its highest form and noblest uses—life bestowed upon every human being, and for which every one of us, married or unmarried, woman as well as man, will assuredly be held accountable before God." A woman must therefore spend her time wisely, purposefully, and usefully. Not only did her heavenly future depend upon this, but so too did her earthly happiness. Work, said the popular British essayist Anna Jameson, "is at once the condition of existence and the condition of happiness."[38]

Noble work of high purpose provided the only meaningful satisfaction in life. The author of *Single Blessedness* reminded readers that earthly happiness, including the joy of family relationships and human love, rests in the material present and is therefore transitory. He recommended taking a long-term view which emphasized the more lasting joys of spiritual growth, moral action, or dedication to one's God-given calling. Mulock advised young women to consider carefully the "choosing [of] a definite profession." She recognized that the selection of a vocation rather than a husband required a woman to "quit the kindly shelter and safe negativeness of a private life, and assume a substantive position." Granted that "women's natural and happiest life is when [they lose themselves] in the

exquisite absorption of home, the delicious retirement of dependent love,"
Mulock asserted it to be no "small thing for any woman—be she governess, painter, author, or artiste—to feel that, higher or lower, according
to her degree, she ranks among that crowned band who . . . are elected to
the heaven-given honour of being the Workers of the world." Jameson
defined happiness and harmony for women, as she did for men, as consist-
ing of "finding in our vocation the employment of our highest faculties,
and of as many of them as can be brought into action."[39]

Single blessedness, then, assured unmarried women eternal grace and
social approval if they assumed a noble work in a good cause at the
inspiration and command of their God. An aura of holiness surrounded
such women. As one social commentator wrote: "She ranks with the
glorious sisterhood, who have gone to the rest of the sainted. Let her soul
be baptized into the spirit of God, let his glory be the seal of her deeds,
and she shall at length join that great company, who 'neither marry, nor
are given in marriage,' but are as the angels of God."[40] In 1832, the
Ladies' Magazine and Literary Gazette recorded the story of Charlotte
Lander. As a young woman, she took it upon herself to raise her two
brothers after her parents' deaths. She founded, taught, and administered
a school. She demonstrated the qualities of Christian charity, usefulness,
and good character. She did not marry, because "hers is not a nature
which needs worldly distinction, or a virtue which rests upon earthly
supports. She is a candidate for a higher prize, even the crown of glory
which fadeth not away." Single blessedness preceded and was the earthly
corollary of that "purer stage of existence" which would last through
eternity.[41]

Single women were commonly described as belonging to the "maiden
sisterhood." Many believed that they followed a sanctified path and spoke
of having taken on the life and the ritual of a novitiate. Lucy Larcom, for
example, thought of the communion service "as a marriage supper," a
symbol of the reunification of her life "to the divine life." Elizabeth Blackwell talked of "tak[ing] the veil" when she dedicated herself to medicine.
Mary Moody Emerson referred to herself as a religious recluse and to her
abode as a monastical cell. She subjected herself to daily spiritual examination and acknowledged certain "days of appointment" when she withdrew
from human society to meditate and live "alone with God." Ellen Maitland
described her life as a "pilgrimage." Such language suggests participation in
a formal religious order and, though familiar terminology in a Catholic
country, is striking in Protestant New England.[42]

The imagery of godliness, sanctification, and the novitiate which characterized the Cult of Single Blessedness associated singlehood with celibacy. It identified the spiritual love of God as more holy and of greater
eternal value than the carnal love of man. In this way, the cult promoted

singlehood as a purer state of being than marriage. This view owed much of its weight to that early-nineteenth-century ideology which correlated women's greater moral purity with their lesser sexual drive.[43]

In 1842, *Godey's Lady's Book* published the story of "Aunt Mercy." It illustrated the virtues of celibacy and spiritual love and portrayed the dangers inherent in unregulated desire and passion. Young Fanny lived with her Aunt Mercy and found in her life of Christian devotion, abstemiousness, purity, and discipline an estimable serenity and spirituality: "[T]hey created in me a thirst for sacred knowledge, a spirituality of feeling as sublime as it was novel—I could exclaim with a more heavenly ambition . . . 'I feel immortal longings in me.' "

One evening, Fanny asked her aunt about the past. Why had she remained single when most women married? Fanny thought that perhaps Mercy "believed it sinful to love any one else but God." The question stimulated a frightful display of grief and agitation as Mercy remembered the tragic consequences of a youthful passion. From this scene, Fanny drew the following lesson:

I trembled when I reflected on the might of human passion—"Terrible, terrible," thought I, "must it be in its strength, if even in decay it can triumph over the coldness of age, and roll its wild waves over the traces the spirit of God has written on the soul." Let *me* be spared its desolating power; let me live on as I now do, calm and passionless, striving to walk in the path of duty, with an eye directed to heaven, and a heart devoted to God.[44]

The author denied to Fanny her state "secure from temptation." Fanny devoted herself to passionlessness and taught her disciples its virtue. She converted her husband to Christianity and encouraged him to give himself over to the ministry and an ascetic style of life. Fanny's influence also transformed her sister—a willful, sexually alive, emotionally unrestrained woman who had heretofore spoken derogatorily of Aunt Mercy's ways. When her desperate grief for a dead husband drove the sister to madness, Fanny persuaded her to adopt Aunt Mercy's discipline. For the first time in her volatile life, she found peace of mind.

Other antebellum literary portraits acknowledged God's sanctification of the celibate. In Catharine M. Sedgwick's *Married or Single?* the married sister wrote to her unwed sibling approving her dedication to a life of single blessedness: "I am almost willing to admit that yours is the highest calling, and to receive St. Paul's opinion, as still of authority, that 'the single are happier if they so abide.' " Harriet Beecher Stowe's novel, *The Minister's Wooing*, revolved around the promise of young Mary Scudder to marry the local minister after she received false confirmation of her beloved's death at sea. Mary sadly decided that she must honor her commitment, despite the error in which it was made. On learning of the changed circumstances, the minister held counsel with himself: "What is it that thou art fretting and self-tormenting about? Is it because thou art not happy? Who told thee that thou wast to be happy? Art thou nothing but a vulture screaming for prey? Canst thou not do without happiness? Yea, thou canst do without happiness, and instead thereof, find blessedness." Having concluded that blessedness had been Christ's portion and so might do as well for him, the minister released Mary from her promise.[45] As in the story of Aunt Mercy, however, a certain ambiguity remained. Stowe's bachelor and Sedgwick's spinster eventually married. Both authors resisted the fully alive portrait of the happy and fulfilled celibate.

Didactic literature debated the merits of celibacy in relation to physical health, happiness, and spiritual well-being. In the early nineteenth century, celibacy carried few of the negative connotations associated with it today. Science and religion upheld the value of preserving the "life forces" rather than expending them in intercourse or masturbation. It was only in the second half of the century that doctors began to espouse the theory that the use and lubrication of the sex organs through intercourse was necessary to physical and mental health.[46] Commentators, philosophers, and critics debated Paul's admonition to the Corinthians to remain unmarried. Had the apostle meant to confer greater heavenly blessing on the single life? The Reverend John Clowes, in a book-length treatise, argued that Paul proved inconsistent in his advice and listed chapter and verse in which the Bible upheld marriage. "Nowhere," he asserted, had God "ordained celibacy, either by command or by commendation." The author of *Single Blessedness* heartily disagreed, insisting that celibacy emanated directly from Christ's example, from his approval of the beloved siblings Lazarus, Mary, and Martha, and from Christian doctrine. "Paul nowhere intimates that the reasons, which he concedes may induce a person to marry, are based on any thing that dignifies, or ennobles, or spiritualizes human nature. But he does say, that a single life is favorable to our spiritual well-being and growth in grace." While some questioned whether the apostle's words or example had "ever prevented a man or woman from marrying," they agreed that his words provided "a great deal of encouragement" to the celibate.[47]

In America, as in England, proposals occasionally arose to institutionalize single blessedness in the form of a nondenominational religious order. The idea generally held less appeal in this country, lacking as it did both an established church and the Anglican hierarchical structure.[48] The single woman in New England was not envisioned as a woman of the cloth. As Catharine M. Sedgwick said of Civil War nurses, "What a different consecration from that of nuns! How blessed are the single women of our country, who have found such new and blessed channels for those affections which crave and will have a channel!"[49] "New England

Nuns" were unbound by convent walls. Their piety took active form. Their spirituality increased not by the repetition of prayers or observation of the canon, but by the cultivation of the intellect and a commitment to human welfare.

Even so, some Protestants spoke enviously of the support which dedicated women found within the Catholic church. Catharine Beecher, for example, mourned the financial failure of her Cincinnati school and denounced the shortsightedness of the Protestant community that allowed it to be replaced by a Catholic girls' school.

The clergy and leaders of the Catholic church understand the importance and efficiency of employing female talent and benevolence in promoting their aims, while the Protestant churches have yet to learn this path of wisdom. The Catholic clergy exert their entire influence in creating a *public sentiment* that sustains, and even stimulates women to consecrate their time and talents to benevolent enterprises.[50]

Beecher hoped to see the Protestant world unite to support and sustain women who gave their lives to the betterment of society. Established religious institutions could provide individuals with structure, funding, recognition, community, and support staff. Although never institutionalized in this fashion, the Cult of Single Blessedness, with its affirmation of the vocational life of the unmarried woman and its celebration of celibacy, provided an ideological framework that upheld spinsterhood as a worthy state of being.

Approval, however, was limited. The literature defining single blessedness adhered to a narrow spectrum of appropriate activity and correct decorum. Women were expected to undertake their work in a truly feminine spirit of humility and selflessness. The radical implications of an ideology that placed such emphasis on the individual interpretation of God's will and the value of a substantive life were not generally acknowledged.

Both the cult's approval of singlehood and the restraints it placed upon single women were embodied in the new images of spinsters that arose in the popular fiction of the early nineteenth century. These portraits of "old maids" presented admirable women, women of courage, integrity, goodness, and loyalty. The new spinsters were feminine women, loved and valued by their families, their communities, and their disappointed beaux.

Stories featuring these model antebellum spinsters attributed to them remarkably similar characteristics and defined for them two appropriate roles—the "Maiden Aunt" and the "Sister of Charity." They were not beautiful, but womanly. They came to be single through the tragic end of a love affair or the death of a loved one to whom they remained eternally faithful. They proved to be dutiful daughters and selfless women who cared first for their parents, then for other relatives, and finally for the poor, sick, orphaned, or sinful of their communities. They found the inner peace with which to submit graciously to their fate through religious or intellectual instruction.

Derogatory images of single women and negative attitudes about spinsterhood continued to exist in early-nineteenth-century culture. Popular songs such as "The Old Maid's Lament" and "My Grandmother's Advice" ridiculed the woman who wiled away her courting opportunities. Numerous stories in women's literary magazines featured a character who exclaimed, "I do not wish to remain an old maid!" or "I won't be a nun!" Poems depicted the unwed as the devil's subjects, cramped with spite.[51] But the unmarried women of these songs, poems, and stories were based on character types typical of eighteenth-century European satire. Antebellum American authors utilized these familiar stereotypes in their presentations of Miss Lister, the aging coquette; Flora Enfield, the emotionally unstable pedant; Prudence Hook, the conniving husband hunter; and Hepzibah Pyncheon, the inept and naive child.[52] That such cultural fossils continued to surface in antebellum literature is not so significant, however, as the evidence that these eighteenth-century stereotypes gave way before a more modern and positive characterization of the single woman.

One of the numerous portraits of the new spinster, "The Old Maid of the Family," appeared in the 1830 *Atheneum*. Its heroine, Ellen Percival, fell in love with a neighbor, Edward Neville. Neville's father refused to sanction their marriage when the Percival family lost its fortune. Ellen's parents died, and she took a job teaching in order to support herself and her invalid sister. Some time later, having made his fortune and lost his father, Edward returned to claim Ellen's hand. But Neville had broken his health with hard work, and died in Percival's welcoming arms. The invalid sister ultimately married and took Ellen into her home to assist in the care of house and children. The author concluded his tale with this moral: "No longer an isolated useless being she saw a family who looked up to her as a parent . . . and found that the great exercise of nature, without either talents or splendid beauty, can render their possessors happy, and crown with joy even the last days of 'the old maid of the family.' "[53]

This moral, inappropriately tacked onto the story, reflects the tensions inherent in the Cult of Single Blessedness. The author proved reluctant to endorse Percival's singlehood despite his approval of her character and role. His patronizing tone and the nature of his conclusion contradict the strength and consistency attached to Percival's character throughout the story. Hers was a richly textured emotional life. She never appeared either isolated or useless. She exhibited tremendous talent, dedication, and intellect. She modeled the virtues of antebellum femininity. She was cheerful, patient, and contented. She found her strength and consolation in the Bible. She was pure, pious, and submissive. She lived primarily a domestic life as a surrogate mother and housewife. Essentially, then, she embodied all the qualities of "true womanhood" while remaining unwed.[54] Yet the author felt compelled to add an afterword to ensure that his readers recognized the transitory nature of Ellen's independence, necessitated as it was by family circumstances. She had chosen marriage, although it was denied her. She manifested her dedication to God appropriately in domestic pursuits and family service.

Another portrait appeared in *The Universalist and Ladies' Repository*. A description of the old maid's physical appearance took up much of the copy. Given the stereotype of the unmarried woman as possessing some physical defect which marred her attractiveness and ruined her prospects, the heroine's appearance could not be dismissed without diluting the moral impact of the story. According to the author, Hannah Lane was not conventionally pretty.

Her eyes were most unpoetically gray, no golden ringlets . . . but locks of darkest brown were bound in smooth unpretending folds about her head; she had a complexion by no means dazzling, and considerably variegated by . . . freckles, a form altogether more *embonpoint* than is justified by the approved models of sylphic delicacy; and hands—alas! . . . that in these days of rosy-tipped fingers and lily-white palms . . . should have been red and toil-hardened!

While lacking the beauty of a romantic heroine, Lane nevertheless presented a heroic figure, that of a medieval abbess, a queen, or a classical goddess:

Hannah's eye was . . . lighted with the purest and most intellectual expression, the deepest and tenderest affection. Her cheek . . . [reflected] the ever varying scintillations of a heart susceptible to every ray of joy, and every breath of awe. Her brow was Juno-like in breadth and strong developments. . . . Her form had uncommon dignity and her carriage was eminently commanding.[55]

The author evoked a vision of womanly power and intellect.

Lane came from a poor background. Her parents, at some sacrifice, educated her so that she might marry up in the world. She fell in love with a man "of excellent character and cultivated mind" but too poor to win parental approval. They forbade her to encourage him. Being a dutiful and grateful daughter, she "crushed her own hope, and checked the dawning aspirations of one who sincerely loved her." Remaining true to this first love, Hannah kept other potential suitors at bay. She turned to education for solace and joy. A humble woman, she never flaunted her knowledge, although "that godlike brow of hers was filled with the rarest poetry, almost bursting with its intensity." She dedicated herself to others: "a treasurer of the poor, a physician to the sick, a saviour to the sinful, she lived and died an honored, respected and beloved maiden." Like Ellen Percival, Hannah Lane provided a model of female piety, and though a more complex character, she fulfilled the traditional role of female benevolence.[56]

The decisions of such women to remain single demonstrated courage and depth of moral character. Their actions reflected values of love, loyalty, and integrity. As womanly women, they lived useful social and domestic lives. As a result, they were respected by their communities, in which they were well integrated members. At no time in these stories were they identified as odd, isolated, or deviant. Yet the social approbation implied by this literature was clearly conditional.

Only so long as these women enacted certain roles, those traditionally associated with the female gender, did antebellum women's literature affirm singlehood as beneficial to women, to their families, and to their communities. Only so long as spinsters exemplified the qualities of true womanhood, self-abnegation in particular, were they portrayed as womanly despite their marital status.[57] Furthermore, the circumstances by which they came to singlehood indicated that these women did not freely choose their status but made the best of difficult, even tragic, situations. Such qualifications suggest that single blessedness existed in a social context in which the single life remained carefully circumscribed.

Whatever the inherent contradictions in the Cult of Single Blessedness, its emergence, along with that of other more liberal views of singlehood and the single life, provides evidence of dramatic changes in early nineteenth-century America. What floodtide had so rearranged the cognitive and emotional landscape? What sea change had come to the Northeast? The shifts in these surface currents were the result of upheavals on the ocean floor. For changing attitudes both influence and reflect changing behavior and social structure. Although the general population statistics for the eighteenth and early nineteenth centuries remain incomplete, data generated by a number of separate community studies indicate a demographic trend toward delayed marriage and increased singlehood beginning in the last decades of the eighteenth century and continuing through the nineteenth.

An analysis of Quaker marriage and family patterns at the end of the eighteenth century found growing proportions of women never marrying. A study of Philadelphia Quakers in the industrial age confirmed this trend: by the generation of 1840, some 40 percent of these women would never marry. Greater singlehood among the daughters of the Hingham, Massachusetts, well-to-do began in roughly 1780. In 1830, 14.6 percent of native-born women in Massachusetts never married. By 1855, some 17 percent of native-born white women in one western city in New York State were still single from age thirty to thirty-nine, well beyond the average age of marriage for women of this period.[58] A variety of social and demographic factors contributed to this trend and established the familial and societal context which gave birth to the Cult of Single Blessedness.

2

"Hymen's Recruiting Sargeant"

Factors Influencing the Rate of Marriage

"Why is Single Life Becoming More General?" asked *The Nation* in 1867.[1] One traditional answer attributes the increase in nineteenth-century American spinsterhood to a discrepancy in the ratio of men to women in the northeastern population. As early as 1765, women outnumbered men in some parts of New England. By 1850, some 20,000 "surplus" women inhabited the New England states, and another 19,000 lived in the Middle Atlantic region. These figures doubled in the following decade.[2] The outmigration of men from more established to less settled areas of the region or to the West shrunk the pool of prospective husbands for women in Massachusetts, Connecticut, and Rhode Island. The reverse situation on the frontier meant that "the spinster preserved her single 'blessedness' only by insistent struggle."[3] While the sex ratio is one factor that influences the rate of marriage, it accounts for the phenomenon of proliferating female singlehood only partially. It merely provides a rough indicator of available partners.[4]

The sex ratio is determined by taking the number of men and women in the population at a given time in a given place with no view to their past, present, or future marital status or eligibility. However, a number of factors mediate between the absolute number of men and women in the population pool and the number of mated couples which emerge from it. The means of mate selection and cultural definitions of eligibility are such factors. These are discussed later in the chapter. Demographic definitions of eligibility are also important.

The age distribution of the population and the ratio of men to women within marriageable age groups influence the rate and age of marriage. A simple sex ratio obscures the fact that the majority of the population in the late eighteenth and early nineteenth centuries was less then twenty years of age, and that marriage during one's teens was a rarity. Nativity is an additional factor influencing marital eligibility. Among the foreign-born in America, there were more women than men. An examination of

the native-born population in Massachusetts in 1860 indicates that
women outnumbered men by roughly 20,000 individuals out of a population of some 960,000. "Excess" women, then, made up only 2 percent of
the entire native-born population. The sex ratio for the state of Massachusetts was 96 for the native-born, hardly a sufficient cause for a 17 to 20
percent rate of singlehood among those women in the thirty-five to fifty-
four-year-old age group.[5]

A close study of that same 1860 Massachusetts census reveals population patterns which tell us more about the factors influencing the rate of
singlehood than does the sex ratio per se. It suggests that unmarried
women followed employment opportunity. Six counties represented almost three-quarters of the total "surplus" of women. All of these had
manufacturing or commercial centers. Men continued to outnumber
women in rural agricultural areas and small towns.[6] The "surplus" of
women reflected local employment patterns and consisted, to some extent, of a temporary, mobile labor force that followed established trade
routes in search of economic opportunity in newly emerging regional
markets. Roads, canals, turnpikes, and navigable rivers connected manufacturing and commercial centers to rural areas, villages, and towns. Geographic mobility carried young women away from their families and communities in their premarital years and facilitated their return to areas with
more favorable sex ratios, as they prepared to marry.

In the antebellum Northeast young women, in numbers as large if not
larger than young men, commonly left their parents and siblings and set
out to work. In 1830, girls aged fifteen to nineteen formed a smaller
proportion of the population than boys of comparable ages in the villages
of Middlesex County, Massachusetts. These women swelled the populations of the nearby city of Portland and the neighboring mill towns.[7]
Among the Lowell, Massachusetts, mill girls, 97 percent of whom were
single and 80 percent of whom were aged fifteen to thirty, some 36
percent returned home to marry men from their home towns, while
another 23 percent sought out partners from other rural communities.
Such women temporarily delayed marriage in order to procure an economic advantage. They married late or they married men of equal or
younger years; but 85 percent of them eventually married.[8]

An examination of the Boston census of 1845 reveals the frequency of
marriage for men and women, and the age at which both married. A
higher percentage of women than men married over the course of their
lifetime in Boston. At any given age, however, a greater percentage of
men than women lived in the married state. Men married at older ages
than women and tended to remarry more frequently when widowed or
divorced. A higher percentage of women than men married during their
twenties. Men began to marry in percentages equal to women in their

early to mid-thirties, and thereafter married at a higher rate than women. Boston was a merchandising and manufacturing center which attracted young women for whom there were substantial numbers of jobs. Some 30 percent of women in the still eligible age group from thirty to thirty-nine were single. No doubt some of these women were widowed or divorced rather than never married.[9]

The pattern suggested here is similar to that of Utica, New York, ten years later. The majority of native-born white women in Utica remained single until the age of twenty-five. Between the ages of twenty-five and twenty-nine, 45 percent remained unmarried. Seventeen percent were still unwed at ages ranging from thirty to thirty-nine. As in Boston, males in Utica married later than did females. Only 18 percent were married by the age of twenty-five, and only 50 percent by age thirty.[10]

The significance of these figures rests with the transformation of the family economy in America between the mid-eighteenth and mid-nineteenth centuries. The family economy was based on a domestic system of production, tied to the cultivation of farmland or the exercise of a craft in a small shop. This way of life was characterized by generational continuity. Gradually, unimproved land, land which could be handed down from one generation to the next, disappeared across New England and the Middle Atlantic states. The lives of one generation could no longer parallel or better those of the previous generation, at least not in the same community. Then, after 1789, when Slater's mill was founded, America entered the industrial age. The growth of commercial markets drew young people, both boys and girls, away from the farm. The development of urban economies, characterized by the decline of artisan production, the rise of the factory, and the increase in white-collar work spurred individual family members to disperse in search of wage income and career advancement. Family members no longer worked as a unit—each with his or her own tasks and each contributing a necessary part to the whole. Now, the labor of each family member was divisible into separate wages, salaries, or profits—for each had individual access to the marketplace. The family economy now depended on the willingness of family members to contribute to it. They might equally well reject family loyalty in favor of individual goals.[11]

Unmarried women followed traditional women's work as it moved out of the home between 1790 and 1835. Whether they were working for their own advancement or that of their families, they chose their occupations carefully to obtain those positions which provided better pay, geographic location, and benefits. As necessary or advantageous, they moved from domestic service (everyone's last choice), to shoe-binding, hop-picking, sewing, teaching, or mill work (the highest paying occupation).[12]

During the second quarter of the nineteenth century, unmarried women found themselves actively recruited to serve as the primary labor force in the textile mills of New England. They made ideal laborers, for they were eager to leave rural communities for more cosmopolitan settings and were free of domestic restraints and concerns, desirous of the wages offered, intelligent, and highly motivated. Most women worked in the mills for only three to five years. A few made of mill work a highly paid, highly skilled, and high-status occupation prior to 1850, when managerially imposed measures raised hours, lowered pay, and undercut benefits, causing many native-born, single women to leave the mills.[13]

Women were also gradually recruited as teachers. America needed a greatly expanded, publicly supported school system. Technologically sophisticated modes of production required educated workers. A participatory democracy demanded an educated electorate. A nation intent on self-sufficiency sought the ideas, inventions, and creative consciousness of an educated population. The expansion of public education provided more teaching opportunities than young men could fill. They were absorbed in advanced education or professional training. As early as 1760, a few women found jobs in public schools as summer replacements. By the 1830s, district schools began to hire women to teach in the winter sessions as well. Between 1825 and 1860, roughly one-fourth of all native-born, New England women taught school for some years of their lives, usually the years prior to marriage.[14] The channeling of unmarried women into teaching paralleled the increasing responsibility borne by women for child-rearing and socialization. The transmission of culture from one generation to the next received greater and greater attention in these years and became more clearly identified as women's work. As economic development produced social change that both expanded the need for education and spread the responsibility for that education beyond the home, women's social mandate to acculturate the young enlisted the unmarried. They could provide a mobile work force and devote large amounts of time and attention to their work.

Americans recognized the importance of the role played by unmarried daughters in a transformed economy. The Massachusetts State Legislature evaluated the economic role of single women in their state at mid-century. Social concern over the welfare of 29,166 "surplus" women led the governor to propose that the state ship these women to Oregon and California, where the predominantly male population created a more propitious environment for marriage. Upon investigation, the legislature concluded that the disproportion of the sexes should be left to regulate itself, because the sudden emigration of these women (some of whom were foreign-born Irish immigrants) would shatter both the state's economy and its standard of living. "The whirring music of millions of spindles would be silent as a sepulchre, while the mistresses of more than a hundred thousand dwellings would be in consternation, from the catastrophe of such a withdrawment of one, two, or three, or more domestics from their premises." The legislature concluded that those persons concerned with providing young women with husbands must realize that it was "not the single women who have most need of sympathy, as regards maintenance and happiness . . . they are, as a class, as industrious, as successful, as independent and as cheerful as are their married sisters."[15]

Young antebellum women moved in and out of their parents' homes many times before leaving permanently, if ever, to marry. Some went to "make their fortunes" or win their independence in the same fashion as their brothers. Others participated in a communal effort to protect or augment family resources during an economically volatile period. Families utilized the labor of daughters in order that sons might continue educations or training to prepare them for high-status, well-paying, professional, or white-collar jobs. Many sons, particularly those in cities, lived at home well into their late twenties or early thirties during this period, relying on family support for an extended time. When upwardly mobile sons finally left the paternal home on the road to career advancement and a home of their own, their unmarried sisters returned to care for aging parents. No longer did the son who once inherited the family land or shop also inherit the responsibility for care of his parents.[16]

Whether out of love, loyalty, or a well-internalized sense of duty and responsibility, daughters assumed their new role. They were proud of their ability to earn wages, support themselves, and contribute to family well-being. But the relationship between a daughter and her family had significantly shifted. Families now might rely on the earnings of daughters without the authority to command their wages. A tension and a balance existed which had not before and which differed from family to family according to circumstance and habit.

Several examples illustrate the range of responses. Elizabeth Jennison of Maine was quite independent. Her assistance was sought by her family after a particularly bad series of harvests. Her father requested the money and assured her of repayment. In a second instance, the Woolson family held sway over daughter Elizabeth, dictating the type, place, and timing of her employment. Elizabeth Woolson undertook a variety of occupations, mostly on a temporary basis. She felt that the Lowell mills offered "privileges" in excess of those to be found elsewhere, and so hoped to extend her tenure there. Her sister Martha, however, summoned Elizabeth home to Milford, Massachusetts, in 1833, saying that she counted on her help with the family for the winter. "I have always depended upon your coming till now and do not feel willing to give it up," she wrote.[17] Later, when her parents objected to a return to Lowell because the mills were too far away and too unhealthy, Woolson found less desirable employment closer to home.

In a third situation, Louisa May Alcott felt primary responsibility for her family's financial well-being. She regularly contributed to the family finances, while keeping her own counsel about how much to spend and for what purpose. Louisa May felt keenly the embarrassment and want of a childhood in which her philosopher father, Bronson Alcott, could not provide for his family. She remembered her mother begging her grand-father for the means to keep them after the deprivation of months spent on a nonproductive collective farm inappropriately named "Fruitlands." Alcott grew up with a fierce determination to support herself and pro-vide for her family. When her oldest sister Anna left their Concord, Massachusetts, home for a teaching position in Syracuse, New York, Louisa decided that it was time to "seek [her] fortune." As she later recalled, "I set forth with Mother's blessing one rainy day in the dullest month in the year."[18]

Alcott engaged in several occupations over the course of her working life: seamstress, governess, teacher, nurse, housemaid, and author. She noted in her diary her accumulated earnings from each source. In April of 1855, for example, she recorded her winter's earnings as fifty dollars for teaching school for one quarter, fifty dollars for sewing, and twenty dollars for writing stories (published in the *Saturday Evening Gazette*). Always her goal was first to support herself and then to help her family. "I want to realize my dream of supporting the family and being perfectly indepen-dent. Heavenly hope."[19]

Although concerned about family needs, Louisa May clearly governed her own employment and allocated her own wages. She delighted in buying her mother a shawl, in paying for art lessons for sister May, and settling the family debts one by one. But *she* decided which debts to pay and when, and which items to support and how. She expressed all of this in a letter to Anna, in November 1858.

Mrs. L[overing, for whose daughter Alice, Louisa served as governess] is to pay me my "celery" each month, as she likes to settle all bills in that way; so yesterday she put $20.85 into my willing hands, and gave me Saturday P.M. for a holiday. This unexpected $20, with the $10 for my story (if I get it) and $5 for sewing, will give me the immense sum of $35. I shall get a second-hand carpet for the little parlor, a bonnet for you, and some shoes and stockings for myself, as three times round the Common in cold weather conduces to chilblains, owing to stockings with a profusion of toe, but no heel, and shoes with plenty of heel, but a paucity of toe . . . and if any of my fortune is left, will invest it in the Alcott Sinking Fund, the Micawber R. R., and the Skimpole three per cents.[20]

In struggling to meet her family's obligations, controlling the distribution of her wages, and taking responsibility for her own support, Louisa May Alcott gained considerable individual autonomy. "Things go smoothly," she wrote to her father, "and I think I shall come out right, and prove that though an *Alcott* I *can* support myself. I like the independent feeling; and though not an easy life, it is a free one, and I enjoy it. I can't do much with my hands; so I will make a battering-ram of my head and make a way through this rough-and-tumble world."[21] If she did not make a "fortune," she ultimately lived rather well on her writing. By the age of forty, she felt that she had accomplished her mission, having made herself and her family secure.

The importance of a daughter's contribution to the family economy, when combined with her move out of the parental home in search of wage work, augmented her importance and independence within the family constellation as well. It contributed to a changing self-image and encouraged women like Alcott to think of themselves as individuals. Harriot Hunt, for example, recognized the connection between the independence of paid work and the growth of individual autonomy. Taking a paid position set her apart from other young women of her age and class. It carried a personal significance greater than the sum of her wages. "Hidden within," she wrote, "was my own consciousness of its importance." She labeled this as her first year of "individual responsibility" and attributed to it a growing sense of personal destiny.[22]

With the shift in the traditional family economy came a decline in patriarchal authority. One of the first things to give way was parental control over their children's courtship and marriage. An increase in premarital pregnancy suggests that family and community control over courtship practices weakened after 1740. Participants rather than parents would seem to have governed premarital behavior.[23] Women also began to marry out of their birth order with greater frequency after 1780.[24] Had parents retained control over their daughters' marriages, they presumably would have marketed them sequentially, thus maximizing each daughter's advantages and insuring the marriage of all of them.

Historical and cross-cultural experience indicates that when the authority for selecting marital partners rests with the family of origin, early and universal marriage results. A system of "free" or individual choice operates somewhat less "efficiently" because men and women must be old enough to make a mature choice, learn appropriate courtship rituals and skills, and undergo a trial-and-error selection process.[25] Changes in both the means of mate selection and the norms defining marital eligibility influenced the rate of marriage after the revolutionary war.

The shift in the process of mate selection accompanied a transformation in the meaning and purpose of marriage. Northeastern families of property and standing gradually separated marital concerns from those of lineage and economic advantage. No longer did they view marital alliances primarily as a means of augmenting family status or assisting in the accumulation of additional resources. Some five hundred eighteenth-century literary magazines reflected a trend toward perceiving marriage in affective or companionate terms, with an emphasis on mutual love and respect. Evidence from eighteenth-century women's writings also shows that personal happiness replaced family considerations as motives for marriage in the minds of many well-to-do marriageable women.[26] Changes in both the definition of a good marriage and the process of mate selection modified the norms which defined an appropriate partner. As daughters demanded more control over the choice of a husband, and as they entertained a new conception of the marital relationship, they looked for different attributes in their suitors.

The selection of a mate absorbed much personal and cultural attention. Considerations of property, status, or influence were easier to measure than those of affection, respect, and potential happiness. All understood the significance of the marital choice when marriage "bound man and woman together for life and subordinated woman to man."[27] A potential mate might not turn out to be all that he appeared during courtship. Because social custom granted to men the initiative in courting, women looked carefully to their defenses. As Eliza Southgate observed in 1800, "The inequality of privilege between the sexes is very sensibly felt by us females, and in no instance is it greater than in the liberty of choosing a partner in marriage; true we have the liberty of refusing those we don't like, but not of selecting those we do."[28]

Counselors and commentators warned young women to take extreme care in courtship. "Better had she been bound to the dead . . . than bound to a living mass of pollution, to one whose principles became more . . . her horror, as they are daily betrayed," advised Artemus B. Muzzey in *The Young Maiden*. A woman so rash as to throw caution to the wind had only herself to blame and only God to turn to in her despair. "She must dwell upon her sorrow, which her own folly hath produced," admonished the didactic literature of the day. Women should marry *only* when convinced that religion provided the "operative principle" in the character of her intended. His religion served as security for his marital behavior. "In common prudence," she should "consider [it] as wanting, until she is thoroughly convinced of its existence."[29] Cautioned the poet, "Link not thy life and fate to His" without looking good and hard, because:

> . . . thou with cowering gaze wouldst start
>   To see the monster there,
> The demon sleeping in that heart,
>   The shrine of dark despair . . .

His soul is shorn of every good,
  There's crime within his blasted heart,
Upon his crimson hand there's blood,
  Gaze at the picture, now, and start![30]

The character of a potential husband concerned prospective brides because of his power over them. But romantic ideation also played a role.

The emergence of romanticism with its emphasis on romantic love led to the development of a cultural "beau ideal" whose character was as clearly defined as that of the "true woman." According to *The Ladies Counsellor*, an ideal suitor should be:

pure-minded, sincere and spotless in his moral character . . . a *self-denying* man; rejecting the wine cup, tobacco, and all other forms of intemperance. . . . He should be an *energetic* man, or he will sink in seas of difficulty. . . . He should possess a *cultivated intellect*, otherwise he will either keep you in obscurity, or subject you to incessant mortification by his ignorance. He should be industrious; if he is a drone he will pluck down ruin on your habitation. He must be *economical*; a spendthrift husband will sow the field of your afterlife with the seed of . . . thorns and briars. He must be *benevolent*, since a covetous man, who sacrifices his own soul at the shrine of the gold demon, will not hesitate to immolate your happiness on the same accursed altar. He must not be a proud man; for pride is always cruel, selfish, remorseless. He should not be *clownish* on the one hand, nor *foppish* on the other, because a stupid clown and a conceited fop are alike mortifying to the sensibilities of every woman of good sense. He should not be deformed or badly disfigured . . . [or] your heart will recoil from him. Above all things, he ought to be *religious*. No man's character is reliable, if his virtues are not founded on reverence and love for his Creator.[31]

"Spare no efforts," advised the author of *The Young Maiden*, "in ascertaining how near the individual who addresses you approaches this glorious ideal. An utter failure, should present . . . an insuperable obstacle to a connection with him for life."[32]

By the 1840s, some commentators ascribed to great expectations the rising incidence of singlehood in the northeastern United States. "With this transcendental view of the passion," wrote one, "a young woman is likely to conclude that, for herself, she shall never see the person whom she can love. No angelic being in human form, will ever cross her path, and therefore she shall always remain single." Another asked how "is any man or woman to blame for living single if they cannot find a person that has a 'celestial' ingredient in the 'compound?' " *The Nation* suggested that one result of better education was that fewer cultured people married because they looked so carefully at potential mates and found it so difficult to identify individuals with whom they might bed down in lifelong partnership. "Their requirements are more exacting; their standards of excellence higher; they are less able to find any one who can satisfy their own ideal."[33]

Women confirmed that high standards presented an obstacle to marriage. Catharine M. Sedgwick, for example, wrote that romantic imaginings "may account for my never responding to the sentiments of those who sought me." She doubted whether a "true man" could be found in America. Elizabeth Blackwell (while teaching in Kentucky) admonished her family, "Do not imagine I am going to make myself a whole just at present; the fact is I cannot find my other half here, but only about a sixth, which would not do." Cornelia Hancock reported back from her Freedman's Bureau school that, "Men, as the generality of them appear in public life, have few charms for me, and if thee has any lingering hopes of my yet in my advancing years committing matrimony. thee must keep thy anticipations in good check for the Freedman's Bureau or Secessia will not be likely to send to thee a valuable son-in-law."[34] Phoebe Cary's poem "Do You Blame Her?" described the rejection of a suitor by a woman who claimed to value fully both the suitor and the proffered alliance.

> And yet, though never one beside
>   Has place in my thought, above him,
> I only *like* him when he is by,
>   'Tis when he is *gone* I *love* him.

> But if he were here, and knelt to me
>   With a lover's fond persistence,
> Would the halo brighten to my eyes
>   That crowns him now in the distance?[35]

Not likely, she concluded. These women demonstrated a remarkable degree of self-assurance as they measured their suitors' qualities and found them wanting.

"Marital trauma" resulted from the separation of marriage from property concerns and family control, the romantic idealization of the marriage partner, and women's greater freedom to chose a mate.[36] Given women's perception of the gravity of the marital choice and the perils of misjudging male character, it is hardly surprising to find that the approach of the age for marriage, the appearance of a suitor, or the promotion of a proposal induced great anxiety. Spinsters Catharine M. Sedgwick and Susan B. Anthony both suffered nightmares in which they envisioned the terrible consequences of marrying unworthy men.[37]

The decline of patriarchal authority in both family and marketplace had one other powerful effect on daughters. They began to differentiate themselves from their families of origin and to develop an individual identity. Letters and diaries of early-nineteeth-century spinsters suggest that the process was well under way. Mary S. Gilpin and Sallie Holley consciously set out to distinguish themselves. Like many another daughter in this period, Gilpin was named for her mother, Mary Dilworth. She chose to change her name in 1829, at the age of nineteen, to differentiate herself from her mother—a highly assertive act for the time. Remarking that, "I do often find myself under the necessity of signing 'junior' which I dislike very much," Gilpin solved her problem by adding a middle name. She considered the selection crucial in representing her personality, values, and self-concept to the world. She sought a pretty name, but feared that an exotic one might suggest too frivolous or romantic a nature. Gilpin considered the names of two close friends and chose "Sophia." Thereafter, she consistently signed her name "Mary S." or "Mary Sophia Gilpin."[38]

Sallie Holley asserted her individuality by changing the spelling of her name in the 1850s. Named "Sally" for her mother and grandmother, she altered the ending when she became an antislavery lecturer and agent. In her early thirties, Holley proclaimed her new identity and new vocation with a change in name.[39] The psychology of renaming one's self, that is, the desire so to differentiate one's self from one's forebearers, implies a new sense of individuality and independence on the part of women. Families respected and used these new names, thereby acknowledging the separation of their daughters' identities from that of the corporate paternal family.

Americans required an intellectual framework within which to understand and define the new roles of various family members given the changing composition and function of households. As the economic importance of the household shifted from its capacity for production to that of consumption, the wife and mother was no longer appreciated for the yarn she spun, the clothes she made, or the food she grew and prepared. She purchased such items and gave her time and attention to the intellectual development of her children and the emotional support of a mate who worked outside the home to supply his family with needed goods and services. Both the cults of domesticity and of single blessedness emerged to legitimate the new order, reinforcing a gender division of labor which placed women in the home to bear and rear children, to guard family privacy, and to care for the affective, spiritual, and intellectual needs of their families.

The ideology of "woman's proper sphere" glorified the autonomous nuclear family. In return for her contribution as guardian of morality, keeper of the private realm, cultural arbitrator, and socializer of the young, a woman was promised domestic harmony, financial security, the love and gratitude of husband and children, the praise of the community, and a home of her own. The contract implied by the cult of domesticity—that which allocated to men the public and economic sphere and to women the private and domestic one, which balanced responsibilities and promised

equal rewards—often broke down through no failure on the part of the wife
or mother. Every nineteenth-century woman knew in her immediate circle
about those women who were abused, widowed, or deserted by their husbands, about wives suffering economic privation due to a husband's business
or personal failure, about children left without mothers and husbands without wives due to their deaths (often in childbirth), or about parents left
unprovided for in sickness and old age by children who had moved away in
search of economic mobility. The autonomous nuclear family, so revered in
the contemporary iconography, could not sustain itself.

Into the emotional and financial turmoil resulting from such "failures,"
were urged a "reserve army" of unmarried, available women. They moved
in and out of the homes of siblings, parents, and more distant kin in order
to nurse family members, care for elderly parents, aid sisters in childbirth,
keep house for widowed fathers, bachelor brothers, or invalided sisters,
and nurture motherless nephews, nieces, or younger siblings. Their presence and participation in the household enabled middle-class Americans
to cope with the social upheavals of economic development and population redistribution.

Unmarried women provided similar social services in the community,
caring for the welfare needs of a rapidly urbanizing and industrializing
nation that had not yet developed social or governmental agencies to
provide for the health and social service requirements of its working population. In an earlier time, social welfare had been the concern of church
and civic leaders. They took responsibility for the indigent, orphaned,
mad, or widowed of their small towns. Their response took the form of
exiling the needy from the community, assigning their care to a local
family in return for such labor as the dependent could provide, or requiring some service to the community in recompense for modest (even mi-
serly) maintenance.[40] The rigor of such a system lent to it a certain
efficiency. People perished or moved on. But such a solution could not
begin to address the sheer magnitude of the problem in the early industrial
period. While many of the social service needs of the transient, unem-
ployed, or new industrial workers continued to be met by households,
increasingly private charity and reform associations organized relief systems, libraries, orphanages, literacy and Sunday school classes, temperance societies, and hospitals. Single women played an important role in
staffing and enacting the programs of these associations.[41] They brought to
all a bracing mixture of human concern, financial assistance, and moral
coercion.

During this transition period, the services of single women eased the
costs of social and economic change and made viable the family structure
which characterized the new industrial order. By promoting the positive
images of Maiden Aunt and Sister-of-Charity, the Cult of Single Blessed-

ness affirmed the importance of the domestic support and social benevolence provided by these women. The Reverend George Burnap, for example, in his *Lectures on the Sphere and Duties of Woman*, referred to single women as Providence's "corps de reserve." "As no wise general brings all his forces into the field at once, but keeps back a part to supply deficiencies, to remedy accidents, to throw in their aid at emergencies," he wrote, "so are unmarried women stationed up and down in life to aid the weak, to take the places of those who are cloven down in battle, or of those who refuse to do their duty." In his view, single women provided comfort and aid to the destitute and forgotten, toiled over household duties neglected by gay young things, aided overburdened mothers and sisters, or nursed the ill.[42] Others agreed that, the "present life would lose many of the comforts, and much likewise of what is absolutely essential to the well-being of every part of society, and even of the private home, without the unmarried female." The woman who served in such a capacity could be assured of a respected place in the community. Dinah Mulock asserted confidently that the "old maid who deserves well of this same world, by her ceaseless work therein, having won her position, keeps it to the end. Not an ill position either," but "often higher and more honourable than that of many a mother."[43]

The ideologies of "woman's proper sphere" and "Single Blessedness" emerged in response to women's new roles in industrial America. Increasingly, they also shaped those roles. Antebellum America became a gender-differentiated society characterized by the separation of women's lives, tasks, and identities from those of men. Women lived in a female world, ordered and defined by female priorities, rituals, relationships, and activities. The emotional viability of singlehood during this period rested in part on the deeply satisfying nature of women's relationships with other women, structured as they were and given meaning by this "separate sphere."

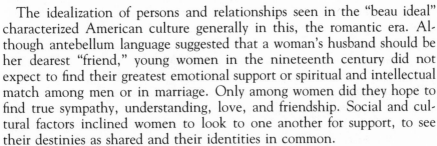

The idealization of persons and relationships seen in the "beau ideal" characterized American culture generally in this, the romantic era. Although antebellum language suggested that a woman's husband should be her dearest "friend," young women in the nineteenth century did not expect to find their greatest emotional support or spiritual and intellectual match among men or in marriage. Only among women did they hope to find true sympathy, understanding, love, and friendship. Social and cultural factors inclined women to look to one another for support, to see their destinies as shared and their identities in common.

Women were raised and educated, matured, grew to adulthood, and passed through the major turning points in their life cycles in the context of a largely female world. Rich interactions between women across the generations often provided a strong base for female peer relationships that fostered and celebrated love between women. Women characterized these "romantic friendships" as beautiful, caring, pure (i.e., morally based and not sexually oriented), and "disinterested" (that is, not rooted in the misleading physiological attractions of sexual conquest or in the economic trade of sex for support). In characteristic fashion, Maria Mitchell wrote, "The love of one's own sex is precious for it is neither provoked by vanity nor returned by flattery; it is genuine and sincere. I am grateful that I have had much of this in my life."[44]

The private papers of antebellum women provide numerous expressions of the value that these women placed on the love of their own sex, the joy with which they gave and received such love, the longing with which they searched for it, and the sorrow with which they regarded its absence. Lucy Larcom wrote frequently of her need for "some one who could understand me fully, love me, and have patience with me through all." In a eulogy to friendship, she wrote:

I do not know if now there is any such friend for me; yet dear friends I have, and more and more precious to me every year. If these were my last words, I would set them down as a testimony to the preciousness of human friendship; dearer and richer than anything else on earth. By them is the revelation of the divine in the human; by them heaven is opened, truth is made clear, and life is worth the living.[45]

Many friends populated Larcom's life: her mentor, Philena Fobes, her student, Sarah Paine, her "sister confessor," Esther Homiston, her idols Elizabeth and John Greenleaf Whittier. She never found a "special friend," but rejoiced in the opening of each new heart to her gentle prodding. As she recorded in May 1861: "Such a glimpse, such a half-unveiling, one has given me today, out of a soul-deep, long-repressed longing for 'something to love.' Ah, that sorrowful need of every woman's heart, especially; yet more joyful than sorrowful, because the longing shows the fulfillment possible—yes, certain. . . . And I am thankful for one more to love."[46]

Some of these women looked to female love to protect them from the dangerous incursions of alien male beings. Men had different values, different qualities, different interests than women. Yet their very mystery was seductively attractive. Marriage required female subordination, loss of self, and separation from beloved family and friends. Yet marriage was supposed to open new vistas to women. In defense against men and marriage, women often turned to other women. As Graceanna Lewis wrote to Mary Townsend, "Thee would shield me from every danger, dearest . . . thee *is* with me to guard and preserve me from many a folly." Carrie A. Rowland urged Emily Howland to send her homilies on spinsterhood so that she might resist the temptation to succumb to the flattering attentions of one or another beau. Rowland dreaded the idea of submitting to marriage, but she loved the fun, the flattery, and the game of courtship. She depended upon Emily to keep her head from being dangerously turned.[47]

Women provided one another with moral and intellectual support, vocational affirmation, and protection from men. They sometimes fulfilled very human needs for affection and sensuality. These relationships existed in a culture that discounted female sexuality. Women might express their devotion through physical expressions of caring—kissing, hugging, holding hands, cuddling in bed—all with a serene lack of self-consciousness. Some single women may have shared carnal relations, but the nature of their activity and its meaning is almost as hard to recover as any evidence of their lovemaking.[48] On the one hand, women wrote to one another in a very suggestive manner. Said Graceanna Lewis to Mary Townsend, "To-night—how I do want to be rubbing thee—to see the flesh and blood of thee." Sarah Pugh wrote to her "darling Mary" Anne Estlin during a tour of Switzerland that she felt cut off by the mountains and wished she might become a bird able to soar over the wall and find herself, "once more nestling by your side."[49] Yet, in a culture that valued female asexuality, spiritual and intellectual love between women was praised for its celibate nature. Margaret Fuller found it "so true that a woman may be in love with a woman, and a man with a man." She believed such love to be regulated by the same laws governing heterosexual love, "only it is purely intellectual and spiritual, unprofaned by any mixture of lower instincts, undisturbed by any need of consulting temporal interests." Mary Grew described her lifelong relationship with Margaret Jones Burleigh as a "closer union than that of most marriages. We know there have been other such between two men and also between two women. And why should there not be. Love is spiritual, only passion is sexual."[50] Women's ability to meet their emotional needs outside of marriage enhanced the satisfaction of the single life.

It is important not to romanticize singlehood in the early nineteenth century. While the very real social supports of female relationships eased the social isolation of the single life and the Cult of Single Blessedness eased the social stigma previously attached to spinsters, the unmarried life was by no means an easy one. The new freedom which young women experienced as a result of the decline of patriarchal authority in the family and enhanced opportunity in the workplace enabled some unmarried daughters to leave home in search of personal and economic independence. But the changes brought vulnerability as well as liberty.

It bears repeating that the trend to increased female singlehood began among the daughters of the elite but became both a familial and personal strategy among the daughters of the middle classes. Even though some 50 percent of the unmarried native-born females in Utica in 1855 were secure enough financially to be spared entry into the ill-paid female labor force, the other half struggled to support themselves or their families.[51] The spinster who relied solely upon her own earnings led a precarious existence. Unmarried women faced economic disaster and stark poverty upon the loss of a job. The "weary, wasting struggle for self-preservation," preoccupied the late-eighteenth-century lace-maker and author Hannah Adams. Constant pressure flavored her outlook with dour fatalism and disappointment. Elizabeth Blackwell radiated a similarly "unhappy atmosphere." "I hope as her practice increases and her pecuniary prospects brighten she will grow happier," wrote her sister Emily. "At least that she will not feel that nervous oppressive discomfort that she does now."[52]

Economic insecurity occasionally caused women to act greedily, ruthlessly, or connivingly. When the Western Female Institute closed, for example, cutting off Catharine Beecher's livelihood, she appropriated all monies from the disposition of the property, including furnishings and tuition. Beecher left her economically dependent assistant Mary Dutton and her married sister Harriet Beecher Stowe to absorb the loss. She bickered with close supporters over trifling amounts of money. Her querulous behavior can only be explained by her desperate fear of insolvency.[53]

Many spinsters dreaded their old age. The relaxation of family obligations to parents and siblings worked both ways. The unwed sister or daughter had only a limited right to family support. Here, too, was a new balance and a new tension. Few working women could afford to set aside an annuity. Mary A. Dodge speculated occasionally on what would happen to her when she could no longer write or teach. Dodge had lost the sight in one eye as a child and dreaded losing the other. She told a friend of her attempts to "bargain with God" and so ensure her vision: "If he will only give me my senses and a usable degree of health I won't mind any amount of work or disappointment, or abuse, or anything of the sort." Lucy Larcom ended her days an invalid. Capable of writing only intermittently, she pondered on her life's course: "I sometimes wish I had earned or inherited money enough not to have to think of the future but doubtless the Lord knows just what I need. It is not best for us all to have life made easy for us, in that way." Larcom eventually accepted a one-hundred-dollar annuity anonymously arranged for her by John Greenleaf Whittier through some Philadelphia Quakers, but she never rested easily.[54]

Although social commentators decried the conflict between the economic and romantic aspects of marriage, and advice books railed against marrying in order to procure a livelihood, the practice remained a last resort for many women. The *Lady's Aid* and the *Young Woman's Counsellor* both cautioned young women not to give their hands where they could not give their hearts, whatever the temptation or need. "Marriage is regarded too often as a Business transaction," admonished Artemus B. Muzzey. "In our country, where all things take the form of traffic, there is a special danger that the most sacred bond which men can form, will bear a mercantile aspect, by being rudely exposed in the marketplace." Mary A. Dodge argued strongly that, "marriage contracted to subserve material ends, however innocent those ends may be in themselves, is legalized prostitution."[55]

Whatever their beliefs in the matter, economics continued to recruit women into marriage. Many an unwed woman considered becoming some man's wife and housekeeper in exchange for her keep. Lucy Chase recorded in her diary the story of one Miss Lynch, a schoolteacher who lost her job and feared for her future and that of a dependent mother. According to Chase, Lynch considered, rejected, and then fortunately "was preserved" from three alternatives: suicide, a fate worse than death (prostitution, presumably), and marriage.[56] Even the resourceful and determined Louisa May Alcott briefly entertained the idea of marrying as a means of economic salvation. After one dreadful day of washing, baking, picking hops, and writing, Alcott sat pondering her situation: "If I think of my woes I fall into a vortex of debts, dishpans, and despondency awful to see," she wrote to her sister. "So I say, 'every path has its puddle,' and try to play gayly with the tadpoles in my puddle, while I wait for the Lord to give me a lift, or some gallant Raleigh to spread his velvet cloak and fetch me over dry shod."[57] Financially speaking, the gender divisions of the new economic and social order left women of the middling and working classes in an unenviable position, forced to choose between economic dependence in marriage or a life of struggle to earn their keep.

The expansion of the single population from 1790 to 1865, then, was rooted in the transformation of American society from a production-based domestic economy to a consumer-based household economy. Young men emigrated, as land which could be farmed and passed down from one generation to the next became scarce. Migration produced something of an imbalance in the male-female sex ratio because men often migrated alone and either married women in the newer communities, delayed marriage until late in life, or remained unmarried. As artisan production declined with the emergence of manufacturing and the development of an urban-based commercial economy, families of the middling sort sought to ensure their future well-being and to give their children a start in life by educating sons for white-collar work or professional careers. Young women of premarital age or older unmarried daughters held an important place in family plans because their labor provided economic support for brothers during educational years. Women were drawn to the merchandising and manufacturing centers where jobs were most available. The concentration of such activity also had an effect on the ratio of men to women. The increased visibility of such women, clustered as they were in urban areas, augmented social concern for their status.

While women delayed marriage, encouraged in their singlehood by romantic ideas, brotherly love, family responsibility, a poor choice of available partners, or the lure of economic advantage, they also chose to remain unmarried in order to be independent, pursue some vocation, or accomplish some goal. For women as well as men participated in the spirit of individualism that characterized the early industrial age. Daughters pursued their independence and individuality in a different way than sons. In an era when marriage and domesticity demanded self-abnegation from women, the route to female autonomy and selfhood lay in singleness. It becomes important, then, to understand the nature of antebellum marriage as seen by these women, for the marital bond served as the protagonist in the nineteenth-century drama of female autonomy and achievement.

3

"To What Thraldom Her Noble Spirit Is Subjected"

The Meaning of Antebellum Marriage

The women in this study *chose* not to marry. Like Aunt Mary, a character in Harriet Beecher Stowe's "Eliza," such women had "failed in being pleased, rather than in pleasing." They remained single because only "by a rare conjunction of planetary powers, [can] a very superior and fastidious woman ever . . . be exactly suited."[1] Catharine M. Sedgwick declared at the age of thirty-nine, "[T]here has been no period of my life to the present moment when I might not have allied myself respectably, and to those sincerely attached to me, if I would."[2] These women were not losers in some numerical mate-matching lottery. Many rejected proposals from men valued as "good prospects."[3] Sallie Holley of Rochester, New York, received the courtship of Joseph Williams, an eligible bachelor—handsome, well-to-do, a Harvard graduate. Astonished when she turned him down (because she did not like his black eyes and his amoral attitude toward slavery), a family friend demanded: "Has the lady no friends to advise her to make this brilliant and eligible match? What prospect has she of doing better?"[4] But Holley had no interest in making a more advantageous match. She had no interest in any match at all.

Antebellum spinsters turned down numerous proposals. At least four men seriously courted Emily Howland, and one, Colonel Charles W. Folsom, much attracted her.[5] Nevertheless, she did not marry. Both forty at the height of their friendship, Howland and Folsom were settled in their independent ways. Folsom, like Howland an ardent abolitionist, refused to take the temperance pledge, a ritual of the utmost moral significance to Howland. Nor did he fully sympathize with the cause dearest to her, the political and social equality of women. Although they parted company, Folsom wrote to Howland regularly until his death in 1903. "He does not forget neither do I," she confided to her diary, where she recorded the receipt of Folsom's letters, analyzing them for those small nuances that gave her clues to his state of mind and health. She enjoyed receiving his missives and looked forward to their arrival. Nevertheless, the appearance of letters often depressed her. She wondered at this reaction, little acknowledging her ambivalence about the nature of her relationship with Folsom.[6]

Some spinsters rejected proposals from men whom they deeply loved. Sarah Grimké, for example, received a matrimonial proposal from Israel Morris, a Philadelphia Quaker and widower. Morris had been Grimké's spiritual mentor. She had lived in his household with his wife and family on her arrival in Philadelphia, and then lived for some time with his unmarried sister, Caroline. Grimké seemed genuinely to have cared for Morris and annually marked in her calendar the date of his proposal, September 16, 1862. She refused him, although she found it "hard work to give him up . . . I have even thought if death had taken him from me I could more easily have yielded him."[7] For eight years Sarah struggled with her feelings. Israel renewed his suit. Again she rejected marriage, apparently because of a growing awareness of the constraints of married life. Sarah had dedicated herself to the Quaker ministry, and perhaps felt that her vocation demanded the sacrifice of all "earthly love." Self-renunciation characterized much of her life. The care and responsibility of Morris's eight children also may have deterred her. They represented both an emotional and a practical investment of time and energy that would have competed with the fullest expression of her calling as a minister.[8]

The decisions of Grimké, Howland, and Holley suggest that among the crucial factors influencing their singlehood were the nature of the marital bond itself and the definition of woman's role within marriage. As women began to question traditional assumptions about marriage and women's role in society, American culture developed an ever more restrictive social ideology that defined woman's role as valuable but limited, identified woman's sphere in terms of the home, and confined woman's concerns to marriage and motherhood. By the second decade of the nineteenth century, the cult of domesticity proclaimed marriage to be the duty and vocation of womankind, the sole source of female fulfillment, and the primary context for female development. Although women had traditionally remained within the home, now for the first time Americans felt compelled to define woman's role in society. They mustered the most comprehensive effort to make this single institution and narrow range of activity the sole source of female well-being. Charles Burdett provided an extreme expression of this viewpoint in his archetypal novel, *Blonde and Brunette*. "Woman is made for love, conjugal and maternal," he wrote, "and when the powerful sentiment which seeks this necessary completion of the end for which she was created has . . . been awakened . . . [h]usbands and children . . . become necessary to her moral organization." In *Married or Single?* novelist Catharine M. Sedgwick bemoaned the ideology that taught women, "by books, by all the talk we hear from old and young, married and single, that marriage is not only the felicity of woman, but that her dignity, her attractiveness, her usefulness depends on it; that in short it is a sine qua non."[9]

The highest stakes rested on the marital decision: earthly well-being and eternal bliss, or hell on earth and eternal damnation. Wrote John A. James, in *The Family Monitor,* "They who enter the marriage state cast a die of greatest contingency, and yet of the greatest interest in the world, next to the last throw for eternity. Life or death, felicity or a lasting sorrow, are in the power of marriage."[10]

The metaphor employed by James is crucial here. Such words as *gamble* and *lottery* were commonly used to describe the institution of marriage.[11] Conventional wisdom held that women rarely knew what kind of man they had "won" until it was too late and the "die cast." With luck rather than character or individual merit dominating the scene, impressionable and eligible young women naturally experienced some anxiety at the approach of marriage. They must have read with fear and trembling the words of the famous Unitarian clergyman, the Reverend George Burnap, who cautioned them that "Marriage comes as the great crisis of a woman's existence."

Perhaps if she knew what life has in store for her, she would shrink back. The marriage festivity would not be without its fears . . . so many whom I have united for life have I seen overtaken by calamity . . . that to me there is ever an undertone of sadness in the wedding's mirth; and when that bright being approaches, upon whom every eye centers and for whom every heart palpitates, I can almost fancy her bridal attire transformed to mourning, and her blushes changed to tears.[12]

This picture of marriage as a relationship productive of much misery and rooted in chance dominated the didactic literature and advice manuals of the late eighteenth and early nineteenth centuries. It resonated with the experience of women who saw little around them to induce their handicapped participation in a game of sport with such enormous consequences.

Rebecca Gratz said that from her own experience she could see that "there appears no condition in human life more afflictive and destructive to happiness and morals than an ill-advised marriage." Catharine M. Sedgwick observed, "So many I have loved have made shipwreck of happiness in marriage or have found it a dreary joyless condition where affection has died of starvation, so many have been blighted by incurable and bitter sorrows." Both Lucy Chase and Sarah Stoughton recorded with foreboding the weddings of their friends Sarah Mason and Maria Johnson. "I always think when I see a 'new made bride,' " concluded Chase, " 'Oh, her happiness will not last.' " Emily Howland remarked on the loss of a sister spinster, "I believe I do not enjoy the prospect of people's marrying much more than my dear mother use to. I know its human nature, but it seems little else than an increase of misery all round to most."[13]

Not only did marriage bind man and woman together for life, in whatever joy or misery they might find, but marriage also subjugated the woman to the man. Christianity indicated no "perfect equality of rights" between husband and wife, according to antebellum advice givers. God "convey[ed] to the former a certain degree of superiority over the latter." So did the laws of man, subordinating wife to husband in economic, political, social, and sexual terms. Warned Charles Butler, in *The American Lady,*

Let it be supposed not only that the parties were to be bound during their joint lives . . . but that in all circumstances their interests were to be inseparably blended together. . . . [L]et it also be supposed that the two parties were not to engage in this association on terms of complete equality; but that one of them was necessarily to be placed . . . in a state of subordination to the other. What caution would be required in the party destined to subordination. . . ![14]

Even fanciful literature emphasized the position of women within marriage. "What happy creatures Old Maids are," a poet wrote:

> How smoothly she glides down the current of life;
> No one to control her, she has her own way,
>   While the girl who submits to be hail'd as a wife,
> Is bound by her *honor* to love and OBEY.[15]

The literature of the period rarely rejected the appropriateness of man's superiority in marriage, however. Like Butler's manual, it merely urged young women to consider very carefully their course of action in a matter of such importance. Yet the very choice of words and images used by such authors contributed to the anxiety with which young women awaited the fateful event.

Commonly, but not necessarily derogatorily, American culture equated the marriage bond with that between master and slave. This view informed a conservative advice book, for example. Woman, it said, by an ill-sorted match, "is enslaved by a perpetual master. Piteous is her doom." An advertisement for the radical free-love movement used similar language. "The great wrong of slavery consists in the power which it gives to one human being over another. A husband has almost precisely the same power over the wife that the master has over the slave." Even moderately inclined social commentators remarked that, "Every man becomes a tyrant as soon as he is married, and every woman a slave."[16]

Many a young woman clearly recognized the potential for abuse in a relationship characterized by the legal domination of wives by their husbands. Their language reflected the same master/slave image so common in the culture at large. But the meaning they attached to the words carried

far greater emotional impact and intellectual weight, and far more negative connotations than most commentators would have imagined. Thus
Anna Blackwell recalled her grandmother's admonition not to listen to
the blandishments of men, "seeing that all that *ceases* when they'd got a
woman to marry them, and then the poor girl found what a dreadful
master marriage had given her." Emily Blackwell, her younger sister,
confided to her diary on the marriage of a friend that "marriages are so far
from what they should be, they so often fetter and narrow the parties that
I am not willingly present at one." Catharine M. Sedgwick wrote to her
brother Robert about her sister's disastrous submission to the inept financial decisions of her husband. "[She] cannot consent to it but in obedience to his wish, which she thinks she has no right to withhold." "Poor
Frances! My heart bleeds for her, when I think to what thraldom her
noble spirit is subjected." Out of resistance to such subjection, Elizabeth
Tappan, of Bradford, New Hampshire, confided to Elizabeth Douglas that
she considered remaining an "old maid" because "most married women are
not better than slaves."[17]

The potential for spiritual and intellectual (not to mention physical)
bondage within marriage influenced these women in their attitudes toward
singlehood. For the greatest problem with the antebellum definition of the
marriage bond, and with the role and duties of women within it, lay in
the loss of individual goals, pursuits, and even will. At the heart of
nineteenth-century domesticity lay self-abnegation. Women were asked to
find self-fulfillment in self-sacrifice. They were expected to spend their
lives serving the needs, wants, and interests of others in the family and
the household.[18]

Over and over, women spoke to this concern. Elizabeth Payson, at the
age of twenty-three, recorded in her journal some thoughts about the
changing complexion of letters sent by a former teaching colleague who
had left school for marriage. "I was struck with the contrast between [the]
youthful and light-hearted fragments [of her previous correspondence] and
her present letters, now that she is a wife and mother. I wonder if there is
always this difference between the girl and the woman? If so, heaven
forbid that I should ever cease to be a child." Although Payson eventually
married, she delayed far beyond the average age of marriage for that time.
Her hesitancy grew from the fear of losing herself. "I think that to give
happiness in married life a woman should possess oceans of self-sacrificing
love and I, for one, haven't half of that self-forgetting spirit which I think
is essential."[19]

At stake was female autonomy. Marriage demanded the molding of the
female to the male. Only in singlehood might a woman retain her independence and develop her individuality. Mary A. Dodge agreed with
Elizabeth Payson about the essential nature of the marriage tie and resisted

being drawn into that institution, "whose tendency is to absorption, something that makes you *want* to live all your life with somebody else, makes you *want* to give up all your own life and make it seem no risk to risk everything." As one spinster to another, Susan B. Anthony revealed her deepest thoughts to a sympathetic Lydia Mott:

In the depths of my soul there is a continual denial of the self-annihilating spiritual or legal union of two human beings. Such union, in the very nature of things, must bring an end to the free action of one or the other, and it matters not to the individual whose freedom has thus departed whether it be the gentle rule of love or the iron hand of law which blotted out from the immortal being the individual soul-stamp of the Good Father.[20]

Antebellum marriage did not contain room enough for the expansion, the development—the growth—of women.

Just as the law assumed the incorporation of the female wife into the civic personage of the male husband, so these women feared the abolition of their souls, their identities, their purposes, their unique selves in an institution that did not acknowledge their separate existence. Elizabeth Blackwell recognized that "in all human relations the woman has to yield, to modify her individuality—the strong personality of even the best husband and children compels some daily sacrifice of self." Susan B. Anthony admitted that she would not object to marriage, "if it were not that women throw away every plan and purpose of their own life, to conform to the plans and purposes of the man's life." Young Carrie A. Rowland declared passionately:

"Wedlock, wedlock is a strife," never never marry never! ! I want to find friends but I dont want a companion for life. Im afraid of having my wings clipped instead of "stretching away, stretching away, On the wing, Ever & aye, Ever and aye as I sing." I have a dread of settling down to a stated round of earthly duties, I want my heart ties to be spiritual ones. I fear anything that shall mar the development of soul and turn me from a learner to a teacher alone.[21]

The unmarried spoke of an overwhelming desire for spiritual and intellectual growth, for the opportunity to develop native talents and abilities, for a chance to exercise their full potential, for the freedom to explore, and for the expanse of time to pursue excellence, truth, and self-actualization.

Antebellum American culture, which prized individualism and lauded self-reliance, did not value female autonomy. Eighteenth- and nineteenth-century political and social thought considered self-direction, self-exploration, self-fulfillment, and independence important issues. Liberal thinkers (such as Condorcet, Godwin, Thompson, and Mill) steeped in the traditions of both the eighteenth-century Enlightenment and the nineteenth-century Romantic movements, wrote frequently about the relationship of the individual to the state or the community. Much of their attention focused on the role of the family as mediator between the two. They emphasized the importance of limiting the state's coercion of the individual by insuring rights to political freedom and economic independence. They discussed the importance of education, both within the family and without. They talked about the need for privacy and the role of the state in ensuring it. These philosophers stressed the development of the individual personality, the exercise of individual will, the fostering of self-awareness and encouragement of self-expression, the formulation of an individual (as opposed to a family, religious, or national) identity, and the promotion of self-reliance. Such were the critical issues for the most influential thinkers of the time.[22] All agreed that the growth of autonomy was an important developmental stage for boys. But they did not place equal, perhaps any, value on female autonomy. On the contrary, girls had to learn to curtail their will and submit to dependence upon both the earthly and heavenly fathers in preparation for their initiation into adulthood through religious conversion and marriage.[23]

But despite the gender limitations associated with the growth of autonomy, these values permeated late eighteenth- and early nineteenth-century American culture. Young women, experiencing the easing of patriarchal authority in the family, achieving a modest level of education, and acquiring a certain independence in the marketplace, eagerly assimilated such values, which influenced young women's evaluation of marriage and singlehood. Women recognized the nature of the duties required of wives and mothers. This knowledge augmented whatever resistance a young woman might have felt as she contemplated her future. Popular writer Artemus B. Muzzey spoke for his society and culture when he wrote, "Woman was not created for . . . absolute and unlimited ease. If she enters the marriage state with any other design than to devote herself to her family, to toil more, instead of less, than she now does, either by mental or manual exertions . . . let her be assured of a fearful disappointment."[24]

Young women knew only too well the demands of housewifery. As unmarried daughters they helped their mothers in the home, and as younger sisters they watched the transformation of older sisters from maiden to wife and, all too often, to drudge. Lucy Beckley recorded in her journal a poem to her "New-Married Sister," which said in part:

> Now you have left your parents wing.
> Nor longer ask their care.
> It is but seldom husbands bring
> A lighter yoke to wear.

Sallie Holley witnessed firsthand the debilitating cares of her older, married sisters, consumed as they were with housekeeping and child-rearing during those same years in which she contemplated her future course.

Holley contrasted their lives with those of several single siblings with whom she boarded for a time after her father's death. Nancy Flynt, although she struggled to support herself as a single woman, compared her sister's married life unfavorably with her own because of "the many hours of confinement and other necessary duties that deprive the married woman of a thousand innocent girlish enjoyments." Lucy Larcom, who accompanied her sister and brother-in-law from Beverly, Massachusetts, to Looking Glass Prairie, Illinois, decried their attempt to build a suitable life on the plains. As she wrote home in 1846:

Talk to me about getting married and settling down here in the West! I don't do that thing till I'm a greater goose than I am now, for love or money. It is a common saying here, that "this is a fine country for men and dogs, but women and oxen have to take it." . . . If ever I had the mind to take the vestal vow, it has been since I "emigrated." You'll see me coming back one of these years, a "right smart" old maid, my fat sides and cheeks shaking with "the agey," to the tune of "oh, take your time, Miss Lucy."[25]

The problem with domestic work, as women saw it, lay not so much in its level of difficulty as with its isolation, its trivial and ever unfinished nature, its lack of intellectual import or personal significance. After her sister's marriage, Emily Howland received one letter after another attesting to the limitations on her time because of the demands of housework. "Oh Emily," she wrote, "the days are *so* short and pass *so* quickly that I cannot accomplish half that I wish even by rising at five." Elizabeth Neall Gay, an abolitionist, wrote to her spinster friend and colleague, Sarah Pugh, that her invalid daughter again required care, and that she could not make weekly committee meetings. "All my life, I have not been able to do any work well—it is only half done." In a conversation on women's role on society, Maria Weston Chapman described maternal duties as stultifying. "I see reason enough why women have never produced so many works of art, or systems of philosophy as men in the fact that they do not pass their lives in producing works of art," she wrote.[26]

Spinsters resisted submitting themselves to a state that would hobble them. Astronomer Maria Mitchell wrote in her diary in 1853 that she objected to the emphasis on needlework in the domestic education of young women. "Once emancipate her from the 'stitch, stitch, stitch,' and she would have time for studies which would engross as the needle never can." Why, she wondered, must women learn and fulfill all domestic tasks when men were never required to do all of their own mechanical work? "[W]oman is expected to know how to do all kinds of sewing, all kinds of cooking, all kinds of any woman's work, and the consequence is that life is passed in learning these only, while the universe of truth beyond remains unentered."[27]

Mary A. Dodge agreed with Mitchell that "[t]he best women, the brightest women, the noblest women are the very ones to whom [housework] is most irksome. . . . A woman who is satisfied with the small cares, the small economies, the small interests, the constant contemplation of small things which many a household demands, is a very small sort of woman." Dodge urged a "noble discontent" as woman's safeguard "against the deterioration which such a life threatens and her proof of capacity and her note of preparation for a higher [life]."[28]

Beyond the burdens and limitations of housework lurked the dangers and cares of too frequent and unplanned pregnancy. For many women, their mothers' experiences stood as a warning of the dark side of marriage. Both Catharine M. Sedgwick and Alice Cary attributed their mothers' early deaths (and Pamela Dwight Sedgwick's descent into insanity) to overwork and constant childbearing. Sedgwick watched in despair as her sister Eliza followed in their mother's footsteps. She characterized as "painful drudgery" the bearing and nurturing of twelve children. Lucy Stone, who married in her mid-thirties, though only after three years of indecision, remembered her mother's frequent pregnancies. She described her memories as "revulsions of feeling" (while her husband-to-be, Henry Blackwell, downplayed them as "unfortunate impressions"). Harriot Hunt always felt that the difficult and prolonged labor by which her mother delivered her, and her own near miraculous survival, set her apart for some special role. She saw her destiny as beyond (and therefore, free from) marriage and the frightful experience of giving birth and rearing children.[29]

Other spinsters commented on childbirth as an "ordeal," a "severe anguish," or that "infernal arrangement" of "appalling suffering." Emily Howland showed enough distaste for the process that her brother refrained from recounting in detail to her the birthing experience of his wife and child. Susan B. Anthony never forgot nursing a cousin through the last month of a difficult pregnancy and assisting during the labor, only to lose the young mother from complications. "It is rather tough business, is it not Mother?" she sighed.[30]

Membership in the Shakers (the largest and most permanent of the early-nineteenth-century utopian communities) peaked during the period 1810 to 1860. Women of childbearing age (twenty to forty-five years) constituted a significant proportion of new converts to the community. Shaker diaries suggest that these celibate, sex-segregated, and highly structured communities "were a haven for women who preferred celibacy to traditional marriage and its concomitant danger to their own lives and to their possible offspring."[31]

How many women of marital and childbearing age entered Shaker communities out of discomfort with sex (in addition to the dangers of childbirth), no one can say with certainty; however, an exchange of views between Charlotte Cushman and a young Shaker girl provides an insight into the way in which such women viewed the celibate life in the 1830s. Cushman published her poem in *The Knickerbocker Magazine* and addressed it to the Shaker community. It said in part:

> Mysterious worshipers!
> Are you indeed the things you seem to be,
> Of earth—yet of its iron influence free—
>   From all that stirs
> Our being's pulse, and gives to fleeting life
> What well the Hun has termed 'the rapture of the strife?'
>
> You too! What early blight
> Has withered your fond hopes, that ye thus stand,
> A group of sisters, 'mong this monkish band?
>   Ye creatures bright!
> Has sorrow scored your brows with demon hand,
> Or O'er your hopes passed treachery's burning brand?
>
> Ye would have graced right well
> The bridal scene, the banquet, or the bowers
> Where mirth and revelry usurp the hours—
>   Where like a spell,
> Beauty is sovereign—where man owns its powers
> And women's tread is o'er a path of flowers.
>
> Yet seem ye not as those
> Within whose bosoms memories vigils keep:
> Beneath your drooping lids no passions sleep;
>   And your pale brows
> Bear not the tracery of emotions deep—
> Ye seem too cold and passionless to weep![32]

An actress, Cushman loved the "rapture" of the stage and the public eye. Her beauty and charisma served her well in her career. Perhaps her main objection to the Shaker life-style lay in its abstemiousness—its isolation, constriction, and regimentation. But the poem evinces some sense of admiration as well as incomprehension of the disciplined lives of Shaker women. Like these women, Cushman never married. She enjoyed her sovereignty and gave no institution power over her life.

A Shaker girl took it upon herself to answer Cushman's poem and to defend her life-style. She explicitly upheld celibacy as female liberation and portrayed the Shaker community as a rich alternative to a culture that confused lust with courtship, prostitution with marriage, and rape with sex. She upheld her life as far preferable to marriage, an institution that encouraged a husband to indulge in his own double standard of morality and gave him the right to abuse his wife sexually, whether by too frequent demands or displeasing practice.

In "bridal scenes," in "banquets and in bowers!"
Mid revelry and variegated flowers,
Is where our mother Eve first felt their powers.
The "bridal scenes," you say, "we'd grace right well!"
"Lang syne" there our first parents blindly fell!—

The bridal scene! Is this your end and aim?
And can you this pursue, "Nor own your shame?"
If so—weak, pithy—superficial thing—
Drink, silent drink the sick hymeneal spring.

The bridal scene! The banquet or the bowers,
Or woman's [bed of thorns, or] path of flowers,
Can't all persuade our souls to turn aside
To live in filthy lust or cruel pride.

. . . .

But here "Beauty's sovereign"—so say you—
It lies upon the surface of the skin—
Aye, Beauty's self was never worth a pin.

. . . .

"Man owns its powers?" And what will not man own
To gain his end—to captivate—dethrone?
The truth is this, whatever he may feign,
You'll find your greatest loss his greatest gain.[33]

This Shaker woman's attitudes toward celibacy and sexual practice in antebellum marriage were not unique. Other spinsters, outside the cloister, admired the Shakers for upholding celibacy. Physician Harriot Hunt had many friends she regularly visited among the Shakers. Hunt believed that the rejection of marriage on which their community was based "originated in that general *abuse* which has marked [marriage] in the world, presenting it in a most gross and sensual form." She believed that the Shakers might one day welcome marriage among them, "But *not* until physiological laws shall be understood and recognized as the regulators of the marriage relation. *Not* until the rights of woman shall be acknowledged and secured. For *not until then* can this institution be placed upon a high and safe foundation, free from . . . the mire of pollution and sin."[34]

Many Perfectionists shared this attitude toward sexuality and believed it desirable to subordinate sexual passion to reason and to certain physiological laws. They emphasized the importance to both the individual and the race of curbing excesss "expenditures." They agreed with the essentially evangelical attitude that salvation requires the placing of spiritual before carnal love.[35] Although Mary Moody Emerson's philosophical roots were more tangled, she too chose celibacy as a way of augmenting spirituality. Early in 1807 she wrote in her diary after a visit to a suitor, Captain

Dexter: "—sick—promised never to put that ring on." A few weeks later, she committed herself to singlehood, casting her "polluted disordered soul into the arms of divine love": "Henceforth the picture I'll image shall be girded loins, a bright lamp, fervent devotion. My condition in life is singular, and presses me on the throne of my Master with peculiar strength." As had the Shakers, Emerson modeled her life after the faithful handmaidens of the Bible who lit their lamps and awaited the heavenly bridegroom, that "perfect Being" arrayed in all "his physical and moral perfections."[36]

Both single and married women experienced sexual aversion on occasion, but little in their private letters illuminates its role in their decision to remain single. Lucy Larcom, for example, wrote a flawed poem called "Sea and Shore" which suggests a certain subconscious fear of sexuality and sexual relationships. The last stanzas read:

> Some gathering of his billows, risen in wrath,
> Far out of landsmen's ken, some headlong crash
> Of surge with surge, has roused the Ocean's heart
> To frenzy, and he rushes to the shore,
> As a boy does to his mother, with the tale.
>
> She gives no answer, only reaches out
> Her arms in speechless welcome. On her breast
> He throws himself and his impetuous grief,
> Then glides back, soothed, to the inevitable strife,
> His pulses beating evenly, with calm tides!
> Ah! would that every sea could find a shore![37]

The poem begins with the sexual image of the male ocean gliding in and out of the female shore. The sea moves from friendly and secret intimacy with the shore to the broiling up of a "mad passion," the rousing of a "frenzied heart." But just as the poet develops the image of a powerful, lunging, male sea about to crash down upon an open, receptive, female beach, she emasculates it. Larcom transforms the passion of the adult male into the woe of a little boy in search of comfort. Awkwardly, disjointedly, and abruptly, she changes passion into anger and anger into grief. Larcom either could or would not carry through the poem the single and terrifying image of a surging sexuality. She quiets the pulse and dispels the arousal, providing release without orgasm. In so doing, she eviscerates her own poem.

Single women probably felt no more sexually inhibited than their married sisters.[38] The early Victorian period did not encourage open discussion of sexuality among "good" women of either state. But whether or not women felt influenced by an aversion to sex or by sexual inhibition, some rejected sexual domination by men and demanded their right to abstain from sex (or to control its frequency). This, they believed, preserved both their health and their autonomy.

In addition to their concerns about the health (mental and physical) of women in pregnancy and childbirth, to their fears and inhibitions with regard to sexuality, and to their rejection of male domination, most antebellum spinsters also objected to the consequences of frequent or unplanned pregnancy for their work, their occupation or nondomestic vocation. Graceanna Lewis, of Media, Pennsylvania, noted the repeated pregnancies of female relatives and the disruption that these caused. In 1843, at the age of twenty-two, she taught at her uncle Bartholomew Fussell's newly established York, Pennsylvania, boarding school. Her aunt Rebecca Fussell became pregnant while primarily responsible for housekeeping at the school. Wrote Graceanna: "Such scrapes are very inconvenient. I think people might have more consideration than to get into them, when there is such a poor way of getting out, but I suppose . . . they are willing to make sacrifices 'for the sake of replenishing the earth.' Very dubious! They deserve sympathy in their benevolent enterprise." Sympathy, perhaps, but not emulation! Although her aunt's pregnancy was but one factor, the school soon closed. Anne Warren Weston, a Weymouth, Massachusetts, abolitionist, wrote in consternation to her sister Deborah, in 1836. "I have a fearful piece of news to communicate," she said, for Maria Weston Chapman was again "in the family way." "The thing that I care most about," acknowledged Anne, "is that it will break up her going to N[ew] York" to the annual antislavery convention.[39] All these women had things they had to do and wanted to do—things that could not be accomplished given the stress and responsibilities of frequent childbearing.

In an unfinished novel, *Diana and Persis*, Louisa May Alcott dramatized the struggle of two friends seeking to develop and survive as artists and as women. Persis resolved to go to France to study drawing. "I feel power of some sort stirring in me, yet I cannot put it into any shape that satisfies me," she told Diana. Diana urged Persis not to look for inspiration in marriage, for art was a jealous mistress. She feared for Persis's future because of her need for external reinforcement. Diana pleaded with Persis not to live alone in Paris but to surround herself with other women artists. Yet from the beginning Persis was doomed to marry and loose her artistic self. Persis felt the temptation even as she left her friend in Boston: "I have a hungry heart [unlike Diana's marble one] as well as an ambitious spirit and art alone does not seem to satisfy me as it does you."[40] Diana's single-minded dedication to her work promised greater accomplishment, whatever the degree of her talent, than Persis's divided one. And indeed, at the end of the novel Persis, married and a mother, sits oblivious to the beauty of a setting sun, planning a breakfast menu—her artistic sensibility numbed and her ambitious spirit quenched.[41]

The novel provides a rich text for the analysis of the conditions, constraints, and conflicts under which female artists struggled in the nineteenth century. Alcott proposed singlehood as a precondition for serious artistic development. The thought was widely shared by creative and intellectual women of the time. Sculptress Harriet Hosmer reflected the same frame of mind as the Shaker poet when she found herself a "faithful worshipper of Celibacy," whose service fascinated her more the longer she remained in it. Declared Hosmer:

Even if so inclined, an artist has no business to marry. For a man, it may be well enough, but for a woman, on whom the matrimonial duties and cares weigh more heavily, it is a moral wrong, I think, for she must either neglect her profession or her family, becoming neither a good wife and mother nor a good artist. My ambition is to become the latter, so I wage eternal feud with the consolidating knot.[42]

Emily Dickinson recognized the restraints of marriage on the growth of female imaginative power. She wrote of the submergence of creativity in the marital relationship:

> She rose to His Requirement—dropt
> The Playthings of Her Life
> To take the honorable Work
> Of Woman, and of Wife—
>
> If ought She missed in Her new Day
> Of Amplitude, or Awe—
> Or first Prospective—Or the Gold
> In using, wear away,
>
> It lay unmentioned—as the Sea
> Develop Pearl, and Weed,
> But only to Himself—be known
> The Fathoms they abide—[43]

In "awe" of words, enthralled by their power and her own as she arranged them, Dickinson had every intention of pursuing "amplitude." To direct her course along the path of artistic development, she renounced marriage. In this way, she maintained her own perspective and avoided the self-abnegation of wifehood.

Antebellum women rejected marriage with a clear understanding both of what they were giving up and of what they were seeking. They dedicated their separate, individual lives to specific purposes. The majority of the unwed described here felt themselves "called" to a vocation that could not be fully realized in married life. Maria Mitchell, for example, said that she did not marry so that she might be "more vigilant in her work." Confirmed by her circle of female friends, Harriot Hunt saw herself so wedded to medicine that, after twenty-five years of practice, they all celebrated her "silver anniversary." Martha Wright pondered aloud whether "if some Boston Adonis of mature age should be accepted by Hunt someday, it would be considered bigamy and whether succeeding patients would be less legitimate than previous ones." Elizabeth Blackwell spoke of "an antagonism between love and work [such that] the man who stood nearest should have the least sympathy with the woman in the expression of . . . the very part of her nature which really colours her love and makes it so noble and precious to him."[44]

While shocking in a woman, such considerations in the minds of ante-bellum men surprised no one. The concept of a vocation was central to nineteenth-century culture. A vocation, highly valued as the vehicle by which a good citizen and a godly person participated in God's work and in society's progress, served a number of important social, religious, and personal functions. It set one on the road to perfection. It enabled one to develop God-given talents that might otherwise find no outlet. It pro-vided the physical regimen and emotional discipline deemed necessary for the well-lived life. Having a wide variety of choices before him, a young man searched for and reverenced his calling as part of the process of social and personal maturation. No such act was expected of young women. As Emily Howland recalled of her early adulthood: "I was leading the aimless life that was required of young women. The more imperative necessity of being employed to ensure health of body and mind was neither recognized nor understood."[45] A woman should await an opportunity to assume the inherent, biologically rooted vocation of motherhood, by which all of her sex might serve their God, race, and country.

The gender division of labor in the new industrially based commercial economy made undesirable any large-scale movement toward female au-tonomy or self-expression through career paths in the public sector. Spinsters, however, increasingly saw themselves as maneuvering around the edges of the gender system. They did not reject the notions of women's particular nature or character, nor did they greatly challenge contemporary notions of femininity. In fact, they tended to believe that because of their particular sensibilities, creativity, and role as acculturators of men and children, women had a particular responsibility for "what belongs to the spirit—its powers—its affections—its unutterable life of thought." They aspired to cultural hegemony. To their minds, woman's sphere was active, generative, and multifaceted. Wrote Mary A. Dodge, "All knowledge is its providence. Whatever tends to enlarge the mind, as well as increase the sympathy, belongs to woman. Politics, art, science, all are hers, subject only to her choice, subordinate always to her freedom."[46]

Because of their seeming release from household duties as wife and mother, single women claimed responsibilities beyond the domestic realm. Said Maria Mitchell, "A sphere is not made up of one, but of an infinite number of circles; women have diverse gifts, and to say that woman's sphere is the family circle is a mathematical absurdity." Catharine Beecher argued that unmarried women "of superior mind and acquirements have risen to a more enlarged and comprehensive boundary of exertion, and by their talents and influence have accomplished what, in a more circum-scribed sphere of action, would have been impossible." Catharine M. Sedgwick felt that unwed women had demonstrated that they could "per-form with grace and honor, duties from which wives and mothers are exempt by their domestic necessities." Given this wider responsibility, single women demanded the freedom to select their vocation and the training and experience to make the most of it. Said Sedgwick, the single woman "has an independent power to shape her own course, and to forge her separate sovereign way." Limited to "no peculiar class of ministra-tions," such women acknowledged only divine guidance in defining their individual spheres of action.[47]

The Cult of Single Blessedness provided a rubric under which, and a vocabulary with which these women justified their vocational lives and aspirations. Lucy Larcom spoke of her "call" in the following terms: "I am very thankful for the few talents I have, not because they are mine, but because they can be given to God, to receive His inspiration, and to be worth something to others besides myself—Ah! living is not mere exis-tence, when God breathes into [it] with the breath of life!"[48] Larcom explained her ambition to write and her craving for the intellectual life, her aspirations for fame and influence, by attributing these things to God. Religious inspiration was an appropriate motive for stepping outside the domestic sphere, according to the constructs of single blessedness.

Some spinsters carefully pointed out their passive role in adopting a nondomestic vocation. Catharine M. Sedgwick described her success as a novelist: "When I feel that my writings have made any one happier or better, I feel an emotion of gratitude to Him who has made me the medium of any blessing to my fellow creatures. And I do feel that I am but the instrument." Mary A. Dodge described her highly visible position as a journalist and political gadfly in similar terms. "For every power God has given me I feel utterly glad and grateful. I rejoice in myself. I am delighted that God did not make me dull, indifferent, and heavy, and I am . . . awed, that He has, I believe, made me the medium through which He conveys some of his truth and consolation."[49]

With these words, women placed their work within an appropriate, socially acceptable context. In private they acknowledged their strivings. Rachel Stearns wrote in her diary of her ambition and desire for recogni-tion in terms which contrasted greatly with the humility so admired by those in her chosen field of religious life. "I cannot rest contented with low *attainments* in religion. It is my desire to be *eminently* holy, for it I *strive* and pray, and though sometimes discouraged I still continue to strive . . . I do want to live holy, to be a *distinguished* Christian." Emily Howland set her sights on accomplishing "in this short life the growth wh[ich] all eternity is given to do." Lucy Larcom acknowledged having experienced since childhood a desire to "be something to the world" in which she lived.[50]

In public, however, women shielded their pursuits. Lucy Larcom maintained the fiction of her work having been thrust before the public eye against her will. She actively sought out literary criticism and publication, even connived to have her work endorsed by the popular poet, John Greenleaf Whittier. But when a small magazine published some of her verses in 1860 (without compensating her), she wrote: "I should have regarded the thought of publishing as premature; but most of my friends are not artistic, and do not look upon my unripe fruits as I do."[51] Catharine M. Sedgwick protested a bit too much when acknowledging the compliments of the Reverend Dr. Ellery Channing on the publication of her novel, *Live and Let Live.*

I can not tell you how much your very kind letter has gratified and encouraged me. I thank Heaven that I am not now working for the poor and perishing rewards of literary ambition. Unattainable they might be to me, but, whether so or not, they are not my object; and I think the time has gone by, or, perhaps has not come to our country, when they are legitimate objects.

What were the "legitimate objects" for which she worked? As she explained:

With the great physical world to be subdued here to the wants of the human family, there is an immense moral field opening, demanding laborers of every class, and of every kind and degree of talent. Neither pride nor humility should withhold us from the work to which we are clearly "sent."[52]

Doubting her reception (and her ability) even as she felt compelled to write, sculpt, minister, or heal, the antebellum spinster carefully shrouded herself within the protective but fragile covering of the Cult of Single Blessedness.

In maintaining the appearance of hesitation and humility women guarded themselves against charges of ambitiousness. Antebellum literature warned women, and spinsters in particular, against the snare of ambition, that most unfeminine of qualities. This hostility indicated an awareness of women's desire to expand their horizons and to accomplish something of moment. Much of the criticism was made in the vein of the short story "The Sisters." Jane Ruthven was acknowledged to be "a superb beauty" but was, alas, a woman of many faults. Chief among these was her ambition. According to the author N. Thorning Munroe, Ruthven "wished to shine in the world, and to be one of those to whom the proud and gifted would bow as unto a kindred spirit. She had great powers of mind, and of all she possessed, she was fully, too fully aware." Munroe approved of genius when exercised in the proper manner, in the proper sphere. She proclaimed genius "a noble thing in women when it is employed for purposes of usefulness and of good unto our fellow beings. It glorifies and adorns a woman when she makes it subservient to the best feelings of her heart." However, Jane Ruthven did not hold her ambition in check and let her mind rule her heart in a most unfeminine manner. Said Munroe censoriously, "her principle aim in life [is] to let the world know that she has that gift. When the best, noblest feelings of her heart are made a sacrifice unto its shrine, and she in all things consults her ambition, before her love and affection, then it ceases to be a blessing, and it would be better, far better if she possessed less of the dazzling quality."[53]

Few women had the self-confidence or idiosyncrasy to pursue public achievement or to relish their accomplishments. When necessary, the Cult of Single Blessedness might be utilized in defense of both. Mary A. Dodge thanked Henry James the elder for his fan letters. Said Dodge: "I shall not pay your sagacity so poor a compliment as to deprecate my worthiness to receive them, but I can answer for it that they do not fall upon unappreciative ground. One ought to do what is given him to do, whether men will bear or whether they will forbear, alone as well as with a multitude. Nevertheless, I think recognition is one of the most delightful things in this world."[54] Speaking sardonically to her mother's fears that in taking on a medical career she had jeopardized her spiritual welfare by stepping outside woman's proper sphere, Elizabeth Blackwell argued that, to the contrary, "I am but living religion all the time."

Isn't it my meat and my drink to do the good will of God, didn't I use to sit in the lecture-room and send up a whole cannonade of little prayers; and didn't a whole flood of answers come straight down from the throne of grace? And what am I doing now? Do you think I care about medicine? Nay, verily, its just to kill the devil, who I hate so heartily—that's the fact, mother; and if that isn't forming Christ in one, the hope of glory, why I don't know what is.[55]

While in part an expression of her frustration with Hannah Blackwell's narrow orthodoxy, the remark also demonstrates that Elizabeth had enough awareness of the values of her culture to use them in support of her individual course of action. At the same time, she was sufficiently distanced from those values to make fun of the entire construct. Blackwell recognized the value placed on religious motivation and pious character in the single woman's "proper" calling.

In her poem "The Unwedded," Lucy Larcom expressed the attitudes of most women described in this study. Larcom's heroine rejects the heavy cares of marriage. In adherence to such concepts as God's call to the vocational life, the beau ideal, evangelical piety, and woman's moral superiority (as reflected in her sexual purity), she chooses singlehood. The poem describes an independent and self-confident woman, who knows herself and her value. She sets a high premium on her autonomy. She prefers to trust her own sense of right and truth rather than marry and be subjected to another's. "For all men have not wisdom and might," and a wife, her vision blinded by love, "will follow by faith, not right." Wrote Larcom:

> "Did she choose it, this single life?"—
>   Gossip, she saith not, and who can tell?
> But many a mother and many a wife,
>   Draws a lot more lonely, we all know well.
> . . . .
> "But is she happy, a woman alone?"
> . . . .
> There are ends more worthy than happiness.
>   Who seeks it, is digging joy's grave we know—
> The blessed are they who but live to bless.
> . . . .
> For the heart of woman is large as man's;
>   God gave her His orphaned world to hold,
> And whispered through her His deeper plans
>   To save it alive from the outer cold.
>
> And here is a woman who understood
>   Herself, her work, and God's will with her.
> . . . .
> Would she have walked more nobly, think,
>   With a man beside her, to point the way,
> Hand joining hand in the marriage link?
>   Possibly, Yes; it is likelier, Nay.

Living in single blessedness, giving as well as given blessings, keeping her integrity and devoting herself to duty, Larcom's "The Unwedded" described her life as "a beautiful Now, and a better To Be."[56]

———◀◉▶———

Women in late eighteenth- and early nineteenth-century America, then, began actively to make decisions about the future and to question the necessity and benefit of marriage. They turned instead toward an alternative—the vocational life of single blessedness. They based their choice on specific values. First, they actively pursued self-development and personal growth. Wrote Anna Dickinson, "I would make every woman understand that she was born for herself and not for another. . . . Woman was *made for herself*—to round out herself. Let her live to the full and make a complete woman of her in every respect." Women also entered singlehood in order to evade male sovereignty. Harriot Hunt kept a vase on her desk inscribed with the words of Elizabeth Barrett Browning:

> The honest earnest man must stand and *work*,
> The woman also;—otherwise she drops
> At once below the dignity of man.
> Accepting serfdom. . . .[57]

Finally, although their culture demanded the subservience of the female self, some women asserted their independence; they remained single and undertook their callings in an effort to achieve autonomy and experience self-actualization. As Elizabeth Blackwell said: "How good work is—work that has a soul in it! I cannot conceive that any thing can supply its want to a woman. In all human relations, the woman has to yield, to modify her individuality . . . but true work is perfect freedom, and full satisfaction."[58]

4

"When I Get My Freedom"

Visions of Liberty

Antebellum spinsters aspired to a life untrammeled by husbandly domination and unconstrained by wifely submission. As they envisioned a future open to their own construction, certain images came to represent the freedom they sought in such a life. Susan B. Anthony, for example, joked about taking off for the goldfields of California. Emily Blackwell's inclination was to "assume a man's dress and wander freely over the world throwing away the constant weary shackles that custom and poverty surround [women] with so closely."[1]

Most of these articulated visions of the independent life coalesced around three specific themes: economic security, a room or home of one's own, and the opportunity to expand intellectual horizons and develop one's mind. Each of these was valued in and of itself. Each was further valued for its role in promoting female autonomy.

Middle- and upper-class women of the late eighteenth and early nineteenth centuries had the benefit of some education. They enjoyed a new degree of independent decision-making within their families. They experienced something of the world beyond the home or village during their youth. These developments in women's lives enabled some to step outside of their immediate situation, to evaluate its limitations, and to formulate ways in which to change their circumstances. Such women had come far enough along the road to independence to recognize their dependence. They knew that without earning power and economic security of their own they would remain tied to the financial largess of men. Without economic independence, they could not develop their talents or follow their callings. Lacking money in their pockets, they could neither rent nor buy the necessary privacy in which to pursue their own thoughts. These women recognized a connection between their social and their intellectual dependence. They feared that without the freedom and opportunity to develop their minds, women would never break the chains which bound them.

Integral to single women's pursuit of autonomy was their desire for economic independence. They both appreciated the value of earning their own living and hoped to stave off want—or better yet, to achieve economic security. Everyone required what the nineteenth century called "a competency," a sustaining economic resource, as the first step toward independent living and independent action. Women recognized that financial dependence curtailed freedom of thought, action, and person. Beyond that, some women believed that the process of earning one's own living augmented self-esteem, reinforced moral integrity, and encouraged the development of latent talent and capacity.

Susan B. Anthony championed the principle that autonomy rests on earning one's own livelihood. In urging women to assert their individuality and to claim their freedom, Anthony said:

What women most need is a true appreciation of her womanhood, a self-respect which shall scorn to eat the bread of dependence. Whoever consents to live by the sweat of the brow of another human being inevitably humiliates and degrades herself. . . . No genuine equality, no real freedom, no true manhood or womanhood can exist on any foundation save that of pecuniary independence. As a right over a man's subsistence is a power over his moral being, so a right over a woman's subsistence enslaves her will, degrades her pride and vitiates her whole moral nature.

Maria Mitchell agreed with Anthony. She advocated the "dignity of occupation—in general the higher dignity of paid occupation." She saw no better school for moral and intellectual growth than that of employment. Mitchell feared that a woman who "learns to expect to be held up . . . ceases to stand upright."[2]

Sarah J. Stoughton learned from personal experience the relationship between autonomy and economic independence. Stoughton lived with her parents as something of an invalid. She contributed stories to contemporary magazines and newspapers. Her writing provided her with a mechanism for self-expression. She hoped it would also free her from the economic constraints of her living situation. Wrote Stoughton in her journal: "One of my little pieces came in the last *Child at Home*. I am glad! for I want to do something. In short, I want to *write!* I wonder if I shall ever be the author of a book—God grant it. I not only want to write, but I want to earn some money for myself. It goads my spirit to be so dependent." Stoughton wanted at least some of that money in order to pursue her vocation and her continuing development as a writer. She did not want to be dependent on anyone else's assessment of how time and money should be spent. When her father suffered financial setbacks due to a poor crop one season, Stoughton rightly feared that the family's penny-pinching mood would deny her money with which to buy a new diary and writing materials. She mourned the loss of her journal, described as a "necessity" because she attached such importance to writing in it daily.[3]

Mary A. Dodge had a different definition of economic independence. She interpreted economic freedom as freedom from market pressures, from dependence on wages, and from the need to obtain and to hold a job. Dodge believed that by entering into the wage economy, women sacrificed their "disinterestedness"—that quality which set them morally above and apart from men. She argued that woman's great contribution to social life emanated from her role as an observer in life and from the objectivity and moral purity inherent in such a position. "It is always a sorrowful thing," wrote Dodge, "for a woman to be obliged to compete with men, that is, to earn money. She can do it only at the constant torture, or the constant sacrifice . . . of something higher than can be brought into the strife."[4]

Dodge did not believe that women belonged in the home. She celebrated those who pursued a study or vocation "beyond the common range," "because the very strength of [their] purpose, overcoming the natural disinclinations of [their] sex, shows it to be of celestial origin and therefore worthy of respect." But Dodge did not want such women to have to worry about earning a living. She hoped that the men in their lives would support them so that they need not submerge their callings in the pettiness, materialism, and strife of the working world.[5] Economic security rather than independent earnings promoted autonomy, according to Dodge.

Many spinsters agreed and gratefully accepted male support. Laura Towne resisted taking a salary from the benevolent society which sponsored her work in a freedman's school. Towne valued her status and independence as a "volunteer." She succumbed only when it became clear that without the salary her work and her home would be threatened. An endowment from her brother eventually enabled her to continue working as long as she wished. She relinquished the salary with relief. Emily Howland appreciated both the income conferred on her by her father and the periodic infusions of his capital which supported her efforts to ease the plight of "contraband" slaves. Nevertheless, Howland felt that the ability to support one's self was a measure of both character and capacity: "I feel proud of the fact that I have earned wages and received them and could earn my own living if I had a chance. There are many other facets of my character [which are] very humiliating."[6]

Howland frequently returned home to take up daughterly duties and domestic functions, a measure perhaps of her sensitivity to the obligation encumbent upon the acceptance of family funds. Towne felt no such constraint in her "dependence" on her brother's money. Both women valued their vocations more as a means of self-expression and of social contribution than as a livelihood or a measure of their independence. Their endowments enhanced the autonomy of the one while both supporting, and to a degree limiting, that of the other.

Few women, however, had the resources available to Howland or Towne. Nor could an independent-minded woman find fiscal self-sufficiency in a marketplace where few occupations provided both respectable and well-paid work. Most, therefore, struggled to survive and to keep their dream alive. Author Alice Cary provides one example.

Deprivation was the theme of Cary's life. During her formative years her beloved mother and two dear sisters died. Her father remarried and left his children in the original family home while he moved his new wife into another house on the property. Cary viewed her stepmother as a humorless, stingy, cold, and oppressive woman who pushed the young Carys to do household chores to the exclusion of reading and study. She was said to have enforced economies which left Alice and her sister Phoebe to write their poems in the dark or by the light of rags soaked in oil. The sisters felt obliged to hide their manuscripts under the front stairs.

In late adolescence, Cary suffered another emotional loss when the man she loved married another woman. At the age of fifty, when ruminating about her life, Cary clearly felt that fate had not been kind to her:

for the first fourteen years of my life, it seemed as if there was actually nothing in existence but work. The whole family struggle was just for the right to live free from the curse of debt. My father worked early and late; my mother's work was never done. The mother of nine children . . . I shall always feel that she was taxed far beyond her strength, and died before her time. . . . I pined for beauty; but there was no beauty about our homely house. . . . We hungered and thirsted for knowledge; but there were not a dozen books on our family shelf, not a library within our reach. There was little time to study, and had there been more, there was no chance to learn but in the district school-house. . . .[7]

All of Cary's psychic distress—her feelings of deprivation, loss, and neglect—coalesced around the subject of economic independence. She swore never to live in debt. She was determined to afford her own home and to live in style. She left the family homestead at the age of thirty and headed east to New York City, where she vowed to earn her living with her pen. She wrote at least a poem a day for most of her life and published in a wide variety of magazines and newspapers.

Cary never experienced the rewards of independence, either in self-esteem or in financial security. She found the remuneration for her work inadequate and unjust. Poets, she wrote to her publisher, James T. Fields, are "*seedy* and *needy* and *greedy*." Cary feared that the quality of her writing suffered from the necessity of turning it out in such quantity.

Always the past rankled: "I don't like to think how much we are robbed of in this world by just the conditions of our life. How much better work I should have done, how much more success I might have won, if I had had a better opportunity in youth."[8]

Not all spinsters were as driven by the dream of financial security as Cary. But to one degree or another, depending on personal and family issues and circumstances, the early nineteenth-century woman had to confront her dependent status, her economic need, and her desire to be independent of the constraints imposed by that need. The successful journalist Mary A. Dodge calculated that she needed $10,000 in order to make herself independent. "I want to be independent . . . and I think 600 a year will enable me to live in the country, as long as I do live, above want, and in a state of comparative ease and elegance." Lucy Larcom, who never adequately supported herself with her writing, taught school as her only viable option. Larcom felt that the demands of teaching impinged upon the time she needed to write and inhibited her creative faculty. "I like my freedom," said Larcom, "and if I can afford to keep it, I shall. I am sure it is not good for me to live in a school."[9]

Rachel Stearns hoped to attend a female seminary at Wilbraham, Massachusetts. She proposed to prepare herself for teaching. Her father's early death imposed upon her the necessity of supporting herself. Assured of admission, Stearns was granted permission to defer the payment of her tuition until she could earn it, if someone would guarantee the loan. She turned to her prosperous uncle, Franklin Ripley, for assistance. He refused to help, apparently fearing to set a precedent. She deeply resented the rejection, all the more because her mother had made sacrifices as a child in order that her brother Franklin might be well educated. Stearns bemoaned the "friendless, pennyless, the utter loneliness" of a woman's economic dependence.[10]

Few single women in pursuit of the elusive goals of financial security and independence had the self-confidence, the relaxed nature, the nonchalance of Cornelia Hancock who, earning one dollar a day teaching school, could say: "There is always a way provided for me to get along and I know for any one who tries to do his or her duty that there always will be. I never look ahead one day for there is no certainty about anything in these diggings, so there is no use fretting."[11]

Whether their definition of economic independence required or rejected a paid occupation, antebellum spinsters associated financial security with intellectual freedom and personal autonomy. They recognized a need for certain resources to free them to follow their minds and spirits in whatever direction these commanded. Among these resources were a private room or a home.

Lacking sufficient finances, most single women lived with their parents or siblings, exchanging domestic labor for room and board. The situation was often difficult. Under the best of circumstances, neither wife, daughter, nor sister had any privacy within woman's so-called "domain." A woman's physical (and even emotional) space in the world belonged to her husband, children, and brothers. According to the same ideology which defined the domestic sphere as properly hers, she could not bar from her presence those very people for whom she created this refuge from the outside world. More than other women, spinsters lived according to the dictates of other household members because of their position as dependents. Their time, activities, and attention were guided by another's purse, schedule, guests, and interests. The limitations of the situation galled them.

Catharine M. Sedgwick, whose earnings as an author never provided her with the money to support her own establishment, reflected on both the social and personal implications of this arrangement: "Never perhaps was a condition of inferiority and dependence made by the affection of friends more tolerable than mine—Still I hanker after the independence and interests and power of communication of a home of my own." Harriot Hunt, who lived happily first in her parents' and then her wedded sister's home for many years, finally recognized that despite the love and respect which she found there, she had to board separately. "If there could be but one family in a house, it is tolerably clear there should be but one head," she wrote. "It cripples one not to have a home of one's own."[12]

The death or economic collapse of a male head of household had a deleterious impact on everyone. For the single daughter, sister, or aunt, it often meant finding or begging another home. Eunice Callender experienced the trauma of having the family home sold out from under her following her father's death. Fortunately, a family friend bought the house at auction and permitted Callender to remain there as a tenant. Hannah Adams moved in with her brother and his family after her father's business failure. She felt unwelcome. The experience marked both her personality and her behavior, leaving her emotionally constricted and subject to attacks of anxiety and insecurity.[13]

For all these reasons—the insecurity, the dependency, and the lack of privacy—single women dreamed of and worked for a place of their own in which they were neither intruded upon nor intruded. They identified such a place as vital to their individual development and well-being. Personal space provided what Harriot Hunt called "a centre" for women, a focal point for their being. Women controlled and defined this space.[14] In it, they moved on their own business according to their own impetus. Here they were free to explore and come to terms with their inner selves.

Women could stamp their own dwelling place with their individual taste, personality, and organization. Their room(s) thus lent support to their sense of self by reflecting this back at them. They controlled access to such places, excluding those who did not contribute to their well-being. Given this, they might then risk new styles of living, new intellectual configurations, new modes of cultural expression, and new kinds of vocational commitments.

Antebellum women testified to the importance of private space in order to think their own thoughts, search their souls, examine their beliefs, reflect on their feelings, explore the depths of their creativity, and mine the inner reaches of their individual natures. Mary Lyon, in an 1832 proposal for a New England Female Seminary for Teachers, included plans for a boardinghouse "to furnish each member with a small chamber, exclusively her own." Said Lyon in explanation, "the great advantages of such a privilege can scarcely be realized, except by those who have often felt that they would give up almost any of their common comforts, for the sake of such retirement as can be enjoyed only in a separate apartment."[15]

Elizabeth Smith of Worcester spoke of her joy on returning from a round of fall visits in 1850. She felt closer to her God and her spirituality in her own home. Here her daily devotions, recorded ritualistically in her journal, went uninterrupted in an atmosphere hallowed by years of regular practice and the memory of shared worship with another woman long since dead. Lucy Larcom yearned for some place of her own: "I want a corner exclusively mine in which to spin my own web and ravel it again if I wish."[16] She never acquired her own home, and rarely had even a room to herself. She lived with siblings or in boarding schools for most of her life. When leaving her rural farmhouse for the last time in 1851, Mary Moody Emerson spoke of "hours surpassing all it ever fell to my meagre capacity to enjoy or think in any other place." Each of these women believed that intellectual development, creativity, and moral strength grew according to the quality of reflection possible only in a private place. "The thoughtless need home for discipline," said Harriot Hunt, "the thoughtful can breathe in no other atmosphere."[17]

Just as a room of one's own was necessary for the cultivation of thought and the experience of psychological and spiritual growth, so too it was a necessary component of vocational life. For writers, artists, and thinkers, privacy was the well-spring of creativity. They required a place cleared of other voices—obstructing and domineering cultural patterns, theories, and influences. Lucy Larcom, for example, spoke of understanding herself and therefore of producing more authentic work in a "retired situation." She sought release from stultifying forms and expectations. "I want the winds from every point of the compass to visit me freely," she wrote.[18]

Spinsters hoped to evade unsolicited and unwanted demands on their time and attention. Louisa May Alcott sought release from family cares and domestic chores in her room. From early childhood the dream of a room of her own haunted Alcott. At the age of twelve, she wrote: "I have been thinking about my little room, which I suppose I shall never have. I should want to be there about all the time, and I should go there and sing and think." A year later, she recorded having "got the little room I have wanted so long, and am very happy about it." Was it coincidence that, having occupied her own room, Alcott proceeded to "make a plan" for her life as the first priority? As an adult, Alcott frequently removed herself from the family home in Concord to a series of rooms (and ultimately a town house) in Boston. "I can't work at home," she wrote, "and need to be alone to spin, like a spider."[19]

Many spinsters required their own place because the exigencies of their work interfered with household routines and rules in a parental home or boarding house. Emily Howland, working with ex-slaves, determined to get a house "and be a housekeeper again." Explained Howland, "I must have a home, and no other person's house should be burdened—and I think no one would endure a boarder with such an extensive acquaintance." Freedmen and women, soldiers, doctors, nurses, and representatives of government agencies and benevolent societies all pursued Howland for advice, aid, and information which she dispersed at all hours from her residence.[20] Harriot Hunt also needed a separate establishment in which to practice medicine. The Hunt sisters, Harriot and Sarah, lived with their mother and shared a joint medical practice. When Sarah married, Harriot came to live with her as a way of sharing her new family life and continuing joint consultation on medical matters. But Hunt soon realized that this means of structuring her life and time lead her away from professional activity into an increasingly family-oriented existence. Hunt had to choose between living with her medical practice and family living with all its distractions.[21]

A separate living space offered the vocationally oriented woman a place of refuge, safety, rest, and repose. That which married women created for others, these spinsters sought to acquire for themselves. As Susan B. Anthony wrote, "A home of one's own is the soul's dream of rest." Here a woman might return and renew her sense of purpose. Here she might retire periodically to regain a sense of mental perspective and physical vigor. Lucy Larcom was fond of quoting Elizabeth Barrett Browning's poem Aurora Leigh: "Make room for rest around me; That in great calms of space my soul may right Her nature."[22] In her own home, a woman found the physical and spiritual nourishment which enabled her to pursue the demanding life of reformer, intellectual, or artist.

Just as their work required a certain kind and amount of space, so too did the personal and social lives of single women. Female friends and networks provided these women with important personal and vocational support. Their friendships were cultivated and flowered in extended visiting. But how could one offer hospitality to an intimate or a colleague if she lived as a guest in another's house? The desire to have a place in which to gather one or more selected others appeared frequently in the musings of single women. Emily Howland wished that her Virginia house was finished so that she might extend a summer invitation to Mary Reed, an early mentor and highly regarded colleague. Lucy Larcom dreamed of building her "long-planned home among the mountains," where, she said, "my friends shall bivouac with me all summer."[23]

Catharine M. Sedgwick wrote to her sister that, "If I had a home (alas! how many sweet visions are comprised within that impossible *if*), I should wish F[rances, her niece] to pass the next year with me." A home of one's own did not necessarily mean a home alone. The question was one of control not distance or separation, of privacy not isolation. Many antebellum women made homes with one another. Others planned for communal retirement, envisioning a group home of congenial elderly maidens. For, as Maria Mitchell observed, "a woman needs a home and the love of other women at least, if she lives without that of man."[24]

For many a single woman, having a home was in one important way different from having a private place or room in someone else's home. It meant not only having privacy, but also a place where she was truly sovereign. Aside from desiring a place in which to grow, and the freedom and privacy in which to do it, single women also wanted the authority, the independence, and the status attached to the traditionally male position as head of household. For while American culture spoke of women as ruling the domestic sphere, the antebellum mother, wife, and housekeeper had mainly responsibility for managing the household and but limited authority over it. In reality, the home was never so isolated from the world as the ideology of domesticity would have had it. In those areas of interaction between home and society (making of major purchases, schooling of children, representation in the community, church, or government), the husband held sway. Single women reigned supreme within their homes in actuality as well as in name. Female householders were to be the first women granted political power through the franchise.

Female reformers Harriot Hunt, Susan B. Anthony, and Catharine Beecher feared that many women married solely to become mistress of their own homes. In the belief that their position as proprietress would bring them relief from parental domination, stature as an adult in the community, and influence as a wife and mother, such women forgot that in entering marriage they gave up parental rule only to acquire that of a husband, and donned not only the status of adult but also the domestic duties of wife and mother. Reform-minded spinsters adjudged that the naive expectations of young women for position and even power were rarely fulfilled in marriage. A wife and mother had only the power of supplication and the limited authority of helpmeet. While sympathetic to the desire of young women to become mistresses of their abodes, these spinsters deplored the route of marriage as self-defeating. The advancement of women in antebellum society might well be tied to the home, but not, in their opinion, to the institution of marriage, to the domestic sphere, or to the female roles of wife and mother. Such reformers dreamed of women launching out of the domestic sphere with the stature and authority of householders and the independence of proprietorship. [25]

Harriot Hunt prophesied that all women would one day have their own homes when "sexual education is abolished and the law of sexual remuneration is annulled." Hunt looked forward to a time when women would no longer be socialized and educated only to be wives, exchanging sex and domestic labor for material support. Susan B. Anthony agreed. She predicted that America faced an era of singlehood. Because marriage in the nineteenth century was based on the subjugation of women, Anthony speculated that women would increasingly reject it. For their own self-respect, as an education in sex equity for men, and as a necessary step toward independence, such women would make comfortable and attractive homes for themselves and one another. [26]

Catharine Beecher defined her life's work as being, "to *train* woman for her true business and then pay her so liberally that she can have a home of her own whether married or single." She urged women to make their homes with one another. Together, then, women would emerge from these female strongholds, taking their concerns about health, welfare, education, and moral well-being into the world at large. In her later years, Beecher rejoiced in the "increasingly open avenues to useful and remunerating occupations for women, enabling them to establish *homes of their own*" where they might take in and care for the orphaned, neglected, and ill. Although associated with the Cult of Domesticity, Beecher ended her public life in promoting female-headed households and family units. [27]

For the most part, the spinsters of this period cast their unfeminine desires for privacy and power in feminine guise. Although "A home of one's own is the want, the necessity, of every human being—the one thing above all others, longed for, worked for," according to Susan B. Anthony, she based women's claim to private, personal places not on individual rights but on the "natural love of woman for home, which no outside occupation can eradicate." In 1877 Anthony wrote a speech for the Slayton Lecture Bureau entitled "The Homes of Single Women." It was inspired by the life of Dr. Alide C. Avery of Denver, in whose home she had resided during the suffrage campaign in Colorado. Anthony argued that despite popular misconceptions the home instinct was as natural in professional women, spinsters, and feminists as in other women. In addition to Avery's dedicated work on behalf of women's suffrage and her devotion to medicine, she "found time for just as careful marketing, house-keeping and gardening as before," wrote Anthony. "All this is done from *pure love of home;*—no spurious second-hand domesticity *affected* for the praise of some man, or conscientiously maintained for the comfort of the one who furnishes the money;—nor, because she has nothing else to busy herself about,—but her own impelling motive, is from the true womanly home instinct—unsurpassed, by that of any of the women who 'have all the rights they want' [i.e., in marriage]."[28] Anthony thus claimed for the spinster the social virtue of love for home in a measure equal to, and perhaps purer than, her married sister. In her demand for a home of her own, or perhaps particularly there, the single woman was a "true" woman after all.

Nineteenth-century women longed for a place in which to be alone with their thoughts and inspiration because they valued the life of the mind so highly. They dreamed of the day when women would have access to the same educational opportunities that had enabled men to expand their intellectual horizons and cultivate their spiritual growth. Indeed, intellectual development symbolized liberation to many women. Their letters and diaries reveal the pleasure, the fulfillment, and the growth which they sought in education.

Hannah Adams gravitated early to the intellectual life. She read widely in her father's considerable library. The "happiness of Heaven" meant to her the gratification of her thirst for knowledge. Sarah Grimké wrote of her "passion" for learning. The longing for an intellectual life and a sense of its total absence in her native Farmersville, New York, characterized letters written by Caroline F. Putnam. Having left Oberlin after only one year (due to family pressure), Putnam wrote longingly, even jealously, of her classmate's greater educational opportunities. To Sallie Holley, she said:

I am greatly puzzled why *you* should have been born with the perennial Mind-Tree already planted beside your very cradle—with ample liberty to pluck its choicest, fairest fruits, and browse upon its most delicious foliage at your leisure and pleasure—while I with the same hunger and thirst, have been stinted and starved with the fewest possible leaves that the four winds could have scattered.[29]

Many women spoke of reading material as that which held for them the greatest value in life.[30]

Such attitudes on the part of young women were neither widely re-spected nor encouraged. Parents and guardians denigrated many a desire for formal education, frustrated the search for intellectual stimulation, and blocked attempts to participate in the broader culture of the day.[31] The main impetus for woman's education in this period lay in a desire to create better wives and mothers, not in a justification of the pursuit of ideas for their own sake.[32] The precocious Sarah Grimké was unusually blessed in having her father's permission to study the rudiments of history, Greek, natural science, and botany. She was forbidden to undertake advanced studies in these areas, and her request to learn Latin was refused on the grounds that its sole value lay in its usefulness as a prerequisite for college or professional training—neither of which were open to the women of Grimké's generation.[33]

The pursuit of learning required a commitment of time, money, and sustained effort incompatible with domestic duties or schedules. Women complained of the "fragmentary," "irregular," and "scrappy" nature of their education. Hannah Adams bewailed the lack of rigor in her training. Catharine Sedgwick decried the absence of system and consistency in hers. Emily Blackwell longed for undivided time in which to study. Sallie Holley bemoaned the superficiality of her knowledge.[34]

Although denied an adequate educational base, many spinsters took extraordinary measures in pursuit of learning. Myrtilla Minor picked hops in order to buy books. Mary Moody Emerson read voraciously, "feasting in books." She borrowed from every private and public library in the region. Maria Mitchell took a librarian's job on Nantucket in order to have access to books. She read devotedly before, during, and after hours.[35] Women's education was a life-long pursuit. At the age of forty-five, Abigail Kimber took leave from her teaching responsibilities in order to study advanced mathematics in Philadelphia. At thirty-six, Mary Reed enrolled in chemistry classes at the Philadelphia Female Medical College. At forty, she attended Oberlin for a summer, but could not afford to continue. It "has been a very hard [year] for teachers," she explained. "We have had to pay about double for board &c. and the salaries in private schools have been no higher." She followed a rigorous reading schedule on her own, however. "Please understand," she wrote to a friend, that "when I speak of 'reading' that I mean reading Virgil. I could not have read so well, had I not gone to Oberlin . . . I wish something might happen to send me there for a year, and then I should be satisfied."[36]

The high value placed on intellectual development among unmarried women stemmed, however, from something more than the pleasure of acquiring knowledge for its own sake. These women aspired to intellectual independence, for the exercise of independent judgment provided a keystone for the autonomous life. Such women understood that their lack of formal education reinforced their subordination as women. To Maria Mitchell, "the strangest thing is that women ever study at all," for in the eyes of men "learning is not a help but a hindrance. The dependence of

woman is one of her chief attractions—her independence is repulsion."
Sarah Grimké agreed. She believed that male opposition to female debate
about women's roles and responsibilities stemmed from "a desire to keep
[woman] in unholy subjection to man, and one way of doing this is to
deprive us of the means of becoming their equals, by forbidding us the
privileges of education to fit us for the performance of duty." She attributed
her own passivity and dependence to her lack of formal study: "Oh, had I
received the education I desired, had I been bred to the profession of the
law, I might have been a useful member of society, and instead of myself
and my property being taken care of, I might have been a protector of the
helpless, a pleader for the poor and unfortunate."[37] The unwed struggled to
free herself from subordination and dependency—whether her political dependence on male citizenry and leadership, her economic dependence on
male relatives, or her religious and intellectual dependence on "received
truth." Enlightenment provided the first step toward entitlement.

Two kinds of intellectual development comprised enlightenment. Self-
knowledge enabled a woman to establish her individuality. Independent-
mindedness reinforced the intellectual and psychological stamina which
had impelled her on her unusual course and sustained her in it. The
pursuit of autonomy began with self-knowledge. A woman had to begin to
think of herself as an individual with wants, needs, talents, a personality,
and a personhood distinct from others. She advanced her self-knowledge
through introspection. The writing of a daily journal provided the means
for regular reflection. Said Mary Moody Emerson of this exercise, "My life
I would occupy only in the study of its wonders—in arranging my ideas of
its real character." Rachel Stearns commenced her journal at the time of
her conversion to Methodism with the purpose of recording her growth in
godliness. "I love to examine myself," she wrote. Periodically, she reviewed her writings and evaluated her progress. On her twenty-second
birthday, Stearns acknowledged that while she had not enjoyed her religion so much during the past year as previously, she had "gained in
self-knowledge, in knowledge of human nature, and self-control."[38]

Devout men had begun to keep such journals in the seventeenth century. Calvinism encouraged the pious to keep watch over themselves as
they opened their souls to God. Self-scrutiny provided a measure of one's
progress toward heaven. Only constant examination could reassure one of
his or her "election" as a candidate for eternal salvation. While many
male diaries survive from the seventeeth century, few from women's hands
exist. In addition to the fact that there were fewer literate women than
men, the activity of journal writing may have been less common among
women because they were encouraged to look to their husbands for reas-
surance as to their religious standing.

The ability of women to read and write virtually doubled from 1780 to

1840.[39] This opened the way for women to record their responses to the religious tracts they read, to copy verses or daily devotions as part of their religious observance, and to summarize weekly sermons.[40] Being records of their spiritual lives and an attempt to measure their growth in the Lord, Rachel Stearn's journal and Mary Moody Emerson's almanac appear fairly traditional in orientation. However, in their efforts consciously to formulate and expound upon their own thoughts, to explore their own feelings, and to analyze politically their lives and circumstances, both diaries have a more modern cast.

The many diaries of women from this period in New England's history testify to women's increasing interest in self-exploration. Mary Moody Emerson spoke of her journal as "a letter to me when unable to think—or feel, which is worse," a "conversation with my old chamber," a means of transmitting prayer from "my soul to its Author." Louisa May Alcott kept a journal throughout her life, accepting her mother's counsel to "make observations about our conversations and your own thoughts. It helps you to express them and to understand your little self." Emily Howland regularly exercised a "clear seeing into myself." In periods of self-doubt, she probed critically into the deepest recesses of mind and heart. "I feel like talking to myself," she wrote during one such episode, "therefore I will seek this old book containing waifs of my life in some of its most important tenses and write . . . verily I am a riddle to myself." Lucy Larcom was not altogether comfortable with journal writing. "A journal of the subjective kind I have always thought foolish, as nurturing a morbid self-consciousness in the writer," she said. "And yet, alone so much as I am, it is well to have some sort of a ventilator from the interior."[41]

In addition to her search for self, the unmarried woman with visions of autonomy aspired to strength of mind. Such women possessed a certain amount of psychological stamina and ego-strength to begin with, but they valued the independent mind as both a means of self-preservation and as a means to the end of self-determination. The courage to question a premise, the ability to analyze an idea for one's self, to direct thought, to sustain a logical progression, to solve problems, and to arrive at a conclusion consistent with the data all required a disciplined and discriminating mind. Because most lacked the benefits of a systematic education, these late eighteenth- and early nineteenth-century generations of women looked for ways in which to evaluate received truth and propose new formulations. Maria Mitchell urged her sisters to reject traditional ways of thinking and doing. "Who," she asked, "settles the way? Is there anyone so forgetful of the sovereignty bestowed upon her by God that she accepts a leader who shall capture her mind?" Mitchell was convinced that "Until women throw off reverence for authority they will not develop. When they do this, when they come to truth through their own investigations, when doubts lead them to discovery, the truth which they get will be theirs, and their minds will go on and on unfettered."[42]

It was not easy either to determine one's true duty or to carry it out. In the first place, as Mitchell acknowledged, it was difficult to know exactly what "one ought to do." Every woman's capabilities, responsibilities, and peculiarities were different. And second, society itself frowned on those who took too idiosyncratic a path. Harriet Martineau, British journalist and commentator on the American scene, warned that "the whole apparatus of opinion is brought to bear offensively upon individuals among women who exercise freedom of mind in deciding what duty is, and the methods by which it is to be preserved."[43]

Ultimately, one had only one's self-respect with which to maintain standards. As Mary A. Dodge put it, "There is nothing in life but to go on perfectly self-poised, satisfied that you are doing what is best under the circumstances . . . and that while we should pay proper deference to man's opinion the real dignity of life is to be independent of it." Abigail Williams May felt so strongly on this point that she decided her niece should learn it early. Eleven years of age was not too soon. She urged Eleanor G. May to "depend more" upon herself. "What you want to do in life, is to help along the world in any little way that God permits. Another first best step towards helping others, is being able to do for yourself."[44]

As women dreamed about freedom, they realized that an expanded intellect was a necessary first step in the pursuit of autonomy. In knowing herself and in developing independence of thought and strength of mind lay the possibility that a woman might make her own way in the world and do her duty in such a fashion as to fulfill her particular destiny. As Alice Cary wrote to an unknown correspondent: "Let me admonish you to stand more strongly by your own nature. God gave it to you. For that reason alone you should think well of it, and make the most of it." She urged her acquaintance to "live a higher, more expansive, and expressive life" because she was "entitled to it."[45]

Emily Howland spoke of the bitterness of being forced to betray a newly gained sense of self. When her parents brought her home from school in Philadelphia because "it was not considered an advantage for women to have an education," she "came home and tried to live. Nobody can tell the unspeakable misery of a young person who has a vision before her and has to live below it. There was no distinct thing that I wanted to do but I wanted to go on."[46] Howland's life was shaped by her efforts to identify, pursue, and live up to her own vision.

Single women who thought about their freedom associated it with economic security and independence, a home or room of their own, and

intellectual development. These were the prerequisites for personal autonomy to which they aspired. Antebellum spinsters believed that these three
things supported the vocational life. They knew that their vocations
fostered self-development and self-regard while promoting accomplishment. Despite the elusiveness of these goals, they continued to work
toward them.

When wearied by overwork, when struggling with the stresses and
strains of an unprofitable and unfulfilling occupation, Lucy Larcom often
played a mental game of "when I get my freedom. . . ." The specific
meaning she attached to her freedom changed over time. Sometimes she
preferred the privacy and time in which to write well. At other times she
sought refuge from the loud and demanding voices of her students, release
from constant remedial study, escape to a life in the woods, independence
from the dogma and orthodoxy of her native New England, or security
from financial pressure. Larcom acknowledged the likelihood that she
would never be free in any of these senses. Few antebellum single women
ever acquired financial security, a place of their own, or higher education.
Later generations would have such benefits largely as a result of the path-
finding efforts of these early pioneers. But for the spinsters of this study,
liberty remained largely the subject of fantasy.[47]

5

"I Have Reached the Age for Action"

Vocational Identity and the Growth of Autonomy

The path to independence differs for each generation, much as the meaning of personal autonomy does. In colonial America, for example, conversion to one or another radical religious sect was an important medium through which women might extend their experience and expand their intellectual outlook. The Quakers, Antinomians, or Grotonists promised more freedom in the individual relationship with God and larger roles for women in the church. These sects provided more room for the development of female autonomy than did the confines of Puritan orthodoxy. In the last quarter of the twentieth century, it could be argued that the physical realm has been the arena in which many have sought to grow and to achieve. Men and women have devoted themselves to various forms of physical exertion and sexual experimentation—some in the name of conditioning, but others as a form of liberation and self-expression, a route to self-awareness and autonomy. The visions of liberty held by the single women of the early nineteenth century were the product of a specific set of historical circumstances and relationships. The means by which, the direction toward which, and the constraints within which these same women pursued their autonomy also emerged from their situation, for the road to independence varied in America according to gender and marital status.

Antebellum women operated within a set of assumptions regarding woman's nature and sphere. Those who sought to pursue self-knowledge and self-actualization did so in the shadow of these assumptions. As the heroine said to her husband in a novel written by Mary Clemner Ames (biographer and friend to several of these spinsters),

Darling, I never had an equal chance with you since I was born. As a woman I could not have had it if I had been born of the same condition in life. Truer words were never spoken than [that], "There is nothing so barbaric as for a human being to say to another that this far shall [s]he be developed and no farther; and that there is no other subject on which so much intolerable nonsense is laid as upon the sphere of women."[1]

Spinsters, then, pursued their autonomy in the one area where the spheres of men and women overlapped—the vocational life.

The primary task of their maidenhood was to develop a vocational identity—one strong enough to withstand both family and social objections. Given that there were few structures in which they might shape such an identity, experiment with and test it, the task required ingenuity, courage, patience, and time. Women rarely concluded their efforts before their thirties, and some continued to struggle well into their forties. A woman emerged from the trial as a butterfly does from the chrysalis, a new creature, no longer wholly daughter nor future wife and mother, but now an intellectual woman, a female artist, a scientific woman. The expressions used are those of the time, for the nouns *intellectual, artist,* and *scientist* were male and signified professional identities.[2] Women's vocational identities were significant because they enabled individuals to detach themselves from the limitations of their immediate environment and the activities expected of women of their age and standing. The assumption of a new identity prepared women to embark upon new, vocational lives.

——————◄◆►——————

Women began to formulate vocational identities when they reached a certain age. The age varied from one individual to another but usually came in conjunction with the end of their schooling, the approach of marriage, the process of conversion, or the end of marital eligibility. These events signified turning points in women's lives, times when they questioned what they would do in the future. At these junctures, women experienced a new sense of accountability for their lives, their talents, their time, and their actions.

Americans did not agree on a specific age or point at which women became accountable for themselves. Independent status was limited for women and came in bits and pieces. Women came of legal age at eighteen but assumed few rights and little independence at that age. Although they acquired property rights, they were permitted to assert them only so long as they remained unwed. When they married, control of their property went to their husbands. Women gained no rights as citizens at any age— the rights to vote and to serve on a jury were both circumscribed during this period. In practice, the coming of legal age largely meant the right to marry without parental approval, or the right to freely subject oneself to the authority of a man other than one's father.

Still, some daughters felt a certain liberation in the release of parental authority and chose to exert their new "majority" in the limited manner open to them. Frances Willard was determined to underscore her changed position on her "freedom day" and plunked herself down in the family living room to read a forbidden novel. When admonished by her father, she asserted, "I am eighteen—I am of age—I am now to do what I think right, and to read this fine historical story [*Ivanhoe*] is, in my opinion, a right thing for me to do."[3] The act was the largely symbolic one of a largely symbolic transition.

Women noted that their "coming of age" brought fewer rewards, less social recognition, and less independence to them than to their male peers. "I am about to embark on twenty-one," wrote Emily Howland in her diary, "that beginning of so many responsibilities, to the other sex, as in common parlance they assume the right of self-government, no such important consequences await the advent of my birthday." Twenty-year-old Emily Blackwell remarked that her labor provided her with only half the earnings of her fourteen-year-old brother, despite the fact that it was *she* who had educated *him*. Frances Willard watched her twenty-one-year-old brother setting off to vote with the men of the household. Blinded by tears, she turned to her sister Mary and asked: "Wouldn't you like to vote as well as Oliver? Don't you and I love the country just as well as he, and doesn't the country need our ballots?" Her sister responded fearfully, "Course we do, and course we ought—but don't you go ahead and say so, for then we would be called strong-minded." The gender-specific restrictions on women's lives created a feeling of relative deprivation in the minds of ambitious young women. Their coming of age did not provide them with an expanded sphere of action, greater responsibility for self, or more freedom of person or movement.[4]

As they reached their early twenties, they began to confront the limitations on woman's sphere and to experience a sense of impending crisis. Jane Maris, a young Philadelphian, suffered a deep depression as she approached her twenty-third birthday: "[A]m I getting old and disagreeable to every one?" she asked. Graceanna Lewis spoke humorously, but with emphasis, of herself and her friends as being among those who were " 'a little more than twenty.' " Emily Howland acknowledged her twenty-fifth birthday with a "Heigho a quarter of a century old to-day only think of it! the first leap down the precipice of old maidism taken."[5]

Howland's words provide one clue to the disquieting nature of the transition among these young women as they noted the passing of a somewhat flexible age for marital eligibility. In colonial America, the mid-twenties had signified the beginning of spinsterhood. Physician John Higginson, for example, spoke of two young women "like to continue ancient maids . . . being twenty-five or twenty-six years old."[6] Although many in the early nineteenth century continued to perceive the mid-twenties as demarcating marital eligibility, others recognized that, as men married at older and older ages, spinsterhood was no longer inevitable for women in their thirties or even forties. Eunice Callender, twenty-three in

1808, admonished her friend Sarah Ripley for labeling a person of twenty-six or -seven a "maiden Leady." "Was you sensible of what a tender point you was striking upon? how in the name of wonder came you to think they were maiden Leadies at that age; I never heard of it before; and only think how *very* few years must elapse before you must address your letters to a *Maiden Leady!!*"[7]

The passing of marital eligibility did not cause these women their greatest concern with regard to their diminished opportunities for marriage, however. It did underscore the passage of time and the need to determine the use to which they would put their time and energies. Women fretted about deeds undone, goals unachieved, and opportunities foregone or foreclosed. Jane Maris wrote to Esther Jane Trimble on the approach of her twenty-third birthday, saying, "such a creature as I to be twenty-three. 'Can thou realize it?' I cannot. . . . What good have I done in the past years?" Emily Blackwell noted that at twenty-five she could no longer think of herself as a young woman and believed that she had "reached the age for action, for great deeds and what is accomplished? How terrible it must be to look back upon a long life of error and failure."[8]

In their own eyes, these women had reached the age of accountability. Some strode forward into spinsterhood with a sense of destiny and purpose. Some recognized that under their particular family or economic circumstances they must make a place for themselves in the world. Marriage might or might not come in its own time. Others edged toward a separate life out of the recognition that, married or not, they would ultimately stand before their God alone, responsible for the use to which they had put their time and talents.

----◄●►----

The experience of conversion propelled many women along the route to autonomy by providing an institutional structure and an ideological framework in which to construct a self and a vocation. The religious identity obtained in the conversion process served as the touchstone for their vocational identity.

Conversion was an act expected of young people, a ritual that marked them as having fulfilled one of the tasks of youth and therefore as having well and firmly placed their feet on the path to adulthood. Conversion meant that an individual had passed through a period of self-examination, prayer, and communion with God. She opened her heart to His word, and to His will for her life. She subordinated her desires to His. She acknowledged and repented past sins, pledged to resist the temptation to sin anew, and dedicated herself to a life of Christian observance. In formal recognition of her taking God as Lord, a young woman made application for membership in the church and subjected herself to examination by the elders that they might determine the extent of her sincerity and transformation. Both men and women were expected to convert before leaving home for the last time.

Some passed easily through the ritual, adopting the form and substance of conversion with relatively few pangs of anxiety. Others experienced conversion, or the pressure to convert, in conjunction with another life crisis. Often these were identity crises of one or another kind, when a woman faced a life change and attempted to align herself with her God as a means of coping with the change. For a spinster like Eunice Callender, who had lived and worked at home thoughout her life, the crisis might not happen until middle age. The death of her parents left her alone for the first time, bereft of her role as family caretaker and stripped of her identity as daughter. Feeling the loss of an assigned role or familiar identity, Callender turned to religion for solace and instruction.[9]

For other young women, the crisis of conversion came with that of proposed marriage. Young women were expected to convert before marrying. Conversion itself signified a readiness to enter the Christian institutions of marriage and motherhood in an appropriate frame of mind. For some, like Catharine Beecher, the transformation held out to her by suitor and church were not altogether welcome. While both marriage and conversion signified progress toward adulthood, marriage did not increase autonomy, and the two in concert connoted the end of one's progress from a dependent to an independent status. While Beecher agreed to a marriage proposal urged upon her by her father, the Reverend Lyman Beecher, she resisted the process of conversion, which he valued fully as much. Her resistance grew from the understanding that "A young man might exercise briefly his submission to God and then recover his sense of independence and self. For a woman, however, submission to God might be but the prelude to a lifetime of earthly submission to a husband."[10] Released from her promise to marry by the premature death of her betrothed, Beecher transformed the language and purpose of conversion into a lifelong public vocation, as high priestess of Christian womanhood and the Cult of Domesticity.

Beecher's conversion experience was particularly rigorous, drawn out, and painful. Heightened in her case by the strength and will of both father and daughter, Beecher's struggle nevertheless was not unique. Others resisted the dependence and self-abnegation of conversion even as they expressed themselves in the rhetoric of pious submission and humility. Women commonly referred to conversion as a turning point on one side of which lay frivolity and freedom from accountibility while on the other came responsibility, self-denial, and self-sacrifice. Many women found that the transformation reinforced, not feminine dependence and submissiveness, but female independence and assertiveness.

The adoption of a religious identity allowed women to assert themselves in both public and private ways—to move into the public sphere in one or another moral or religious vocation, or to indulge in a kind of "holy-self-ishness" or self-absorption at home.[11] Spinster Elizabeth Smith of Worcester, Massachusetts, lived quietly in the family home immersed in piety. Her diary recorded daily and annual summaries of the state of her spiritual self. At the age of eighty, she was still experiencing the "earnest desire to examine myself more strictly this year . . . than I have ever done." She sought the Lord's help that she might "walk worthily [in] my holy vocation and ever more serve him in righ[teousness] and holy[ness] all the days of my life."[12]

Missionary women were among those who moved out of the domestic sphere, spurred by their Christian conscience and identity. Before mid-century, women went to the mission field primarily as wives of male missionaries. In the eyes of the church, they served an auxiliary function and were not God's workers in their own right. Gradually, single women sought to follow their Lord's call to minister to the heathen. Cynthia Farrar sailed in 1827 with an appointment from the American Board of Foreign Missions. She was to superintend female schools in Bombay, India. Farrar was thirty-two at the time. With the exception of a two-year hiatus in the United States, Farrar served in India until her death at the age of sixty-seven. In 1828, the American Board sent four single women—Maria Ogden, Delia Stone, Mary Ward, and Maria Patten—to the Sandwich Islands. Sarah Cummings became the first single woman sponsored by the American Baptist Board. She went to Burma in 1832. When she died after a year of service, Caroline Harrington replaced her. Over the next ten years, single women went to Ceylon, Liberia, Greece, China, and Persia.[13] Others took their beliefs and skills to the native population of their own country.[14]

Officially, their purpose was "to comfort and aid the wives of the missionaries in their various cares and domestic duties, and to improve the condition of the native females."[15] The mission societies emphasized the former, but, in the name of the latter, women established schools, developed teacher-training programs for native women, translated religious works into indigenous languages, provided medical assistance and training, and taught the word of God in their own way. Although they retained the rhetoric and demeanor of Christian humility, they moved out of the private sphere and into the public as independent women of God. Following their own definition of a new religious identity, these women embarked on a vocational life through which they expanded their intellectual and personal horizons through their contact with various human cultures and material conditions. They had to face alien definitions of women's status and thus learned tolerance. They grew in their faith. As they met the physical, emotional, and intellectual challenges of new worlds, missionary women gained in self-knowledge and self-esteem.

The experiences of Fidelia Fiske, first spinster missionary to Persia, offer an example. Fiske's initial journal was both difficult and frightening. The company sailed from Boston to Istanbul, then continued overland through almost eight hundred miles of mountainous, unsettled territory inhabited primarily by thieves and raiders. It was an experience to daunt the spirits of anyone, but particularly a young woman who had never traveled far and who professed both a fear of the unknown and a preference for the settled domestic life.[16] Fiske summoned untapped resources of both physical stamina and emotional courage. She conquered doubts and fears and made the best of the experience not only for herself but for the entire party.[17]

During her years in Persia, Fiske drew enormously upon her reserves of emotional and physical strength to meet both the daily duties of keeping home, mission, and school together and to cope with the extraordinary calls for nursing a sick student or staff member, mentoring and guiding young women who sought to emulate her role, and traveling to other missions or schools as consultant, substitute, or trouble-shooter. Through all this, Fiske enjoyed far better health and more happiness than she had at home. Her well-being reflected the healthy exercise of mind and the enlargement of spirit made possible by work. Fiske learned Persian so that she might write and instruct her students in their native language. As she took on new work and met new challenges, she gained confidence in herself and in her calling. She also grew in faith. "I have learned here," she wrote a friend, "as I never did in America, that He who fed the five thousand with the portion of five, can feed the soul, and richly feed it, too, with what I once thought were *only* the *crumbs.*"[18]

After fifteen years, Fiske came home to America. She fully expected to return to the mission field once she had seen to the needs of her mother and sister. People urged her to remain in America, perhaps to take Mary Lyon's position at Mount Holyoke Seminary. In response, Fiske detailed the value of a lifelong commitment to a religious cause for antebellum women such as she.

I do not think so much of what I can reasonably expect to do [in Persia], as of giving up the work. It seems to me that there is much in *abiding in our work,* even if we can do but little. I think of the influence upon others; and more, I trust, of what my Heavenly Father desires. My four years in America have been very pleasant, and I should go back with the feeling that there is before me more of self-denial and trial than I should be likely to meet here; but I am afraid it would not be right to stay here; and, if not right, I could not be happy in staying.[19]

The virtues of dedication and stick-to-itive-ness, of carrying a work through to completion, surviving a hostile environment, continually meeting new challenges, testing one's ingenuity, courage, resourcefulness, and skills, doing one's duty to God—all these made of missionary life an exercise in personal and professional advancement. Fiske chose to remain in America and become Mount Holyoke chaplain, but she never fully accepted her decision. She died feeling that she had lost something vital by leaving the mission field.

The point here has to do not merely with religious enthusiasm or even self-assertion in the name of piety. During the religious upheavals of the 1830s, women exercised a certain autonomy through conversion. Some half of the female converts who joined church joined singly, without accompanying relatives of either sex. Two-thirds joined without male relatives.[20] They acted to resolve the contradictions of female status and role by defining their own identity and asserting it in church membership. For Fiske and other female missionaries, the act of conversion and the adoption of a religious identity was one of self-definition.

The life of Rachel Stearns provides a more subtle example of religious conversion as self-definition. In 1833 she moved with her mother and siblings to Greenfield, Massachusetts. Stearns was twenty years old and dreaded the approaching time when she must profess her faith. Sarah Ripley Stearns, her mother, was a deeply pious woman and expected that her daughter would confess her devotion when examined for membership by the orthodox Congregationalist elders of their new church. Said Rachel, "Religion appeared gloomy; but something I must have, in order to be prepared to die."[21]

One year later Stearns evidenced a greatly changed attitude. By then, she had found in religion something that prepared her to live. Stearns had attended a Methodist revival. While the rituals of orthodoxy left her cold, the emotional fervor of the camp meetings stirred her inner being. "Everything is changed," she wrote. "I seem to live in a new world. I almost doubt my identity sometimes. Indeed, I am not the same, I have been born again."[22]

But the change did not come easily. Stearns remained insecure in her new identity. Although she gave herself to God on October 11, 1834, she did not join the Methodist church for another year. Even then, her diary records pangs of doubt and episodes of backsliding. Some of the difficulty had to do with the diverse social standing of Methodists and Congregationalists in her community. In evaluating the "sacrifices" of Methodist affiliation, Stearns wrote: "I must descend from the rank in which I have been educated, and be looked upon by those whom I have considered my equals as an inferior—and—I must bear all manner of reproaches, be looked upon by my relatives as insane—crazy—self-willed—obstinate—

influenced by the opinions of others—.[23] In converting to Methodism, Stearns chose to adopt and flaunt a social position into which she had been forced as a result of family economic reversals.

Stearns's father died when she was four years old, leaving the family without resources. Sarah Ripley Stearns raised her daughter on social pretentions, with expectations that could not be fulfilled. Rachel's sense of relative deprivation worsened through comparison of her family's existence with that of her uncle, Franklin Ripley's. He and his family lived the well-to-do life in Boston, at some emotional and geographic distance from his "fallen" sister. Rachel resented the fact that she had to dress below her class, borrow money for schooling, and struggle to support herself and her mother while his family lacked for nothing. An outcast from her rightful social position by virtue of circumstance, Stearns chose to make herself a social and religious outcast as well. In consciously and willfully joining the despised sect, she reconciled herself to her fate and gained emotional strength by taking control over her caste and, through this, her life. She transformed social inferiority into moral superiority. As her sister complained, "Rachel thinks she can't do wrong. She thinks she is perfect."[24] Rachel Stearns cloaked her "dishabille" in self-righteousness.

Stearns felt drawn to Methodism by women's greater public role and freedom of expression within the sect. While teaching school in Leominster, Massachusetts, she concluded that duty required her to open class with a prayer. "It is well I am a Methodist," she confided, "otherwise I should think it wrong for a woman to pray before a man." Stearns often spoke before public prayer meetings, much to the dismay of her mother, who suggested that "perhaps there has been a great deal of vanity and pride" mixed with Rachel's sense of duty. Even admitting the possibility, Stearns would not desist. She regretted the lack of a Sunday school class in Leominster such as she had taught at home in Greenfield. She determined, however, to put her experience to good use by advising Mr. Bullard of the Massachusetts Sunday School Society on the content of his Sunday talks. She rationalized her assertiveness: "Satan told me not to go—it was not proper. O this cold propriety—I did tell [Bullard] and if it did any good, I don't care if it was not proper."[25]

A woman who hoped to make a name for herself as an eminent and distinguished Christian, Stearns had found an institution in which her ambition could be accepted as inspired by God.[26] The style of worship was such that her assertiveness need not be seen as abnormal, unfeminine, or egotistical. Stearns taught school as her occupation and consciously provided a Methodist presence as part of her work.

Rachel Stearns moved to end her cultural and familial dependence by asserting her independence in the matter of religious affiliation. She acquired her new identity by undergoing a long and difficult conversion process. In doing so, she adopted new patterns of religious observance, answered a vocational calling, and distanced herself from the values of her family and community with regard to female activism, class identification, ritual behavior, and doctrinal orthodoxy. Resolved Stearns, "I have set out to be different from other people, and I will be, no matter if there is not another person in the world like me, I am my Lord's and he is mine, and I will serve him, with my whole heart."[27]

Stearns sought a vocation to match her new identity, one that would serve the full measure of her ambition and exercise the full amplitude of her being. She hoped that the Methodist affiliation would provide such an opportunity. On occasion she thought about going west with a group of missionaries or founding a Christian academy. Finally, she left New England for Mississippi to work as a teacher to planters' daughters. Even in this capacity she sought to enlarge her work and give it a Christian cast by attempting to open a school for slavechildren on the plantation.[28]

The conversion experience, then, was an important catalyst to increased autonomy for many. As a young woman faced her God, she also faced a number of questions, the answers to which further shaped her sense of self. She confronted her church's definition of women's religious role, and with it whatever contradictions might exist between that definition and her own persuasion. She asked for what purpose she was put on the earth. As a corollary to this, she pondered her definition of duty: What was the nature of her calling? What talents and abilities had she? What desires? These questions brought her to account for the use to which she put her time, her opportunities, and her talents. From this new perspective, she reassessed the values represented by her family, denomination, or community and chose either to accommodate or to resist them. The self-scrutiny required by conversion began a process through which certain women established a separate identity and thereby redefined their social role.

———◆———

The "age" of accountability came in contexts other than conversion, as women searched for their vocational identity during the transitional years of their youth and early adulthood. The end of schooling, for example, brought home to many young women the social prohibition that they should go so far and no farther on the road to development and independence. Women experienced a hiatus when they left school, whether that schooling was a period of sporadic attendance at a finishing school or extended enrollment at a private female seminary. During this stage of their lives, young women taught school or undertook domestic duties while attempting to clarify the future. Frances Willard described the two years after her graduation as "often very dull and sometimes very gay," but "the most difficult in [her] life," for she had not yet "found her 'vocation.' "

Friends wait and watch. Materfamilias fears and paterfamilias hopes. It is a time full of unuttered pathos for a gentle, refined and modest girl. The truth is, she ought never to be put into a position so equivocal—one whose tendency is to tinge her soul with at least a temporary bitterness. Girls should be definitely set at work after their school days end, even as boys are, to learn some bread-winning employment that will give them an independent status in the world of work. Better still, this education of the hand should be carried on for both, side by side with that of the head and heart.[29]

Willard found herself preoccupied, continually evaluating her character and talents with an eye to determining what she might do with her life. The lack of occupation and clear vocational identity undercut her self-confidence.

I remember that I used to think myself smart. I used to plan great things that I would do and be. I meant to become famous, never doubting that I had the power. But it is over. The mist has cleared away and I dream no longer, though I am only twenty-one years old . . . I have come to this point: I think myself not good, not gifted in any way. I can not see why I should be loved, why I should hope for myself a beautiful and useful life or a glorious immortality at its close. Never before in all my life have I held myself at so cheap a rate as since I came home this last time . . . I can not quite content myself to belong to. . . "the happy mediocrity." Is it, then, inevitable that I am to account myself one of the great "commonality" during life? . . . *What you believe of yourself is vital to you.* Let others think as they will, if you feel "the victory is in you," as my father says, all things are possible.[30]

Such introspection and self-castigation haunted many young women at this same point in their lives.

After Emily Howland's parents brought her home from school in Philadelphia, she struggled for years to recapture the self-esteem, the sense of potential, and the independence that she had experienced at school.[31] Her birthday musings recorded her efforts to transform vague longings to be of some use and account in the world into a specific calling. She sought a cause or project worthy of her moral commitment, in need of her skills, and sufficiently interesting to hold her attention. Year after year she restated her desire for such an activity, her frustration at not yet embarking upon it, and her fear that she might never do so.

She looked back from her twentieth birthday, recalling that at fourteen she had expected by twenty to have acquired useful and interesting training. "Those years have passed," she wrote, and "what am I now? But little that I anticipated." At twenty-one, she mourned that "the course of my career moves on as ever, neither wiser, or better." "I am often a perfect marvel to myself," she wrote despairingly. "Why a life so useless should ever have been granted or why perpetuated . . . is the most unaccountable of our Creator's providences." At thirty, she recorded that she was "yet waiting for something to turn up." "I still want, hope, fear and despair alternately as I have done so many years. One year ago I thought this is my last record, before another [twelve] months life will have become a reality, I shall have an employment. But here I am as far apparently as ever from my object in life."[32] For a woman who felt that she could not live if she did not express herself in some vitally interesting work, the years of waiting proved frustrating and difficult.

Howland's correspondence indicates that she filled her time with many of the usual female pursuits: reading, studying, cultivating an herbarium, keeping house, nursing, and visiting friends and family. She shared her ambition with selected friends and relatives, seeking support in her search for a vocation. These discussions sustained Howland during this difficult juncture in her life's course.

Carrie A. Rowland, a younger woman of less serious mien than Emily, nevertheless understood her ambition. When Howland bemoaned her impotence and irresolution in undertaking some worthy task, Rowland reassured her that:

The feeling I have of thine is that thee is restless, uneasy, thinking that thy life is passing and thee is not acting up to the power within thee. Thy main purpose in life does not appear clearly enough to thee. But I think this, that now is the time of retirement, study and reflection. The dazzling romantic dreams of girlhood have passed—the time for them has passed and life appears before thee clothed in its majesty—its reality. Thou art to be a worker in the vast arena of the world, it is no light task—can we devote so many years to worldly education and shall we be impatient because our spiritual training demands equal time for its completion?[33]

Rowland urged Howland to offer God a willing heart and a prepared mind. She asked that Emily consider the possibility that this trial of patience was to be her testing ground, and that God awaited only her acceptance of His will and His time schedule before providing her with a task in life. Wrote Carrie, with a maturity beyond her years:

I do not misjudge thee. I know thy spirit craves a high and holy life beyond that this outward world can give, and I would strengthen thee. I would encourage thee, not to sink down helpless and disponding, but work steadily onward and though thy advancement may seem slow to thee and when the time cometh and the word goeth unto thee, "come for all things are now ready" thou shall find thyself possessed of powers of which thou hast taken no account, they have grown so silently.[34]

Howland heard similar advice from several women. As one after another prospect for a position, task, or role presented itself only to prove illusory or unsatisfactory, they begged her to "take courage and remember that many efforts must be made in any enterprise before we can succeed in our wishes and everything in nature that has been in an accustomed channel for a long time seems to make great efforts before it can be reversed or changed."[35]

In 1856, Emily heard about a school run by Myrtilla Miner for young black women in Washington, D.C. After so many tentative steps in first one direction and then another, Howland felt that at last she had received the call. She would go to Washington to assist Miner in her work. Despite Emily's assurance that this was the right step, several factors intervened to slow her departure. Emily's mother appeared set against her leaving home. Fearing her mother's grief and disapproval, Howland delayed telling her about her decision. In addition, Emily doubted her own capacity to fulfill the political responsibilities of the post. Lastly, she recognized that she had no teaching experience. In order to put off informing her family and to gain experience, Howland began a period of practice teaching in her cousin Phebe Coffin's school. At the age of thirty-one, she found in the classroom a "pleasure and satisfaction and cheerfulness" previously missing from her experience.

For some twenty months Howland postponed her departure. During that time she approached female friends and relatives for help and approval. Although she received conventional advice about the responsibilities of an unwed daughter to her parents, she also heard much that endorsed her decision. Some "rejoiced" in the prospect of Howland's entry into her "field of action." "It may seem strange and unnatural to your friends that anyone should recommend one in your situation absenting [her]self from the *near ties of home* but I think it very important for every one to do something if not at home go abroad—we can never know whether there is anything of us until we are proved. It is a great satisfaction to do that we can respect ourselves for," one wrote. Another commented upon the curious fact "that parents are less resigned commonly, to give up their daughters to be wedded to any interest however deserving—as being for the benefit of Man on the broad scale of humanity—than wedded to *one man*."[36]

Among the most important of those with whom Emily Howland discussed her future plans was her Aunt Rebecca. Rebecca adhered to a more orthodox, less activist Quaker belief system than Howland practiced, having a more conservative view of social and family relations. Nevertheless, she recognized the righteousness and sincerity of Howland's call to teach. Wrote Rebecca:

I have thought of thee much of late, very much, especially in relation to thy leaving home and launching into the world on thy own responsibility, and leaving thy afflicted and lonely mother; this however others do who marry, and some do well, and become excellent and valuable help meets, and raise families to usefulness and even valuable members of Society; others make shipwreck. The former feel quite sanguine in believing [what] would have been the happy result of a rightly formed connection [which] in thy own case, and even now, is not too late, but I would not prescribe for thy tossed and troubled mind; thou art of an age to set up for thy self. . . .

Rebecca validated Emily's decision to leave the nearer and dearer relationships of family and community for the broader fields of God's service. Although shocked by the letter which told her of Emily's plan, she nevertheless had foreseen the arrival of something like it. She had long believed that her niece's spirit and dedication would call her beyond the domestic sphere:

I said to myself this is a wonderful age of advancement, in mind and matter, [as] strength is given even to timid females to out do even themselves. I have long thought and felt that there was a burning desire for something beyond thy sphere of life, that would ere long [bear] down upon us. I have thought thee might turn Author; but I believe I have most of all desired for thee that thee might find thy talented and active mind enlisted in the cause of our holy Redeemer imparting and spreading the light of the Gospel of our saviour, and the immediate influence of his holy Spirit as believed in by our worthy and excellent [F]riends. . . .[37]

In her own words, Rebecca recapitulated the major tenets of the Cult of Single Blessedness, justifying Emily's position to her personal satisfaction. She acknowledged the value of the single life as compared with marital discord, the importance of social as well as domestic usefulness, and the religious justification for the vocational life. She also exhibited a certain dismay at having to offer support for such an unusual course of action. She took Emily's plan seriously, knowing that the commitment was a deep one. "On the great principle thee has in view I have had little time to reflect; therefore can have little say; I however am not disposed to laugh at it as wild or visionary. It appears thee has given the subject much thought, and has had a great struggle to come to the Crisis. The sacrifice must be great to thyself, and a severe trial to thy friends, if I may be allowed to judge from my own feelings."[38] She knew the dangers involved: the horrors of slavery that would be witnessed, the martyrdom experienced by abolitionists in the upper South, and the distance from home to be suffered by all.

Rebecca honored Emily for her choice and stamped with her approval her new vocational identity and proposed vocational life. Both were suited to the talents and personality of her niece, and both were appropriate, given the religious and social values of her time and faith. After twenty-two months of preparation, garnering support and polishing her skills, Emily Howland committed herself to the advancement of the black race. The support and encouragement of women whom she loved and admired made this choice possible. The long struggle sanctified it.

The Civil War opened to women new opportunities for service and individual advancement. By definition war is an abnormal situation. It calls for everyone to make sacrifices, to extend themselves in order to meet the emergency. Under the guise of war work, many women found not only their occupation but also their vocational identity. Propriety encouraged patriotic women to work at home, rolling bandages, collecting medical supplies, or sewing clothing. Some women, however, ignored social convention and seized this chance to distance themselves from family and community regulation. Dorothea Dix, Clara Barton, Abigail Williams May, and Emily Elizabeth Parsons found new identities and vocations in army nursing. Their overall responsibilities and the specific nature of their work provided them with a powerful sense of purpose and a surer sense of self.[39]

For the youthful Cornelia Hancock, the shock and trauma of warfare— the sounds and smells of battle, the sights of burned, maimed, dying, and maddened humanity—fulfilled a function not unlike that of immersion in a foreign culture through missionary service. Through the immediacy, importance, and even agony of this work, she grew strong and independent. She formulated a commitment to a life's work among the nation's needy and outcast.

Demonstrating a youthful stubbornness as well as a burgeoning strength of character, Hancock circumvented the wishes of her parents and the regulations of the nursing authority (she was younger than the minimum required age of thirty) to arrive at Gettysburg with a small group of volunteer nurses two days after the battle. She described what she found there: the stench of decaying flesh, piles of unburied dead, an operating table that ran red with blood for seven long days, wagon loads of amputated limbs, and rows of still living but gradually dying men laid out on the bare ground, too severely wounded to be helped by the surgeons working unceasingly on men with a greater chance to survive. "So appalling was the number of the wounded as yet unsuccored, so helpless seemed the few who were battling against tremendous odds to save life, and so overwhelming was the demand for any kind of aid that could be given quickly, that one's senses were benumbed by the awful responsibility that fell to the living. Action of a kind hitherto unknown and unheard of was needed here and existed here only," wrote Hancock.[40]

Amid all this horror, Hancock demonstrated remarkable satisfaction, even happiness, with her task. As she wrote to her mother after the first shock at Gettysburg: "I have eight wall tents full of amputated men. The tents of the wounded I look right out on—it is a melancholy sight, but you have no idea how soon one gets used to it. Their screams of agony do not make as much impression on me now as the reading of this letter will on you."[41] It was not that Hancock was hardhearted at twenty-three years' old, but rather that she was vitalized and empowered by the responsibility thrust upon her, by the capacity discovered within, and by the expansion of views and interests inspired by the experience. "You will think it is a short time for me to get used to things," she tried to explain to her mother, "but it seems to me as if all my past life was a myth, and as if I had been away from home seventeen years. What I do here [one] would think would kill at home, but I am well and comfortable."[42]

What Cornelia Hancock meant by "well and comfortable" astounds the reader today much as it did in 1863. The nurses rested on mattresses of sticks and pine boughs in tents open to the elements. As they slept in their clothes, it was not uncommon for women to awake in garments so wet with dew that they had to be wrung out before being redonned for another day's wear. Their diet consisted of what they could scavenge from neighboring fields and farms. Aid stations moved with the fighting and occasionally experienced shelling.[43] Life behind the lines offered a decrease in such stress, but nurses continued to work with limited supplies under primitive conditions caring for appallingly mutilated men. They fought rats and filth rather than imminent death and fear of enemy attack. Hancock often recalled the frustration and sorrow with which she heard of men whom she had nursed and seen convalesce return to battle only to be killed.[44]

In spite of these trials, Hancock welcomed the experience. "The main reason for my staying, aside from duty, is that I am so well, if it only lasts. I feel like a new person, eat onions, potatoes, cucumbers, anything that comes up and walk as straight as a soldier, feel life and vigor which you well know I never felt at home. The place here is very healthy." The contradiction between the ugliness of her experience and the pleasure she took in it confused Hancock. As she said, "I cannot explain it, but I feel so erect, and can go steadily from one thing to another from half past six o'clock in the morning until ten o'clock at night, and feel more like work at ten than when I got up at home."[45]

Between field placements, Hancock worked with Emily Howland in the contraband camps around Washington, D.C., aiding displaced blacks released from slavery as the Union army marched through the upper South. Like them, she lived in a barn with lath nailed over the cracks. She shared the poor quality and minimal quantity of their food. She was exposed to the same diseases that raged through their ranks. And through it all, she nursed the ill, distributed food and clothing, placed orphans in schools and families, attempted to teach basic language and mathematical skills, and negotiated with the federal bureaucracy and the army for needed supplies. She thus gained considerable skill in the areas of medicine, administration, social work, and education.

After the war, Hancock moved to South Carolina to teach ex-slaves under the auspices of the Freedman's Bureau. Twenty years later, she returned to Philadelphia to work among the poor and disadvantaged of the city's immigrant slum neighborhoods. Always, she said, as she had written from South Carolina, "I greatly prefer being where I am to being [at home with the family]. It seems as if I cannot have my health living a sedentary life and that I am blessed with [health] is all that makes one place more desirable to me than another. Then too, I believe I am well fitted for this business and every person is not."[46]

Hancock's vocational identity rested in social service. In her case, traumatic experience, physical exertion, intellectual challenge—the occupation of mind, heart, and body—produced a self-directed, self-actualized, and independent woman. The immediacy of violence and destruction, the shared lives of soldier or refugee, all served to expand her universe. These introduced her to needs, capacities, fears, joys, and abilities that she had never known. Her activity challenged her stamina, as it forced her constantly to push back the boundaries of the known, the comfortable, and the tested. It was "good discipline," she wrote, "in patience and perseverance."[47] Having witnessed the worst that war, poverty, and racism could impose upon human beings, she developed a richly textured sense of human strength and limitation. Her personal journey toward autonomy involved an effort to exert mastery over an environment destructive to human survival and to exercise rationality in the midst of irrationality. She sought to build a better world. In her time, such tasks were usually performed by men.

The life of Emily Dickinson provides the quintessential example of the antebellum spinster whose pursuit of autonomy progressed through the expansion of her imaginative and intellectual faculties. Dickinson's maturing sense of her identity as a poet occurred only gradually. During her twenties, Dickinson explored various roles and identities that the nineteenth century offered to young women. Driven by a need to express herself and propelled by her talent, she rejected all except daughterhood, and this identity she projected into her art.

Dickinson approached conversion as did all young women, but found no comfort or sense of calling there. She acknowledged to her close friend Jane Humphrey that she felt isolated in her resistance to this important ritual: "Christ is calling everyone here," she wrote, "all my companions have answered, even my darling Vinnie [Lavinia Dickinson, her sister] believes she loves, and trusts him, and I am standing alone in rebellion, and growing very careless." Like Catharine Beecher, Dickinson recognized the enormity of her "rebellion" in the social context of the day and both delighted in her idiosyncrasy and feared for her obstinate soul. "I really think I envy them," she wrote of those who experienced the change.[48]

Dickinson also realized that she was not domestic, while her sister Lavinia excelled at household management. The two sisters divided life into two compartments—the material and the intellectual. Lavinia ruled over the household and Emily over the mind. Vinnie was "head of the committee on arrangements," and she appears in the Dickinson letters in constant motion as she tended garden, cleaned house, cooked, sewed, and served her family. Although Emily teased Vinnie about her domestic vocation ("we consider her standard for superhuman effort erroneously applied"), she depended upon her to keep order in the house and to protect the time and solitude she herself needed to be creative.[49] Although Emily enjoyed such domestic tasks as baking bread, she prayed to be preserved from "what they call households" and the "prickly art" of housekeeping.[50]

Dickinson also rejected a role as Sister of Charity. She felt no calling to tend to the emotional or intellectual needs of the citizenry of Amherst by visiting the sick, teaching in the Sunday school, leading the female literary society, collecting signatures on petitions opposed to slavery, or gathering monies to support foreign missions. These tasks comprised the formula for the useful and worthy life as it was advocated by Mary Lyon at nearby Mount Holyoke, which Dickinson had briefly attended. But such a role interfered with her attraction to a different calling:

I came to the conclusion that I should be a villain unparalleled if I took but an inch of time for so unholy a purpose as writing a friendly letter—for what need had I of sympathy—or very much less of affection—or less than they all—of friends—mind the house—and the food—*sweep* if the spirits were low—nothing like a little exercise to strengthen—and invigorate—and help away such foolishness—work makes one strong, and cheerful—and as for society what neighborhood so full as my own? The halt—the lame—and the blind—the old—the infirm—the bed-ridden—and superannuated—the ugly, and disagreeable—the perfectly hateful to me—all *these* to see—and be seen by—an opportunity rare for cultivating meekness—and patience—and submission—and for turning my back to this very sinful and wicked world. Somehow or other I incline to other things. . . .[51]

Whether sinful, improper, or unfeminine, the art of writing called Dickinson. She reveled in the joys of language and the mysteries of poetry. Dickinson acknowledged the error of her ways, but remained aloof when the local female sewing circle gathered for its first meeting: "—now all the poor will be helped—the cold warmed—the warm cooled—the hungry fed—the thirsty attended to—the ragged clothed—and this tumbled down world will be helped to its feet again." Notwithstanding her "high approbation" of the tasks at hand and the women who engaged in them, Dickinson could not bring herself to participate. "I am already set down as one of those brands almost consumed," she confided, "and my hardheartedness gets me many prayers."[52]

During the 1850s, Dickinson discovered her talent and with it her desire to be a poet. Aside from an earlier letter to her brother, William Austin, at school, informing him that he could expect some sibling rivalry in the matter of poetry writing, Emily had indicated little leaning in this direction.[53] Progressively, if somewhat obliquely, Emily slowly revealed her new sense of self and her new identity. To first one friend and then another, Dickinson hinted at changes.

To Jane Humphrey she provided perhaps the first glimpse: "I have dared to do strange things—bold things, and have asked no advice from any," she said. "Oh I have needed my trusty Jane—my friend encourager, and sincere counselor, my rock and strong assister! I could make you tremble for me." She confessed that she had found a new experience, that "life has had an aim, and the world has been too precious for your poor—and striving sister!" She contrasted her path with that of friend Abiah Root. "You are growing wiser than I am, and nipping in the bud fancies which I let blossom—perchance to bear no fruit, or if plucked, I may find it bitter. The shore is safer, Abiah, but I love to buffet the sea—I can count the bitter wrecks here in these pleasant waters, and hear the murmuring winds, but oh, I love the danger!" She more clearly revealed her new interest to Joseph Lyman: "We used to think, Joseph, when I was an ungifted girl and you so scholarly that words were cheap and weak. Now I dont know of anything so mighty. There are [those] to which I lift my hat when I see them sitting princelike among their peers on a page. Sometimes I write one, and look at his outlines till he glows as no sapphire."[54]

Then, in the early 1860s, the poems themselves emerged. These spoke hesitantly, then with growing confidence, of Dickinson's development as a poet. In approximately 1860, Dickinson celebrated her glorious gift, her as yet "unsteady tongue."

> For this—accepted Breath—
> Through it—compete with Death—
> The fellow cannot touch this Crown—
> By it—my title take—
> Ah, what a royal sake
> To my necessity—stooped down!

> No Wilderness—can be
> Where this attendeth thee—
> No Desert Noon—
> No fear of frost to come
> Haunt the perennial bloom—
> But Certain June!
>
> Get Gabriel—to tell—the royal syllable—
> Get Saints—with new—unsteady tongue—
> To say what trance below
> Most like their glory show—
> Fittest the Crown![55]

The crown she so desired, the title to which she aspired, was that of poet. In another early poem, Dickinson explicitly named her vocation. Here she explained the overwhelming importance to her of writing. Not yet secure or confident enough to take the title of poet for herself, she nevertheless implied her new identity by utilizing the plural, "Poets—All."

> I reckon—when I count at all—
> First—Poets—Then the Sun—
> Then Summer. Then the Heaven of God—
> And then—the list is done—
>
> But looking back—the First so seems
> To Comprehend the Whole—
> The Others look a needless Show—
> So I write—Poets—All—[56]

This period gave rise to numerous poems that reflect Dickinson's search for her vocation, her desire to join the ranks and adopt the name of poet. Her approach was cautious, however. Many poems despaired of lost voice or failed language. Yet, while inadequacy haunted these poems, they also resounded with the joy of articulate expression. The poetry stood as a passionate confession of the extraordinary importance to Dickinson of the creative life. She was desperate to succeed.

> *One Life* of so much Consequence!
> Yet I—for it—would pay—
> My Soul's *entire income*—
> In ceaseless—salary—
>
> *One Pearl*—to me—so signal—
> That I would instant dive—
> Although—I *knew*—to *take* it—
> Would *cost* me—*just a life!*
>
> The Sea is full—I know it!
> That—does not blur my Gem!
> It burns—distinct from all the row—
> *Intact—In Diadem!*[57]

Here Dickinson suggested not only the importance of her gift, a gift worth dying for, she also celebrated its distinctiveness. Hers was a unique talent rooted in an individual sensibility. She sought to control language, to develop her craftsmanship in order to express her particular vision.

To make the most of her gift, Dickinson severed past identities and ties. She renounced all claims to her time, her mind, her strength, and her devotion. She submerged herself in the struggle to create a new self, a new role. She would make her way as a poet and meet the world as an intelligence, a sensibility, an artist—not as a daughter or yet a wife.

> I'm ceded—I've stopped being Their's—
> The name They dropped upon my face
> With water, in the country church
> Is finished using, now,
> And They can put it with my Dolls,
> My childhood, and the string of spools,
> I've finished threading—too—
>
> Baptized, before, without the choice,
> But this time, consciously, of Grace—
> Unto supremest name—
> Called to my Full—The Crescent dropped—
> Existence's whole Arc, filled up,
> With one small Diadem.
>
> My second Rank—too small the first—
> Crowned—Crowing—on my Father's breast—
> A half unconscious Queen—
> But this time—Adequate—Erect,
> With Will to choose, or to reject,
> And I choose, just a Crown—[58]

Thus, Dickinson confirmed her arrival, her embodiment as a poet. Baptized anew and by her choice, Emily took on a new identity.

When Dickinson appropriated the mantle of poet she undertook a new mode of living. She honed, focused, and condensed her life until she lived primarily within the walls of her own room, with sister Vinnie as the keeper of the house and guardian of the gate. But as her physical realm shrank, Dickinson's intellectual universe expanded. Her beloved books nourished her mind. The intense interpersonal relationships within her family, particularly her love for her sister Lavinia and her adoration of her sister-in-law Susan Gilbert, charged her emotional nature. Her art—the distillation, refinement, and condensation of her entire being—fortified and sustained her.

By 1863, Dickinson felt the strength and certitude of her vocational identity. She had expanded the boundaries of her consciousness and in the process achieved both personal and artistic independence. This she celebrated in one of her most powerful poems.

On a Columnar Self—
How ample to rely
In Tumult—or Extremity—
How good the Certainty

That Lever cannot pry—
And Wedge cannot divide
Conviction—That Granite Base—
Though None be on our Side—

Suffice Us—for a Crowd—
Ourself—and Rectitude—
And that Assembly—not far off
From furthest Spirit—God—[59]

The "Columnar Self" is a potent image. It suggests individuality, autonomy, self-reliance, and self-confidence. It stands an awesome monument
to the mature sense of self, the sure sense of artistic identity, and the
proud expression of the independent-minded intellectual female.

Creative women such as painter Fidelia Bridges, actress Charlotte Cushman, sculptress Harriet Hosmer, and historian Frances Caulkins all attempted to transcend the "double bind" of the female artist or intellectual:
the impossibility of self-assertion for a woman and the necessity of self-
assertion for the artist.[60] In *Diana and Persis*, Louisa May Alcott described
the process of artistic development as experienced by antebellum women.
The talented Persis feels the stirring of her creative powers and seeks to
refine and develop her drawing skill. Yet when her first show proves a
popular success, she is uncomfortable. "My work is not thoroughly good,
only striking," she sighs, "for I aimed high and audacity always tells at
first; but when the novelty of style wears off, the poverty of the material
will show. I know I can do better if I can only get more criticism and less
praise; find the right atmosphere, the right inspiration, and really do my
best."[61] The patronizing attention given the female ingenue, the little
woman with the (implied little) talent, did not provide the serious and
tough criticism needed by a self-respecting artist.

While Persis went to Paris to study (and instead fell in love, married, and
essentially gave up her art), the less original Diana worked away on her
sculpture in Boston. Like a nun in her cell, she dedicated herself to her
work. She was rewarded with a "growing ambition, and the sense of power
that strengthened every year." Persis, "the lark," named Diana an "eagle"
and recognized in her the strength of perseverance and commitment.
"However high I go," she said, "I shall find you before me, for you can look
at the sun with unwinking eyes and your wings never tire; while I can only
twitter up a little way and tumble down again all out of breath."[62]

Alcott craved that "growing sense of power" which she attributed to
this character. She, like other antebellum spinsters, expressed the belief

that she had never achieved her desired proficiency, never lived up to her own high standards of artistic excellence.[63] Alcott recognized, however, the stages of development that both drove the creative artist and rewarded her for her devotion to her art: the definition of a unique artistic sensibility, the acquisition of skilled technique, the extension of control over one's medium, the expansion of vision, the gradual accumulation of a body of work, the growing ability to give an informed and selective response to outside criticism, and the satisfaction of accomplishment. Creative women found that progress through these stages reinforced their vocational identity and enabled them to "push back the verges toward autonomy."[64]

Single women of antebellum America initiated their search for independence by establishing a vocational identity. They extended the margins of their experience and incorporated into an existing psychic economy new levels of consciousness and understanding. Approaches varied, but certain commonalities prevailed. Some found themselves and their calling in the development of a religious identity or artistic sensibility. Others gained entrance to new realms by throwing themselves into new experiences. In the shock of war or a foreign culture they found new levels of self-awareness, broad understanding, and growth impossible to those who followed more familiar paths. All were tried and rewarded for their attempts at greater independence. These women struggled to free themselves from the constraints of domesticity—or more accurately, to define themselves and their callings in opposition to the domestic—so that they might explore the realms of imagination, spirituality, or human experience. Perhaps the visionary Mary Moody Emerson said it best as early as 1817: "Alass, with low timid females or vulgar domestics how apt is this [moral grandeur] to lose its power when the nerves are weak. . . . but give me that oh God— it is holy independence—it is honor & immortality—dearer than friends, wealth & influence. . . . I bless thee for giving me to see the advantage of loneliness."[65]

Few, however, eluded woman's "proper sphere" entirely. Emily Dickinson achieved her independence, both artistic and personal, by remaining locked up in her father's house, impersonating the daughter who never grew up. This pose—as child, submissive daughter, or, in some poems and letters, student—served Dickinson in her growth and development as a poet. But she paid a high emotional price. Although Dickinson went free of the constraints of nineteenth-century marriage, wrote innovative, powerful, and voluminous poetry, and gained "amplitude" of being, she confined herself to a nursery of her own creating. The pose became a habit, a way of being as well as an artistic persona. The other side of Dickinson the assertive poet and "Columnar Self" was Dickinson the strange woman in white and the madwoman of Amherst—the ghostlike presence glimpsed only at a distance through her upstairs window.[66]

The childlike posture adopted by Emily Dickinson, in literature and in life, provides only the most dramatic example of a crucially important factor that structured the lives of young women in the antebellum period. The making of a self was a private, individual task which took place primarily in the domestic sphere among family, kin, or friends. Few outside institutions validated a woman's choice or supported her struggle. With the exception of those for whom the Civil War provided a very different and abrupt departure from home, young women sought to find themselves and to test new roles, primarily at home, or perhaps briefly at school. Women's role and identity within the family were first and most important. While a woman might, and these women did, choose not to submit to the demands of wife and motherhood, they had little choice about those of daughterhood. Its status and responsibilities came with birth and remained until death. Perhaps the most significant psychological task that faced women of these generations was the integration of the new vocational identity with the primary identity of daughter.

6

"A Daughter, an Immortal Being"

Family and Vocation

Whatever an unwed daughter's age, her parents never recognized her as fully self-governing. No woman in this period was. Whatever her vocational commitment or duties, the single woman's parents expected that she could be recalled at need. Until he gave her hand to another, a father retained responsibility for his daughter and held a claim on her services. The tasks of daughterhood had to be forgiven as they were foregone. Daughters required parental permission to venture abroad, leaving father's house and mother's hearth. Thus a young woman's vocational identity, her status as an independent being, was forged in a furnace heated by personalities, expectations, responsibilities, love and guilt, needs and wants. Family participation was a given. Family approval provided tensile strength to the finished product. The lack of it could produce sometimes long-hidden cracks and weaknesses.

Emily Dickinson's solution to the duality of roles and identities (daughter and poet) was to withdraw from the household without leaving the house. Hers was a rare solution, and it worked in part because she had a sister to pick up the pieces of domestic management. Equally unusual was the response of Cornelia Hancock, who ignored parental demands. Hancock's parents bombarded her with reports of their physical ailments and financial problems. They urged her to come home from the South and attend them. In February 1866, Hancock's mother wrote, "I suppose thee prefers being there but it does seem as if thee was a great way from home and Father says write for her to come home."[1] Hancock turned a sardonic eye on parental persuasion. She consulted with her sister Ellen Child as to the legitimacy and urgency of the parental need, then held the family at bay:

I received a letter from Ellen yesterday with a pressing invitation to come home before you all got mad. I think you should all have sufficient control over your tempers not to be mad with me for doing what seems to me to be best. If I had been unfortunate enough to have married some forlorn person and been obliged to stay in some disagreeable part of the country, you would not feel you could control me in coming home at your discretion. Now in that case it might be very humane to send for me. In this, I am pleasantly located with congenial friends and congenial employment and an independent home but am not allowed to stay in it in peace.[2]

The unusual nature of these responses merely underscores the fact that however much antebellum spinsters valued their vocational lives and identities, few could divorce themselves from family responsibilities and household tasks.

⋯⋯◄◆►⋯⋯

There were essentially three reasons for the difficulty. In the first place, antebellum women appreciated those special gifts attributed to them by their culture. Susan B. Anthony, for example, copied into her diary an extract from Elizabeth Gaskell's *Life of Charlotte Brontë*, in which Gaskell described Brontë's life as divided between that of Currer Bell (her nom de plume) the author, and Charlotte Brontë "the woman." While men commonly deserted old responsibilities in order to undertake new ones, while they rejected old roles and adopted new careers at will, women did not. Wrote Gaskell, "no other can take up the quiet, regular duties of a daughter, the wife, or the mother, as well as she whom God has appointed to fill that particular place." Most Anglo-Americans agreed with her that:

A woman's principle work in life is hardly left to her own choice; nor can she drop the domestic charges devolving on her as an individual, for the exercise of the most splended talents ever bestowed. And yet she must not hide her gift in a napkin; it was meant for the use and service of others. In a humble and faithful spirit, must she labor to do what is not impossible, or God would not have set her to do it.[3]

Anthony, who left home to teach in 1838, was concerned about her mother's health and well-being. She worried that her mother did not take good care of herself and that no one at home properly looked out for her. On at least one occasion, Susan dreamed that her mother had died, and that the death was directly attributable to a daughter's neglect.[4]

Spinsters felt that they must maintain both their commitment to their vocations and their responsibilities in the family. Both were legitimated by the Cult of Single Blessedness and both were beloved of God. Competition between the two was intolerable. It suggested a conflict that threatened the entire ideological and psychological structure within which these women operated. They had to meet both sets of requirements if they were to feel right about undertaking nondomestic vocations.

The second attitude which complicated women's pursuit of autonomy and vocational fulfillment was their belief, in conjunction with society's teachings, that the domestic role was crucial to their own health and happiness. Many spinsters agreed with Louisa May Alcott's contention that "the home-making, the comfort, the sympathy, the grace and atmosphere that a true woman can provide is the noble part, and embraces all that is helpful for soul as well as body."[5] However much they abhorred the drudgery of housework, antebellum single women valued homemaking as sincerely as did their married sisters. To be sure, they preferred to make their own homes, but the activity held merit for them in either context.

Last, women felt a conflict between their vocational lives and their domestic duties because they loved those to whom they rendered service. To neglect activities that eased the lives of loved ones, whether those tasks (as defined by a particular family) were real or imagined, necessary or inflated, caused pain and sorrow. Torn between her personal desire to contribute to the antislavery movement and her responsibility as a daughter to assist her mother, Caroline F. Putnam described herself as engaged in a battle with "Peet-dom," her stepfather Peet's uncouth and intransigent rule over her mother's abode.

I have entered upon that sharp trial to which Truth has in all ages subjected its faithful followers. . . . "He that loveth Father or Mother more than me is not worthy of me," with what keen sensibility Jesus must have said that, "For I am come to set a man at variance against his father, and a daughter against her mother"—"And a man's foes shall be of his own household!"

The spirit of struggle conveyed by Putnam was commonplace. Many felt embattled, both internally and externally, as they tried to determine their "proper" sphere.[6]

Guilelma Breed, for example, sorrowfully rejected an offer from Emily Howland to join her in the mountains for a summer's rest, reading, and recreation. Although Breed recognized that "health would be strengthened and soul gladdened" to be in Howland's "freer atmosphere," she acknowledged that "duty will keep me [at home]." Breed's mother was ill and too weak to accompany her. Breed's sister refused to take sole responsibility for their mother's care. Guilelma stayed home but "sigh[ed] for a different life—freer and wilder."[7]

The resolution achieved by many single women required that they periodically immerse themselves in dedicated domesticity. As they pulled away from the private sphere and the role of devoted daughter, sister, or aunt, spinsters concurrently and contradictorily bound themselves the more tightly to family life. It was almost as if they sought to exorcise their self-centered vocational drive through periodic acts of self-sacrifice. They underwent penance in a humble and contrite spirit, expressing only resignation, not resentment.

Sarah Pugh spent two years in England working with Mary Anne Estlin in the Bristol antislavery movement. She helped to edit *The Anti-Slavery Advocate*, an abolitionist newspaper. She organized local antislavery associations in the American manner. She maintained Estlin's antislavery correspondence, which linked reformers in the United States and the British Isles. Pugh took great satisfaction in her work. It eased the emptiness in her life that followed her mother's death. It provided her with a sense of self-worth which ten years of caring for her mother had gradually eroded.[8] Yet when her brother came to fetch her home to Philadelphia, Pugh went. She found one cousin dying. While Pugh was nursing her, a sick aunt called for her assistance. Still another lay ill and unattended not far away. Although Sarah's return signaled the end of her full-time antislavery work and brought to a close one of the most rewarding and productive periods of her life, Pugh accepted her personal sacrifice as necessary. "Very thankful am I," she wrote to Estlin, "that I am here to share—and in a degree to lighten the labors of love that have been crowded into these weeks. I have never felt that I staid away too long, yet very often that it was well that I came home last autumn."[9] She could not rest easy knowing that there were family needs unmet, nor could she set aside family requirements for her own interests or even those of her cause.

She remained conflicted, however. On her fiftieth birthday, Sarah Pugh pondered on life and measured herself against a high standard of godly excellence and human achievement. "Almost a life, and how spent?" she asked. "What am I? Where am I? What must be the record? My life as a whole has been aimless, objectless." Although she felt that she had finally given up the "ascetic condemnation" of herself in which she had indulged for many years, Pugh still wondered whether she had any power to do anything of importance in the world. "May what there is of ability in me be so employed as to obtain the reward above all others, 'well done, good and faithful servant,' " she prayed. Looking back on sixty years, Sarah saw only the endless striving to achieve restrained by the "petty trivialities" which had engaged her time and attention.[10]

Abigail Kimber found her family to be a conservative influence on her public activity. She was a member of the Philadelphia Female Anti-Slavery Society, one of the more radical abolitionist and more outspokenly feminist organizations in antebellum America. With her cousin, Sarah Pugh, Kimber crossed the Atlantic in 1840 to attend the World Anti-Slavery Convention in London. It proved to be a momentous experience for these women individually and for the woman's movement. In rejecting the credentials of the female American delegates, the convention raised in Britain the "woman question" that had so divided American abolitionists. It also raised the consciousness of British women and provided one spark that would later explode onto the American scene in 1848 as the Seneca Falls Convention on women's rights.[11] For Kimber, the convention was a time of expanding horizons. She traveled on the Continent with Sarah Pugh; she met and talked with outstanding British women such as Harriet Martineau, Elizabeth Pease, and the Ashurst sisters; she defied and debated the preeminent men in Anglo-American reform; and she cemented a commitment to the cause of human freedom.[12]

Throughout her early adult life, however, Kimber was unable to give more than passing attention to the cause. The Kimber home was a stop on the Underground Railroad and Enoch Kimber, Abigail's father, was an ardent abolitionist. Yet the family did not encourage Abigail to pursue reform work as a career. Along with her sisters Gertrude and Martha, Abigail taught in the Kimber school and helped with its administration.[13] Her father so dominated her professional life, that Lucretia Mott, the Quaker minister, hoped her friend would marry in order that she might remove herself from her father's authority, household, and school. Said Mott, "Her father has a great idea of being 'monarch of all he surveys,' and has ever kept his family in greater subjection to his will than accords with my view of right." Mott believed that when a daughter reached the age of forty, as had Abigail, her independence should be respected, particularly when what she had gained in social and professional position and livelihood was "the product of [her] own labor."[14] Whenever Kimber could leave the school, she came into Philadelphia to stay with her cousin and to participate in the deliberations of the Anti-Slavery Society. Even with all her responsibilities—to the antislavery movement, the Kimberton school, her own botanical observation and research—when an uncle became seriously ill, Abigail nursed him herself despite Sarah Pugh's plea that she hire someone else.[15]

These women experienced the conflicting pulls of family responsibility and vocational commitment. They veered between the two. In love, devotion, and (perhaps) guilt, they strove to accomodate competing demands on their time and attention. Said Mary A. Dodge, when a creeping paralysis foreshadowed her mother's death, "I seemed to see before me a freedom that was dreary."[16] Release from family service meant both liberation and loss, not only of a beloved parent but also of an important role and identity.

Women who rejected domestic responsibility as daughters carried a substantial burden—particularly those who placed considerable geographical distance between it and themselves so as to ensure their independence. Fidelia Fiske wrote of the concerns she felt in leaving her widowed mother to go to Persia: "those remembrances of and anxieties for my mother were peculiarly chastening. My heart would not thus have clung to my work had it not been riveted to it by a mother's sacrifice. Those dear Nestorian girls were all the more precious in my eyes, because they had taken me from my mother." Laura Towne agreed. "I have felt all along that nothing could excuse me for leaving home, and work undone there, but doing more and better work [in the Sea Islands]."[17] Having made the difficult decision to give God's call and her own inclinations more weight than her family's needs and wants, the antebellum daughter felt that she must stick to her decision at all costs and complete her appointed task.

The nature of the social behavior expected of unattached daughters exacerbated their internal conflict. Family claims left little time for substantive study or work. Parents, siblings, nieces and nephews, aunts, uncles, and cousins expected a spinster to have no particular occupation and therefore freely sought her companionship, business assistance, nursing, housekeeping, and babysitting services. Social conventions of the early- and mid-nineteenth century required that young, middle-class, unmarried women spend part of every day engaged in social visiting. The task of maintaining a family's social connections continued to be the responsibility of adult spinsters. The institution of family visiting provided a way for middle-class women to come together to talk about mutual business, friends, community needs and doings, to make matches, and to guide social behavior through censure or praise.

Women's work consisted of rendering service. Because their services were ongoing in nature, and because these services demanded constant renewal, the spinster never felt that her obligations had been met, and therefore that her time was her own. The single woman remained "on call" throughout her life. While she saw something wrong in the way that most wives and mothers submitted so totally to what was a noble and necessary occupation, she herself had difficulty setting limitations on family demands. It did not help that the Cult of Single Blessedness upheld the role of the Maiden Aunt devoted to the private sphere. To hear Benjamin Howland say to his sister Emily, "No one has the right to demand of thee the sacrifice of thy happiness and of all thy most cherished plans. Thee has done enough for Father and Mother—do something for thyself now,"[18] jars anyone versed in the private documents of the early nineteenth century because so few thought in such terms.

Not until 1865 did Mary A. Dodge publish such sentiments in *A New Atmosphere*. Dodge reflected on the changing lives of women and spoke to the struggle of the vocationally committed unmarried daughter whose aspirations conflicted with her parents' desires. "The mere fact of a daughter's services being needed at home is no reason why they shall be claimed after she has become of age, either through years, or maturity of character, when such service is distasteful to her, or other service is tasteful and possible," wrote Dodge. She acknowledged that many readers would find her argument unnatural and undutiful but insisted that there were rather remarkable notions around regarding nature and duty. "In our eagerness to enforce the claims which parents have on children, we seem sometimes ready to forget the equally stringent claims which children have on parents," she noted.

Here is a daughter, an immortal being, accountable to God. Surely, when she has become a woman, she has a right to direct her life in the manner best adapted to bring out its abilities. No human being has a right to appropriate another human being's life—even if they be mother and daughter. You say that she owes life itself to her parents. True, but in such a way that it confers an additional obligation on them to give her every opportunity to make the most of life, and not in such a way as to justify them in monopolizing it, nor in such a way as to render her accountable to them alone for its use.

Dodge argued that if filial unfaithfulness was a sin, then so was parental unfaithfulness, for while the first violated the relationships which it found when it came into life, the second violated those which it created. Dodge did not claim, she said, that a daughter did not do well who "chooses to sacrifice her inclinations—by inclinations I do not mean the mere promptings of self-indulgence, but the voice of her soul calling her to a work in life," she merely stated that a parent had no right to demand such a sacrifice.[19]

Dodge's tract, written at the age of thirty-six, provided a clear directive to younger women. But her own generation lived by another code—a set of cultural priorities that upheld submissiveness as the most feminine of virtues. Both a patriarchal family and a patriarchal religion demanded of women the submission of the self to the will of others. Sacrifice, acquiescence, and duty were ruling principles of women's lives. Women fought to control their willfulness and to suppress their unfeminine desire for a substantive life, in an effort to adopt genuine female submissiveness. Most did not see their struggle as one of role conflict, a cultural and social issue of profound significance.[20] The power of this culturally imposed demand for female submissiveness, and its cost, can be seen in the lives of many antebellum spinsters.

In her fiction Louisa May Alcott portrayed this battle with submissiveness. Sylvia Yule, the heroine of her most ambitious novel, *Moods*, was an unconventional, frank, intelligent tomboy, a woman disappointed in herself. Says Yule:

I cannot be like others . . . I don't try to be odd; I long to be quiet and satisfied, but I cannot; and when I do . . . wild things it is not because I am thoughtless or idle, but because I am trying to be good and happy. The old ways fail, so I attempt new ones, hoping they will succeed; but they don't, and I still go looking and longing for happiness, yet always failing to find it.

The task the author set for Yule was to overcome a passionate, willful, and undisciplined nature. She must control herself and internalize the cultural norms of true feminine behavior.[21] Ultimately, Yule rejects an unconventional passion (unconventional in its intensity and in its object—a man other than her husband) and a conventional marriage in order to dedicate herself to a single life of usefulness and discipline in caring for her father. She joins, "that sisterhood called disappointed women; a larger class than many deem it to be. . . . Unhappy wives, mistaken or forsaken lovers; meek souls, who make life long penance for the sins of others; gifted creatures kindled into fitful brilliance by some inward fire that consumes but cannot warm."[22] Anguish more than disappointment was the experi- ence of women who sought to conquer their "immortal longings," to drown their resistance to traditional female roles, to subsume their grief over lack of achievement and lost purpose. Alcott's private writings ex- hibit the full range of her personal efforts to make herself more feminine, more selfless, more humble and submissive. "I hope success [in publishing *Moods*] will sweeten me and make me what I long to become more than a great writer, a good daughter," she wrote.[23]

The intensity of this effort is evident, for instance, in the writings of Laura Stebbins. Stebbins longed to join Emily Howland in her work with the freed slaves, "But we cannot move otherwise than God appointe, and *my* cross must be, to stay in this sequestered spot, and minister as well as I am able, to those who seem to need me—who have none other to look to for aid." The forces tying her were not current but potential family needs. Said Stebbins, "my eldest Aunt, almost eighty, is so very frail and feeble, that I ques[tion] very seriously the propriety of my leaving—for both [aunts] are very helpless and in case of sudden illness—or of accident, they might suffer much; and then I should reflect upon myself exceedingly."[24]

To stay at home in the *prospect* of future need galled Stebbins. "When in their ordinary health, my stay here is not attended with either interest or usefulness—and it seems hard to lead such a life." She was determined, however, to fulfill the task that God had set for her in order to win a moral battle of tremendous importance in her journey toward immortality. "Oh for a willing cheerful spirit to meet duty in whatever form it presents itself," she wrote. "I am trying to gain victory over my wishes, wh[ich] seem so to clash with present obligations." She provided Howland with a glimpse into the conditions under which she fought. Because her aunts read her correspondence, Laura begged Emily not to allude specifically to the subject, for "it would give them pain to know how I feel in this matter, and how prison-like, it is, here in my childhood home." Not only did Stebbins struggle to submit herself to potential rather than immediate duties, and not only did she thereby give up an important sense of her self as an actor in the world, but she did so in silence, unwilling to broach the issue with her family for fear of hurting their feelings.[25]

Patty Rogers resisted efforts to encumber her with family cares. Unlike Stebbins, she did not seek a specific vocation but rather longed for meaningful social and intellectual interaction outside the immediate family. As the sole unmarried daughter in the Rogers family, Patty was responsible for nursing her father. The state of his condition governed life in the household. In February 1785, Rogers wrote in her diary, "no person here got comfortably thro[ugh] the day." A week later, she again commented, "O my Fathers disorder will kill us all." Rogers's father was a difficult and demanding patient. The entire family seems to have lived in fear of his rages. Patty's well-being was sacrificed to his. Sibling disapproval discouraged her from leaving the house, for they feared the consequences of her absence. In late March the attending physician urged Patty to participate in a town function because the confinement and nursing were taking a toll on her constitution and psyche. Rogers sadly rejected this advice. "The distress of the Family were so great—it would not be prudent in me to appear there."[26]

Regular entries in Rogers's diary demonstrate her emotional swings between resentment of her role and rededication to it. She felt anger about the situation and guilt about the anger. Patty's efforts to resign herself provide heartrending reading.

May 7, 1785
Sat with my F[ather] all day—talked of Senia, Socrates, Cicero, and Demosthenes to divert his melancholy hours! I find the *mind may* be diverted and drawn off these disagreeable objects which obtrude themselves upon it, in its *solitary* hours! Then *ought* I *not* to try to my utmost, to disapate those gloomy clouds which hang upon the brows of a *dear* parent? I certainly will, as for months past I have sacrificed *my* happiness for *his*. I'll do so still! away ye *gay scenes!* Cease to please *me!* while I have a *tender* parent to *please* by my presence!

July 27, 1785
spent the afternoon with my father—felt some *tender emotions* which excited a flood of tears!—I longed to have it in my power to do good to somebody or other!—Can I by any thing, said I, relieve my fellow *Creatures!*—I was disolved in tears, and *felt* emotions I would not have *exchanged for all the gaities in Life!*

October 1, 1785
arise early found my Father very ill. O! may he be spared yet a little while!—twill be *hard* to loose such a parent! how *severely shall we feel it!—very dull and really unhappy! Committed myself to Heaven, to the great preserver, the friend of the friendless!*

November 4, 1785
denied seeing my friends!—O! make me contented, *grateful,* and *happy,* tho[ugh] *denied of all Earthly* enjoyments—Every Day, and hour convinces me more and more of the *Infelicity of human* Life!—Tis frought with ill—O! *unhappy—unhappy* ever to have come into the world—What *tortures* have I gone through and *what future sorrows I know not*—But hope to preserve a Calm and steady temper; how ever r[ough] the paths I tread may be. Man is born to sorrow; as the sparks fly upwards—And shall I alone escape; who am the least deserving of all Gods creatures? *Surely not*—Then be Content and *know tis for thy good.*[27]

Rogers hated the isolation, the confinement, and the narrowness of such a life. She came close to wishing her father dead and herself freed from his care. Yet, like a good daughter and a good Christian, she tried valiantly to fulfill her responsibilities. She wanted to embrace nursing for her own sake as well as her father's, but it was a truly difficult path to Heaven.

Given the set of assumptions by which these women lived, most found it difficult to balance the demands of their families with those of their vocations. Their inability to define priorities and to claim adequate time for themselves and their callings resulted in several serious consequences. The constant interruption of vocational life and the subsequent denigration of vocational commitment proved distracting and, ultimately, intellectually crippling. Sarah Pugh, for example, lamented the many antislavery letters that remained unwritten due to claims of friends and family. She contrasted the ninety-two letters written in one month by her friend Mary Anne Estlin with her own lack of productivity. She despised her "round of petty employments"—"reading a *little*, writing a little, and then as a refreshment from the *labor*, walk or drive!"[28] It was not that Pugh lacked genuine reform work to do. The problem was her inability to escape from domestic activities which nibbled away at her time and will.

Abigail Kimber recognized the ennervating nature of the domestic and social duties required of the spinster. "This frittering away of life, this abrasion from the veriest trifles is," she said, "very much like walking over a soft sandy plain—you leave no foot prints that the next breeze will not efface—you make no progress—you feel your strength wasted without seeing that you have done any thing more today than was done yesterday, and will be done tomorrow." Gradually, Kimber felt so demoralized that she no longer acted "as though any change was desirable." That frightened her, because, "Then you sink into placidity and stupidity—and seem to be good sort of folks, because you have just energy enough to be gladdened when good active folks are busy in the world around you and are *doing* while you wish to do."[29]

Domestic and social tasks could certainly be stultifying and draining. But, by way of contrast, the relative tranquillity of domesticity could also undercut such will and determination as a woman was able to muster on behalf of her cause. Particularly in missionary or antislavery work, but even in the creative arena, women were expected to undertake tasks for which their domestic lives and limited educations had not prepared them. The glare of publicity was focused on women who acted in the public sphere. They were subject to ridicule, even danger. To sustain their commitment required strength of will, force of mind, and physical stamina. These came with practice. Periodic submergence in domesticity ate away at women's courage and confidence. It undermined their strength of purpose. As Susan B. Anthony wrote to Lydia Mott, "It is so easy to feel your power for public work slipping away if you allow yourself to remain too long snuggled in the Abrahamic bosom of home. It requires great will-force to resurrect one's soul."[30] Anthony feared that she might come to prefer the relative calm and consistency of the domestic sphere to the stress and strife of reform work.

Periodic interruptions eroded the spinster's confidence in her ability to contribute to public life. She felt demoralized and mediocre. Mary Grew, who held a well-deserved reputation as a local speaker, refused to take the stand at national antislavery meetings. "My gift for speaking," she said, "is not for such occasions."[31] Despite her "earnest longing for light and truth," Sarah Pugh felt,

the continued sense of inability to accomplish anything beyond the petty trivialities of the day, the dwelling in little things, not from the love of them, but from the want of effort and the feeling of power to escape from them; for these little things must be done to make the lives of others and my own comfortable, and why should I not accept them as my work, as gifts for accomplishing greater things are not mine?[32]

Similarly, Carrie A. Rowland, enmeshed in domestic cares, acknowledged the passing of her adolescent fancy to be something and someone important. She described herself as plodding along in the knowledge that, "I won't be much of anything after all the fine dreams of my early years about woman's influence, &c, &c, and I am getting reconciled by degrees to filling a very little 'measure,' having a very tiny 'career' indeed." She did not give up all ambition but continued to absorb "mental nourishment" in the hope that she would perhaps be "a great bush if not a tree."[33]

The structure of the domestic sphere—the pace of life as determined by the tasks of cleaning, working, and nursing—was hardly conducive to sustained and focused intellectual or professional activity. Although the late eighteenth and early nineteenth centuries witnessed changes in the place and process of making goods, household manufacturing remained important well into the 1830s. Daughters experienced much continuity as well as change in the nature and place of their work and their gender role. Whether daughters went out to work in the textile factories of New England in the 1820s and 1830s, or to teach in the schools of the 1830s and 1840s, whether they lived at home or boarded outside of the home, whether they took their wages for themselves or contributed them to the family coffers, these daughters retained considerable family loyalty. Engaged in making a female self, in pursuing autonomy, and achieving some place and purpose in the world, these early spinsters only modified, they did not revolutionize, their position in the family.

The ongoing significance of both the domestic role and family identity for antebellum spinsters meant that they expended considerable time and energy on attempting to harness together the two worlds of family and vocation. A remarkable series of letters testifies to the efforts of unmarried daughters to bend parental will to filial purpose. The final step in the forging of a vocational identity, and the first in embarking on a vocational life, appears to have been an effort to engage parental sanction. The texts of these letters exude the traditional language of female submissiveness. Yet the subtext is assertive, independent, and determined. The letters represent one important movement in a carefully choreographed battle. Although this skirmish resulted in defeat on occasion, the culmination of several combined actions promised a breach in the family walls that encircled the unmarried daughter. She could then forge ahead with her life's work.

Emily Howland carefully planned her assault on the bastion of parental consent. For some months after she first verbalized an interest in joining Myrtilla Miner, Howland consolidated support for her course of action. As already seen, she approached a variety of female friends and kin, and her brother, who was glad that "thee has finally decided to do what thee ought (for thy own happiness) to have done long ago."[34] Emily had already undertaken her practice teaching before she broached the subject to her parents. This she did in a letter rather than in person—an indication of the anxiety engendered in her. To her mother she wrote:

May I give a little of my life to degraded humanity? May I work a little while for that class which has so long enlisted my closest sympathies? May I try if I really can to make the world a little better for having lived in it? Can't thee spare me a while to do what I think my portion? I want to do something which seems to me worthy of life, and if all my life is to go on as have the last ten years, I know I shall feel at the end of it as tho[ugh] I had lived in vain, others with perhaps not as much capacity had reared noble, worthy families, contributed their share to the world and I had done nothing, [merely] dwindled away. I know thy health is very poor but I can do nothing for it, and as long as no one would think of its deterring me from marrying and leaving home forever if I choose, (Most think very strange that I do not, doubtless) it certainly can no more be urged against my taking a few years or months perhaps, for a benevolent enterprise.

Emily explained that she had inherited such a desire to work that she could not remain at home as did other daughters. "If I am different from the stereotyped kind I can't help it," she wrote. "I must be filled. For the last thirteen years, I have been busy about nothing, it does not satisfy me, it never can, until I have done something more." Howland reassured her mother about the distance she expected to travel and promised to be home in two days should there be some family emergency. She begged her mother to acknowledge the importance of her chosen work. "Do not ask anyone but thy own self whether to let Emily go or not," she pleaded. "It is not a question of propriety, how it will look and what people will think, I have allowed my ideas of duty often to be crushed by such counsel. Nothing, no good thought or work was ever given to the world that did not look queer to the most of folks."[35]

Howland crafted her letter carefully to meet all possible parental objections: distance from home, propriety of action, support of friends, carefulness of consideration, preparation, and significance to God and country. Howland wanted her mother's understanding and her approval. She would not have left for Washington without permission. Emily Howland was thirty-one years old when she wrote this letter. She was an adult unencumbered by husband or children. Yet first and foremost she was a daughter.

Many letters were written in similar circumstances by single women to their parents. Emily Elizabeth Parsons had begun nursing early in the Civil War. She had trained in Boston hospitals and volunteered for duty at Fort Schuyler, New York. Her parents could not accept her occupation, although she worked far from the battlefield. When Parsons fell ill in 1862, they wrote asking her to give up nursing and return home. "I am in the army just as [my brother] Chauncy is," wrote Emily, "and I must be held to work just as he is; you would never think of requesting he might not be sent on picket duty because it was hard work."[36]

After recuperating for three weeks, Parsons received an urgent summons to a Saint Louis military hospital. She telegraphed her father for permission to accept the post. He had meanwhile found war work for her that could be done at home in Boston and hoped this would meet Emily's earnest desire to contribute to the war effort. It did not. She wrote saying:

I feel bound to accept the position offered me. . . . The extreme distance will be an objection to you, but in the work to which I have pledged myself there can be no such limit as to time or space. I received your letter relative to the agency this morning; it is out of the question my undertaking such a work—I am not fitted for it. This St. Louis opportunity gives me what I can do, and wish to do, and I believe it to be my only chance for just what I could wish.[37]

She urged her father to telegraph his consent and begged her mother to be "trustful."

Parsons left New York without hearing from her father. So great was her distress that she wrote to her mother enroute: "If you think at any time that father would be happier to have me at home, or that it is best for me to be there, you must let me know, and I will do what you say. I hope I shall be guided to do what is right."[38] This letter, like Howland's, was carefully crafted. Its effect was disingenuous. Although she couched her terms in capitulatory language, Parsons merely regrouped, she did not surrender. She sowed dissension in an effort to divide and conquer. Parsons urged her mother to unite with her in following "the right" and in persuading her father to grant his consent for her mission. Emily certainly understood her father's wishes in the matter. Although she could not overtly defy him, neither was she willing to obey. She must appear to have misunderstood. If she could then turn one parent to her cause, her rebellion would not seem so complete. All this posturing occurred in Parsons's thirty-ninth year. She was no child, daughter though she was.

Fidelia Fiske received her call while at Mount Holyoke seminary working with Mary Lyon. From the time of her conversion in 1831, Fiske had felt that her "home was to be on missionary ground." One night, as she sat listening to the Reverend Dr. Justin Perkins tell the students and faculty about his work in Persia, Fiske felt God call to her. She stepped forward when Perkins asked for volunteers to accompany him on his return to the Middle East.[39]

Fiske's family and friends vehemently objected to the idea, citing her poor health. She decided to write her mother a letter calculated to win her approval:

Oh, it is a precious privilege to be consecrated by believing parents to the Lord in the early dawn of infancy! And, more than this, to have this consecration often renewed as years roll away. Oh, it does lead one to feel, and strongly feel, that one is not one's own! You, my dear mother, together with my dear father, have, I believe, thus often consecrated your children; not only in a sick, and, as you supposed, dying hour, but in days of health and prosperity. That you were sincere in this consecration I doubt not for a moment. I have had evidence of your sincerity in your efforts to promote my usefulness, and willingness ever to have me go where Providence directed. And now, my mother, one more opportunity presents itself to renew this consecration before you leave from this vale of tears. Shall I tell you how? I almost shrink from it. But why should I? Why fear to ask the Christian mother to do what perhaps she loves to do? I will not. No; I will tell you what my Father has presented to me, which I must present to you. The question is this: Are you willing that Fidelia should leave you to dwell the rest of life in a foreign land? to spend the rest of her days in pointing heathen souls to the Lamb of God? These questions have been, this week, proposed to me. The ground is Persia my employment to teach. . . .[40]

Fiske reminded her mother that she had dedicated her daughter to God's will and work. She implied that her mother would be hypocritical if she failed to sanction her daughter's call. By raising the subject of sincerity, Fidelia suggested its opposite. She cast herself as a dutiful daughter, submitting to the teachings and devotions of a lifetime, the education and example of a Christian mother, and the inheritance of a sainted father. She posed as fearful and diffident, yet confident that a mother's love of God would equal in kind and degree that of a daughter. Fidelia imputed to her mother assumptions which were far more hers and Mary Lyon's than Hannah Fiske's, and in so doing tried to establish the terms of the negotiation. She dared her mother to prove her faith by agreeing to the test set by her daughter.

Hannah Woodward Fiske resisted her daughter's emotional blackmail. She recaptured the terms of the debate, regaining for herself the high ground of principle. She said that Fidelia was needed at home by her family. This was a Christian daughter's first and most important duty. In fulfilling it, she would please her God and her mother. Such service being blessed by God, it was all the sanctification Fidelia required in this life.

Although initially dissuaded, Fidelia renewed her suit and approached Mary Lyon for help. Although Lyon had hoped that Fiske might stay at Mount Holyoke and share her own work, she agreed to intercede with Fiske's family. She had taught Fidelia the value of female service and acknowledged that work in the Persian mission field embodied the Mount Holyoke ideal.[41] Together, the two women drove a sleigh through thirty miles of snowy countryside from South Hadley, Massachusetts, to Shelbourne, Connecticut, to confront the Fiske family. Aroused from their sleep, the Fiskes reluctantly gave permission for Fidelia to go abroad.

Sarah Chase, a young Quaker woman from Worcester, Massachusetts, was visiting in Philadelphia when the Civil War broke out. At the age of twenty-five, she wrote home asking her father's permission to go to the battlefields as a nurse. "I feel fully prepared in every way: Thy consent only is wanted, and I *depend* upon it."[42] The Chase correspondence demonstrates with what seriousness even the most liberal families regarded such requests.

Anthony Chase found the responsibility of giving his approval a fearful one—"I wish it was not laid upon me." He worried about his daughter's safety, her companions, and her arrangements. But he acknowledged the righteousness of her request and granted her a certain respect for making it. "The idea is creditable to thy humanity," he wrote. "We are all here for a purpose—we have missions, and if we are true to ourselves we shall seek to know what that mission is, and knowing, endeavor to fulfill it." He asked whether she had thought about her capacity to endure camp life and the horrors of war; whether her experience, health, and constitution were adequate to meet the demands that would be made upon them; and whether she would be properly cared for and not exposed to danger or insult. If she had carefully weighed these matters, he would not interfere with "a daughter's wishes, 'who is of age and can answer for herself' and is responsible [to God] for neglect of duty."[43] He submitted her request to her brothers and sisters, however, for their consideration as well. Sister Elizabeth and brother George consulted, and responded in kind:

We have no objection to make, *provided* thee has thought of these things: First, with whom thee is to go; under whose leadership, as to their standing, character, etc. Secondly, the contingency of what may happen to thyself, and Thirdly, whether, all thy family consenting, thee is *sure* it is best to go. We say this not to prevent thee from going, but, if thee is strong in thy decision, to add to thy strength by our loving interest All our fears, as well as all our hopes. What do Pliny, Lucy, and Lizzie say? Our Heavenly Father's blessing shall be thine dear Sarah, and Mother is perhaps now repeating that Bible verse of thine, "Many daughters have done virtuously, but *thou excellest them all.*"[44]

Ultimately, Sarah did not go to the battlefields. After the war, however, she and her sister Lucy went south as teachers to the freedmen. Elizabeth joined them for awhile. The family's concerns were met by the end of hostilities, the supervision of the Freedman's Aid Bureau, and the company of siblings to insure safety, propriety, and companionship.

The definition of the parent-daughter relationship was such that changes or continuances in a woman's vocation required updated parental approval. Emily Howland required continual extensions of her "leave of absence." The very term connoted the temporary status with which her family viewed her vocational commitment. In May 1863, Howland wrote to her parents from Washington, D.C.:

I suppose the time which I proposed staying here, when I left home is about expired. . . . I feel as tho' I had just learned how to work with some efficiency. I will come home if you say so, but if there is no suffering need of me there, I know there is here. I would like to have a longer leave of absence . . . I want you to be willing I should stay, otherwise I can't feel right about it.[45]

Howland had shown her obedience to parental summons in 1858, when she returned home for five months to care for her ailing mother. She would return again in 1867 to take up her father's housekeeping after her mother's death.[46]

After fifteen years, Fidelia Fiske returned from Persia to Connecticut to care for an aging mother and an invalid sister. Hannah Fiske had used every family crisis in the intervening years as an opportunity to impress upon Fidelia the domestic costs of her chosen work. Although Fiske long resisted the pressure to return home, she had frequently worried about the righteousness of her priorities. Ultimately she felt compelled to respond.[47]

———◆———

Early-nineteenth-century families did not ordinarily consolidate and direct their resources to providing daughters with an advanced education, career training, or a financial start in life. More commonly, an unmarried daughter's contribution to the household economy or to domestic management enabled a family to provide for sons, whose success would redound to the family's social and financial credit in the community. Despite changes in family governance and women's emergence from the home in search of work and wages, parents thought of their daughters in traditional terms as inhabiting the domestic sphere and serving family or even parental needs. An unmarried woman of any age remained first and foremost a daughter. The Cult of Single Blessedness did not suggest otherwise.

But if family or the domestic sphere constrained female autonomy and achievement in antebellum America by ordering the vocational lives of its daughters and restraining women's emerging individuality, they also aided in the making of an independent female self. The family provided the structural support and emotional environment necessary for female growth toward independence. While, on the one hand, Emily Dickinson's image of the "Columnar Self" suggests strength, maturity, and autonomy, it also implies solitude, separation, and aloneness. Yet even in Dickinson's case, the single woman neither grew in isolation nor stood alone in her completeness and integrity. For the fires of the female intellect were fanned by the flames of female association and friendship, both of which were rooted in the private sphere of home and family life.

Dickinson refined her voice as a poet through the inspiration of her beloved sister-in-law, Susan Gilbert. In the early 1850s, while she groped toward a vocational identity, Dickinson fell passionately in love with Gilbert. "How vain it seems to write when one knows how to feel," she said. "Susie, forgive me Darling, for every word I say—my heart is full of you, none other than you in my thoughts, yet when I seek to say to you something not for the world, words fail me. If you were here—and Oh that you were, Susie, we need not talk at all, our eyes would whisper for us, and your hand fast in mine, we would not ask for language—."[48]

Dickinson's passion for Gilbert demanded that she find a language with which to express the depth of her emotion. Susan was Emily's inspiration, her muse, and sometimes her "text."[49] Dickinson's devotion to Gilbert released her creativity. In the context of their relationship she explored her individual voice. Emily wrote almost three hundred poems to Susan. They included poems celebrating every possible theme, occasion, or feeling. Emily gave Susan drafts of some poems, revisions of others, and final copies of still others. Susan Gilbert responded to these with a critical reading. Gilbert was Dickinson's "most consistent audience, and, from all appearances, her most intelligent and responsive mentor."[50]

Although it remained an underdeveloped theme in the book *Diana and Persis*, Louisa May Alcott also suggested the importance of female collegiality, inspiration, and love as essential components of the creative life. Alcott felt keenly the lack of an external source of inspiration, succor, affirmation, or meaningful artistic criticism. She wrote for a popular audience; she wrote for money. The exigencies of her life demanded this. But she knew that she had better work within her. Her struggle with the novel *Moods* exemplifies this. Alcott reworked this novel in an effort to say something meaningful about women's lives in the nineteenth century.[51] She required a Persis to her Diana, a Susan Gilbert to her Emily Dickinson. She needed a sustaining force that would also nurture, a compatible mind that had an intuitive grasp of the experience from which the artist drew her subject matter, and an analytical presence that could challenge her to refine her best work. In other words, Alcott recognized that the creative woman in the nineteenth century must have other women who would not confine her within the domestic and maternal realm, but would free her to soar with the eagles.[52]

When thinking of the development of an artistic sensibility as popular as Alcott's or as singular as Dickinson's, we picture, perhaps, the male model, the scholar in his study enmeshed in his own thoughts, alone with his books and papers. Women's learning, however, was not an isolated activity. Women's art was created in the context of shared lives and relationships. Perhaps because men considered the female intellect to be of lesser quality, women required the confirmation and encouragement of other women. The academies of higher learning were closed to women, so female education occurred in and was structured by informal institutions—reading circles, "conversations," public lectures, the exchange of letters and ideas between friends, acquaintances, and kin.[53]

Letters record the drive of women for intellectual expansion, their compulsion to read, their striving to clarify thoughts and refine expression. Female friends and kin played a prominent role in women's intellectual development. Emily Howland's extensive circle provides one example. Mary Reed, a Philadelphia schoolteacher, structured her vacations around books and the reading of them with this beloved companion and respected intellect. As she wrote one summer: "We will have a plan, and go by it. Do tell me what books to bring in; I will bring any thing you say. . . . I am quite crazy to come." Carrie Rowland apologized for monopolizing a recent visit, saying that "for some time I had not had a good talk with any one about books, and I felt that thee so thoroughly appreciated the subjects that had been filling my mind that the impulse to talk of them was irresistible. Oh if we only had had more time." Rowland feared the loss of motivation, the blunting of intellect, the dampening of spirit, the curtailment of growth inherent in her domestic position. Cousin Phebe Coffin longed to continue the intellectual discourse shared with Howland while she was practice-teaching. As Coffin took time from a busy day to indulge herself by reading the *Atlantic Monthly*, she thought, "Now I wish my friend Emily was here to talk to me to read the *Tribune* to me (always knowing how to select the readable matter), to talk to me about Byles and Dr. Cheever and Beecher and all our favorites. I can't bear to think that those days are all over. How much I learned, how my mind grew and expanded in the light of your general intelligent conversation. I am not ashamed to own it. It was . . . culture of the highest kind, a feast of fat things to me."[54]

Female reading circles also played an important role in the informal education that inspired and encouraged women. Some proved disappointing in their lack of seriousness and rigor (the very disappointment suggests the motivation of the members), but others provided rich food for starving minds. Elizabeth Palmer Peabody provided her friend Maria Chase with a detailed account of one such "blue-stocking club" in which she participated. Comprised of sixteen young ladies, the group met once a week to read and sew for the poor. Discussion generally stopped about half past eight, when young men were admitted and the group took on a more social and superficial air. Hannah Adams reported "a few dear friends" who met regularly to indulge their "taste for reading" and to present the poetry they wrote for praise and criticism. Frances Elizabeth Gray recorded in her diary the formation of a "reading party." She, the sisters Louise and Helen Amory, and a Miss Newton were to meet regularly to talk about the books they had read. Laura Lovell participated in a history reading circle with her friend Eliza Nelson.[55]

Formal "conversations" led by women of learning provided an opportunity to expand their horizons. Elizabeth Palmer Peabody held such classes in Boston and Salem in the 1820s. Her class met three times a week for one to three hours. The reading included "Some articles on Poetry etc. of the Heroic ages from several sources; Herodotus' History;—Schlegel on Dramatic Literature as far as it is applicable to Greece; and the times of Socrates." A tall order for women unaccustomed to read critically and to discuss ideas, but Peabody was convinced that this could be accomplished "in three months if we meet regularly."[56] Margaret Fuller gave similar courses in Cambridge in the late 1830s. Here, too, the women met once a week and for a fee received "inspired guidance." Fuller believed that women's education had failed fully to address their intellectual potential and so retarded their intellectual development. Unlike men, women had no opportunity to sharpen and exercise their minds or expand their capacities. She hoped that her "conversations" would provide an ordered structure, an intellectual community, "a place of stimulus and cheer," a point of union for "well-educated and thinking women." For Fuller believed that the interaction of minds was a necessary aspect of learning.[57]

Encounters with intellects such as those of Peabody or Fuller led women to discover their own intelligence and to establish friendships distinguished by the search for knowledge. In the company of females, antebellum women found "room to think in," respect for their mental gifts, permission to grapple with their ignorance, and aid in obtaining knowledge and practicing scholarship. In 1842, Fuller translated the correspondence of two German women for an American audience. Just as Emily Dickinson said of Susan Gilbert ("Susan is imagination"), so Bettine von Arnim wrote to Caroline von Gunderode, "Thou shinest on me with thy intellect, thou Muse."[58] The intellectual excursions of these women into literature, philosophy, natural science, and religion emerged from their mutual devotion—the one inspiring, reflecting, and challenging the other.

In America at this time, the path to female independence and achievement was a shared one. Women journeyed together, in pairs or groups, among kin or close friends. Women's separate sphere shaped that course for better or for worse.

7

"My Earthly All"

Sisterhood and the Search for Autonomy

Antebellum women were educated, grew to adulthood, and passed through the major turning points of their lives in a largely female world, solidly rooted in the domestic sphere. A regulated daily existence whose rhythms, purpose, and tasks were shared with other women was given meaning by the enduring nature of the emotional bonds within it and the ideation of woman's separate sphere outside it. The making of a female "self," the growth of female autonomy, and the kindling of female ambition occurred within this separate world. Female institutions, whether formal academies and associations or informal reading circles, fostered female achievement. Female friendships provided emotional and logistical support for vocational lives. Female kin played a crucial role, for it was in the family that women formed their gender identity and established their primary relationships. The strength of these relationships enabled a small group of women to assert themselves in personally, socially, and culturally significant ways.[1]

For the women of this study, the route to the essential self, the passage to female autonomy, and the pathway to achievement originated in female, peer, and particularly sibling relationships. Female support and encouragement provided the necessary audience, criticism, inspiration, and partnership for vocationally oriented women. Shared lives eased domestic, economic, and familial responsibilities. On the psychological level, women whose emotional ties were strong and whose interchangeability was culturally prescribed, struggled to establish individual limits of mutual identification and dependence. The process strengthened women's sense of self and promoted female autonomy. Among the women in this study were an extraordinary number of siblings, sisters who loved one another with such devotion and primacy that they spent their lives together in single blessedness: the five Smith sisters of Glastonbury, Connecticut; the five Blackwells of Cincinnati; the four Spear sisters of Newton, Massachusetts; the four Motts of Albany, New York;

the four Westons of Weymouth, Massachusetts; the three Lewis sisters of Media, Pennsylvania; or the three Chase sisters of Worcester, Massachusetts. Pairs of sisters were particularly numerous in the spinster population: Margaretta and Sarah Peale of Philadelphia, Alice and Phoebe Cary of New York City, Hannah and Eliza Brown of Boston, Emily and Lavinia Dickinson of Amherst, Margaretta and Elizabeth Morris of Philadelphia, Susan and Mary Anthony of Rochester, Mary and Hannah Townsend of Philadelphia, Sarah and Rebecca Lee of Boston, Sarah and Mary Gilpin, and Clementina and Harriet Smith of the Brandywine River Valley. This phenomenon of sibling attachment emerged in the early nineteenth century and appears to be linked both to changes in the middle-class family and to the transformation of American society from a transgenerational to a peer culture.

Spurred by changes in the nature, place, and timing of work, the democratization of the family, and the emergence of institutions directed toward the young, girls looked to one another for a sense of shared values, for understanding of their particular experience, for clarification of expectations about the future, and for recognition and support in attaining their goals. As young women moved away from the family, they idealized family ties. *Sisterhood,* like *fraternity,* was a term of crucial political, intellectual, and social significance, and gained its power from an idealized and romanticized sibling relationship.[2]

Sibling love represented an individual's greatest potential for intimacy. The nineteenth century promoted the idea that all women shared certain intellectual, emotional, and character traits, that they behaved in certain predictable patterns because of their common biology. Among women, sisters uniquely shared a lineage, a past, and an inherited world view, in addition to common personality and physiological traits. So similar were sisters believed to be, that they often substituted for one another—in the serial marriage of one man to a succession of siblings, for example.[3]

Reared in such a culture, and often in a family where older sisters took care of younger ones, it is not surprising to find deep emotional resonance to the term and relationship implied by the word *sister.* Women bestowed the title on their closest female friends. Missionary Fidelia Fiske called her colleague Susan Rice her "dearest sister," and indeed they lived as such, sharing a domicile, work, and leisure. For many years, the two women cared for one another's physical and emotional needs. Elizabeth Smith, a deeply private woman, noted in her diary the death of a beloved friend "with whom I have lived as a sister." Women spoke of the "maiden sisterhood," denoting a "band" of women united by their single status, their shared experience, and their particular interests and spheres of action.[4]

Antebellum women held high expectations for the sisterly relationship and invested it with great emotional significance. Carrie A. Rowland, for example, wrote that she looked within herself for strength, courage, and independent-mindedness, "for having no sister I am more dependent on my friends, and they are getting married off at a most alarming rate."[5] Eunice Callender described the death of her sister Susan in highly romantic terms.

It has pleased the Almighty to deprive me of a beloved sister!—one who was the delight and pride of our hearts and with whom I fondly hoped to have long taken sweet counsel, to have walked in the same path, and have shared her joys and her sorrows—no one can tell how I have anticipated her return home [from a family visit], how much joy I had laid up in store! and how I rejoiced when I thought of having a companion, a friend, and a sister return.[6]

Susan was much younger than Eunice, so the two had yet to develop a mature relationship. Eunice spoke, then, out of a cultural expectation surrounding the nature of sisterhood. She grieved for her dreams about what their relationship might have become rather than for the death of what had been.

The primacy of the sibling relationship and its significance for female autonomy and achievement in the early nineteenth century is most dramatically seen in cases where sisters were forced to separate. Many women dated the great turning points of their lives from the marriage or death of a sister.[7] Either occasion resulted in enormous stress. Both stimulated the reformulation of a woman's sense of self and sense of purpose. Some experienced the disruption of previously shared lives as a betrayal and could not accept it. Others, making the effort to carry on, found it a liberating if no less traumatic transition.

In her early thirties, Hannah Adams lost her older sister, Elizabeth. According to Hannah, Elizabeth had been calm and even-tempered, while she was immoderate and irritable. Elizabeth had been judicious, steady, persevering, and disciplined, while she was indecisive, impulsive, enthusiastic, and undisciplined. Elizabeth had been cheerful while she was melancholy, courageous and strong while she was timid and weak.[8] The comparison contains an element of hyperbole and self-denigration. Hannah was sufficiently disciplined to write at least five books, and strong enough to support herself by writing at a time when authors were paid little, had no copyright protection, and were overwhelmingly male or male-protected. Nevertheless, Hannah cast Elizabeth as her other half, believing that together they presented a formidable front to a hostile world.

"I placed the strongest reliance upon Elizabeth's judgment," said Hannah, "and as she was older than myself, she seemed the maternal friend, as well as the best of sisters. In short, 'she was my *guide*, my *friend*, my earthly all.' "[9] The phrase, "my earthly all," was conventionally reserved to describe a wife, not a sister. Its use, and that of adjectives such as *mated* or *widowed*, indicates that many sisters thought of themselves as wedded to one another in a relationship more intimate and meaningful than many marriages, and carrying equal social significance. Hannah's love for her sister bore not only the weight of idealized sisterhood but also gathered emotional momentum from the great trauma of her twelfth year—her mother's death and father's immediate remarriage. It was then that Elizabeth became mother as well as sister to her.

Elizabeth's health declined steadily for two years before her death. She tried to prepare Hannah for her passing, but Hannah would not listen. "If [Elizabeth] were taken away, I should surely die," said Hannah, for "there was but one heart between us." Although Hannah did not follow her sister to the grave as did many others in this situation, she nevertheless acknowledged that "for years after my sister's death it was a struggle to live."[10]

Hannah Adams memorialized her sister in poetry, seeking to immortalize their love.[11] Writing poetry had redemptive value. It eased her sorrow and shifted her attention away from death. One fragment illustrates the flavor of her work:

> Dearer than life, or aught below the skies,
> The bright ideas and romantic schemes
> Of perfect love, and friendship, fancy paints,
> In her I realized.

> And she is dead! My life, my all is gone.
> The world's a desert. Nothing now on earth
> Can yield me joy, or comfort.[12]

The death of so intimate a soulmate, so beloved an other, of one whose "interests were so closely blended that I nearly identified her existence with my own," left Hannah Adams in profound loneliness. Now isolated in an alien world, she described her previous sense of integration:

> Of sacred friendship, was my love to her
> Our minds expanding, each succeeding year
> Heightened our mutual friendship. Not a joy
> Ere touched my soul, but when she shared a part.[13]

Hannah's identity, her sense of self, her growth and development were intertwined with those of her sister. At some basic emotional level, she never recovered from Elizabeth's death.[14]

The devastation that could be wreaked by a sister's death was unmatched. A sister's marriage, however, and the transference of her allegiance, attention, and love to a male interloper resulted in another kind of emotional shock. Feelings of great loss infused women's descriptions of their sisters' weddings. Catharine M. Sedgwick was only seven when she experienced the "first tragedy" of her life, the marriage of her older sister Eliza.

She was my mother-sister. I had always slept with her, and been her assigned charge . . . I remember where the bride and groom stood, and how he looked to me like some cruel usurper. . . . When the long consecrating prayer was half through, I distinctly remember the consciousness that my sister was going away from me struck me with the force of a blow, and I burst into loud sobs and crying.

Sedgwick later remembered her brother-in-law attempting to reassure her by saying, "I'll let your sister stay with you this summer." That she was now dependent upon his will for her sister's presence impressed upon Sedgwick the enormity of the change. Sedgwick cried herself to sleep that night and awoke in tears the following morning. Thereafter, she found weddings more sad than joyful.[15]

Louisa May Alcott dreaded the marriage of her sister Anna and depicted the wedding ceremony in funereal terms. "I moaned in private over my great loss," she wrote, "and said I'd never forgive J[ohn] P[ratt] for taking Anna from me." On the day of the wedding, the gray dresses the sisters wore and the roses they carried symbolized to Louisa sackcloth and ashes, "for I mourn the loss of my Nan and am not comforted."[16]

Among the important losses occasioned by sibling marriage was that of a shared vocation. Sarah Hunt left not only a sister but also a partner when she married. Three years apart in age, Harriot and Sarah had grown up together, sharing schoolwork, domestic responsibilities, and a professional practice. Their partnership began when their father's sudden death left the family in severe financial distress. In an effort to generate income, Harriot and Sarah opened a school. Then, at the age of twenty-two, Sarah fell seriously ill. Harriot took both classes so that Sarah could rest. Forty-one weeks of illness and 106 professional calls compelled the sisters to take charge of Sarah's treatment themselves. Harsh purges of leeches, blistering, and prussic acid had achieved nothing but discomfort. The sisters began to study medicine in the hope of understanding Sarah's illness and finding a less painful, more organic cure. Sarah gradually regained her health. The sisters apprenticed with homeopathic doctors before establishing their own practice, which flourished.

Sarah's marriage threatened all that the sisters had built up over five years. She assured Harriot that she retained a deep interest in medical work and was available for consultation. The newlyweds planned to live with Harriot and her mother, Kezia Hunt. Sarah hoped that proximity would ensure continuing medical practice, but Harriot recognized that her life, her work, and her sense of self were changed: "Who that has had an only sister married but can understand my feelings! My life had now assumed more distinctness—more identity. I knew I must act now, in a great measure, act alone. There was a widowed feeling about me, which passed away somewhat in time; but it has never wholly left me. The word 'we' spoken professionally, sometimes escapes me now!"[17]

Hunt mourned her sister: their lost intimacy, unanimity of purpose, unity of mind, shared work and play. But she also found that the separation provided an opportunity for personal growth. For the first time, Harriot differentiated herself from her sister, and her vocation from Sarah's. Their allegiance of heart and alliance of mind was broken. Harriot realized that she must leave her sister's house if she were to survive professionally. Although Sarah begged her to stay, Harriot knew that she must forge a distinct life in a separate place.

My practice told me of the need for a separate home. My profession seemed hallowed to me, my patients were my family; and a new purpose to labor more effectively for women, seized my soul. Individual responsibility became more defined: the significance of the word physician, became more apparent. . . . My love for my sister had become stronger. She was now my all. But she was a wife and mother, and I must be wedded to Humanity. The thought of living with her was only transient.[18]

Although Sarah might be Harriot's "all," the sisters no longer had a perfect sharing. Harriot found autonomy thrust upon her. She did not welcome it or the marriage, and would have preferred their continued partnership of life and work. In the end, it was her commitment to medicine and her drive for achievement that prevented her from subsiding into the role of maiden aunt.

Other sisters pursued autonomy and achievement without the trauma of sibling death or marriage. In the lifelong sharing of occupation, vocation, and domesticity, the Weston sisters of Weymouth, Massachusetts, demonstrate the meaning of antebellum sisterhood. As a group, the Westons united "the highest education and the first of abilities with the purest philanthropy. They have warm hearts, clear heads, wit, humor, spirit, literature, and most of them the virtue which every woman should have if possibly she can, beauty."[19]

Two of the six sisters married, the oldest, Maria, and the youngest, Emma Forbes. The others seem not to have seriously contemplated the prospect. They did not reject marriage in principle so much as they shied away from their suitors. Anne W. Weston, for example, described the proposal of a Mr. Bigelow. She was twenty-four at the time and had met the man in Groton, Connecticut, at the home of a dear friend (and rumored suitor), Dr. Farnsworth. Bigelow called on her in Boston and asked permission to continue his attentions. "I assented thereto," wrote Anne, "but felt pretty well frightened for I knew what was coming well enough." Queasy about facing the ordeal but knowing that she must see it through, Anne awaited his call. As she told her sisters about "the hot coal business": "he made me a down right offer and I as down rightly declined. It was a trial to me, but on the whole I got through with it better than I could have thought. I never could for a minute have entertained the thought of making any other answer than I did but truth compels me to say that I think the man a very good one."[20] The only man Anne seems to have truly loved was married and lived abroad.[21]

Edmund Quincy, a family friend and fellow abolitionist, believed that the sisters' love for one another precluded marriage. "Nothing but a most desperate falling in love could carry them off. They are married to each other and cannot imagine at present, that any possible man could supply the society of their sisters." He and Richard Dana Webb, an Irish abolitionist, prided themselves on the intimacy of their friendship with the women but also consoled one another about the boundaries of that friendship. The Westons excluded all but one another from the innermost ring of their "magic circle."[22]

The Westons lived and worked together. The parental home in Weymouth served as their geographic and emotional fulcrum. From here, they moved between Maria Weston Chapman's Boston home and various teaching positions (in Boston, Roxbury, and New Bedford). Later, they visited the European home of Chapman's widowhood and stayed at their brother's house in New York. On occasion they set up housekeeping on their own. Caroline and Anne, for example, ran a Boston boarding school for a time.

The sisters stayed together despite the centrifugal forces of economic exigency. In 1836, both Caroline and Anne had lucrative offers to teach far from home. Both discussed the matter with their sisters and decided not to go. Said Deborah the following spring, "I am very glad that Caroline is not going to Providence. I do so hate to have her leave Boston." She herself sought work closer to home than the New Bedford post she then occupied. Ultimately Deborah gave up teaching in order to rejoin the family. "I am sorry to have you lose your dollar a day," said Anne, "but of course glad to have you back again this winter."[23]

The attachment of the Weston sisters is evident in their correspondence. Anne told of sleeping in the same bed with an acquaintance, Sarah Thaxter, on her first night away from home. Poignantly, she told of waking abruptly in the night. "I thought I was with Deborah and finding that was not the case, my trouble was so great that it waked me entirely up so that I could not get to sleep again." Deborah grew so excited about a weekend with her sisters that "thought of it almost stops my breath." She confessed that the receipt of a letter from home aroused her senses in the same fashion as reading romantic fiction.[24]

The sisters depended upon the exchange of letters and journals to maintain their communication. They noted every break in the flow of correspondence. Chastised Deborah: "Why you good for nothing sinners have you not written. It is now more than three weeks since I have heard a word. One of the school girls told me the other day that she saw the marriage of Miss Anne Weston in the paper and I really think it must be you. Nothing else will excuse your laziness. . . . Write if you have not written the moment you get this."[25] Through the exchange of diaries, the sisters shared events, feelings, and thoughts with an immediacy matched only by common experience. Wrote Deborah to Caroline, "I wish you would keep a journal *faithfully* and transmit it to me as fast as you fill a sheet." She, in turn, assured Lucia that she would "keep a journal for your edification" while nursing Maria.[26]

An analysis of the relationships among the Westons sheds light on female autonomy in the early nineteenth century, for it was in the context of sibling relationships that the struggle for individuation took place. Sisterly love enabled women to develop and express self-love and self-respect. Although antebellum culture promoted abnegation of the female self, sisterly love provided opportunities to strengthen autonomy, support initiative, reinforce individual will, confirm vocational identity, and promote the aspirations of that other being who most closely resembled one's self.

It has been suggested that the placidity of the domestic environment and the psychodynamics of child-rearing in the early industrial family left an imprint on female personality. Women did not develop a striving, competitive, rational character because, unlike men, they did not struggle to individuate from a parent of the opposite gender. Reared in a female world characterized by gender and family solidarity, women may have found individuation difficult.[27] Certainly middle-class Americans increasingly emphasized the affective role of the mother in child-rearing. The mother-daughter relationship assumed special significance in those cultures and families where daughters learned their social role from their mothers with relatively little trauma. Yet mothers born before (and even slightly after) 1800 experienced frequent pregnancy and childbirth. Catharine Beecher and Catharine Sedgwick remembered mothers too absorbed with household management, production, and childbirth to help their children beyond infancy. Others, like Emily Dickinson or Guilelma Breed, had invalid or inept mothers who essentially abdicated any important place in the household. Many, like Frances Gray, Catharine Seely, or

Hannah Adams, lost their mothers at an early age. It may be, then, that the placidity of the domestic environment and the close relationship between mother and daughter have been overstated for this early period. Perhaps they developed with the decline in fertility that came in the mid-nineteenth century. If so, such family life emerged concurrently with industrial and educational opportunities that drew daughters into worlds far different from those of their mothers and into environments far from home.

Many of the subjects of this study lived in households where female kin played important roles as nurturers, teachers, confidantes, and disciplinarians. Maiden aunts tutored the Blackwell and Weston sisters. Catharine Sedgwick and Hannah Adams found solice with older sisters. Sarah M. Grimké and Alice Cary acted as guardians for younger siblings. That girls of these generations had a variety of older women to emulate and love may have aided their psychological development by defusing identification with a single individual.

However, the unavailability of the mother left some daughters competing for the attention and approbation of the women in their lives. As peer attachments became increasingly important, sisters vied with one another for position, love, and attention. Mary S. Gilpin, for example, experienced her older sister Sarah as critical, opinionated, competitive, self-righteous, exclusionary, and domineering: "Her chief intercourse with me has been what she *calls* giving me advice, but which to me seems like saying things so severe and censorious, as to awaken all the irritation of my nature . . . things she has said have been as sharp piercing daggers running in so far that it has required an effort indeed and time to draw them out one by one and regain peace [of mind and soul]." Mary resented Sarah's usurpation of a daughter's place at their mother's side after their father's death. Sarah refused to share the role of companion, nurse, and housekeeper or the privileges of wealth and comfort that went with their mother's estate. Mary lamented "that disposition, or I should say resolve for a paramount and undisputed sway in S[arah] which seems to merge the love of kind in the love of power so completely as to make her alert to frustrate every wish small or great which might possibly encroach on it."[28] Being healthy and comfortable, her mother did not require the assistance of two daughters. For her own peace of mind, and for her mother's, Mary deferred to Sarah in domestic matters. Because she had no desire to live under Sarah's tyranny, she sought an independent home and livelihood. Some such relationships between siblings, cousins, or even intimate friends resulted in the loss of individual identity and increased emotional dependence.[29]

Yet other girls found their personalities strengthened in the effort to define a personal identity and to maintain separation within the extraordinary closeness of the female kinship network. Relationships among the Weston sisters illustrate the subtle forces that militated against individuation among siblings. The sisters submitted to popular assumptions about female and sibling interchangeability in various ways. They adopted strategies for resisting such forces and thereby were able to forge independent identities.

One Weston sister frequently found herself substituting for another in a variety of roles. In the domestic sphere, for example, although the sisters' particular characteristics and skills differed widely, one did as well as another in an emergency. Henry Chapman arrived at Weymouth to retrieve his daughter Elizabeth from her aunt's care. "He wanted to carry me back," confided Deborah, "but I would not go, so Emma was carried off by the hair of her head."[30]

In teaching, too, the sisters completed one another's terms when necessary or took up a position vacated by another. Caroline, for example, wrote to Deborah telling her that the family had had a conference and decided that an offer from the Morgan School was too good to pass up. Therefore Deborah "had better close with it at once." Caroline coached her sister on the fine points of bargaining for salary and benefits. She urged Deborah to "say it is *possible* that your health may not permit you to begin [January 1] but if it *does not* one of your sisters will act for you till you are ready." Anne assured Deborah that she would fill in if need be. Anne and Deborah regularly rotated the New Bedford job between them for many years.[31]

Even in their political activities, where their personalities, skills, and interests most clearly diverged, the sisters were seen as interchangeable. Everyone (including themselves) assumed that each could and would substitute for the other in passing petitions, organizing fund-raising events, lecturing the public, or conducting meetings. Apprehensive about serving as a delegate to the annual New England Anti-Slavery Association convention in 1839, Anne nevertheless reported for duty. "When I first arrived in town, Caroline told me that if I did not go she should; that it would be inconvenient to her, and might perhaps injure her school, but that she was resolved that one of the family should be there. . . . Maria thought the same."[32]

Despite their presumed domestic and public interchangeability, the sisters struggled to form separate identities and to distinguish themselves one from the other by carving out separate spheres and testing their individual talents. They recognized, if they did not always appreciate, one another's unique qualities. Maria dominated the family circle. A handsome woman, she had a dynamic personality and was a charismatic leader. In awe of her political powers and attracted to her personal ones, author Harriet Martineau described her as having "reasoning powers which can never be baffled, learning and literary *fullness* I cannot fathom or compass; and knowledge of the world which the worldling cannot suppress." Yet she ascribed to Chapman "the sweetest womanly tenderness that woman ever manifested."[33]

Caroline, the second eldest, felt most keenly the comparison with Maria. She proved impatient with, and perhaps jealous of, references to her sister's personality and appearance. In comparing the two, people found Caroline to be "a delightful woman, not so handsome or majestic looking as her sister, but with perhaps more sweetness of manner and a good deal of the same energetic frame of mind."[34] Nicknames given the sisters by political rivals underscored their similarities and differences. Proslavery forces in Boston referred to Maria Weston Chapman as "Lady Macbeth," a reference to her connection with William Lloyd Garrison, the "diabolical" antislavery leader, and to her leadership of the antislavery movement. The name reflected all the elemental force and raw drive of Shakespeare's villainess. Caroline was labeled the "Dutchess of Sutherland." Having spent some years in Britain, she displayed the genteel mannerisms, the self-confidence, and the imperiousness which characterized this aristocrat.[35] The sobriquets suggest Caroline's refined authority and Maria's stark power.

Anne Warren Weston described herself as being molded in a "less heroic strain" than her two sisters. Edmund Quincy called her a descendent of Bunyan's "Much Afraid."[36] On her own ground, however, Quincy found her to be much the best conversationalist, male or female, that he had ever met: "charming, fresh, and original."[37] Anne succumbed to a variety of nervous complaints but nevertheless carried on a career in reform.[38] It was she, not Caroline, who filled Maria's shoes as director of the annual Boston Female Anti-Slavery Society Fair (a large and important money-raising event) and editor of *The Liberty Bell* (a gift-book of essays, poetry, and fiction written by prominent international abolitionists and published yearly to raise money for the cause).

Deborah, nicknamed Dora, was the family's "indispensible housekeeper and care-taker."[39] She was "the angel of the house"—the favorite teacher, devoted nurse, beloved aunt, and neighborhood benefactor. Deborah cared for the Chapman children when needed and remained in Weymouth, "attending to . . . the thousand little duties of a country neighborhood. . . . Visits, parties, hikes, road mending, sewing meetings, Freedman's Aid Societies, all are in her hands and keep her very busy."[40] Deborah resisted a leadership role in the antislavery movement, although she passed petitions, attended meetings, and followed events in her own locale. "[I am] sorry to disappoint you," she responded to Maria's importunings, "but I am afraid I must bang to your glorious door again—I am never going to take upon myself the management of any society matters, such as 'passing resolutions and voting supplies'—I feel no call and certainly no ability for the thing—Indeed I have an oath in Heaven against it."[41] Every sisterly grouping, however large or small, required one "Dora" to keep things organized on the domestic front.[42]

Just as the Weston sisters' temperaments and specialities differed, so too did their principles and ideas. They disagreed quite freely. Edmund Quincy laughed at a colleague's assumption that the sisters thought alike. "You know them very little," he explained, "if you think they are influenced by [Maria Weston Chapman] or anybody in making up their minds. Mrs. C. has no more influence over them, nor they over her than you or I have . . . . They differ in the most animated way on all kinds of subjects but without the least *aigresse* and with perfect good temper."[43]

It was not easy to establish and maintain both individuality and mutual devotion. Anne acknowledged the toll extracted by a high level of constant intimacy. She felt her privacy violated by the frequency and ease with which the sisters walked in and out of one another's minds, hearts, and rooms. Anne sometimes felt that the sisters were overly involved in one another's lives. Continual discussion of everything from lesson plans to politics was "the cross" she bore. She admitted to "an envy [of] people that stand alone in the world never having had any remembered ties of blood."[44]

Yet that very intimacy which at times overwhelmed her enabled her to carve out for herself a sense of her separate identity and an important degree of independence. Shared lives provided a firm foundation upon which to build prominent vocations in the antislavery campaign—arguably the most significant political movement of their generation. The Westons were sensitive women, afraid to walk alone down Boston's Washington Street for fear of the store clerks' rude jests. Together, however, they defied not only adolescent clerks but also delegations from Boston's mercantile and religious elites. When British abolitionist George Thompson spoke to the Boston Female Anti-Slavery Society in 1835 and a threatening mob surrounded the building, it was Maria Weston Chapman and her sisters who led the membership out through the abusive crowd to safety. In May 1838, during the Women's National Anti-Slavery Convention in Philadelphia's Pennsylvania Hall, Maria's conspicuous bravery and self-possession held the convention's attention while a clamoring crowd threw bricks and excrement through broken windows. Hidden in the home of abolitionists James and Lucretia Mott, Anne and Maria sustained one another's courage while a mob searched for them.[45]

The Weston sisters' reform activities clearly depended upon their mutual assistance. The degree of their financial support is implied but not detailed in surviving personal documents. Deborah, feeling isolated and lonely in New Bedford, took comfort in being "able to do something to help us along." The sisters readily made gifts and loans to each other: dressing gowns and patterns, best Sunday clothes, teaching materials, and modest amounts of cash. Caroline made by far the best living, earning at her estimation some $25,000 by teaching. Given that her life-style seems not to have differed from that of the others, it would seem that all shared in a family economy. No sister suffered want or would have allowed another to do so.[46]

In many other families sisters replicated the Weston pattern of living, loving, and working in concert. All maintained a tenuous and complex weighting of mutual dependence, independence, and dependibility. In many, the mixture promoted autonomy and achievement. Emily Blackwell, pioneer female physician and medical educator, consciously patterned herself after her older sister Elizabeth in an effort to make a name and a mark for herself in the world. The intensity of Emily's desire to excel and her need for Elizabeth's approval and love spurred her intellectual and professional achievement.

"When Elizabeth Blackwell announced her determination to become a physician, Emily, then a girl of eighteen, made up her mind to do the same, in order to make an independent life for herself, and to help in opening the door for other women," said Alice Stone Blackwell, her niece.[47] Much of the attraction to medicine lay in Emily's romantic dream of two confident sisters sharing both the opprobrium and the glory of pioneering women's role in the discipline.

Emily doubted her ability to make her own contribution—doubted that medicine was her true calling and feared that, should Elizabeth be prevented from completing her work, "I shall never be able to fill her place," thus implicitly comparing herself and her worth to her older sister's. She always felt the spur of competition—competition with her sister for the approbation of others, and competition with others for her sister's love and attention. As she sought to draw ever closer to Elizabeth, Emily's fear of rejection and her dislike of dependency caused great pain and marked her personality with a certain constraint. "I ask myself often," she sighed, "if I do not expect too much sympathy and companionship from Elizabeth and life sometimes appears cold and lonely in the future."[48]

Elizabeth encouraged Emily to see their futures as linked. She wrote to her in November of 1850, "I look forward with great interest to the time when you can aid me in these matters, for I have really no *medical friend;* all the gentlemen I meet seem separated by an invincible, invisible barrier, and the women who take up the subject partially are inferior."[49] While Elizabeth reckoned that it would not always be so, for the time being the two sisters would have to rely upon one another.

In January 1850, Emily began her professional journey by accepting Elizabeth's old job teaching school in Henderson, Kentucky. She hoped to earn the money necessary for medical training. "My home life has closed, my solitary life of struggle has commenced and painful has the introduction been," she recorded in her diary. Blackwell expected a great deal of herself and measured her potential against her sister's accomplishments. She confided to her journal:

It is the age of moral martyrdom to those who would become perfect as *he* is perfect. How deeply my own indecision, weakness, selfishness, and listlessness pressed on me. . . . Ah my Father, willingly would I be purified and strengthened though it were by fire but I fear the elements in some respects are wanting. When I look upon such women as . . . Elizabeth, [her] devotion and still more [her] practical efficiency, I feel most bitterly my own deficiency.[50]

Blackwell hated teaching but could not afford to quit. She missed her family and felt estranged from Southern culture. When a chance to teach in Cincinnati was offered to her, Emily rejoiced. She would live with her family and earn three hundred dollars a year toward her educational expenses. "I looked round on my room where Elizabeth lived her career," she wrote, "where so many sorrows tried me, where while I fought the Devil all day I met God 'in the cool of the evening.' "[51] She thanked Him for the spirit and thought which animated her existence—and for her release from this burden.

During her last weeks at Henderson, Blackwell lived in anticipation of leaving. Once home, she suffered an inevitable letdown. After "wasting" several weeks which she "should" have used for study, she lapsed into a deep depression:

Here end four restless painful weeks . . . I have suffered intensely from irresolution, self dissatisfaction, and disappointment, but why should I suffer so, with God, and his universe around me, is not Heaven ever open to those who truly seek it. Did a true and noble self devotion fill us we should not be so utterly discouraged even by our failures, by our deficiency. It is my ambition and self love as well as my true self respect that are wounded. I feel at once a terrible self-distrust. . . . Could I entirely lay aside selfishness and devote myself with a true and single purpose to the service of Truth, in spite of disappointment and sorrow, surely a true faith and happiness would dawn upon me.[52]

In January, Blackwell began her new job. On weekends she studied medicine but continued to doubt herself and her course. "I would that I knew clearly what my work was. I have thought much about it. I think that I have chosen the position for which I am best fitted, but my purposes and powers are not yet clear to me."[53] She recorded symptoms of increasing emotional stress: an inability to concentrate, drowsiness, and torpor.

By late summer, Blackwell was thoroughly disgusted with "the most detestable occupation," as she called teaching. For five years she had labored, loathing the work and feeling a complete lack of talent for it. She had managed to save only five hundred dollars toward medical school. "I long with such an intense longing for freedom, action, for life and truth. I feel as though a mountain were on me, as though I were bound with invisible fetters," she wrote. "I am full of furious bitterness at the constraint and littleness of the life that I must lead, and God is so far off, I can not realize His presence." Emily Blackwell had sufficient social and feminist consciousness to recognize that some part of her problem stemmed from the female condition in America. "I can not comprehend our limited, bounded, suffering, ignorant life," she wrote.[54]

Elizabeth wrote Emily urging her to come to New York. Emily's heart leapt at the thought. "It seems almost impossible to toil away the next seven months teaching and I do so earnestly long to be at work, not to feel as each month passes a painful feeling that it has done nothing worth mentioning. O for a truly noble life—to be—to do great works for Humanity."[55] Emily asked that Elizabeth specify arrangements between them and describe the medical training available in New York. The reply was not all that she had hoped. "She repeats her advice to come east," Emily confided to her diary, "but not strongly. There appeared to me to be a little irritation in the letter and I felt so forcibly how desirable it was to stand independent that I resolved on the spot to teach the rest of the year unless I could obtain admission to some college."[56]

Emily knew that Elizabeth was under great personal and professional stress at the time, struggling to establish a practice and earn a living despite the great prejudice against women in medicine. Nevertheless, she felt rebuked by Elizabeth's reply. Throughout her life, Emily would exhibit extreme sensitivity to Elizabeth's every action, mood, and expression. With the younger sibling's greater appreciation for the differential presence and use of power in family relationships, she continually measured who loved, needed, and wanted more from whom. In an effort to remain free of obligation, she was tempted to reject any assistance not freely tendered. She loathed the dependence she so clearly felt.

Nevertheless, in the summer of 1852, Emily traveled east to look at medical schools and to visit Elizabeth. Elizabeth had started a public lecture series, and Emily looked on admiringly. "She certainly has some of the qualities of a really great woman," she acknowledged, "she has the power of making things succeed." But Elizabeth's public influence only added to Emily's ambivalence about their relationship. "I want to see her to judge how far I can work with her and whether we can be really friends."[57] The visit went well, and for five days, "[W]e talked over her whole course—her position, plans and prospects—and I liked E[lizabeth]. She was not nearly as particular and fidgety as I had the idea."[58] The fact remained, however, that Emily came as a junior partner. The plans, dreams, and policies were Elizabeth's. To Emily were allocated the tasks of administrator and drudge.

That fall Blackwell applied to medical school in Philadelphia. Although encouraged by several doctors, she was denied admission. "For a moment my bright light went out, then my will rose firm." Emily turned to God, her usual source of comfort at such times. But the proper attitude of Christian humility eluded her. "Why am I alone," she cried, "perplexed in a labyrinth of impenetrable mysteries, fettered in restraints within and without, and not I only but every human soul that thinks and feels and aspires in vain for its life—its life—its home. . . . God if thou art our father—Christ if thou art our brother, speak to me."[59]

With enormous effort, Blackwell persevered, applying to schools in Cleveland, Cincinnati, and Columbus. Rejected for admission in Cleveland and lacking other encouragement, Emily borrowed money and traveled eastward. There she applied and was refused entrance at Dartmouth, Pittsfield, and Geneva (her sister's alma mater, censured by the state medical association for graduating Elizabeth). Finally, Elizabeth Blackwell and Horace Greeley used their combined influence to have Emily admitted to rounds at Bellevue Hospital in New York City.

For two months Emily participated in these clinical evaluations, recognizing that the exercise provided her with no credential, however much it contributed to her medical knowledge. She despaired. Some of her depression may have resulted from continuing ambivalence about her relationship with Elizabeth. "I do not feel completely clear that I can establish myself in New York and work in concert with E[lizabeth]. On many accounts I should like to, but whether I could not work more effectually elsewhere I have not yet decided."[60]

Blackwell went to Chicago where, in November of 1852, she enrolled as a medical student at Rush College. She gained valuable clinical experience by working with a local physician but he asked her to leave when a female patient complained that women had no place in a doctor's office. Blackwell longed "exceedingly for those free untrammeled opportunities of study a young man would have." When, on her return from the summer break, Emily was denied readmission, she transferred to Western Reserve Medical School in Cleveland. At the age of twenty-seven, her future looked "black with a golden glow beyond it."[61]

Finally, in February 1854, Emily Blackwell graduated with high honors. "Now I am free," she exclaimed.[62] It had taken two years of extensive study and practice on her own and at various institutions, but she had accomplished her goal: five years younger than Elizabeth, she had graduated five years later. In March, Blackwell fulfilled a lifelong dream by journeying to Europe to complete her medical education. There she gained knowledge of female diseases and experience in the early use of anesthesia by working with surgeon James Simpson at the University of Edinburgh. She interned at Children's Hospital and Bartholomew's in London. She studied with Dr. Pierre Huguier in Paris and learned obstetrics at La Maternité, perhaps the foremost institution of its kind in the world. Hers was a superb medical education, surpassing in breadth and depth that of most contemporary physicians.[63] Blackwell returned from Europe in 1856, at the age of thirty, prepared to join Elizabeth and Dr. Marie Zakrzewska in opening an infirmary and a dispensary for women. Elizabeth served as director, Emily as surgeon, and Marie as resident physician, housekeeper, and manager.

After only two years at the Infirmary, Elizabeth returned to England, where she too had studied medicine and had contacts among prominent and well-to-do women. There she lectured on the medical achievements of women in America and the value to women of gaining physiological and medical knowledge. Lady Byron urged her to remain in England and head up a women's hospital endowed by the Countess de Noailles. At the time, Elizabeth was dependent upon Emily's administrative abilities, medical skill, and emotional support. She would consider the offer only if Emily were part of the scheme. "I will accept nothing that is not offered to us both," she wrote, "we cannot separate in practice."[64] While Elizabeth lingered in England, Marie Zakrzewska took a position managing a hospital attached to the New England Female Medical College in Boston. Emily was left with sole responsibility for the New York Infirmary.

Emily's self-doubts resurfaced. In June 1858, she wrote despairingly in her journal:

A terrible trial has fallen upon me. An agony of doubt has burnt in my heart for months. Oh my God, is the end of all my aspiration, of my prayers and dreams, to be that this long earnest struggle has been a mistake, that this life of a Physician is so utterly not my life that I can not express myself through it—and worse—worse—that I might have done more in other ways. Oh my Father thou who seeist how pure and true were my motives, leave me not—"My God my God, why hast Thou forsaken me?" I could bear anything but the feeling of failure, show me the way, be with me![65]

The choice of medicine as a profession had been Elizabeth's. Emily followed her and then felt abandoned. Still, she carried forward the medical and educational goals established by her sister for the rest of her career.

When Elizabeth returned from England in 1859, she established an outside medical practice and lectured extensively. The Infirmary bore her famous name, but she played little role in its administration. Although she decided to stay in America for a time, she described herself as merely "reconciled" to this course.[66] The sisters founded a medical college for women attached to the Infirmary in November 1868. The college had been an integral part of Elizabeth's long-range plan for expanding the role of women in medicine. She appointed herself Professor of Hygiene and made Emily Professor of Obstetrics and Diseases of Women. The college offered a combined theoretical and practical course of study, and was one of the first medical colleges in America to require a four-year curriculum. At the end of their first year of operation, Emily proudly wrote that the college had achieved success—"better than anything we have had yet." It was "a step forward."[67]

In the face of this, her greatest triumph, Elizabeth returned to England in 1869. She spent the rest of her life there. Kitty Barry, her adopted daughter, would later say that the sisters seriously disagreed about many things, and that Marian Blackwell, the elder of the three, had warned Elizabeth that she risked alienating Emily by the way in which she handled their problems.[68] For the next thirty years Emily capably nurtured, guided, and expanded both the college and the infirmary. Though the college closed in 1899 when the Cornell Medical School opened its doors to women, the infirmary continued to operate. Despite her enormous contribution to the management of these institutions, Emily always felt that they were Elizabeth's work more than her own. In April 1908 she reported to her sister that "The Infirmary is thriving, it now has one hundred beds, a large out practice and quite a staff of women doctors connected with it. Your work has borne fruit in many ways."[69]

As for herself, Emily felt "footloose." She retired with a younger colleague, Dr. Elizabeth Cushier, an eminent gynecological surgeon. In this relationship Emily seems finally to have found the combination of shared love, work, and housekeeping that she had longed to have with her sister. "Dr. Cushier," she told Elizabeth, "is sincerely attached to me, and would never wish to leave me."[70]

Descriptions of Emily Blackwell portray a woman powerful in her own right—striking in appearance, authoritative in manner, and decisive in action. As one student recalled, she was "tall, broad-shouldered and commanding . . . but . . . it was her face and head that arrested your attention." Noble was the only word adequate to describe her. "When she entered a room full of students, there suddenly seemed to be only one person in that room and that person was Dr. Blackwell. . . . Her voice was low and calm and of an uncanny quality."[71] Beneath an exterior that exuded strength, courage, power, and authority, Emily Blackwell longed for a life in which love and mutuality gave meaning to independence and achievement. She had gained professional and economic freedom, but within a structure largely determined by another. Her personal and professional identities were deeply intertwined with those of her sister. Although the relationship was not all that she wanted—neither as devoted nor as equalitarian—yet it provided a context in which Emily could pursue her own goals. And it offered power, status, and more opportunity and approbation than she could have found in the male medical establishment. Given Emily's personality, her emotional dependence and inner conflict, it appears unlikely that alone she could have set in motion the institutions envisioned and founded by her sister. Her achievement, no less than her struggle, was structured by her relationship with Elizabeth.

Writers Alice and Phoebe Cary provide another illustration of joined identities and lives. Originally, there were seven Cary sisters: Rowena, Susan, Rhoda, Alice, Phoebe, Lucy, and Elmina. Alice devoted herself to Rhoda, the nearest sister in age, and to Lucy, a special charge. Both girls died within a month of one another in 1833, when Alice was only thirteen.[72] In her grief and shock, Alice turned to Phoebe and Elmina.

Phoebe and Alice shared a love for poetry and a calling to create it. They began to write, they said, as a release from household chores demanded of them by their stepmother. Alice was eighteen and Phoebe fourteen when their first poems were published in a local Ohio newspaper. In 1849, a book of collected verse brought them one hundred dollars and a small amount of national attention. Alice Cary left Ohio for New York City, determined to make a name for herself as an author.

One year later, she sent for Phoebe and Elmina. Although Elmina soon married, her life remained tied to Alice. When she fell ill, her husband sent for Alice to nurse the invalid. He purchased a town house in which the sisters might live together while Elmina convalesced. She never seems to have recovered sufficiently to resume normal connubial relations. After her death, Alice and Phoebe continued to reside in the house, which Alexander Swift left to them.

Alice wrote prolifically. In addition to her volumes of poetry, she published seven books of prose, including three novels. The manuscript for a fourth novel remained unpublished at her death; yet another was in serialization. Phoebe did not have the drive that propelled Alice. She never worked in as diligent and disciplined a manner as her sister. In fact, she wrote little and published nothing for almost eight years. Over her lifetime, however, she produced three volumes of poetry. Phoebe and Alice published several collected editions. For a short time, Phoebe edited a feminist journal, *The Revolution*. Perhaps Phoebe felt overwhelmed by Alice—by her determination to be both financially and personally independent, and by her ambition to be an influential writer. To write was to adopt, or certainly to participate in, Alice's agenda for their lives because Alice infused the creative process with these considerations.

Alice also wanted her own home. She needed a place in which to write and a setting for her literary gatherings. She enjoyed having a structure to mold and manage. She required a refuge for her troubled spirit. By living frugally, Alice and Phoebe managed to support themselves by their writing and with Swift's assistance, they also had a home. Alice dominated the domestic sphere as she did the literary one. She planned the menus, did the marketing, directed the servants, and kept the house.

To some extent, Phoebe was aware of her dependence upon Alice in both their domestic and artistic lives. In 1867, she received a proposal of marriage from a man for whom she apparently cared. She consulted Alice, who refused to consider the idea. Phoebe rejected her suitor. She knew that Alice could never live comfortably anywhere but in her own abode. She also recognized that some of the appeal of the proposal stemmed from a desire to establish a separate sphere. Wrote Phoebe, "When I think of it, I am sure I never lived out my full nature, having never lived a complete life. . . . My life is an appendage to that of Alice. It is my nature and fate to walk second to her. I have less of everything that is worth having, than she; less power, less money, fewer friends. Sometimes I feel a yearning to have a life my very own; my own house, and work, and friends; and to feel myself the centre of all. I feel now that it is never to be."[73] Phoebe Cary's autonomy, her full development as an individual and a writer, were confined by Alice's need of her—and by her own devotion to Alice.[74]

Mary Stevens Robinson recalled having once urged Phoebe to pay her a visit. Phoebe stalled and finally agreed to come only because Alice was away from home. Said Robinson:

> I discovered afterward that this cheery soul, who could sing songs, get books into market, and whose plentitude of spirits was apparently unfailing, whose very gait, at once smooth and rapid, expressed swift and direct force, this hearty, happy woman, pined somewhat when severed from her mate. In the stillness of the house her gayety drooped, and she had no one to think of. The tender curve of her mouth, the arch of her eyelids, something round and child-like in the whole contour, betokened this dependence of affection in her.[75]

Phoebe loved Alice. She basked in her sister's affection and her reflected light. Their dependence was mutual, as the circumstances surrounding their deaths reveal.

Alice had been ill for some time with a creeping cough and Phoebe nursed her as always. In the days immediately preceding Alice's death, Phoebe herself collapsed from the long hours of watching and waiting and the lack of fresh air, good food, and exercise that accompanied her nursing. She lay in bed next door to Alice, "sick unto death." After her sister's demise Phoebe wrote, "Alice, when she was here, always absorbed me, and she absorbs me still; I feel her constantly drawing me." She told a friend that she simply could not function without her sister. She tried to write but found no words; tried to keep busy around the house but could not sustain the effort. "I do not know what is the matter with me," she said. "I have lain down, and it seems, because Alice is not there, there is no reason why I should get up. For thirty years I have gone straight to her bedside as soon as I arose in the morning, and wherever she is, I am sure she wants me now."[76] Although Phoebe appeared to have been a robust and healthy woman, she faded rapidly after Alice's death. She died a mere five months later.[77] Apparently, she could not continue without her sister's force of will.

This relationship was symbiotic. Alice needed to be loved; she wanted to rule. Phoebe loved her and accepted Alice's domination. Less driven than her sister, she was motivated to write by Alice's example and encouragement. Alice served as critic, muse, and inspiration. "How lost I feel now!" she said after Alice's death. "When I have written anything I feel as if I did not know what to do with it. Half the charm of writing is gone, since I have no one who loves me to see what I do!"[78] Her friends and admirers, her feminist colleagues on the staff of *The Revolution* and in the Sorosis Club, could not replace Alice. The Carys' interdependence provided an avenue by which they might live unusually independent and creative lives as literary women. Only together could they travel that road.

Eliza Perkins Cabot recalled her mother saying that she "thought any of her daughters were fools to marry anybody. They had all they wanted at home."[79] Many sisters knew instinctively the truth of this judgment and acted accordingly. In a culture which discouraged female attainment and proscribed female autonomy, women found that only among their own could they assert themselves and their ambitions. If they did not find total acceptance and support, they did find far more dependability and understanding here than they could elsewhere.

Relations between these sisters suggest that the role of sister mediated between the role of daughter and that of independent woman. Siblings could relate to one another as peers united against established authority outside the family, supporting one another in their search for autonomy and their quest for achievement. They could also forge alliances against the parental authority that continued to circumscribe a daughter's independence in the early industrial period. The Chase family found it more acceptable to send two, even three, sisters out into the world together than to send one alone. Propriety, safety, and, to a degree, family governance were all served in this fashion. Mary Grimké urged her retiring daughter Sarah not to allow her more flamboyant sister Angelina to contract alone as an antislavery agent. Painful as it was to see her daughters turn on the system in which they were raised, she could more easily reconcile herself to this public and highly political vocation if the two siblings supported and protected one another.[80]

"Families" of single sisters formed during this transitional period. Structured horizontally, these peer families enabled women to leave the domestic sphere while remaining within a female and, to some extent, a private world. At the height of the consolidation of woman's separate sphere, strain developed between the generations which inhabited that sphere. Released from paternal domination of the family, daughters who owed their gender identity and strength to the domesticity of their female kin began to resist the domination of mothers and to develop nondomestic vocational identities and roles. The divisions within the female world posed problems for mothers and daughters that would become more fully visible at the end of the century with "the passing of the home daughter."[81] Nevertheless, during the early and mid-nineteenth century, siblingship enabled some daughters to emerge from the domestic sphere without relinquishing the security and dependability of family ties.

Sisters were related, however, because they were daughters. Some of the limits of their individual independence and some of the emotional struggles in which they engaged developed precisely because their role as daughters impinged upon their role as sisters. As parental authority declined during this period, as older sisters mothered and mentored younger sisters, some of the authority symbolized by parenthood informed and, to an extent, diminished the democratization of the sibling relationship. The Westons, Carys, and Grimkés helped one another to resist the assertion of parental authority experienced by Emily Howland, Emily Parsons, or Fidelia Fiske. However, they incurred certain stress in taking on and looking to one another for the essentially parental roles of establishing rules, defining responsibilities, and assigning tasks.

All in all, the evidence suggests that greater independence in daughters resulted when they rebelled against paternal authority in the family and/or male domination of the public sphere. This was particularly true of those cases, such as the Grimké sisters and Emily Parsons, in which the daughter had at least the tacit approval and support of the mother. Rebellion against the mother, on the other hand, was fraught with ambivalence and guilt. A daughter journeyed from the family with greater ease when she went with her sisters, or when additional siblings—largely other daughters or daughters-in-law—picked up the domestic responsibilities left behind.

———◆———

Female relationships moved out from the family as women emerged from the home. Although sibling relationships remained central to the lives and purposes of antebellum women, non-kin same-sex relationships also became increasingly important. Over the course of the nineteenth century, friends would replace sisters as primary relationships among native-born, middle-class single women. Maria Mitchell ruminated in her diary about the degrees and kinds of love she held for various women.

I have an entirely different regard for Lauri and Ida. I love Lauri as one loves a sister—I admire Ida and am jealous of her regard for others—it is something like *love* and less generous than that which I have for Lauri, which is affection. But all these affections are weak compared with what one has for kindred—the ties of blood are stronger than those of all other ties.[82]

Emily Howland kept among her private papers a poem to "Pious Friendship." In the romantic and religious language of the antebellum period, it characterized the virtues of female friendship:

How blest the sacred tie, that binds
In union sweet, according minds!
How swift the heavenly course they run
Whose hearts, whose faith, whose hopes are *one!*
To each, the soul of each how dear!
What jealous love! what holy fear!
How does the generous flame within
Refine from earth, and cleanse from sin!
Their streaming years together flow,
For human guilt, for human woe!
Their ardent prayers together rise,
Like mingling flames in sacrifice.
Together both, they seek the place
Where God reveals his *awful face!*
How high, how strong their raptures dwell,
There's none but *kindred souls* can tell!
Nor shall the glowing name expire!
When nature drops her sick'ning fire,
Then shall they meet in realms above,
A heaven of *joy,* because of *love.*[83]

Women looked to one another for the inspiration and strength to do the business of their lives. "The business to be done requires cooperation and autonomy, purposefulness, the use of the whole self—both intellect and passion," wrote one. "So closely woven have been our lives, our purposes and experiences that, separated, we have a feeling of incompleteness—united, such strength of self-assertion that no ordinary obstacles, difficulties or dangers ever appear to us as insurmountable," said Elizabeth Cady Stanton to Susan B. Anthony.[84]

There were many such friendships among the maiden sisterhood. An analysis of one exemplifies the ways in which female friendship paralleled sibling love in structure and approached it in meaning. Sallie Holley and

Caroline F. Putnam devoted their lives to the black cause, first as anti-slavery agents and then as teachers in a black school in Lottsburg, Virginia, after the Civil War. The letters of the two women reveal the gradual shaping of Putnam's character and vocational identity in her relationship with Holley. Here, Putnam learned to draw away from a domineering family, to define her calling, to explore her various capacities, to establish goals, and to give and take in human intimacy over a number of years of shared living.

The friendship began at Oberlin College in 1848. Caroline Putnam, a rural girl from Farmersville, New York, met Sallie Holley, a dynamic young woman from Rochester. Sophisticated and independent-minded, Holley immediately aroused Putnam's admiration. Putnam and Hollie attended several antislavery meetings together. Abigail Kelley Foster inspired Holley to join the abolitionist movement and become an antislavery agent upon graduation in 1851. Putnam left Oberlin without graduating.

Uncertain about her future course, Putnam joined Holley, Foster, Parker Pillsbury, and Sojourner Truth for a six-month lecture tour through Ohio and New York. Holley served as Putnam's intellectual mentor, spiritual advisor, and model for the well-lived life. As Caroline confessed: "I never have in all my life, felt more fully the extent of my obligations to you, how large is my indebtedness to the Truth you had received before me—and of which you became the Interpreter to me. . . . It is indeed a great thing to render so valuable a service to any soul, by which it may attain a higher worth, and is enabled to enter upon a life of superior excellence."[85]

Much as Putnam admired Holley for her courage, she could not sustain a commitment such as hers. She neither felt a calling to lecture nor had the gift of oratory. When her family demanded that she come home, Putnam returned to Farmersville and spent two years in domestic service. These were difficult times for her. She continued to study and to correspond with Holley. The thought of engaging in a broader sphere of action haunted her. As she wrote:

When I read or hear of so much virtue and excellence attained by any human being—of a pure conscience preserved unsullied—I feel a painful suffocation over my heart . . . for it is as if I should burst with longing and aspiration, and then immediately comes the weight, the darkness, or imperfection, of adverse influences, that oppress me and all light and peace are gone—only this one streak to hang a hope upon, that *I want to be good,* and "good for something," and I firmly believe "Seek and Ye shall find."[86]

What sparked Putnam's imagination and inspired her effort was the desire to be worthy of Holley's love and the hope that they could work together. "I would on no account miss the old delight of working, sleeping and talking by your side," she told Holley. In turn, Holley urged Putnam to devote herself to the cause. "With her mind," Holley confided to Foster, "it is a shame to remain idle." Perhaps, she suggested, Putnam might join her as a lecturer on the circuit, or she might write columns for an antislavery journal.[87] Putnam's family objected that itinerant lecturers earned very little, and that irregularly. Putnam herself felt inadequate and depressed.

Over time, the relationship between the women grew from admiring friendship, even infatuation on Putnam's part, to mutual devotion. Although Putnam initiated the relationship, Holley increasingly depended upon her for support in a dangerous and exhausting endeavor. Their relationship flourished primarily on correspondence until the summer of 1854, when Holley came to stay in Farmersville. After three months, Putnam agreed to join Holley on tour. Foster encouraged Putnam to sell tracts, so that she might be more than a companion for Holley and feel a sense of independent contribution to the cause. Putnam agreed to try, and for the next fourteen years she worked with Holley in this capacity. She accompanied her on lecture tour, arranged for audiences, housing, transportation, and meeting halls, sold tracts and subscriptions to antislavery journals, and occasionally wrote letters to newspapers.[88]

Putnam could not help but feel, however, that this was not her calling in life. She sought a more substantive role in the cause, but lacked the energy and force of will, the confidence and independence, to search it out. As she confided to Foster:

It always does me some good, it ought to do me *much* to think of you, what a "hero" you *are* and *have been* "in the strife." . . . Then too, I know dear Sallie how constantly she trims her lamp, and how perpetually is the consecrated gift laid upon the altar of self-sacrifice. . . . I bind these reflections to my heart and think they shall never escape me night or day—They will surely be an amulet causing the lions to banish from the wilderness through which I might fight to the Celestial city. But oh, the power of the worldling's snare, the temptations to self-indulgence, the over-mastering inertia, the sad forgetful sleep. . . . Heaven help me to redeem the coming time! and shame away the feebleness and fluctuation of my character.[89]

Sallie Holley goaded Putnam to make better use of her talents. In 1855 the two women attended a Chautauqua lecture by Wendell Phillips, an abolitionist hero and one of the nineteenth century's most outstanding orators. As Holley reported later:

Mr. Phillips told how *leisurely* Germans enjoyed a landscape, taking ample time to survey in detail, clouds, sky, rocks, hills, grass, water &c—all the simple means by which Nature makes up a picture—and thus securing an indelible impression, which could be a happiness to themselves, forever—Miss Putnam turned to me, in an ebullition of dear self-complacency, and whispered "*I am German*"—By this time Mr. Phillips, was going on to say, how fixedly the *Italian* would stand, with folded arms and positively refuse to be coaxed, or flattered or hired or driven *to do the least thing in the world.* There I quite took down Putty's sails, by quietly remarking "You seem to me, to be more *Italian!*"[90]

Such sarcasm commonly emerged in their discussions. After five months of touring the Midwest, Putnam exclaimed: "How much more I would give for five months in New England than for five months here!" Holley pounced on this assertion, "the audacity" of which offended her. "But you have no idea of giving anything for either," she retorted. Holley had a sharp tongue and was perfectly capable of using it to prod Putnam in the name of the cause and Putnam's potential contribution to it. When the two separated so that Putnam might again visit her family, Holley wrote scathingly of her letters. "Don't write me such gossip—But write me for the cause and my lectures."[91]

Underlying such criticism lay Holley's great need of Putnam's attention, love, and help. During one absence, she wrote, "Oh, my heart yearns toward you this morning, and the heaviest disappointment of my life would fall if *you* should die. Again and again I thank you for all your love to me. I wish I were more deserving of it. Please God I may be some day. How I should love to put my arms around your neck and kiss you!"[92]

Holley's style of extending love and approval then withdrawing both in a storm of verbal abuse no doubt contributed to Putnam's unhappiness with her role and with herself. She began to explore other vocational possibilities, even at the risk of leaving Holley. She considered working as a governess for the abolitionist family of Foster and Elizabeth Buffum Chase. For two years in the early 1860s both Putnam and Holley retired to Farmersville, New York, to rest. Putnam attended to household and family matters. Both women took a role in local reform activities. When Sallie resumed lecturing in 1864, Caroline joined her: the thought of Holley setting out alone was anathema to both women. But the life of an itinerant speaker proved even less satisfying to Putnam than previously. At this point Emily Howland offered her a new career.

Holley, Putnam, and Howland knew one another, as women engaged in the antislavery effort often did. They followed one another's activities in movement literature, searched one another out on tours and visits, met and conversed through the intermediation of others. Putnam and Holley had long encouraged Howland in her teaching career. "Your whole letter has been a rare delight to me," Putnam once wrote Howland, "and I have read it again and again. How rare and precious all your conscientious striving is!"[93]

Howland, like Holley, served as a model for Putnam, who feared that she was not capable of serving as they did. "It is superfluous to say 'God bless you'—for you most certainly have His best blessing in being enabled to *live* this truth so heroically," she wrote Howland. She measured even her capacity for empathy against Holley's greater one. "I am rejoicing with all *my* might that your hitherto pent up genius is diffusing such genial gifts upon the needy minds of 'Africa's Sable daughters.' I say with all *my* might which is of course mere feebleness compared with Miss Holley's— Hers is a deep and profound sympathy—such as can only spring from kindred traits of character."[94]

Holley visited Howland while on a lecture tour during the war. Howland spoke about the need for a school and a teacher for the cooperative farm she had founded in Virginia. "Emily wants you to work and teach among her people," wrote Holley to Putnam. "She thinks you would be an admirable person to go. If ever you will go, you have only to write her to secure a place."[95] Holley did not stand in the way of such a move. She understood Putnam's restlessness. She recognized and respected her need for a place and a vocation of her own. As Holley's own occupation came to an end, she also looked for ways in which the two might continue their work for black freedom and equality.

For almost a year Putnam considered the possibility of joining Howland in Virginia. They talked it over during the summer of 1868. Putnam felt particularly drawn to the life-style suggested by Howland and based on her teaching days at the Miner school. "Your joint school and housekeeping . . . is a kind and style of life that always captivated my imagination—Far more than the ordinary mode of domesticity—the family proper."[96] She longed for an integrated life and sought a way to combine work and home which neither marriage nor itinerant lecturing provided. She longed to engage in her own work, live in her own home, and share both with a kindred spirit.

Howland and Putnam decided to go to Virginia together. Howland would take the school at the cooperative settlement, and Putnam would open another in Lottsburg, some eight miles down the road. In the fall of 1868, Putnam joined Howland in Washington, D.C. They spent a month establishing the school. Among other things, they attended the meeting at which the black freed men and women of Lottsburg organized the school and welcomed to their community the Northern white women who would teach in it. The significance of the meeting fired Putnam's imagination—the community had launched its first free institution. She wrote Holley: "It was a wonderful, wonderful meeting to have in a life-time! I wish *you* of all the world had been here. It seems like something that can never be again, and I can no more give an account of it than I could paint a sun-rise."[97] For all her excitement at this "dawn of civilization," Putnam's joy also reflected her private happiness at having found a vocation and a sphere at the age of forty-nine.

Ultimately, Howland (among others) came to feel that Holley's ideo-logical imperiousness, her strong personality, and her financial control impinged upon Putnam's autonomy and development in negative ways. One quarrel emerged over the government's policy of bringing freedman's schools into the public school system. Holley feared that Southern racism would destroy black education. She felt so strongly that she objected to visits by any of Putnam's friends who supported integration. Wrote Howland: "What a life of struggle Miss Putnam has. I think clinging to Miss Holley has thwarted what should have been her life." To her dying day, however, Putnam rejected this view. She defended Holley from such criticism and expressed her gratitude for Sallie's leadership and love. After Holley's death, she said, "I owed Miss Holley the chief good, and happi-ness of my life."[98]

The two friends experienced some emotional distance in later years. Sallie Holley moved elsewhere in Lottsburg, leaving Putnam and her assistants in the house adjacent to the Holley school. She spent greater amounts of time in New York City at the Miller Hotel with her circle of urban, cultured, feminist friends. The transition was gradual, however. Holley had spent her life in the hard service of the abolitionist movement. She was growing old. She acquiesced to the primitive life in Virginia solely to be near her friend and to continue their work; but she felt its privations. As she wrote while on "annual leave": "I am overjoyed to be here amidst 'society, friendship, and love.' It is an amazing contrast to my exile in Virginia. No going hungry here; no army of ragged, dirty, low-lived whites and freed negros to wait upon in this dear old familiar Miller Hotel. Here I can have time to read books and recreate my mind and sleep the sleep of a happy, unwearied woman."[99]

Then, too, teaching was not Holley's vocation. Putnam thrived on it. Gradually, the power, responsibility, and reputation of the two women shifted. As political attention focused on Reconstruction after the war, abolitionists identified the freedman's schools as a central factor in achiev-ing equal rights for blacks. Putnam and her school became better known than Holley and her lectures. Holley, now essentially retired, had previ-ously represented the duo in public. She may have resented losing the spotlight. Some abolitionists believed that she did. Holley certainly re-gretted Putnam's increasing independence, particularly on issues of a po-litical nature where Sallie had always led.

A story written for abolitionist newspapers that focused on the Holley school but paid far more attention to Sallie's career than to Caroline's teaching precipitated the separation. While Caroline always denied feel-ing any resentment about the story (and her more diffident nature would be consistent with such a stance, for Putnam never enjoyed public atten-tion), Northern friends objected loudly and, what was worse, in print.

Holley felt humiliated. She took offense and blamed Putnam for complaining to her friends and making a scene. As the issue became a subject for private gossip and public debate, Holley withdrew in hurt silence to New York. She felt that her long record of service was being overlooked. Despite Putnam's many attempts at explanation and reconciliation, Holley never felt that her friend had sufficiently cleared the air with the New England abolitionists whose regard she so valued.[100]

Caroline F. Putnam worked over a number of years to build a vocational identity and to acquire independence from her family. Whatever the stresses and strains of their later lives, this process went on largely within the context of her relationship with Sallie Holley and was aided by her. Holley's love, her intellectual challenge, and her financial support all contributed to Putnam's transformation from an insecure, essentially domestic and dependent woman into a vital, confident, effective, and independent worker.

<hr/>

The bonds of female friendship which held Sallie Holley and Caroline Putnam had both negative and positive aspects. In shaping the nature and the degree of female autonomy and achievement they constrained the development of both; for the female world of love and work was a private world, oriented around domestic activity and personal relationships. As Caroline F. Putnam, Emily Blackwell, and Alice Cary found, even when women entered the public sphere the satisfactions and meaning of their work were tied to domestic structures, relationships, and values. This world conceptualized women's occupations in terms of the private vocation, not the public career. Women who pursued either ultimately relied upon the resources commanded by women from the home. These were limited. In addition, the pace of life as determined by household tasks was hardly conducive to sustained intellectual activity. The absorption in daily tasks and the satisfaction and importance of personal relationships all underscored the private orientation of women's lives and encouraged them to invest their psychic energy in tending to these relationships. The very structure of woman's separate sphere proved crucial, then, both to women's emergence from the bonds of womanhood and to the strength of the bonds themselves.

Female friends, sisters, and cousins provided validation, affirmation, and nurturing. They encouraged self-esteem. They taught selflessness and compromise. A firm commitment to the vocational life prevented sisterhood from dissolving into a welter of personality conflicts, guilts, and jealousies. The process of differentiating self from beloved "sisters" was sometimes painful and unsatisfactory, but the struggle strengthened women. Here, and here primarily, existed the possibility of "perfect friendship." Harriot Hunt learned with her sister that love of and trust in self were necessary prerequisites for the exercise of autonomy and creativity, and for the long-term commitment of the individual to a cause, a goal, or a vocation. At the best of times and in the better relationships, siblings and friends helped one another to "belong to themselves" and to achieve.[101]

8

"Heavy Head and Heavy Heart"

Conflicts in the Single Life

Antebellum women who rejected or delayed marriage in an effort to acquire independence, pursue self-development, or accomplish some essential task or calling found support for their efforts in their circle of female friends and relatives and in a culture that applauded Single Blessedness. Changes in family and social life and the needs of a developing industrial economy provided new opportunities for women to make their independent way in the world. However, those women born between 1780 and 1840 stepped out of woman's traditional sphere only tentatively. They lacked models of how to proceed. They pioneered an expansion of female roles in a society that remained inhospitable, if not so hostile as previously believed. The reality of women's lives bore little resemblance to their cherished dreams. Many found that their primary accomplishment lay in their ability to earn a living and sustain themselves, rather than to achieve independence and attain creative, intellectual, or moral goals. They felt betrayed by the lack of freedom gained by remaining single and avoiding the snares of marriage.

Clementina Smith, for example, complained to her friend Sophia duPont about the limitations of the single life. As unmarried daughters, she and her sister Harriet lived largely at home. Clementina grumbled about the drudgery of the housework for which they were responsible and detested making mantuas (the open-front gowns worn by women of her class and time). Although she submitted to her domestic tasks with some grace, she tried to protect her time and independence through a "busy, even aggressive commitment to Sunday School duties" and missionary society work.[1] She longed to do more in the public world of religious reform, "acting a part in the busy scene" rather than taking a "peep at the world from out the loop hole of retreat." But even her visits to close friends depended on parental needs, wants, and plans. As she told Sophia, "Indeed dearest if I could do just as I pleased, I should not be long away from you, but you see that even in a state of single *blessedness* when ladies

are supposed to have their own way they are not always without restraint."
Smith's disillusionment once led her to question the wisdom of her
choice. "Spinsters," she acknowledged, "are no more independent than
married people, if they are as much so indeed."[2]

Rather than a life singly blessed, many an early-nineteenth-century
spinster experienced great strain. It originated in the conflicts and contradictions inherent in the Cult of Single Blessedness, attitudes held toward
women in antebellum society, and their own efforts to define new roles.
Women found their singlehood dominated by the competing demands of
family and self, of vocation and occupation. Because holy callings did not
provide an adequate living, women had to have an occupation in addition
to their vocation. Women's service to God, their search for self-expression
and dedication to a skill or art often conflicted with their family responsibilities. They felt confused (and some were angered) by a culture that
valued female submissiveness but whose God demanded assertion and
whose vocations required it.

Women expended considerable effort to maintain some sort of balance
in the face of conflicting values and responsibilities, and this cost them
greatly. They found their energy, purpose, and direction interrupted and
diffused. Tasks remained unfinished, achievement blocked. Guilt—the
guilt of work undone, initiative stunted, industriousness dissipated—all
decimated self-esteem. Women's physical and mental health were affected
by the enforced dependency of daughters and the deprivation of mentally
engaging activity resulting from traditional female roles.

Like their married sisters, many antebellum spinsters experienced debilitating illness, physical frailty, attacks of languor or morbidity, and even
insanity. Catharine M. Sedgwick suffered throughout her life from the
stress-related ills of dyspepsia and headache. Lucretia Crocker gave the
frequent impression of frailty and suggested to friends some undefined
delicacy of throat and lungs which occasionally invalided her. Mary Grew
regularly withdrew from public life for weeks or months at a time with an
incapacitating illness. Abigail Williams May, Sallie Holley, and Catharine Beecher periodically committed themselves to water-cure establishments to rest and reconstitute their failing strength.[3]

Scholars have focused attention on the psychoneurotic and nervous ills
of nineteenth-century women. They have used the classic psychological
explanations for anxiety, trauma, and hysteria in an attempt to understand why so many women displayed certain kinds of symptoms. There is
general agreement that the roots of female distress grew in the barren soil
of a culture which demanded great submission and dependence of women,
and which encouraged them to find self-actualization in abnegation of
self.[4] In the late eighteenth and early nineteenth centuries, American
women believed themselves to be creatures of their reproductive systems.

Female biology defined woman's nature and restricted her social role. The equation of women's bodies with women's being encouraged the somatization of discontents.[5]

Both married and unmarried women experienced emotionally based illness, but the sources and timing varied for the two groups. Major crises in the single life surrounded the choice, development, loss, or interruption of a vocation. Single women also suffered from thwarted independence. Constraints on either work or autonomy could bring on an attack of nervous illness. The likelihood of physical or emotional collapse was increased by the confluence of two things: physiological changes associated with aging and emotional changes linked to the loss of female friendship.

Women experienced emotional and physical distress at specific times in the life cycle. The nineteenth century defined the single life in terms of biological functions that remained unused or misused. Many spinsters internalized these attitudes and felt a sense of loss during their late thirties, as friends devoted themselves to marriage and childbearing. In their forties and early fifties, unmarried women approached menopause with fear and trepidation. At such times, nontraditional women faced the full implications of their different path and were most susceptible to depression or illness. The unwed reacted strongly to disruptions in their support networks. While death or marriage of a sister or friend often proved devastating, disapproval and rejection could cut equally deep. Changes in the structure or affect of female relationships increased the likelihood of subsequent illness.

------◆------

Personal experience and the example of other women had taught the antebellum spinster that self-actualization required the exercise of her talents. She therefore sought a substantive life which engaged all her faculties. Sarah Pugh, for example, contrasted her work in the antislavery cause (which she called the "blessing of my life") with her duties as family caretaker (which she described as being "less responsible and not so calculated to call forth the powers of my being").[6]

For Pugh, participation in reform work provided an opportunity for personal growth, liberation from domestic routine, interaction with interesting people, a sense of social usefulness, an intellectual outlet, and a structure in which she might productively and politically labor. In their vocational lives, women gave vent to their talents, expressed their ideas, enacted their ambitions, and promoted their personal growth. Such women understood the importance of having a sense of purpose and a feeling of accomplishment. They knew that self-respect and the validation of the self by others were necessary for the good life. Personal happiness and health corresponded with commitment to useful, challenging, and fulfilling activity.

Emily Parsons assured her parents from Fort Schuyler army hospital that "hard work was the condition on which I have either mental or bodily health." From the battlefield at Gettysburg, Cornelia Hancock told her sister, "I am black as an Indian and dirty as a pig and as well as I ever was in my life." Hancock had been sickly as an adolescent, and her family worried about her ability to withstand the strain of army nursing. Hancock reassured them that she had never felt better, for *"There is all in getting to do what you want to do and I am doing that."* Fidelia Fiske suffered from typhoid fever in 1840 and was not expected to live. Her family feared the effects of rigorous missionary life on her health. They believed that her call to serve in Persia was in fact a death knell but Fiske enjoyed excellent health as a missionary. She spoke of it as a special token of God's loving kindness, a dispensation which permitted her to do His work on earth.[7]

When not engaged in their vocations women complained of boredom. Carrie A. Rowland, for example, described herself as "getting 'ennuie' for want of active business," and vascillated painfully between despair at "ever being anything or doing anything" and a determination "not to give up the pursuit of Truth and the proper sphere of usefulness."[8] Rowland, whose domestic occupations involved nursing an invalid grandmother, a sickly brother, and a disabled father, defined her "proper sphere of usefulness" in rather broader terms.

In the absence of vocational activity women also experienced a variety of nervous symptoms. Emily Howland suffered bouts of depression and anxiety approximately twice a year throughout the 1870s. She had given up her work with Southern blacks to care for her widowed father. While engaged in spring cleaning, Howland recorded the frustrations of such a life: "Worked with what ability I possess from about 6 a.m. to 3 p.m., then tidied up and served the rest of the day. In time I could become a humdrum drudge so fully occupied with trying to keep clean and in order as to know or care for little else. I am as neat in idea as my neighbor but my better part revolts from becoming thus absorbed and I shall not."[9] Emily found no solace as the year progressed. Her days were short, busy, monotonous, and uneventful—a far cry from those weighted with the sense of import that had characterized time spent in Washington and Virginia. Howland spoke of the "shriveling" of her mind, soul, and sociability. More than once she resolved to "return to active work for humanity." "I need it," she wrote, "the work needs me." She feared that she was "wasting and growing odious at mere housework."[10]

Margaret Jones Burleigh believed Howland's morbidity to be rooted in her unwilling assumption of a subordinate status. As she withdrew under her father's roof and authority, she gave up autonomy, mobility, and vocation. Burleigh recognized Howland's duty to her father but encouraged her to take time for herself. She urged Howland to make decisions independent of her father's interests. "Surely thou must be thy father's main prop during his decline," she wrote. But how, she asked, could Howland properly minister to him "if thee grow 'worrisome,' or gloomy, with the life which does not sufficiently nourish thy soul or give scope to thy activity?" She reminded Emily that "soul and body have their needs which must not be too long withstood."[11]

Anxious about the state of Howland's mental health, Burleigh urged her to "save" herself from "days of ennui and nights of torturing thought [that] induce a derangement of the nerves which increase the cause from wh[ich] it springs." Burleigh appreciated Howland's description of herself as a ship lying idle on the waves and confided to her the story of a mutual friend, who out of boredom seemed destined to undertake a poor marriage. "With no occupation for intellect and heart," this young woman had devoted her attention solely to love affairs. Burleigh feared that such "a noble nature wh[ich] by a proper occupation of its powers might have been saved, [is] now doomed to wretchedness." She suggested that Howland's salvation, like this young woman's, lay in the productive occupation of her time and intellect.[12]

Among the most compelling conflicts in the single life were those having to do with earning a living. Financial exigency stalked the single woman. Striving and independent, she grappled with her need to support herself and her desire to express creativity, spirituality, or social conscience through a vocation that usually offered little material reward. Cornelia Hancock determined after the Civil War to serve the contraband community. "Poverty I think is now my greatest stumbling block. I have such a horror of organizations that for the last two years I have given my service gratuitously and that has got my purse in such a condition it behooves me to look about for an organization to sail under in my next crusade."[13]

Hancock applied to the logical group, the Pennsylvania Freedman's Aid Society of Philadelphia. Her sister, Ellen Child, and her brother-in-law, Dr. Henry Child, were well known in philanthropic circles there. She explained that she had no desire to teach but wanted to serve as liaison with the federal and military bureaucracies and the emerging state governments to ease the plight of newly freed blacks. She expected that the economic and social situation in the war-ravaged South would require a great deal of facilitating. The Freedman's Aid Society wanted to wait until winter proved the need for such intervention. Meanwhile they stuck to the less political and easier task of providing Northern white teachers for Southern black schools.

Wrote Hancock, "The ignorance of such societies is the most unlimited and I think they show it especially in wanting nothing but teachers to go among [Southern blacks]. I know in any of the large cities of the South there is work and plenty of just the kind I wish to do. I should not ask any body about it only I think justice requires I should be paid for my services and for that reason must await the action of some wise society."[14] A determined woman, Hancock ultimately went south under the auspices of the Pennsylvania Society. She perceived her charter as rather broader than they did, however, and left teaching to those who felt so called.

Some antebellum spinsters never satisfactorily resolved the conflict be-tween their occupational requirements and their vocational needs. Lucy Larcom, for example, experienced a debilitating dissonance between her occupation as a teacher and her calling as a writer of verse and inspira-tional prose. Larcom simply could not make a living from writing. She became well known but commanded only ten dollars for a poem, occa-sionally twenty-five for an extended effort. This did not constitute an acceptable standard of living.[15] Larcom supplemented her earnings by editing a children's magazine, but found it more work than pay.[16] She collaborated with John Greenleaf Whittier on several editions of poetry, but the collaboration was also unremunerative. He provided his famous name and kept the copyright and royalties while she did the editorial work.[17] Larcom's only viable alternative was to teach, and that she did for eight years at Wheaton Seminary for girls. Afterward, she tutored, lec-tured, and gave occasional courses on her own.

Larcom's attempts to balance her creative aspirations with her physical needs provide the substance of much commentary in her private papers. In early 1855 she saw in *The Republican Era* an advertisement for an as yet unwritten book of hers to be published that season. "I had begun to count it among the impossibilites, my time is so completely broken into little bits here [at Wheaton]," she wrote to Whittier. "But when I saw that notice, I said 'Now it *must* be done.' "[18] Yet Larcom found the school a poor atmosphere in which to work. It was a noisy, demanding environ-ment that provided no privacy, little adult companionship, and no time to think creatively. She began to doubt her will, even her capacity to write. Then, "when I feel most like writing, a grave 'must not!' rises before me, in the shape of a lesson in Moral Science, or a pile of compositions to be corrected, forty or fifty high."[19] Since her teaching career provided a living and her writing could not, Larcom attempted to do her best as a teacher and to devote such time as she could to her writing.

The year 1865 typified Larcom's occupational struggle. In February she wrote: "I have spent a very pleasant year in Norton. I should be willing to spend a long time here if I knew that this was *my* place, and that teaching was *my* mission." Somehow, Larcom could not accept that it was. In

November she acknowledged that "teaching has never satisfied me, because somehow I have always felt as if I was not *quite* living when so occupied." Six years later, she continued to vacillate: "I have learned really to love my employment. I thought I should never like to be a teacher, then I had always other employments of my own, which I loved and longed for; I love them still; but I feel that while I teach . . . the rest must be only a relief, a recreation."[20] Larcom's difficulty was that she could not accept her calling to write as mere recreation—it consumed her thoughts during her brief periods of rest and nagged at her during the school term, distracting her from Wheaton responsibilities.

Larcom's inability to devote herself to her writing was due to more than financial insecurity. A life focused on the exploration of her own thoughts and the transcription of those for others seemed too isolated, too individualistic, too selfish and self-centered a one for a woman of her time. How could one embrace this life in a culture that worshiped female selflessness? She tried to explain the problem to Philena Fobes by recalling her private distress when she was assigned a roommate at the Monticello Female Academy. Everyone assumed that, because of her outgoing personality, Larcom loved to keep company, be social, and gossip with friends. But she demanded privacy and could write in no other atmosphere. She abhorred the constant interruptions of people acting according to their own needs and schedules. She wanted to live alone, to think freely and introspectively in a disciplined manner. She was denied this in boarding school, as student and teacher. "It is . . . the uphill work of my life, to be interested in the multitude I must live among," she confided. "I think kindly of *almost* everybody, and think I am not unwilling to do what I know how to do for their happiness—anything but *to be with them all the time*." Nevertheless, Larcom accepted her culture's dictate that "a self-absorbed life is a mean one." She had no desire to live "*that*," but she never could work or relax well in the midst of others.[21]

When faced with a threat to their continuing productivity, spinsters often despaired of future happiness and took to their beds. Almost invariably, women's response to vocational crises involved physical or psychic collapse. In 1861, for example, with the start of the Civil War, Sallie Holley recognized the imminent close of her career as an itinerant antislavery agent. Hers had been a grueling vocation. She traveled from place to place, spreading the antislavery gospel, sleeping wherever she could find a room, eating such food as a supporter might provide, traveling in all kinds of weather by every conceivable sort of conveyance, meeting a gamut of responses from her audiences, which ranged from the violently hostile to the blankly indifferent. At a visceral level, such conditions inspired Holley (like fellow agent Parker Pillsbury, who signed his letters "from a field hand") to identify all the more closely with the slave.[22] For six years Holley worked well and steadily under such circumstances. Then suddenly, in the fall of 1861, she fell ill—too ill to continue her tour.

Holley retreated to the Elmira, New York, water cure, where her disease was diagnosed as "torpidity of the liver." In a letter to Caroline Putnam she acknowledged her exhaustion and her wish to remain "rather than have again the dreadful cold and fatigue and hard work of another lecturing campaign." Holley felt bad about her desertion from the field. "I confess my conscience and heart would not be satisfied with doing nothing for the noble cause, and now of all times, to give up seems to me weak and wrong." A month later, Holley contemplated a new lecture tour, although "every 'cowerin', sleekit, tim'rous beastie' in my character begs and pleads for exemption this winter." She felt she could no longer tolerate the strange faces, massed audiences, poor conditions, and nervous excitement of her calling. She wanted to believe that the peace she had found at the sanitorium was God's way of telling her to stay, but she knew that she should continue her efforts as long as the antislavery leadership deemed necessary.[23]

Holley remained at the Elmira spa for seven months. With the exception of a brief lecture circuit in 1862, she retired from public life. The timing is significant. Holley did not suddenly succumb to the pressures under which she worked; she had thrived under the strain. Instead, she realized that with war on the horizon her job was finished. She no longer had a reason to live. Although much antislavery work remained to be done, Holley no longer commanded the position that had so suited her. Illness and the extended retreat it provided gave her a chance to regroup and a guise under which to contemplate her new status. She was never again so active or happy as she had been as an itinerant antislavery lecturer.

Clara Barton also thrived on hard work and activity. She, too, became an invalid when faced with the completion of her task. In her case the symptoms were those of lost function of body parts. Twice she lost her voice. The first occasion was a few years after the Civil War. As she told it:

Our war closed in the spring of '65. Almost four years longer I worked among the debris, gathering up the wrecks, and sometimes, during the lecture season, telling a few simple war stories to the people over the country. . . .
One early winter evening in '68, I stood on the platform of one of the finest new opera houses in the East, filled to repletion, it seemed to me, with the most charming audience I ever beheld. . . . Gradually, and to my horror, I felt my voice giving out, leaving me; the next moment I opened my mouth, but no sound followed. Again, and again, and again I attempted it with no result. It was

finished! Nervous prostration had declared itself. I went to my home in Washington, [and] lay helpless all winter.[24]

Barton faced the end of her vocation as she had known it. She saw no clear avenue for continuing work. The speaking tour, with its emphasis on past glory, neither sustained her interest nor met her need.

The Franco-Prussian War provided Barton with a new opportunity for service. Having recovered, she went to work nursing the wounded and organizing medical aid. In 1872, however, at the close of the war, her eyesight gave way. Barton spent months recuperating in Karlsruhe and London before feeling and seeing well enough to attempt the journey home to America. She feared that she would become a permanent invalid. Once home, she took to her bed. A hurried trip to Massachusetts to see a dying sister brought on total collapse. Clara stayed with relatives in North Grafton, then entered a Danville sanitorium. She stayed for ten years. Some clue as to the cause of this extended illness exists in a poem she wrote while crossing the Atlantic. Still five days out from New York, Barton ruminated on her war work in Europe:

> I have heard the faint note of the last sentry's call,
>   And seen the white flag flutter out o'er the wall;
> I have bound up death wounds lying dark and alone,
>   And the language that blessed me was strange and unknown.
> The homeless and famished clung wild with despair,
>   And the noble and gentle have cherished me there.
> Still trustingly,—loyally: loving and true,
>   Anxious and glad, I am coming to you.
> Have ye place, each beloved one, a place in your prayer,
>   Have ye *room*, my dear countrymen, room for me there?
>
> How the strength rose and fell in those perilous years!
>   What torture it made of my hopes and my fears,
> When I joyed in its rise or wept for its fall,
>   It was never myself that I thought of at all.
> But if only once more I might tread the loved land,
>   And toil for its weal with my heart, and my hand;
> Have ye place, each beloved one, a place in your prayer,
>   Have ye *work*, my brave countrymen, work for me there?[25]

It was not until she began to organize the American Red Cross, with its first chapter in Danville, Massachusetts, that Clara Barton regained her energy and her health.

----——◆——----

Women also experienced a sense of crisis on finding themselves in overt conflict with established male authority in their efforts to obtain the training, status, or resources needed to pursue their vocations. Not uncommonly, strong-minded, independent, self-willed, vocationally oriented single women collapsed mentally or physically after taking on the university, church, or law. Sarah Pugh noted of abolitionists Mary Grew and Mary Anne Estlin, "Why will you dear good, strongminded ones, be so feeble in body?"[26] The case of Graceanna Lewis of Media, Pennsylvania, is illustrative.

Lewis, an ornithologist and scientific illustrator, experienced a number of career setbacks in the years preceding her illness. In the early 1860s she had applied for a position on the science faculty at Swarthmore College, but stepped aside in favor of a male nauralist whom she felt to be more competent. Maria Mitchell objected that "she weighed her own technical and scholastic learning against that of her rival, and she counted womanly culture and refinement as nothing."[27] Mitchell argued that, given Lewis's outstanding ability, she would be a better teacher than her competitor, for she would be a helpmeet and an example to students as well as a scientific instructor.

Mitchell told the National Congress of Women that they "must not only be ready to help women into new occupations, but we must make women willing to enter them." She encouraged Lewis to apply for a similar position at Vassar, where Mitchell was professor of astronomy. The position represented professional recognition and status for Lewis and could ensure economic security. Despite strong letters of support from John Cassin, curator of birds at the Academy of Natural Science in Philadelphia, and Spencer Baird, secretary of the Smithsonian Institution, Lewis was rejected in favor of a male geologist. The rejection cut more deeply than that of Swarthmore because Vassar was a women's college, because Mitchell (who was highly regarded) had supported her candidacy, and because Lewis herself had actively competed for the post.

The year was 1868, the start of a memorable two years for Lewis. She published her first scientific work in that year, volume one of a projected ten-volume *Natural History of Birds,* a catalogue and general scientific treatise on ornithological classification.[28] It proved a critical and popular success. Lewis also attended her first meetings of the American Association for the Advancement of Science. She presented two papers at the prestigious gathering—one on the plumage of terns and the other entitled "Thoughts on the Structure of the Animal Kingdom." Lewis recorded no reaction to her professional debut, but she must have felt torn. The first paper was straightforward and, considering the accuracy of her observations and the clarity and artistry of her illustrations, no doubt well received. The second paper drew criticism. It presented a teleological orientation to the structure of the animal kingdom, a philosophical perspective already under attack in the natural sciences and one that would lose its last and ablest defender with the death of Lewis Agassiz in 1873.[29]

In 1869, John Cassin, Lewis's scientific mentor, died. She had depended on him for professional aid and advice, recognition and support. In the spring of 1870 the Philadelphia Academy of Natural Science proposed Lewis for membership. Joseph Leidy, professor of anatomy at the University of Pennsylvania, George Tryon, curator of ornithology at the Academy, and Edward Nolan, academy librarian, supported the nomination. Lewis had studied at the Academy for eight years, and was well known by the members. For whatever reasons, they withheld membership. A week later, they reversed their decision and admitted Lewis along with two other women—a scientific illustrator and a minerologist.[30] Though still an honor, membership status had come in a graceless fashion.

During these two years, then, Lewis experienced the pleasure of professional recognition and the pain of professional rejection. She had lost an important faculty position, taken the losing side in a philosophical battle that divided the sciences, received backhanded recognition from scientists who knew her and her work personally, and lost her most important professional mentor. Lewis also faced an economic imperative and returned to secondary school teaching in order to support herself. In her younger years she had enjoyed teaching. Now she found boarding-school life intellectually constricting, emotionally demanding, and physically draining. She spoke of suffering from "the pressure of school duties." After teaching the 1871 summer term at the Philadelphia Friends' School, she fell ill with "an affection of the brain" that confined her to bed for two years. Her sister, Dr. Rebecca Fussell, attended her. The future looked grim for this woman who had found no financially secure base for her scientific research. Her efforts to enter the male preserve had met with limited success. Lewis withdrew into invalidism.

------◄●►------

The single woman who pioneered new social roles and new life-styles during the antebellum period had insufficient role models and cultural supports to legitimate her choice. She lacked a feminist theory to provide a social rather than a personal analysis of her pain and suffering. Although the Cult of Single Blessedness upheld singlehood and valued certain kinds of activities, single women continued to be seen as less than fully female when outside the domestic sphere. Beginning at about mid-century, male medicine and science began to corollate women's beings with their bodies. If some saw celibacy as purity, others defined it as unnatural. Women's "natural" biological functions were aimed at pregnancy; therefore marriage and childbearing were women's normal social roles. This meant that spinsters were considered both biologically and socially deviant.

Many spinsters felt little sense of deviancy, however, either social or biological. They felt supported and cared for in the love of family and friends, and respected for their socially useful work. Others, however, were sensitive to their "difference." Emily Howland spoke compellingly about her feelings of deviancy as an unmarried woman. In the winter of 1861 Howland recorded in her journal a remarkable dialogue with "her darkest self." More than any other contemporary statement, this illustrates the social pressures brought to bear on the unwed:

I have found my place and I feel sure it is the right one. Why then do you have to pit yourself against your pitiless logic to convince yourself of a self-evident truth? You take the position of single woman voluntarily, why falter at the consequences, why care for slights, for lack of caste and place or be chilled by isolation, are you not with the right . . . ? Are you sure you are not living a mistake? I, Earth, teach you in every lesson I give, in plastic matter, that isolation is wrong. Marriage is the law.

I am not proud, I only mean to live as truly and freely as I can, and in thus doing strengthen my weak sisters to the same. With all deference to the Earth in its place, I believe in a Higher Power with my whole soul. . . . It is terrible to be alone, it makes the earthling shiver, but is not the sea alone in its mightiness, is not God alone, are not they harmonious, each, and with the Universe too? Then cannot the human soul be great, true, pure, free alone? Yes, I know it. I feel it, I exalt in it, but alas I am so human, my vanity makes me suffer so, when I see myself passed by because forsooth I am a cipher in the world's esteem if I lack the initial figure of a man at my left.[31]

While few women acknowledged such feelings, a subconscious tension wore away at the self-esteem of some and curtailed the energies and concentration they needed to marshal for their life's work.

Perhaps because they lacked the usual accoutrements of womanhood—husband and children—these spinsters felt their subjection to other measurements of femininity that much more strongly. Mary Grew, the inspired speaker and editor of the abolitionist journal *The Pennsylvania Freeman*, turned down an invitation to speak at an American Anti-Slavery Association anniversary meeting for "want of sufficient voice to fill the Tabernacle." She subscribed to the feminine qualities of delicacy, humility, and physical frailty. Perhaps in her own mind Grew balanced her unfeminine vocation with her feminine style. Sallie Holley spoke of the "shrinking and dislike and suffering" attached to having one's name appear in newspapers. It was commonly held in the nineteenth century that a lady's name should appear in the newspapers on only two occasions—her marriage and her death; a public lecturer's name appeared every time she spoke. In fact, Holley's name often showed up in letters to the editors as well as announcements and reviews of lectures. "I think I can never forget," she said, "the sudden, intense, and overwhelming emotion, I experienced on seeing my name for the first time in a public newspaper. It seemed that every drop of blood in my body, and every feeling of my soul rose up in 'terrible rebellion'—I can never forget the day, the hour, and the spot where it happened." Catharine M. Sedgwick, who occasionally admitted to literary ambition, denied the care and craftsmanship, the emotional and financial investment embodied in her writing by saying (in accordance with the dictates of feminine decorum): "My *author* existence has always seemed something accidental, extraneous, and independent of my inner self. My books have been a pleasant occupation and excitement in my life. The notice, and friends, or acquaintances they have procured me, have relieved me from the danger of ennui and blue devils, that are most apt to infest a single person. But they constitute no portion of my happiness."[32] The adherence of these women to certain standards of femininity limited their contributions to public life and often made their vocational commitment a conflicted and guilt-ridden experience.

Feelings of deviancy and sensitivity to the "unnaturalness" of their state became most problematic at particular points in the life cycles of single women. They were more vulnerable to cultural prescriptions of femininity when their biological clocks marked specific transitions along life's path. The passing by of marital eligibility or the childbearing years increased awareness of their difference and aroused doubts about their chosen track. The process drained the unmarried of emotional and physical reserves and often resulted in psychic or physical distress.

Catharine M. Sedgwick, for example, felt that her "solitary condition" was "unnatural," and she feared it to be unchanging. In the spring of 1828 she wrote a devastating indictment of the single life as she experienced it. Spring had arrived, "the season of life and loveliness, the beautiful emblem of our resurrection unto life eternal." Although the fields had turned green, the flowers bloomed, the birds sang, and the air smelled sweetly of perfume, she despaired. "Hope now seems to turn from me," she wrote. "The best sources of earthly happiness are not within my grasp." At thirty-nine, Sedgwick faced her spinsterhood with all its ramifications and admonished those who might follow:

From my own experience I would not advise anyone to remain unmarried, for my experience has been a singularly happy one. My feelings have never been embittered by those slights and taunts that the repulsive and neglected have to endure, there has been no period of my life to the present moment when I might not have allied myself respectably, and to those sincerely attached to me, if I would. . . . My fortune is not adequate to an independent establishment, but it is ample for ease to myself and liberality to others. In the families of all my brothers I have an agreeable home. My sisters are all kind and affectionate to me . . . their children all love me. . . . I have troops of friends, some devotedly attached to me, and yet the result of all this very happy experience is that there is no equivalent for those blessings which Providence has placed first, and ordained that they should be purchased at the dearest sacrifice.[33]

Sedgwick had not and was not willing to exchange her independence for marriage. But she complained of the lack of emotional primacy in her relationships with others. She "who began life as . . . the primary object of affection to many" had "come by degrees to be first to none," while yet her "love remain[ed] in its entire strength, and crav[ed] such returns as have no substitute." Although she dearly loved her siblings and devoted herself to their children, Sedgwick longed to be the first object of someone's love.

There being no discernible outward reason for Sedgwick's "mental paralysis," her "depression and morbidity"—that is, no substantial change in family relationships or vocational status—it is possible that Sedgwick at thirty-nine accepted fully and for the first time the consequences of her decision neither to marry nor bear children. She experienced a kind of existential loneliness in the pregnant fullness of spring. Although nineteenth-century women bore children into their forties, only rarely did they begin the cycle so late in life.

Lucy Larcom felt the same way at about the same age. Larcom was in her mid-thirties at the time of her blackest depression. At this point, she was forced to clarify her attitudes toward marriage. She and a childhood friend had an understanding that they would eventually marry. But Larcom found both the candidate and the institution wanting. She shared her fears and hopes with her friend, Esther Homiston. "I often wish I had some one to live with me, for whom I could have an absorbing call," she wrote in 1857. "It is rather dreary to feel that no one in the world *particularly* needs you." Six months later she said again: "What I need now is to love, fully and deeply, like the sunshine, the wind, and the dew. I have thought I knew the blessing of such a life, so the shadows seem deeper now."[34]

Larcom talked about marriage as "the highest state of earthly happiness," but acknowledged that she could not imagine marrying. She loved study and privacy and insisted on making up her own mind about things. Larcom also voiced some concern about bearing children. She suffered from a tendency toward scrofula, a form of tuberculosis characterized by the painful swelling of neck glands and joints. She feared that the disease was hereditary and told Homiston that she could not build her "happiness" on the possible suffering of any offspring.[35]

Doctors had told Larcom that scrofula was not necessarily hereditary and that, with careful diet and proper care, it could be cured. Her objection to marriage on this ground, then, may have reflected a disquieted state of mind and have been more an excuse than a valid obstacle. The timing of the discussion is suggestive. As Larcom approached her thirty-fifth birthday and retreated from her fiancé, she faced the likelihood that she would never marry. The foreclosure of this traditional female role heightened her anxiety. A more general loss of confidence, resulting from vocational stress, induced fears about her capacity to fill nontraditional roles as well.

Lucy's distress grew in 1859, when she wrote to her sweetheart and rejected his suit. In February this "middle aged woman" confirmed her sense of having passed a turning point in her life. "I feel almost as if it were another beginning of life," she wrote, "another journey begun;—the afternoon walk must be very different from that of the morning."[36]

As Larcom succumbed to the demands of boarding-school teaching, as she dreamed of creative writing and struggled with her feelings about marriage, she suffered greater and greater pain in her head, neck, and back. "It is not really pain," she said, with insight into the emotional nature of the problem. Her condition so worsened that by October she feared for her sanity. "God preserve me from [madness]! but I have often *dreamed* that was so, within a year or two."[37] The confluence of biological, marital, and vocational crises seriously threatened both Larcom's emotional and physical well-being. The closing off of the role of wife coincided with Larcom's fears that her job would forever inhibit the flowering of her creativity. She sank into depression.

Graceanna Lewis and Emily Howland also experienced a convergence of biological and vocational crises. Both were in their fifties when Graceanna collapsed of her "brain fever" and Emily suffered "recurring morbidity." There remains no absolute evidence to indicate the onset of menopause, but their age makes such an assumption reasonable. Little attention has been paid to women's attitudes toward menopause over the centuries, and particularly to the response of single women to this change of life. It must, however, have been a difficult transition for women living in a culture which so closely defined them by their function as mothers. After years of pregnancy and childbearing, a married woman could embrace menopause as a release from an important duty well done (or at least endured). A spinster, however, learned from science and medicine that "the non-exercise of any functions of the body are not limited to the organs immediately concerned. The whole system participates, and general ill-health or derangement of other organs is sure to result." Advice literature warned that women faced disease in old age if they failed to devote themselves to husband and family in younger years. "Nature gave to each sex certain functions, and the whole system is in better health when all parts and powers fulfill their destiny."[38] Spinsters violated physiological and social laws by committing their "life force" to the training of the mind rather than the exercise of the reproductive organs.[39]

In Howland's case, some literary evidence suggests a link between her depression and change of life in the imagery she used to describe herself after the age of forty-three: cold, numb, life-suspending, and sterile.

I thought why can't I rise from the freezing into life and the kind of beauty I am capable of. Suppose many of the petals of my being are blighted by the frost of snow and time and trial. Have I not something of worth left? My buds like those who have felt the chill may never open; still remembering what they have endured in the icy embrace of winter, their life and beauty is more remarkable than all the glow of a garden in summertime.[40]

This sense of herself as a plant that budded but never flowered pervades her diary and her correspondence in later years.

It was during this period that Howland shrank from receiving letters written by her old admirer, Colonel Folsom. The receipt of his missives, usually so welcome, perhaps increased her confusion and sense of lost opportunity, functioning, and role. "Vulgar sadness someone calls this depression without cause," she wrote. "Why suffer so much for what seem mistakes now. They may not be at all."[41] The convergence of menopause, lost vocation, and submission to dependence and domesticity all contributed to Howland's despair.

———◄◆►———

The confluence of biological or life-cycle issues with vocational crises compounded a spinster's anxiety and damaged her self-esteem. One other factor further aggravated an individual's well-being. The loss of emotional support from female friends or changes in the structure or availability of female networks occasionally pushed an unmarried woman beyond her capacity to cope with life. Like any human being, she required moral, intellectual, and emotional affirmation. Perhaps more than others, she required legitimation of her course. A spinster's physical and mental health were often affected by the loss of a loved one, the betrayal of friendship by an esteemed other, or the absence of a valued friend at a crucial time. Rachel Stearns experienced severe emotional trauma when the dear friend whose support she was depending on chose to pursue a separate life and career. Stearns's diary reflects her physical and emotional collapse.

After years of looking for a way to express her religious convictions and support herself, Rachel Stearns left her native Massachusetts to teach in a Methodist school in Mississippi. That she left alone tried both her faith and her strength, but it seemed a necessary sacrifice. Then, in June 1837, Stearns received a letter from Margaret Wells, a childhood friend, "stating in terms not to be misunderstood, her attachment to the Methodist cause, her desire to come south, her love for me, and her determination to serve her God." Stearns had long hoped for Wells's conversion. She rejoiced, "I no longer wondered what I was made for."[42]

In September, however, Stearns heard from her mother that Wells had converted to Unitarianism. "I calmly bowed my head," she wrote, "and said 'thy will be done, O Lord.' " In anguish, Stearns interpreted these events as a testing time—a test of her religious faith, her self-confidence, and her love for her friend. She pondered her future with dread. "I must go on my journey alone," she wrote, "but I shall never smile more, and as a sense of it would come over my mind like a withering whirlwind, I would sigh . . . night came, I attempted to sleep . . . my soul was sick." Stearns continued to mourn for several days. Wracked with fever and pain, she secluded herself in her room. By day she fought off visions of a future not to be. By night she was visited by nightmares. At one point, she cried aloud, "O my sister, my sister and will you leave me to travel in the weary path of life alone?"[43]

In December, Stearns heard that Wells had gone to Georgia and had relinquished entirely the idea of joining her in a life of Methodist teaching and sisterly love. At the same time Stearns learned of her rejection as administrator of the school in which she had taught. She experienced some failure or embarrassment at the public examinations held at term's end. These combined assaults on her self-esteem—the failures in personal, vocational, and social life—drove her to bed, where she lay seriously ill, hallucinating or unconscious for some time.[44]

----◆◆◆----

So the unwed experienced considerable stress and conflict in their single lives. The Cult of Single Blessedness held up an ideal that could not be realized both because of the contradictions inherent within it and because of cultural attitudes and social structures that inhibited its full expression. Nineteenth-century women could not support themselves as scientists, artists, authors, or builders of new social institutions. Lacking that, they strove to make a living at those few occupations open to women. They found that their jobs consumed the time and energy they would have preferred to invest in their vocations. Society defined woman's sphere and role in terms of her biological function as mother and her social role as wife. The equation of womanhood with the female reproductive capacity caused celibates particular pain as they reached an age when childbearing became unlikely or they underwent menopause. Medicine frightened spinsters with its theories about the origins of decay and disease in "unused" organs. Awareness of biological dysfunction and social deviancy exacerbated whatever doubts women may have felt about their decision to remain single and any lack of fulfillment they may have experienced in their alternative life-styles. Female support, whether of friends or sisters, set women on the path to individual autonomy and achievement. Those same relationships, especially when grounded in common enterprise, similar values, or a shared life, nurtured female health. But any loss in that primary support system proved devastating. Like other women, spinsters frequently somatized their distress and retired into illness or depression.

9

"The Mind Will Give Way"

Assertion and the Limits of Social Tolerance

The majority of women in this study believed that they had important tasks to accomplish in the world. They felt destined to generate new ideas, to build new institutions, to reform existing social structures, to catalogue and describe God's world to His greater glory and man's expanded knowledge, and to create works of art in tribute to the human spirit and capacity for self-expression. Lucy Chase delighted in "laying corner-stones." Although neither she nor her sisters had any assurance that long-standing structures would be raised upon their foundations, they themselves loved the "soul-stirring work." Lucy Larcom spoke in a symbolic way of her affinity for mountains and heights. She detested the "wearisome levels in life": "What is it in us that refuses to love levels? Is it that there is no searching and toiling for anything, up cool heights and down in sheltered hollows?" To Larcom, the ease or comfort of plateaus signified only stagnation. "It would be good for me to ascend oftener to the heights of being," she wrote, "I fear losing the power and the wish to climb."[1]

While Chase and Larcom spoke of laying foundations and gradual ascents, others spoke in more combative tones. Said Anna Dickinson, "The world belongs to those who take it." Sallie Holley preferred to hear hymns that celebrated human existence as "a battle, a warfare, a march on to higher and higher work, under 'the great taskmaster.'" She recalled a favorite: "Be not like dumb, driven cattle, Be a hero in the strife." She believed herself assigned to sacred tasks and devoted herself to their accomplishment. Mary A. Dodge reveled in the challenge of writing exactly what she wished. She refused to accommodate the views of dissenters. "I *want* to upheave and overturn," she told her mother. "Land needs to be sub-soiled, as well as top-dressed. 'The time is out of joint, O cursed spite, That ever I was born to set it right,' says Hamlet, but I don't say so. It's just what I should like to be born for, and I hope I was."[2]

Yet few single women of the early nineteenth century had the training, the opportunity, the freedom, or the strength to scale the heights to which they aspired. All too often, for reasons beyond individual constitution or constraint, their efforts produced as much heartbreak as accomplishment. Their striving to do good and great deeds conflicted with cultural definitions of womanhood. The pioneering of new social roles was not easy. These women burned, as Louisa May Alcott said, "with a fire which consumes but does not warm."[3]

Some spinsters interpreted their conflict as reflecting personal weakness of character, ability, or commitment. "The trouble with me," sighed Mary Reed, "is that I have more to do than is well done. My will and taste are strong, my skill, ability, and talent, wanting, weak—small. Hence there has always been a war within, and always will be." Emily Howland wrote in 1873, "O I am so sick of myself. I do so little, I want to do, I ought to do so much." On her fifty-eighth birthday, she looked back in sorrow wondering "if my life has been a mistake or if I shall ever see it vindicated as wise and useful. It looks poor and a failure to me." On her fiftieth birthday, Sarah Pugh measured her life against a standard of godly excellence and human achievement. "Almost a life, and how spent?" she asked. "What am I? Where am I? What must be the record? My life as a whole has been aimless, objectless."[4] Such women quietly suffered, descending into illness or depression as the battle raged within.

Others waged their struggle more publicly. Their behavior challenged and dismayed a culture that accepted female invalidism as understandable behavior, for it believed women were innately weak physically and emotionally. Excitable, egoistical, and ambitious women who vigorously pursued their goals exhibited behavior deemed unwomanly by family and peers. They were self-centered, single-minded, and strong-minded. They were also competitive, lacking tact and the capacity to compromise. Emily Blackwell admitted to "a great deal of a kind of proud scorn, or scornful pride in my disposition which is no mark of a great character." Rachel Stearns hoped that God had destined her to the same "high station of usefulness" to which she aspired, because she could not be happy doing good in a small or unobtrusive way. She found that the "*pleasure* of doing well, consisted in *excelling others.*"[5] Such women pursued their visions of achievement and autonomy beyond the point where family or community could support them. While they perceived themselves as upholding principle and acting with integrity, others uncomfortably labeled them obstinate, aggressive, proud, idiosyncratic, and manly.

Nineteenth-century culture tended to link female independence and ambition with decreased mental or emotional capacity. A few strong women had sufficient intellectual perspective (and suitably low public profile) to make fun of such attitudes. Carrie A. Rowland, for example, wrote to Emily Howland that "I am glad if thee has had difficulties to conquer, and I shall think it splendid if thee has been obliged to get angry and assert thyself!" She felt that Howland's work for racial and sexual equality had profited her greatly. "But mind you I wouldn't say so to many people," Rowland teased. "Frown and shake my head and say Quixotic and queer, improper &c &c and give all sorts of 'suitable' advice to any rash, unsettled, thoughtless pale who would dream of such a thing."[6]

Those who experienced direct attack in the midst of heated public strife could not take such linkages so lightly. Susan B. Anthony copied into her diary a quotation from another infamous female reformer, Frances Wright: "Ambition is the spur, the necessary spur of a *great* mind to *great* action when acting upon a weak mind it impells to absurdity and sours it with discontent."[7] Perhaps so many countrymen and women had attacked Anthony that she questioned her motivation and capacity.

Society interpreted Anthony's search for female autonomy as an attack on male dominance in America. Certainly some pioneering spinsters saw in male prerogative the frustration of their ambition and independence, and, like Anthony, they developed a critique of gender roles and the oppression of women within them. Others, while rebelling against gender limitations, did not consciously attack them. Catharine Beecher, for example, wove new roles for women from traditional cloth. She never directly confronted the gender structure, with its limitations on female autonomy.[8] Over the course of the nineteenth century, male institutions such as the church, university, medicine, law, and science increasingly responded to any pursuit or extension of female autonomy as a threat to their hegemony. Pejorative labels were attached to independent women. They were called "amazons," "hermaphrodites," and "mannish maidens." Professional and intellectual men broadened their litany of linked deviancies to include singlehood, hatred of men, public activity, and feminism.

As early as the 1830s, women who rejected dependence upon men and strode out of the domestic sphere were viewed by social commentators as being somehow "other" than women. In 1838, *The Mother's Magazine* carried an anonymous article on "Female Orators" attacking women who asserted their independent-mindedness and did so in public. Decrying the activity of women such as the Grimké sisters, who rose to lecture the public on their political, moral, and religious duty with regard to slavery, the author found some consolation in their singlehood. "These Amazonians are their own executioners. They have unsexed themselves in public estimation, and there is no fear that they will perpetuate their race. We treat insanity in all its forms, with allowance."[9] The author reasoned that, unattractive and unfeminine as such "unnatural" women must be, they would never find husbands. Thus they would never have children and could not propagate their deviancy.

The Ladies' Companion contained an article accusing women who pursued education beyond the bounds of ladylike accomplishment of being "semi-women" or "mental hermaphrodites." A new, third sex had been invented—the intellectual female. In 1853, *The New York Sun* responded to the nomination of Susan B. Anthony to serve on the business committee of the World Temperance Convention with an attack on her womanhood in this vein:

The quiet duties of daughter, wife or mother are not congenial to those hermaphrodite spirits who thirst to win the title of champion of one sex and victor over another. What is the love and submission of one manly heart to the woman whose ambition it is to sway the minds of multitudes as did Demosthenes or a Cicero? What are the tender affections and childish prattle of the family circle to women whose ears itch for the loud laugh and boisterous cheer of the public assembly?[10]

Until the 1870s, the association of female autonomy, intellectualism, ambition, and singlehood with man-hating and mental instability was fairly loose—though widely intimated. Eventually, women who stayed single and were aggressively independent would be diagnosed as congenitally deranged and called lesbian.[11]

Even in antebellum America, social constraints were exercised against those women who pursued autonomy, personal development, and public work in self-defined paths. An antebellum woman who rejected marriage could be appreciated in her community and family as a model of single blessedness if she fulfilled certain roles and paid homage to certain norms of female behavior. However, she ran up against the limits of social tolerance if she flaunted her autonomy, ostentatiously acted out her independent-mindedness, overstepped the boundaries of female propriety, or openly challenged male prerogatives.

Mary Sophia Gilpin was such a woman. She was competitive, ambitious, and self-involved. She had few traits of the womanly woman: far from being yielding, serene, submissive, or domestic in nature, she was nervous, high-strung, and overly sensitive to slights and disapproval. She expressed herself with a rigidity of opinion and forcefulness of manner that left little room for diplomacy.[12] She was impulsive and capricious. Once, when attending the annual Episcopalian convention in Philadelphia, Mary found the doorway jammed with crowds of conventioneers; she gained entrance to the hall by climbing through a window. On the other hand, Gilpin had trouble making up her mind and agonized for months over difficult decisions. Gilpin's personality and behavior were neither bizarre nor disturbed according to any current definition of the words. The fact that she was briefly committed to a mental hospital in the spring of 1852 indicates the narrow and increasingly rigid boundaries imposed upon female activity in the mid-nineteenth century and the desperation of one driven further and further into "unfeminine" behavior and nagging complaint when she became frustrated in her desire for a fulfilling vocation and the accomplishment of an independent life.[13]

Mary S. Gilpin aspired to be a personage of some repute in her church and community. She wanted to make a significant and lasting contribution to her society in the area of early childhood education. Gilpin used her family's position and contacts, her friends' influence, and her own assertive personality and perseverance to further her goals. This was the "Age of Jackson" in America, the era of the lone hero pitting his skill and imagination against sea, prairie, or mountain. Deemed eminently appropriate for the nineteenth-century male, such qualities served him well in the business or political arenas. They certainly aided Gilpin's father and brothers, for example.

Joshua Gilpin was an inventor, paper manufacturer, poet, and scholar of natural history. Henry Gilpin, the oldest of Mary's four brothers, had a prominent career as a businessman, lawyer, solicitor of the Treasury, and attorney general of the United States. An intellectual, he edited James Madison's papers and wrote a biography of his friend Martin Van Buren; he edited *The Atlantic Souvenir,* directed the Pennsylvania Academy of Fine Arts, and served as an officer of the Historical Society of Pennsylvania and as a member of the American Philosophical Society. Thomas clerked for American businesses in England and held a political appointment as American counsel in Belfast. Richard farmed in Chester County, Pennsylvania, and pursued engineering interests. Dedicated to the West and to the development of its natural resources and political power, William published several works on natural history and western railroads. He also served as governor of Colorado.[14] Evidently, those qualities in Mary Gilpin which so alienated her community—her intellectualism, independent-mindedness, entrepreneurial cast of mind, and ambition—characterized other members of her family as well. But such qualities were not thought at all suitable in a woman. That such an obviously intelligent, talented, energetic, and endowed individual could find no appropriate sphere for accomplishment says much about the dark side of the quest for female autonomy and achievement in nineteenth-century America.

Mary S. Gilpin received much of her formal education in England. Her mother, Mary Dilworth Gilpin, was a British Quaker. She and Joshua Gilpin had met in England and lived there briefly until the birth of their first child. The family retained close ties with their British kin and attempted to cultivate an English country-home environment on their American estate, Kentmere on the Brandywine. For three years in her early adolescence, Mary S. Gilpin attended a British boarding school. As the rustic American cousin, she apparently was not subject to the same expectations as her schoolmates with regard to discipline or decorum. Her independent-mindedness thrived in such an atmosphere. Her "chief companion and competitor" later reminded Mary that "whenever any thing occurred [of] which [she] did not approve [she] would re-iterate 'I protest against that.'" Gilpin spent holidays with her British cousins, who encouraged her precociousness. They found her unique opinions and youthful posturings entertaining and novel, and so did not hold her to British codes of accepted female behavior.[15]

Returning to the family circle, Gilpin chose to follow her intellectual interests. She took up natural history, her father's avocation, and designed a book on the Brandywine River Valley. She confided her plan to Sophia duPont, a friend who shared her interest in nature. Here Mary met the first of many rejections from her friend, rejections rooted in Sophia's strict sense of propriety. As Sophia told it:

[Mary] proposed to me to assist her in writing a work like the journal of a naturalist about this country. The plan was, we should each keep a journal, and read and obtain scientific information, and afterward condense our observations, lumbrations and informations, into a work like the above cited. She hinted that if we found it worthy afterwards, we might anonymously publish it! Oh dear! I was shocked at the bare idea of any words of *mine* in any way appearing in print!

Either Gilpin ignored Sophia's dismay or Sophia misled her with assurances of secret help. In any case, Mary felt encouraged. Sophia, however, confessed that although she admired Mary, she could never thereafter love her.[16] This ambivalence on Sophia's part—overt encouragement yet covert disapproval, the extension of friendship in public qualified by private reservations—contributed to Mary's emotional distress over the next two decades.

What happened to Gilpin's book is not clear, but it seems never to have been published. She returned to England later in the decade for an extended visit to the ancestral home. While there, her interests took a different turn. She underwent a spiritual awakening under the influence of the British moral reform movement. There, "in the midst of all that was most congenial to my mental tastes and feelings, and to my sense of right and cherished habits of practice," Mary S. Gilpin dedicated herself, with patriotic and religious fervor, to the betterment of her countrymen.[17]

Gilpin's conversion was inspired by the example of a young woman named Savage, whom she met while in Belfast visiting her brother Thomas. The two women planned a joint moral effort of some kind, perhaps an orphan asylum, a pauper's kindergarten, or a Sunday school. They were unable to pursue their idea, however, and parted company, to Mary's lasting grief.[18] The reasons for the separation remain unknown, but Mary's parents called her home to Philadelphia at about this time.

In 1841 Joshua Gilpin died. Kentmere was put up for sale. The family scattered. Mary stood at a crossroads, attempting to sort out her duty, her needs, her wants, and her future plans. She had hoped to engage in moral reform in Britain, and the breakup of the family provided a strong impetus to do so in America. She expected that her network of friends would provide valuable assistance. Mary's mother encouraged her, possibly out of her own religious conviction. So, too, did sister Sarah, although Mary mistrusted her motives, suspecting her sister of merely wanting her out of the way. Thus, while Sarah and Mary Dilworth Gilpin undertook a recu-perative voyage to visit family in England, Mary Sophia remained in Pennsylvania. She developed a scheme for an infant school similar to those which she had seen in Britain.

With the widowed Julia Frances, Mary S. Gilpin rented a farm where they planned to provide residential instruction for young boys aged four to ten. They intended to teach French, English, history, literature, drawing, and dancing. Older boys would be taught Latin grammar. Attention would be paid to religious instruction. Although Frances was a Roman Catholic and Gilpin an Episcopalian, they agreed to disagree on contro-verted points of doctrine or observance and to concentrate on instilling in their students the manners and character of Christian gentlemen.[19] Mary had excellent qualifications for teaching. She read Latin, French, and Italian; she spoke French; and she had a thorough grounding in English literature.

Sophia duPont, Clementina Smith, and other women in Mary's intel-lectual and social circle encouraged her in this maiden effort at teaching and administration. Gilpin actively sought their support, believing it a necessary foundation for a successful operation. Friends might refer pupils, lend the institution social status, provide financial stability, and sanction such an independent course of action. Gilpin clearly felt vulnerable in this regard, for she worried about community criticism and "the comments of those not interested in us."[20]

After six months Gilpin's arrangement with Mrs. Frances terminated. Differing religious and teaching philosophies played some role in the split. Gilpin also acknowledged that her opinionated and authoritarian manner may have been a factor in the separation. "I at first *leaned too much* on the hope of sympathy in my views and harmonious cooperation," she re-marked, "and when this failed, I occupied myself with endeavors to make things right." Thus she aroused both the opposition and the resentment of Julia Frances.[21]

The end of the experiment proved devastating for Gilpin. She lamented the separation from the children and mourned the loss of professional status, identity, and occupation. She also feared the economic and personal upheaval sure to follow—particularly since Sarah and her mother had already made plans for the winter based on the assumption that Mary had provided for herself. She hesitated to face her own mother who, however willingly she listened to the facts of the case, could not sympathize with Mary's feelings about it. She was also apprehensive about facing her sister's biting criticism. Drained and demoralized, Mary feared that "my own capacity for effort is gone, and the patience of my friends is exhausted and I dread to meet them, to inconvenience them."[22] Because of the fanfare with which she had begun school, Mary's failure was a very public one. She suffered incessant, debilitating headaches for nine months. At the urging of family and friends, she traveled to Harrisburg to relax in a rural atmosphere in the hope of regaining health and peace of mind.

While recuperating, Gilpin continued to brood about her failure. "I do not know myself for what I used to be," she confided, "and turn which way I may no hopeful feeling seems to arise—and difficulties and opposition seem to destroy the power to make those efforts which yet I feel to be essential to the restoration and preserving of a healthy mind." If she could only look "forward to some prospect of useful occupation," Mary could relax, take the cure, and refresh her body and spirit. "I seemed to need some special object of interest and pursuit," she wrote; but she found little understanding or respect for this need.[23]

Her family's attitude particularly depressed Gilpin. "The view which they take of my wishes has been a trial of greater keenness than can be conceived, and the little prospect I have of being better understood seems to throw me back continually into a state of perplexity," she wrote. Sister Sarah baited Mary, and brother Richard suggested that she place herself under medical care. Mary insisted that her melancholia was rooted in her disappointment, "and medicine cannot reach the heart."[24]

Friends provided no greater sympathy. Sophia duPont suggested that Gilpin accept her situation as God's will and intimated that her ongoing efforts to secure employment and develop her plans for an infant school were misdirected and flew in the face of heaven. Such criticism from her "best friend" cut Mary deeply. "It did not seem kind in you so to judge me," she wrote. While she seriously considered Sophia's opinion, she concluded that it must be in error. "When I said to you that I had ambition, for which you . . . reproved me, I wished to convey my desire to carry out those views for which I had tried to fit myself rather than to undertake others for which I did not deem myself so well qualified."[25] Gilpin believed that she was acting according to God's will, but was shaken by the disapproval of others.[26]

Mary began to believe that the problem lay within herself—in her audacity, perhaps: "doubtless I need to be humbled far more than I had apprehended yet the severity of suffering and agitation of mind I have undergone seems to have injured my powers both physical, mental, and moral." She lost the ability to make decisions, to take initiative, or to seize opportunities. Her immobility itself greatly disturbed her. With no one to encourage her or to appreciate her motives, Mary could neither summon the energy nor the courage to help herself.[27]

The future augured ill. Her occupational failure called into question the viability of her vocational choice and the potential for fulfillment of life as a single woman. Despondent, Gilpin reflected on her decision to forego marriage and dedicate herself to a broader sphere:

It cannot be known by those who possess them, what is the constant daily *want* of a protecting arm—a strengthening *mind* in the trials which the *world* presents— nor what the heart becomes when domestic sympathies—griefs and joys do not hourly keep it alive—Is it not the unacknowledged anticipation of these natural claims and emotions which forms our early existence, unconsciously perhaps but not the less entirely. I was still young and ardent, and scarcely aware of their full value to life—when I felt called upon to relinquish such. . . .[28]

Despite her choice, Gilpin retained a domestic and affectionate nature and fully expected to exercise it in teaching. She begged duPont to have her friends "undertake for me" and provide some "healthful occupation." For "the fear *will* arise that the strength of my mind will give way unless thought finds a channel away from self."[29] Gilpin, like other single women, linked her mental and physical well-being to the stimulation of a vocational life.

Even as she despaired, however, a healthy and determined part of Gilpin reasserted itself:

I cannot be unaware that my creator has endowed me with capacity and I am sometimes astonished at the vigor it maintains after all it has undergone. I know likewise that it requires exercise, and is capable of far more than it has yet done for I know that the same circumstances which render my path a difficult one, have caused me to conceal and depress my faculties and power of understanding rather than to bring them forward and use them as I should naturally have done.

Mary cautioned Sophia not to take this assessment of her gifts as evidence of vanity. She did not feel vain; she felt humble in the face of the little she had accomplished in life. She did not seek a position out of pride or a desire to display herself; she wanted to "labor and feel that some good purpose" was effected.[30]

Sophia duPont urged Mary S. Gilpin to commit herself to a sanitorium where she might retire, contemplate, and come to see the error of her ways, thus planting the seed that would bear fruit seven years later. Although Mary thanked her for the concern, she argued "that the necessity for this might be saved by a timely removal of the harassing fears and anticipations which I seek to shun in a diligent, retired occupation and regular life." Was she asking so much, she wondered? She sought only "what you yourself and most of my young friends enjoy, only that wanting the same immediate ties [the affections of husband and children], the objects of my care must be drawn together."[31] Thus Mary explained her emotional needs in domestic terms to a very traditional woman. This was hardly a subterfuge or a manipulation, for Gilpin saw herself as a woman with feminine longings and needs, if unfeminine ambitions and aspirations.

Gilpin's depression continued through the winter of 1844. She tried to work while in the country and penned a review of a book of poetry by Margaret Davidson. Back under the scrutiny of friends and family in Philadelphia, however, Gilpin felt her inspiration and motivation dissipate. She anticipated sending her article to the *Southern Literary Messenger*, but took so long to revise it that it was no longer timely. "I should have been glad to have read it to you," she wrote to duPont, "because I am a good deal acted upon by sympathy, the thought that a friend is feeling an interest in a thing sometimes gives me an impulse, which otherwise I have not." The trusting offer, made to one who abhorred Gilpin's desire to publish, demonstrates either Gilpin's misapprehension of duPont's attitude or her desire to incite a response from her. The cumulative effect of the disapproval which Gilpin met was to induce retreat from creative or analytical writing. "I do not feel up to anything more intellectual than translating or copying," she confessed.[32]

Mary continued to search for an appropriate sphere despite the lack of support she received. She had a letter from Columbia, Missouri, offering her a possible teaching position. She avidly pursued the job through the offices of the visiting bishop of Missouri. When neither the bishop nor Gilpin could obtain specifics, she turned to Bishop Lee of Wilmington and explored the possibility of developing a religious school under his auspices. In preparation for such a task, she visited parochial and black schools in and around Philadelphia. Exhilarated by these examples of the "missionary spirit," Gilpin wrote: "never have I felt more the all absorbing importance of doing *all* we can, and of expanding our ideas and hearts to see how much more we *might* do than we do—of really *working* before the night comes."[33]

By late May of 1845, after several bouts of illness (induced perhaps by the anxiety of again committing herself to an educational enterprise), Gilpin had gathered five students with whom to begin her Wilmington school. The small number bothered her, and she questioned the wisdom of investing in desks, books, and a stove on such a slim margin. She hoped, however, that word of mouth and the bishop's support would expand the numbers of her scholars.[34]

The enterprise never flourished. Sophia brought to Mary's attention the concerns expressed by several parents. She blamed Mary's "unfortunate want of tact and practical knowledge of the world" for the fact that the school remained so small despite Mary's "superior teaching." Mary remonstrated that while she was willing openly to discuss or meet any reasonable parental objection, there was a limit beyond which compromise with her methods would subvert her entire system.[35] Clementina Smith, saddened that people "could not make allowances for Mary's eccentricities" and fearing a relapse of ill-health, advised Mary to give up teaching and go live with her mother. Mary believed that her sister Sarah had contributed to the misunderstandings swirling around her and rejected the idea of living at home. "I feel that it is subjecting myself to a sort of power which is not good, and which I have had gradually to escape from."[36]

Although she withdrew from teaching, Mary could not abandon the idea that it was her calling. "I have passed through some very discouraging and depressed hours—not as to the main feature of my occupation which satisfies me that my views for present and future usefulness are well founded—but as to the isolation of my position which diminishes the effect of all my efforts, whilst it causes too heavy a drain on my physical and mental powers for making them." Gilpin lacked those support networks which reinforced the labors of the antislavery sisterhood. Seeing such support of women's teaching in the Roman Catholic church, Gilpin wondered why Episcopalians did not provide in the same way for the education of their young through the good offices of female nuns and laity.[37] Although Bishop Lee listened to Mary's ideas, he proved either unable or unwilling to provide emotional, financial, or institutional support for her school. Perhaps he had no wish to take sides in a parish dispute. In any case, the circumstance further isolated Gilpin.

In early 1846 Mary was offered a position at an academy in Marietta, Georgia. Although she preferred to stay in Delaware or Pennsylvania, she accepted the job. It had the merits of little capital risk, high status (an administrative post heading the female department), and the security of an established niche in the community. Leave-taking from friends, family, and the Brandywine proved stressful. Gilpin suffered acute attacks of self-doubt. She made recriminations against family and friends that seem largely to have stemmed from her forebodings of loneliness.

Yet distance afforded Mary some peace. For the first time, and due largely to her warm reception in Marietta, she recognized the full measure of her "betrayal" by her sister and friends, whose disapproval of her calling had caused her such anguish. She wrote duPont, refuting her intimations that she lacked proper religious feeling. Mary could not accept Sophia's belief that she had brought her problems upon herself because she did not bend to God's will in the true spirit of Christian and female submissiveness. She rejected Sophia's counsel that she meditate upon her deficiencies and pray for humble acceptance of her place. She had reason to fear "the solitary exercise of [the] mind upon itself," and was persuaded "that only by going out of [her]self *could* [she] be the means of conveying benefit to others." Her wish for an occupation was "no whim or chimera," she maintained, but rather a "settled conviction" arising out of her rejection of marriage and domesticity and the "knowledge that [her] nature needed something to replace them."[38]

Gilpin's association with the Scott school in Georgia lasted almost eight months. It ended when the school closed after losing students to a newly opened Catholic school. Gilpin began plans for an infant school but collapsed under the emotional strain of her lost position. She returned briefly to Delaware but found that family "influences" afforded her no rest. Although she tried to submerge her anger with Sarah for the sake of family peace, the effort only increased her level of stress. Her nervous headaches returned. As she put it, "The suppression [of my feelings] has seemed to destroy inward sensibility, and to cause a hopelessness which, restraining prayer, takes away strength, and gives a bewildered sensation which I cannot dwell on as the precursor of more serious derangement of mind." Recognizing that her mental health required distance from her family, Mary returned to Georgia, determined to undertake her "Children's Lyceum."[39]

Gilpin spent six months at this task. During this time she experienced renewed health and vigor. She attributed this state primarily to mountain air, sunshine, and well-water; but she knew that other factors played a role: "When released from the fear of clashing with views of others with which I *could not* agree, I found the task of freely acting out my own and making them acceptable comparatively easy."[40]

For reasons left unstated in her correspondence, Gilpin returned to Philadelphia. She anticipated an attack on her newly won self-esteem and pleaded with duPont to understand the source of her "masculine" persona. "I would ask you *not* to rail in faithfulness as to such faults as your eye may perceive or your spirit discern to have risen up or gained ground in me during a period of contact with comparative strangers," she begged, "and under circumstances where it has been *a duty* rather to *lead* than follow the ideas and experience of others."[41] Gilpin recognized that her success in Georgia had changed her, and she clearly expected to be criticized for it. She could not find within herself the strength to fend off such criticism.

Home again, Gilpin continued to search for a place to exercise her mind and utilize her talents. On hearing a missionary to the Cherokee lecture, she felt that missionary teaching might prove the answer. True to her desires for status and position, she proposed to found a training institute to prepare young women for the field rather than to undertake such a course herself. In preparation for her school, she traveled to Indian reservations and teacher-training institutes in order to learn as much as possible.[42]

She and Sophia again took up their old argument about the source and cure for Mary's discontent. Wrote Gilpin, "[Y]ou bade me strive 'for that peace which has hither to been a stranger to your bosom'—and because I had once used the word *ambition,* you seemed to think this unduly robbing me habitually of a better portion." She had known both the peace of a rich spiritual life and various "trials of faith." Some of the latter, she informed her friend, must be unknown to the likes of one who experienced "outward encouragement and sympathy" from so many. Unlike Sophia, she had been "silenced and at once crushed back within by abrupt charges of vanity—self-sufficiency, and hypocrisy."[43] Mary tried to explain that the source of her depressions and religious crises ("irritations") lay in having been so misconstrued. "I think I must tell you," she wrote, "that my self-examinations on that ambition of which I spoke, have not been unsatisfactory or self-reproaching." "[F]rom a child I do not recall my aspirations to have been of a personal aggrandizement—so much as an impulse leading me on to strive—not *humbly* then certainly—but *generously* and *justly* for those attainments—which I now see to have been as a preparation for what I have since been led on to step by step."[44] But Sophia duPont neither understood nor sympathized with Mary S. Gilpin. To do so would have been to undermine her own sense of woman's lot in life and the redemptive value of female suffering in marriage and childbirth.[45]

By 1851 Gilpin had arranged through Bishop Lee to develop her missionary training school. Whatever had caused him to withdraw support from her earlier venture, it did not close his mind to her. She hoped that affiliation with the church would ensure success, but her letters indicate a continuing sense of isolation. Even though she felt the support of Clementina and Harriet Smith, she shriveled under the disapproval of Sophia duPont. In May, Mary wrote to Sophia, "You say also that 'as usual, you view things very differently from me' which as it is a phrase with which you have generally wound up our conversations of a serious kind for the last ten years—or since you have found me exercising freedom of thought and speech, I am not surprised by." Gilpin attributed these differences to their two different spheres "of observation and information." Having seen something of the world, she felt that her opinions were rooted in experience, while the domestic Sophia remained dependent upon others for their observations and assessments of public issues.[46]

Gilpin began the painful process of withdrawing her trust and love from this circle of friends, and from duPont in particular. She suspected that Sophia viewed her own opinions not only as more proper than Mary's but also as more moral. She felt that the long-standing nature of her vocational commitment indicated its essential sincerity and correctness. "It could scarcely be anything but the inward and not to be resisted conviction that I *ought* to think and speak as I felt, without a *chief* regard to what others might think of it." Mary thanked Sophia for the kindnesses and attentions she had received at her hands over the years. She acknowledged again the love that had first inspired her to adopt Sophia's name as her own. But she regretted her friend's interpretation of her problems and rued Sophia's unwillingness to validate the ideas, experiences, needs, or behavior of one so different from herself. "If instead of personal pity, showing you thought me imaginative and at fault—you could have aided in giving me some effective occupation for others, their good and my own might have been secured." DuPont's view of woman's suffering lot offended Gilpin, for she felt that her suffering had been gratuitous, demoralizing, and unnecessary, providing no means of transcendence, no avenue for redemption or grace.[47]

Mary urged Sophia to be noble, just, and generous—so to redeem their long association. "You once soothed and cheered me when much depressed, by saying I had stimulated you to good," she wrote. "Indeed, I brought with me from England the most earnest desire and purpose to effect it, and perhaps an over-anxiety to do so may have become self-will." Gilpin conceded the possibility that the objects placed in her path might have been intended to humble her. But that, she felt, was not Sophia's place to judge. She sought a rededication to principle on both sides: "What I cannot effect, let others undertake and let us be again united in intention and object and feeling, without regarding too much any natural differences of temperament and disposition."[48]

When the teaching institute failed and the church severed its connection with Gilpin, Mary believed that Sophia had had something to do with the conflict. She sent her an extended letter clarifying her thoughts about their relationship and accusing duPont of hypocrisy, self-righteousness, and narrow-mindedness. "Never after our mere girlhood had passed, was your feeling towards me that of *free* and cordial affection: look at it, and you will see how it became one which you forced yourself to as a sort of duty—and as a sort of meritorious work towards me." She refused to grant duPont homage. "Do not mistake your office," she wrote, "and think you have a sort of justice to measure out, and that you can be the arbiter of others' causes and motives of conduct."[49] Gilpin expressed the hope that they could renew their affection but expected that it could not be done. She was right; the correspondence faded.

Mary S. Gilpin tried to revive her teacher-training institute in Washington, D.C. She gathered testimonials from prominent political and religious figures: President Millard Fillmore, Secretary of State Daniel Webster, Secretary of the Treasury Thomas Corwin, Secretary of the Navy William Graham, Secretary of the Interior Alexander Stuart, Supreme Court Justice Wayne, Horace Mann, and various congressmen and rectors. She presented the prospectus to Walter Lenox, district mayor, and various councils and boards early in 1852.[50] But she lacked the necessary financial, physical, and emotional resources to succeed.

Not long thereafter, following her fortieth birthday, Gilpin entered the mental asylum of the Pennsylvania Hospital under the care of the well-known Dr. Thomas Story Kirkbride. She had no visitors but seemed to fare well under the asylum regimen of structured activity, physical exercise, and kindness.[51] She left after a few months, moving to the health resort at Cape May for a rest treatment of bathing and salt air.

Information on Mary S. Gilpin's later life is limited. There is a vague reference to her as a patient of a New York doctor in 1857, and evidence that she moved south during the Civil War.[52] She apparently lived with her married sister, Elizabeth Maury, and seems to have become a supporter of states' rights. After the war, she traveled. Living in Italy for a time, she adopted a daughter. Nothing is known of the child's fate.

An Englishwoman writing for a Philadelphia newspaper a decade later claimed to have found Gilpin in a far northwestern Indian village, living in a dilapidated hut, surrounded by her beloved Greek and Latin library.[53] Strange as it may seem, her earlier letters suggest a subconscious link between her state of mind and the icy environment of the northern frontier. Late in 1844, Gilpin had written about her alienation from Philadelphia social life in the following terms:

I find myself with regard to my warmer and most heart-felt sensations—among icicles—not to be thawed by any amount of sunshine I can bring: those I meet are not to be moved from one beaten track of feeling or opinion . . . and this is of so constrained and narrow an order that I cannot for my life keep on the track: it seems like clamping myself down and going back years and years in my own experience on almost any topic or information, or intermingling of sentiments.

Gilpin felt that whenever she advanced an idea or an observation it was met by a cold, vacant, or surprised stare. "It seems to me just like those keen frosty days in winter when the bright sun shines its best, and yet can make no impression on the ice."[54] Perhaps Gilpin finally stopped trying to thaw the ice around her and went north, feeling more at home in a land of ice, among a strange people with whom she shared not even a language. There, at least, was no pretense of common culture and shared sentiment. Surrounded by her books, thinking her own thoughts, she may have experienced comfort in just being herself. Perhaps in this way she finally enacted the eccentric role that family and friends had ascribed to her.

Mary ended her days in Denver, Colorado, in the home of her brother, Governor William Gilpin. He and his wife Julia had a violent and very public separation during the course of which three of their six children

(Marie, William, and Louis) were forcibly removed from their mother's care. Governor Gilpin wrote to Mary during the several years of his separation and custody battle, asking her to come care for the children. He had written a decade earlier urging her to come and "assist in the *planting and building* of empire." "I need familiar assistance, such as you have the ability, and ought to have the overpowering inspiration to contribute."[55] Later, when the two siblings quarreled over her attempts to leave his household, William claimed that he had brought Mary to Denver at the request of a clergyman who had found her on an Indian reservation, and that she had been insane for forty years. Mary countered that her brother had held her prisoner for her money. Mary S. Gilpin died shortly afterward, in 1891.

----◄●►----

Not a comfortable woman to be around, Mary Sophia Gilpin was unconventional, willful, opinionated, obstinate, ambitious, loquacious, self-concerned, independent-minded, and self-indulgent. She was also frustrated, vulnerable, lonely, and driven. There is nothing in her personal documents, however, to substantiate her brother's self-serving charge of insanity. A man with her character would certainly have made a place for himself in antebellum America. Her brothers did, most successfully. A spinster who curbed her ambition and adopted a more feminine persona would also have had a place, as did her friend Clementina Smith. Gilpin's periodic depressions, her anxiety attacks, and her hospitalization issued from the constriction of her vocational impulse by her culture, her church, and her community; from the slandering of her character, femininity, and spirituality by her family and friends; and from the repeated obstruction of her independence and intellectual development.

Gilpin ultimately freed herself from the environment that so confined her. She had not the resources, however, to make the break a liberating one. Instead she succumbed to, or perhaps adopted, the role of eccentric old maid. Her behavior, however, had a certain integrity. The moral and cognitive framework within which Mary Gilpin happened to live decried female autonomy and ambition. It is not surprising, then, to find her channeling her resistance to this framework into eccentricity, after long and unsuccessful attempts to invest her energy and talent more constructively.

10

"The Great Social Disease"

On Women and Independence

Women holding a wide variety of political perspectives felt that the increase in single women over the course of the nineteenth century was a healthy sign of women's move toward equality and advancement. Alice Cary, in her address as first president of the New York Women's club Sorosis, proposed in 1868 the following as an agenda for the club women:

the inculcation of deeper and broader ideas among women . . . to teach them to think for themselves, and get their opinions at first hand, not so much because it is their right, as because it is their duty . . . to open out new avenues of employment to women, to make them less dependent and less burdensome, to lift them out of unwomanly self-distrust and disqualifying diffidence, into womanly self-respect and self-knowledge. . . .

Harriot Hunt thought that women should be trained and educated to be self-reliant so that they could make a choice as to whether or whom to marry, a choice based on love and reason rather than necessity. "May it not be affirmed that the prevalent custom of . . . bringing [women] up without an occupation, profession, or employment, and thus leaving them dependent on anybody but themselves—is an enormous evil, and an unpardonable sin." Mary Livermore agreed that women should be educated to be independent and trained in self-reliance. "As the theory that 'all men support all women' does not fit the facts it is time for us to reform our theory as well as our practice. I would give to all girls equal intellectual and industrial training with boys."[1]

Many, however, worried about increasing numbers of single women in America. They began to define singlehood as a social problem of significant proportions. Considerable public discussion followed. "Why is the single life becoming so general?" queried one. "What should we do with our surplus daughters?" asked another.[2] In 1867, the Reverend John Todd spoke to the heart of the matter by saying: "The root of the great error of our day is, that *woman is to be made independent and self-supporting—*

precisely what she never can be, because God never designed she should be. Her support, her dignity, her beauty, her honor, and happiness lie in her dependence as wife, mother, and daughter. Any other theory is rebellion against God's law of the sexes, against marriage, which it assails in its fundamental principles, and against the family organization, the holiest thing that is left from Eden."[3]

Concern about the increasing instability of sex roles and the growing feminist agitation against the exploitation of women in marriage focused attention on the "independent," or unmarried, woman. Women living outside the control of men threatened a gender structure which had subordinated women. Increasingly, then, in the last third of the nineteenth century the singlehood of women became a politically charged issue from which it was clearly understood that spinsterhood and independence were linked and, furthermore, that the pursuit of female autonomy comprised an attack on male hegemony. This recognition inspired a political and cultural backlash which, in the 1920s, returned women to marriage and domesticity.

A number of changes in the decades following the Civil War contributed to this social milieu. One of the most important was the burgeoning of female education in all regions of the country. There emerged in New England a number of private institutions—Vassar in 1865, Smith and Wellesley in 1875. The South first produced a state-funded institution for women's higher education in the State Industrial Institute and College of Mississippi, established by the Mississippi state legislature in 1884. The Morrill Act of 1862 established land-grant colleges as agricultural and mechanical schools in the West and Midwest. By legislation, women were to be admitted to these on the same terms as men. Thus women entered the University of Colorado, for example, at its founding in 1876. By 1900 all but three state universities were admitting women (Virginia, Georgia, and Louisiana), and by 1910 women comprised 30.4 percent of those enrolled in colleges, universities, and technical schools. The secondary school system also grew rapidly. From 1890 to 1920, women comprised 55 percent of all high school students and 60 percent of all high school graduates.[4] But the education of women, and particularly the stated goal of feminists for an education equal to that of men, raised serious qualms in the minds of many educators and physicians. They wrote about the dangers to the mental and physical health of women who diverted too much blood from their reproductive organs and sent it to their brains to fuel their study.

Edward Clarke's famous 1873 treatise *Sex in Education; or, A Fair Chance for the Girls* warned that the female brain could not tolerate the same course of study as the male. "The system never does two things well at the same time," he wrote. "The muscles and the brain cannot functionate in the best way at the same moment." During puberty, then, girls had to be particularly careful to consolidate their energy, putting it into their physical development toward womanhood. In 1879, the renowned gynecologist Thomas A. Emmet recommended that "to reach the highest point of physical development the young girl in the better classes of society should pass the year before puberty and some two years afterwards free from all exciting influences. . . . Her mind should be occupied by a very moderate amount of study, with frequent intervals of a few moments each, passed when possible in the recumbent position, until her system becomes accustomed to the new order of life."[5]

Embued with such ideas, it is not surprising to find a young, gifted, and soon-to-be eminent gynecologist beginning his practice with considerable concern about the effects of study on his young, educated working patients. Richard L. Dickinson did not question innate female intellectual ability or the viability for single women of vocations such as nursing, teaching, and religious or social work. Yet he firmly believed that mental caliber could not be isolated from emotional or physical life and therefore discouraged female scholarship on the ground that "scholarship takes all." In women, "what the emotions could perceive and the mind plan the physical resources could not execute." Female physiology could not "carry on at boiling point long enough, the sustained effort necessary to original work. The needs of the organism seemed to require modifications of the grind toward success which man does not require."[6]

If women did not modify their course, then they would find themselves transformed through its influences. Dickinson reflected the mid-nineteenth-century belief in the sympathetic interplay of mind and body. Should women pursue intellectual development at the expense of physical maturation, the result could only be their masculinization. Clarke himself had forecast the masculinization of the female intellectual, the "hermaphrodite in mind." Although she successfully competed with men by taking up first their study and then their work, she lost both her femininity and the function of her female organs in so doing.[7]

Anxiety about the masculinization of intellectual women was fed by the medical fraternity's conclusions about the physical implications of longterm celibacy for this growing group of unwed, educated daughters. In the postwar period, physicians and biological scientists came to believe in the prominence of the womb in shaping female physical, emotional, and psychological makeup. The woman whose reproductive organs were not fully developed or, once developed went unused, would experience the atrophy and derangement of those functions. A painful menopause was the presumed consequence of reproductive organs that were not regularly bathed in male semen.[8]

Increasingly, the medical fraternity expanded their litany of ills, suggesting that abstinence incurred dysfunction and disease not only in the sexual organs but elsewhere as well. A spinster could look forward to a shorter life span, for example. Warned one physician, "Very carefully prepared statistics show that between the ages of twenty and forty-five years, more unmarried women die than married, and no instance of remarkable longevity in an old maid is known." Celibacy might also lead to insanity: "throughout the civilized world there are every where three to four single to one married woman in the establishments for the insane" and "of those unfortunates who, out of despair or disgust at the world, jump from bridges, or take arsenic, or hang themselves . . . nearly two-thirds are unmarried and in some years nearly *three-fourths.*"[9] Thus, the intellectual daughter would become an old maid, having lost both female attraction and function. A withered being, a masculine female, the old maid must be a degenerate creature because of her abstinence and the abuse or misuse of her "life force." So, by the end of the century, the single state was no longer blessed but cursed. Celibacy became the "great social disease," its consequences feared both because of the large numbers afflicted with it and because of their growing impact on public life.

Changing attitudes toward singlehood were closely related to changes in the structure and meaning of marriage. The expectations that men and women held of the marital relationship shifted in the last third of the century. Marriage was no longer merely affectionate, it was now an exclusive and intense emotional relationship. The new ideal also emphasized the friendship and togetherness of husband and wife. The modern woman looked forward to marriage. It provided her with an opportunity to participate equally in life's major adventure. Marriage was to be that "perfect consummation of both personalities." It would "involve every phase of mutual living." Women expected to be the partners of tender men, to be mutually engaged in providing an appropriate environment in which to raise their children. No longer need they depend upon a male protector/provider. Now they would share the responsibilities, the joys, and sorrows of life with a partner.[10] But the "companionate marriage" was not necessarily mutual or equalitarian. Many women were to be disappointed when the promise did not match reality.

Men, too, had new ideas about marriage. Having lost the authority of their role as pater familias, they increasingly sought the nurturance of their wives as a substitute for submissiveness. A man looked forward to sharing the trials and tribulations of life with a soft-voiced woman who would pillow his burdened head and heart on her bosom. She would be an efficient housekeeper and not nag about money or household details. She would have the time and temperament for a bit of fun, too, and discreet sexual romping.[11] Displays of independence in women threatened this prescription for male/female relationships. Spinsterhood clearly challenged the male need by refusing to meet it or to legitimate its demands on women.

Women's separate wages provided a degree of financial independence that might lure the young or provide alternatives to the unhappily married. And suggestions of premarital and extramarital sex surrounded the single woman with an aura of the illicit. Her potential availability was both tempting and threatening.

Divorce and the control of contraception became major marital battle-grounds in the last third of the century. Divorce was more accessible and acceptable. It enabled women to make choices about their relationships throughout the life cycle, and to leave those marriages which no longer proved satisfying or fulfilling. In 1860, almost two-thirds of divorces were granted to women, and this proportion continued to rise. In 1870, only 1.5 divorces were obtained per thousand eligible persons. The figure doubled by 1890 to 3.0, was 4.5 by 1910, and dramatically increased to 7.7 in the next ten years. Marriage did not meet the expectations of some, and they acted to escape it. [12]

Falling fertility rates also drew public attention. Increased access to means of preventing conception provided women with some control over their bodies and allowed them to separate sexual activity from pregnancy. Birth control clearly worked among the upper segments of American soci-ety and among the more educated population. A study by the Association of Collegiate Alumnae in 1885 showed that only 68 percent of married college graduates bore children. Most of these bore only one or two when 92 percent of married women in America were bearing three to four children each. Furthermore, although some 90 percent of American women married, only 68 percent of upper-middle-class women married, and far fewer among the college-educated. [13] In the context of a debate on the future of the family, inflamed by the feminist critique of marriage and the social purity legislation (which controlled prostitution, censored birth-control devices and information, and found certain sex-education materi-als obscene), the decline in fertility and increase in divorce rates became highly political issues. [14]

Increased immigration and high birthrates among Catholic and Eastern European immigrants and blacks raised the specter of racial decay or, worse, race "suicide" by America's native-born, white, Protestant, edu-cated elite. President Theodore Roosevelt declared vehemently in letters to women's magazines, public speeches, and addresses to legislators and businessmen that "a race is worthless and contemptible if its men cease to be willing and able to work hard and, at need, to fight hard, and if its women cease to breed freely." Woman's responsibility to her race, God, and country was perfectly clear to Roosevelt, as was the cost of her abnegation of responsibility. "If a race does not have plenty of children, or if these children do not grow up, or if, when they grow up, they are unhealthy in body or stunted or vicious in mind, then that race is decadent, and no heaping up of wealth, no splendor of monetary prosperity can avail in any degree as offsets."[15]

In the first decade of the twentieth century, people feared that all those unmarried daughters who were getting an education and pursuing an occupation or vocation in the male world of work threatened the gender divisions in American life. And these divisions were held to be the basis of American—indeed Western—civilization and progress. Female careerism joined divorce, low fertility, and higher education as public issues. Roosevelt's aggressive assertion of masculine virility and leadership in public life and his demand that women do their part by breeding children and nurturing men were partly responses to the so-called feminization of the public sphere. Women, and particularly the daughters of the middle and upper classes, were increasingly to be found in the previously male domains of business and the professions. The percentage of female professionals reached a historic peak in the early twentieth century. In 1870 women in the professions comprised only 6.4 percent of the nonagricultural female work force. They numbered 10 percent in 1900 and 13.3 percent by 1920—growing from 92,000 to almost one million strong. New and highly visible white-collar occupations claimed new workers as secretaries and salesgirls.[16] In 1870, fewer than 1 percent of all women in nonagricultural occupations had been employed as clerical workers; by 1920, more than 25 percent of such women, some two million in all, were so employed. The fields of white-collar and professional work were dominated by native-born, white women of native parentage. Although only 34.7 percent of the total female work force, they comprised 51 percent of clerical workers and 68 percent of all female professionals.[17]

Marion Harland bemoaned the "passing of the home daughter," the "restlessness" that had spread through the "mighty" American middle class. Young women were no longer willing to stay at home and wait for marriage. Rather, they chose to go out and seek the independence of a career, leaving their mothers in lonely despair. Carolyn Shipman decried that "spirit of the age" which furnished the single woman with the "charm of a latch-key and the independence it implies, the comfort of one's club or a cozy apartment, the pleasure of mingling with men and women on a plane of business equality, and the accompanying contact with the world which is denied to the 'protected woman.' "[18] Yet the seeming feminization of the public sphere was greatly exaggerated.

Most of the new workers in the labor force were indeed young and single, but they did not pursue careers. Instead, they worked for a short time before marrying. Although there was growth in the percentage of married women workers over the course of the twentieth century, the majority of these were immigrant or black women rather than native-born, white, middle- and upper-class wives. Then, too, the gains made by women in the public sphere were largely accomplished by 1920. The gender division of labor held firm despite the insurgence of women into the paid labor force. Among professional women, the vast majority worked in the less highly paid and high-status occupations of teacher or nurse. Gains made by women in the white-collar fields were most clearly made between 1910 and 1920. There was little expansion in the 1930s, and the status and pay of clerical workers never equaled that of office men.[19]

Also exaggerated was the financial and personal independence of the "new" woman. The vast majority of young working women who entered the paid labor force at the turn of the century did not experience any great expansion of autonomy or independence, as Shipman suggested. They did not have the opportunities for responsibility or advancement which their brothers experienced. Indeed, by the 1930s, writer Lorine Pruette proclaimed a "lost generation" of American girls, who had been "marking time in a world that allowed them neither security nor opportunity. They have not had to confront the earlier feminist choice of career versus home of their own for many of them had a chance at neither."[20]

Obliquely, and sometimes directly, public discussion of the perils of modern life became a debate on female singlehood. The issues of careerism, education, divorce, declining marriage and fertility—all, to one extent or another, reflected concern about the unmarried daughters of middle- and upper-class America. Several well-known and well-read female journalists engaged in a largely futile attempt to recast the shape of the argument. Ida Tarbell, for example, the infamous muckraking author of the 1904 study The History of the Standard Oil Company and a feature writer for McClure's Magazine, attacked as premature the death knell for the American family as an institution and for native-born, white Americans as trend-setters and policymakers. In the Woman's Home Companion, she argued that women married more freely in the 1910s than they had in 1890 or 1900: some 70 percent of women over the age of fifteen, 81.5 percent of women over twenty, and 86.7 percent of women over twenty-five married. She maintained that the 1900 census contradicted fears that the fecundity of "lower races" (Negro, Native American, and immigrant) had outstripped that of the "true American," causing a decline not only in numbers and position but also influence. She concluded that the true American "was holding his own, making a better showing than at any time since 1870."[21]

Tarbell believed that concern about the feminization of the public sphere was due to the fact that industrial workers and businesswomen were more visible when gathered together in the urban marketplace than when they had canned, woven, and sewn in the isolation and privacy of their own homes. Women's activities were not new, she argued, rather "that she talks, thinks, and wants things that apparently never interested her before. But this is true of men as of women. She, like him, is reacting to a new vision of the possibilities of life. . . . [Women] are putting their hands to new tasks, their heads to new thoughts . . . [but] when you come down to the actual facts . . . you find that whatever the stir on the surface, below, the same great occupation, the woman's profession, claims her as it always has." The "business of being a woman" was still, in her opinion, that of managing to feed, clothe, shelter, nurse, and nurture humankind.[22]

Written by a highly educated and respected journalist, a woman who thought of herself as a feminist (though not a suffragist), these articles reflect considerable ambivalence. Tarbell herself never married—indeed, she prayed from the age of fourteen for God to keep her from marriage. "I could never marry," she wrote. "It would interfere with my plan; it would fetter my freedom." She recognized that singlehood was still the key to female independence. "Four hundred years ago a woman sought celibacy as an escape from sin. Today she adopts it to escape inferiority and servitude; superiority and freedom her aim."[23]

Agnes Repplier, the well-known and much honored biographer and essayist, a frequent contributor to The Atlantic Monthly and The Catholic World, gave a spirited defense of spinsterhood in a 1904 issue of Harper's Bazar. Like Tarbell, Repplier associated her spinsterhood with autonomy and self-development. To those who expected women always to efface themselves in deference to others, Repplier wrote, "But what if she honestly prefers her own interests—a not uncommon attitude of mind? . . . What if, holding her life in her two hands, and knowing it to be her only real possession, she disposes of it in the way she feels will give her most content, swimming smoothly in the stream of her own nature, and clearly aware that happiness lies in the development of her individual tastes and acquirements?" She argued that "the outcry against celibacy as a 'great social disease' is louder than the situation warrants."

It is not profane to plan or to advance an individual career. We do not insult Providence by endeavoring to provide for ourselves. And if the restlessness of modern life impels women of independent fortune to enter congenial fields of work, the freedom to do this thing is their birthright and prerogative. We can no more sweep back the rising tide of interests and ambitions than we can sweep back the waves of the Atlantic.

Repplier found it ridiculous either to glorify or to decry the rate of singlehood. To her mind, both the single and married just followed their destiny in an effort to fit themselves to the style of life for which they were most suited. Neither state called in and of itself for commiseration nor implied moral deterioration, and both offered a means of adding to the happiness of self and the "gayety of earth."[24]

Anna Garlin Spencer emphasized the service that modern spinsters performed. She noted that:

The spinster who is succeeding in efficient and well-paid work in any intellectual or business line, in free and open competition with men and through a long course of uninterrupted personal achievement, is doing an inestimable service to her sex and to society by providing beyond peradventure that the higher education of women and the vocational independency and the economic security of women are socially worth while. Such successful work of the unmarried woman is showing clearly that women in general only lack opportunity and preparation to do a fair share of the world's most esteemed work.

Spencer, however, had no desire to see the perpetuation of "a large class of disengaged or detached women . . . to do the larger social work of womanhood," for "it is the normal and the average that in the long run must serve the purposes of social uplift. The unusual and the 'variant' may serve peculiarly some preparatory process for a higher plane of common life." "Women," she wrote,

must enter all the higher paths of intellectual life and achievement through the hard and fast lines of specialization which men have laid down for their own guidance; and often to the narrowing and mechanizing of the feminine nature. This means that the women who "survive" and succeed in the competitive struggle with men for positions of place and financial power must be, for the most part, those to whom the purely intellectual or the personally ambitious makes strongest appeal. This means again that in those women who can most easily maintain a lifelong and successful equality of effort with men . . . the individuating sense must be keen, and the power of grasping all those opportunities that make for self-advantage strong. This means again that in the long reaches of selective influences, should the day of the spinster continue unchanged by any new social impulse, we might breed a "detached class of women," who should form the intellectual and economic elite of the sex, and leave marriage and maternity for the less developed woman.

Hence Garlin hoped that "the day of the spinster [would be] but a bridge of feminine achievement—which shall connect the merely good mother with the mother that shall be both wise and good."[25] While she believed in the expansion of woman's sphere and lauded female accomplishment, Garlin also considered individuation and ambition deviant ("varient") and feared to perpetuate independence in masculinized spinsters.

Underlying Garlin's fears, Repplier's caustic wit, and Tarbell's defensiveness was the increasing sexualization of spinsterhood that began after 1875 and thoroughly colored discussions of single women by the 1920s. The findings of a new field, sexology, helped to shape public attitudes. From the beginning, sexual researchers and their popularizers focused on "abnormal" rather than "normal" expressions of female sexuality. Physicians, sexologists, and psychologists studied and described what were believed to be significant, perhaps epidemic, increases in such practices as autoeroticism (self-stimulation), for example. Masturbation was most often associated with celibacy and the deflection of normal sexual activity in the absence of its proper exercise in the marriage bed.[26]

The sexologists were fascinated by homosexuality, with understanding its origins and implications. The true "invert," according to Havelock Ellis, inherited her "disease." Having come from degenerate stock, she was congenitally "tainted." She was distinguished from the pseudo-invert, who might act like a homosexual but needed only the proper heterosexual stimulus to find her true path. The pseudo-invert was likely to have been led into homosexuality by a true invert or by the feminist movement, which encouraged female independence and self-support. The true invert could be identified by her "more or less distinct trace of masculinity." Specifically, she exhibited a neurotic desire to reject woman's accepted role in marriage and family, and an "inverted" desire for genital sex with other women.[27]

Gradually, the medical, psychological, and scientific literature outlined a pathology infecting "the modern woman"—hermaphroditism. The hermaphrodite of the sexologists and psychologists realized the worst fears of earlier educators. Here indeed was the masculinized woman—for the hermaphrodite was no woman at all, but rather a newly identified, highly deviant third sex. The hermaphrodite combined a female body and genitalia with the male attributes of independence, intelligence, ambition, and love of women.[28] Although the connections were made earlier in Europe, by World War I Americans increasingly linked together lesbianism, feminism, and spinsterhood. All women infected with such "isms" shared certain characteristics, behaviors, or attributes: independence, self-assertion, careerism, devotion to other women, and a rejection of marriage.

In 1901, William L. Howard, an American psychiatrist and disciple of German sexologist Krafft-Ebing, published a novel called *The Perverts* illustrating these ideas. The central character is a diseased Ph.D. feminist named Mizpra, who expresses her congenital "taint" through a twisted personality that delights in tormenting others. Mizpra is clearly a spinster, an independent woman, a career woman, and probably a lesbian. For the less sophisticated reader, Howard draws the following moral:

The female possessed of masculine ideas of independence, the viragint who would sit in the public highways and lift up her pseudo-virile voice, proclaiming her sole right to decide questions of war or religion, or the value of celibacy and the curse of woman's impurity, and that disgusting anti-social being, the female sexual pervert, are simply different degrees of the same class—degenerates.[29]

Wilhelm Stekel's *Frigidity in Woman*, published in this country shortly after World War I, demonstrated the way in which contemporary fears of race suicide, class dilution, sexual deviancy, female careerism, and single-hood could merge into one long litany of dire complaint against "modern womanhood."

Marriage dread and aversion to childbearing afflict particularly our "higher circles." Increasing numbers of girls belonging to the upper strata remain single. Women of culture withdraw more and more from their roles as mothers and wives. They are "emancipated"; they are growing self-reliant, self-sufficient and, economically, too, they are becoming more and more independent of the male. They are accustoming themselves to get along without love, or they pander to love "without issue."

Such women had sex outside of marriage and either used birth-control methods to prevent pregnancy or, as Stekel said, participated in an "appalling increase in morbid, neurotic homosexuality."

What is the result? The lower social strata are rising in power. This would not be unfortunate if their rise would be accompanied by an infusion of new blood. As matters stand, however, this means that the higher classes cease to count in the transmission of ethical acquisitions and cultural refinements; they do not participate in the task of passing on the lighted torch of humanity's progress. It means that our cultural acquisitions are available to individuals and not to the race as a whole. The spiritual aristocracy of the race is dying out. The progress of humanity is being halted.[30]

Celibacy, often a symptom of that new female sexual disease, frigidity, would result in physical and mental degeneracy. Homosexuality and female independence were degenerate in and of themselves. Thus the epidemic of spinsterhood had to be quashed. The progress of civilization and the health of women depended upon it.

The sexologists' belief in the congenital deviancy of homosexuality was replaced in America in the 1920s by the Freudian notion of childhood trauma and arrested development.[31] Freud was more readily accepted in this society than had been the sexologists, and more widely read. After all, Americans understood the concepts of sublimation and repression. They lay deep in the psyche of this essentially Calvinist society whose rapid industrialization owed so much to both. From the 1920s on, the well-read, psychologically sophisticated American assumed that celibacy was not a chosen or healthy state but indicated some subconscious conflict. The repression of normal sexual expression through celibacy resulted in neurosis. In the 1930s, Frances Donovan said of the unmarried "schoolma'm" that her adolescent devotion to study had probably stunted normal development of her emotional life. Having never learned the fine art of romance and having failed at husband hunting, such women were subject to sexual frustration. It was celibacy which gave rise to the "queer teacher" known for her sternness, authoritarianism, and moodiness.[32] And no longer would such a reader accept at face value an assertion such as that made by Vida Scudder in her 1937 autobiography: "a woman's life which sexual interests have never visited is a life neither dull nor empty, nor devoid of romance."[33] Post-Freudian generations assumed that such innocence was a result of either repression or dishonesty and probably indicated latent if not actual homosexuality.

In the early decades of the twentieth century, the American public became fascinated by sex—it chimed "Sex O'Clock in America," quipped William M. Reedy.[34] Popular culture—including films, dress, and dance— all projected a new sexuality. Increasingly the definition of a good marriage included sexual pleasure and fulfillment. However, this new emphasis on sexual expression contained a "heterosexual imperative." The youth culture of the 1920s was given over to the cultivation of heterosexual bonding. Everyone that was anyone engaged in the sexual dance (although good girls did not "go all the way," since the object was matrimony not promiscuity).[35] "Normal" women experienced the same drive for sexual expression as men, and as "normal" women, the object of their passion was male.

In such an atmosphere, the sex life of the unmarried adult was subject to considerable attention and research.[36] Studies by Katherine Bement Davis and Robert L. Dickinson found homosexual activity to be common among young single women, particularly when living or working together. Of her sample of clubwomen and college graduates born about 1880, Davis found that some 50 percent of single and 30 percent of married women had experienced intense emotional relationships with other women. About half of these were "accompanied by mutual masturbation, contact of genital organs or other physical expressions recognized as sexual in character."[37] So, too, Dickinson, who had kept detailed records of patient complaints since the 1880s, found homosexuality to be widespread among his single patients. When he began his practice, it had not occurred to him to ask about sexual activity, even among women living together: celibacy was assumed. He later discovered (how remains unclear) that of the 350 women whose sexual histories he recorded, some 28 had had genital relationships with other women. Among these he found no evidence of congenital malady. Rather, "Good health and steady occupation is the rule; appearance, dress, and social status are without idiosyncrasy and above the average." A number were college graduates engaged in business or professions. Many shared homes and/or finances.[38]

Over the years Dickinson changed his assumptions about what constituted perverse sexual behavior. By 1934, for example, he accepted autoeroticism as a normal expression of sexual feeling. "Homosexuality," he would write, "has been stressed far beyond its numerical significance or its importance as a harmful interference with normal response. Physiology is teaching us that we are all in some degree bisexual and that we possess some sex traits other than those characteristic of our overt type, with two series of stages between extreme masculinity and complete femininity." He believed that, given the frequency of female homosexual experience, "To stamp such activity a 'perversion,' instead of a deviation or deprivation, is to lack a sense of proportion, if not sound judgment." This was a liberal point of view for the time, although one wonders to what extent his readership appreciated (and exactly how they would understand) the technical distinction between perversion and deviation. Yet despite his liberality, even Dickinson found "non-marriage and non-mating a social and biological thwarting," constituting "the frustration of love-comradeship, child-rearing and home-making."[39]

The point here is that the sexualization of singlehood made it difficult for Americans to view spinsterhood as other than threatening. Fears about the sexual and psychological deviancy of single women and the costs of female independence to American family and social life constrained growing female autonomy in America because they cut off the path to autonomy that was singlehood. Women in the twentieth century subscribed to the marital imperative more completely than their nineteenth-century forebears. The proportion of never-married women in America fell precipitously after 1900. Even among the college-educated, the trend was to early marriage. At Vassar, only two in five graduates from the 1870s were married by the age of twenty-seven, but by the 1920s the majority married well before that age. The mean age of marriage fell steadily after 1890 until the 1950s, when it hit an all-time low of 20.2 years.[40] Competition among women for that all-important marriage certificate was fueled by the radical decline in the historic surplus of men in the American population. From a high of 106 in 1910, the sex ratio fell below 100 in 1945, and bottomed out at 95 in 1970.[41]

Harriet Hosmer had honored "every woman who had strength enough to step out of the beaten path when she feels that her walk lies in another; strength enough to stand up and be laughed at if necessary. That is a bitter pill we must all swallow at the beginning; but I regard these pills as tonics quite essential to one's mental salvation." Hosmer believed that she and other independent single women paved the way for those who would come after, and that "in a few years it w[ould] not be thought strange that women should be preachers and sculptors." She thought that each generation would experience fewer and fewer taunts and blows.[42] Instead, women found that they faced not ridicule but more sinister and subtle attacks on their gender and sexuality; for the correlation made between female independence, lesbianism, and singlehood cast doubt on the nature of women's relationships with other women.

Women of the antebellum period, the pioneering spinsters of the late eighteenth and early nineteenth centuries, shared a fundamental gender identity. This sense of their womanhood was a source of great strength to those who broke the common mold. Spinsters, whether domestically or vocationally oriented, shared with married women a common view of what constituted feminine character, virtue, and values. Disagreement over the limits of their "proper" sphere did not undercut their belief that women had something unique and valuable to contribute as women. Now their very womanhood was in question, for single women were viewed as masculinized women or perhaps hermaphrodites. This cut far more deeply into individual self-esteem, gender consciousness, and gender solidarity than anything else had—or perhaps could.

Twentieth-century women, then, became divided into two camps of mutually distrusting and fearful women—heterosexuals and homosexuals. Shattered was the female world that had given birth to early stirrings of female autonomy and had encouraged and empowered women to move into the political, economic, and professional arenas late in the nineteenth century. Sisters no longer lived and worked together as they had in the earlier period. As women increasingly left the family to enter the urban marketplace or university, they went alone, enrolling as individuals. At a time when middle-class daughters left home increasingly early for school or work, the family no longer provided a center for individual development or emotional and intellectual support. It could not offer quite the same buffer between private and public spheres as it had early in the century. Women continued to rely upon and develop female friendships and supports throughout the nineteenth century, but with the attack on the "normalcy" of such relationships, women's mutual trust and love became subject to suspicion. No longer viewed as pure and disinterested, women's relationships with other women were defined as sexual in nature and stigmatized as abnormal, even pathological.

Although slow to develop, the growth of such ideas created disarray and defensiveness in women's colleges and organizations that had inspired and nourished female achievement. It split women's political and professional networks and associations, as women feared to work with other women and distrusted one another's motives and behavior. It encouraged those who feared the homosexual label to marry. It damned to isolation and self-doubt those who pursued their independent course. Women who nourished and supported other women, who relished relationships in which work and intellectual striving were shared, or who pursued a feminist critique of the gender structure in America, would be deemed dangerous and unwomanly.[43] The twentieth-century spinster would find it more difficult to speak positively about her status than had her early-nineteenth-century forebear.

For the most part, these changes did not affect the women of this study, although many lived into the early 1900s. Antebellum women had just ventured on their quest for liberty. A dedication to God, in whose service their talents and abilities were to be developed, justified their move beyond traditional roles. The Cult of Single Blessedness validated their callings and provided social support for their course. They were strengthened and inspired by their relations with other women. Although family and political life, courtship rituals, and economic opportunity were all tainted in the early nineteenth century by male domination and female submission, female relationships were constituted in a somewhat different way on a different basis. Such relationships offered women a separate social, and a distinct conceptual, view of the world which enabled them to form individual identities, develop latent talents, and follow their own ambitions.

Independence for the spinsters of this study was given meaning by the nature of their obligations and their opportunities. Independence was often structured by the interdependence of family and friends. Its expression had to do with the nature of the family, the gender structure of labor and education, and a definition of female sexuality as passionless. These factors continued to structure the meaning of female independence in the early twentieth century; however, their nature changed. The heightened emphasis on sexuality and the definition of heterosexuality as normal colored women's relationships within and without the family. In addition to casting suspicion on female relationships and directing girls into early competition for male attention and approval, it sexualized the father-daughter relationship, ensuring conflict between mothers and daughters and encouraging women to look to men for identity and role.[44]

The pursuit of autonomy in which women engaged in the early nineteenth century slowed down a century later. Although native-born, white, middle-class women of the 1780s generation only dreamed of intellectual expansion, financial independence, and having a home of their own—one hundred years later, women could seriously entertain such options. But while the antebellum spinster engaged in her vocation and pursued independence with the support of other women, those never-married women born in the 1890s or later felt cut off from, or at the very least confused about, that very source of inspiration and mutual aid. The deviancy attached to the twentieth-century single life strongly contrasts with the holiness of the antebellum Cult of Single Blessedness.

Conclusion

Women who came of age in the first half of the nineteenth century found their values and lives shaped by dramatic changes. These influenced the way in which they thought of themselves, the expectations they held for the future, and the kinds of activities in which they hoped to engage. Among the significant developments were new attitudes regarding their nature and role. Women began to think of themselves as individuals with their own identities, goals, rights, and callings separate from those of kin, church, or community and defined by personal needs and desires, not the prescriptions of gender. Women began to express the very human desire to grow, to accomplish, to succeed—they acknowledged ambition, valued independence, and sought autonomy. They wanted to make their own choices, to be responsible for their own achievements and failures, to establish their own priorities, and to enact them. They differed in degree of self-awareness, range of opportunity, and life-style from the women who preceded and were to follow them.

Among the changes in American life that fostered these desires were increasing literacy and the opening of primary and secondary education to women. As they read and wrote, particularly in groups devoted to the purpose, women began to value the intellectual life, to ruminate on ideas, and ultimately to explore their own selves. Changes in family life undercut the patriarchal authority of the father, increased the authority of the mother, and promoted mutuality in marriage. Ideally, marriage became more an affair of the heart than of the pocketbook or lineage, and so more an individual than a social concern. The qualities of an intended spouse and the characteristics of the institution were subject to new scrutiny. As maternal love and parental suasion replaced physical control and paternal domination of children, and as youth began to spend time in institutions other than the family (factories, schools, associations), young men and women experienced a new degree of independence at an earlier age.

With the emergence of industrialization between 1800 and 1820, change came to the workplace—in both the place and the process of production. Production moved from home to factory, where machines replaced hand-tooling. Industrialization opened work outside the home to both men and women. Young women left rural homes in their early teens, moving to manufacturing towns and commercial centers to take work in domestic service, manufacturing, distribution, or teaching. Their work gave them a new sense of independence and freedom, and a degree of control over their earnings. Men's departure from the home to work in factory or office increased the significance of women's work in the home— whether as mother, household manager, or housekeeper. Many sisters and daughters of middling circumstances contributed the fruits of their labor to the family coffer or their brother's advancement by assisting with boarders or taking in laundry, piecework, or scholars. The opening of educational and occupational opportunities increasingly took young males out of the labor market, to be replaced by sisters whose earnings enabled them to secure a foothold for themselves and hoist their kin up the rungs of the class ladder.

Geographic mobility further disrupted the American social order. Made possible by improvements in roads, canals, and railroads and encouraged by the decline of open land in the more settled areas of the Northeast, such mobility tempted young people to leave their birthplaces. Regional markets drew labor from one place to another, establishing short-term variations in sex ratios and disrupting traditional courtship practices.

Ideas also contributed to a changing America. In the wake of both political and industrial revolutions, and with the emergence of romanticism, women as well as men thought in individualistic terms about the uniqueness of personality and the importance of exercising one's own will, about fostering self-awareness and encouraging self-expression, about promoting self-reliance, about the need to develop a personal identity and adopt an individual calling suited to one's own talents and abilities. The rise of the Cult of Domesticity and the ideas of female purity and passionlessness contributed to an atmosphere in which singlehood came to be viewed as potentially both an individual and a social good. A Cult of Single Blessedness emerged which legitimated the decision of an increasing number of upper- and middle-class women to remain unmarried.

Singlehood meant different things to different people. To some it was a necessity—the product of a family strategy or the result of family circumstances that required a daughter's labor and services beyond the age of marital eligibility. The new emphasis on the special nature of childhood stressed that couples should have fewer progeny and give them more care. The singlehood of daughters enabled families to provide more inheritance to these offspring, thereby consolidating family status and wealth. Such daughters served a new purpose within an old tradition—they subsumed their individuality to the family in its wish or need to conserve or expand its resources. Indigent, sickly, or elderly parents required a daughter's attention more than a son's labor at a time when sons contributed money to support them in old age rather than taking over the family homestead or shop.

While some women experienced singlehood as the result of personal tragedy or limited opportunity, still others remained single more out of choice than chance. A woman might exercise a degree of "choice" for any number of reasons. Some found no appropriate or desirable suitor. Some feared marriage—the domination of men, the danger of childbirth, the unknown territory of sexual intercourse. There were those who rejected the drudgery of housekeeping for a family in favor of work suited to their inclination or talent. Some sought a sphere of public usefulness; still others aspired to fame or accomplishment in the public sphere. Some would not forsake their premarital independence for the marriage bond or commit themselves to self-sacrifice rather than self-cultivation.

Observation of the women in this study suggests basically four values and objectives that confirmed them in their singlehood: (1) a combination of ambition and service orientations, which took the form of a desire for a life of high purpose devoted to glorious and good deeds; (2) the desire to expand the intellect; (3) a desire to explore, to come to understand, to cultivate, and to revere the self; and (4) a desire to be free and independent. Margaret Fuller set forth the issue most clearly when she wrote that "human beings are not so constituted that they can live without expansion. If they do not get it in one way, they must in another, or perish," for "what Woman needs is not as a woman to act or rule, but as a nature to grow, as an intellect to discern, as a soul to live freely and unimpeded, to unfold such powers as were given her."[1]

Meeting such needs was not ordinarily possible within the bonds of nineteenth-century marriage. The family circle smothered development of the female intellect by fragmenting women's time and attention. Daily chores buried mind and spirit in dust, dishes, and disorder. Once women chose to pursue "Truth," however, they began a journey of self-enlightenment that often led them into the service of God, culture, or community. The freedom to attend to one's calling, to commit time, energy, and thought to one's work, signified one's devotion. The demands of husband and children, of woman's "proper" sphere, prohibited realization of the vocational life. Susan B. Anthony, in advising a niece on her future employment, reminded her that marriage was "an *all absorbing* profession!!"[2]

Lucy Larcom found that her search for self, truth, achievement, and independence could be sustained only in singlehood. Larcom experienced the constriction of thought, movement, and behavior, and the interruption of work that resulted from her acquiescence to custom, structure, routine, or the needs and wants of others. She wrote frequently about her frustration in being caught up in a web of another's making. From Beverly, Massachusetts, her childhood home, she wrote that she loved her home but could not live in it. While treasuring the family circle, she did not wish to remain in it, because "it does not seem to me that I can here develop the utmost that is in me. Ought I to be contented while that feeling remains?" She took pleasure in the company of her nieces and nephews, "although they will break in upon me rather suddenly sometimes." She could not learn "to think my own thoughts in the thick of other people's lives."[3]

Nor was Larcom content to rest in the stifling intellectual atmosphere of Boston and environs. "There is not *air* enough in this part of the world for me. . . . There is so much of custom and established order;—even I hardly dare be myself, for I see written on everybody's face, 'Why dont you do as we do.' " She found little satisfaction at Wheaton Seminary. "It is the hardest work to transfer yourself into somebody's fixed way of doing things! I dont believe I shall ever be very acceptable here; for I am either too old or too stubborn to step out of my own notions and habits." She found no fault with the school's management, she simply could not "fall into an established order. I shall have to be myself or nothing."[4] Larcom's desire for a home of her own (or at least a corner where she might "spin her own web") followed from her need to be her own person, to think her own thoughts, write her own poetry, and commune with her God in her own way.

Despite the financial distress, the professional struggle, and the loneliness of her singlehood, Larcom felt that she had chosen well. According to her namesake and niece, Lucy Larcom Spaulding, she died with the word *freedom* on her lips.[5] Perhaps she spoke in thanksgiving, intending to signify freedom from the pain of her last illness, freedom from financial exigency, or freedom from earthly restraints. (Larcom was a devout Christian and fully believed that she went to a better world.) But *freedom* is not the appropriate word to designate these things: *release*, perhaps, or *relief*. Larcom was a poet—she chose words carefully. She was also a romantic and surely utilized the dramatic weight given to "last words." She died as she had lived, naming the value that dominated her life—"freedom"— meaning liberty, independence, and autonomy.

Many an antebellum spinster, sharing Larcom's values, recognized the centrality of her singlehood in her life's work and meaning. There were certain things single women knew could only be learned and done on one's own. Maria Mitchell penned the following poem to Sarah Shaw in illustration.

> Did you never go home alone, Sarah,
> Its nothing so very bad,
> I've done it a hundred times Sarah
> When there wasn't a man to be had.

> There's a deal to be learned in a midnight walk,
>   When you take it all alone,
> If a gentleman's with you, its talk, talk, talk,
>   You've no eyes and no mind of your own.
>
> But alone, in dark nights when clouds have threatened
>   And you feel a little afraid
> Your senses are all supernaturally quickened
>   You study the light and the shade,
>
> Oh Sarah, there's much unwritten lore
>   Unkenned when others are by.
> Which, if you have no chance to learn before
>   You'll learn when you're old as I.[6]

Mitchell here articulated the importance of being alone for the development of an individual perspective, for extending one's own faculties beyond their usual range, for learning courage and independence, and for identifying one's sources of strength while gaining a feeling for one's own power. Describing them metaphorically in terms of a night's walk home alone, Mitchell believed that such tests were crucial to individual expansion, and particularly to female empowerment.

Such assessments characterize much of the private and public writing of antebellum women. Margaret Fuller spoke of women developing self-reliance and fullness of being. This, she felt, was best done alone. "Those who are not intimately and permanently linked with others, are thrown upon themselves; and, if they do not there find peace and incessant life, there is none to flatter them that they are not very poor, and very mean. A position which so constantly admonishes, may be of inestimable benefit. The person may gain, undistracted by other relationships, a closer communion with the one. Such a use is made of it by saints and sibyls." She argued that, in being alone, an individual has need of fortification and must turn inward for it, to the self and to the Divine Being. "We must have units before we can have union."[7]

Phoebe Cary devoted her favorite poem to "A Woman's Conclusions." In more traditionally religious terms than Fuller's, Cary wrote about the power to resist temptation, the strength to abide in God and to seek out spiritual truth—all of which came through the trials of the single life.

> If I could have known, in the years now gone,
>   The best that a woman comes to know;
> Could have had whatever will make her blest,
>   Or whatever she thinks will make her so:
>
> Have found the highest and purest bliss
>   That the bridal-wreath and ring inclose;
> And gained the one out of all the world,
>   That my heart as well as my reason chose;

And if this had been, and I stood to-night
  By my children, lying asleep in their beds,
And could count in my prayers, for a rosary,
  The shining row of their golden heads;

Yea! I said, if a miracle such as this
  Could be wrought for me, at my bidding, still
I would choose to have my past as it is,
  And to let my future come as it will!

My past is mine, and I take it all;
  Its weakness—its folly, if you please;
Nay, even my sins, if you come to that,
  May have been my helps, not hindrances!

Who knows its strength, by trial, will know
  What strength must be set against a sin;
And how temptation is overcome
  He has learned, who has felt its power within!

And who knows how a life at the last may show?
  Why look at the moon from where we stand!
Opaque, uneven, you say; yet it shines,
  A luminous sphere, complete and grand.

So let my past stand, just as it stands,
  And let me now, as I may, grow old;
I am what I am, and my life for me
  Is the best—or it had not been, I hold.[8]

The antebellum spinster by and large evaluated her chosen state in a positive light. Said Catharine Beecher, "I have been for many years a wanderer without a home, in delicate health, and often baffled in favorite plans of usefulness. And yet my life has been a very happy one, with more enjoyments and fewer trials than most of my friends experience who are surrounded by the largest share of earthly gratifications." Emily Howland saluted eighty full years of singlehood in birthday greetings to peers and friends. To Mary Grew, she wrote: "The largess of life is yours dowered with a brain alive to the issues of your time and heart aglow with service for truth, blessed with a friendship [with Margaret Jones Burleigh] as rare as the friend was noble—your joy is all immortal." With Caroline F. Putnam, she assessed their lives as spinsters: "I believe we have more to make us glad than sad that life has given us of its best in the way of health, opportunity and friends, and however far from our ideal of achievement or in the spiritual life we may feel that we have meant well to humanity and have been generous seekers for what it is good and pleasant to know."[9]

Not all spinsters felt this way. Clementina Smith was disappointed with the degree of independence she actually found in the single life. Catharine

M. Sedgwick, who evaluated her own experience in a light comparable to Howland, still did not recommend it to others; for the single life, as constructed in antebellum America, had severe limitations. Although new occupations for women opened with industrialization and the development of regional markets, these were not careers or professional opportunities. Some women, necessarily spinsters, pursued careers as physicians, reformers, creative artists, intellectuals—but the struggle was enormous, the pay poor, and the numbers few. For the most part, women found that they had to create their own intellectual and institutional support. They were not incorporated into the male courts, hospitals, colleges, or churches. They remained on the periphery, working without the status or resources of male peers. Women, even single women, engaged in vocations, not professions.

Singlehood in antebellum America remained a dependent status defined by the family. No matter what her age, work, or position in the world, the unmarried female was seen (as were all women) in a family context, defined by her primary relationships. She had no husband, but she did have parents, siblings, and kin whose needs, judgments, and demands were believed by all to merit paramount consideration. Eliza Fell, naturalist, acknowledged that, "As is often the case of single ladies, who can and want to be useful, I am prone to be ready at the beck and call of many to serve them, thereby I sometimes find I have allowed an unnecessary enfringement upon my time and pleasure [in botany]."[10] Daughters were in little moral, social, or economic position to command respect and support for their individual course, until and unless family requirements were met.

Last, the single life was shaped by the nature and strength of women's relationships. It was in these relationships, particularly those between siblings, that women learned to individuate. Here they tested ideas, constructed value systems, and devised economic and political strategies for furthering their personal goals. Here they rejoiced in common tongue and shared values. Here they found love, intimacy, nurturing, encouragement, and a sustaining belief in the right and righteousness of their chosen course. Being essentially private and domestic, however, such relationships could not provide the resources available to men in the public sector. These had to await the establishment of women's clubs and colleges after the Civil War.

Antebellum single women entered the public sphere and influenced public life in large numbers and more profoundly than women of an earlier age. Among them were arbiters of public health (Dorothea Dix, Clara Barton, Emily and Elizabeth Blackwell), moral reformers (Mary Grew, Sarah Pugh, Frances Willard), educators (Catharine Beecher, Mary Lyon, Elizabeth Peabody), social workers (Cornelia Hancock, Emily Howland, Ellen Collins), philanthropists (Sophia Smith, Caroline Plummer), missionaries (Fidelia Fiske, Cynthia Farrar), artists, writers and intellectuals (Emily Dickinson, Harriet Hosmer, Frances Bridges, Margaret Fuller). Yet few of these women can be said to have left the domstic sphere entirely, and, of these, fewer still felt comfortable in so doing. The sense of place and role provided by emotional ties with other women, ties rooted in domestic life, remained central to this generation's identity and experience.

Yet though their individual achievements were limited by the structure of antebellum work, family, and gender relations, these women played an important historical role. They were pioneers exploring the boundaries of women's separate sphere. They were among the first to articulate the value of female autonomy, among the first to assert themselves and be recognized as individuals—still female persons, but individuals. These women were highly conscious of the model they would provide for others.[11] They were not always comfortable with their position, but they recognized that in women's progress toward equality there must be a generation or more of independent women to lead the way. Both women and men must be shown, they believed, what women could do on their own.

These women believed in the special qualities of the female character, the greater moral purity and goodness of women. It was up to them to define more comprehensively the nature of woman's sphere. Margaret Fuller said that, while "Marriage is the natural means of forming a sphere, of taking root in the earth; it requires more strength to do this without such an opening." She recognized that many had failed in this effort, and in the process had cast doubt on single men and women as a whole by their partiality, harshness, officiousness, and impertinancy. Nevertheless, she rejoiced in the "increase of the class contemptuously designated as 'old maids,' " and looked to them to "help plac[e] women on the true platform."[12]

The antebellum spinster had specific proposals for institutionalizing that which could best produce female independence and achievement. Graceanna Lewis, for example, produced a plan in 1873 which would assure her own "independence and future usefulness" along with that of other women. She hoped to develop a utopian community of eighty acres at Sunnyside, the family homestead in Media, Pennsylvania. She described the project as "an industrial village where any occupation suitable for a woman to study, may be taught by competent instructors without fear of refusal." The community would admit both men and women "believed to be capable of exercising a healthful moral influence, or imparting energy, ability, and character." Lewis envisioned a setting that would provide for all a nurturing, self-sustaining environment. Mary P. Townsend, who died in Boston in 1868, left $80,000 to found a public home for indigent spinsters. Said one who read the announcement, "I haven't felt so independent in years . . . I speak for the first choice of rooms in the proposed building." Both examples serve to illustrate women's efforts to enact their values outside the structure of the family circle.[13]

Catharine Beecher and Susan B. Anthony, women who shared little else in common politically speaking, both advocated the establishment of female-headed households as a step in the direction of female autonomy and advancement. "In women's transition from the position of subject to sovereign," wrote Susan B. Anthony, "there must needs be an era of self-sustained, self-appointed homes, where her freedom and equality shall be unquestioned." Beecher rejoiced in the increasingly "open avenues to useful and remunerating occupations for women enabling them to establish *homes of their own*" in the late nineteenth century. She urged women to make such homes with one another. Together, then, women would emerge from their female strongholds, taking their concerns about health, education, and welfare into the world at large.[14]

Many early-nineteenth-century spinsters expected that female autonomy, social respect, economic independence, and political influence would only come to women after generations of spinsters had demonstrated their competence and had shown men what they could achieve if allowed to expand their personal, intellectual, and occupational horizons. Their advocacy of female independence stood at the center of a broader prescription for social change. Such feminist analysis as emerged in the mid-nineteenth century owed a great deal to the writings and lives of these early spinsters—both those who served in a broader sphere and those whose circumstances confined them within the home.[15]

Emily Howland died in 1929. By living to the age of a hundred and two, she confounded medical authorities, who argued that single women suffered a greater incidence of disease and died earlier than their married sisters. The words she chose as her epitaph capture the essence of her kind: "I strove to realize myself and to serve."[16] Not by accident did she articulate these values, for the two were dynamically linked. Service gave meaning to self-expansion, to singlehood, and to liberty, even as it sometimes constrained them. The single woman of the antebellum Northeast was not a woman alone. She lived with her sisters—those of blood and those of choice. She worked in close conjunction with others in her household, family, or association. Her service was consecrated to God, family, or community. She envisioned her liberty as both autonomy and affiliation. Certainly there was a dark side to the single life: service might become duty, attachment degenerate into obligation; independence could feel like isolation; distinction might be seen as deviance, or ambition as mania. Nevertheless, in this world *liberty* conveyed neither a sense of libertinism nor libertarianism. The happy spinster was a useful spinster. Her freedom enabled her to commit her life and her capacities to the betterment of her sex, her community, or her kin. It was for this reason, then, that liberty was a better husband than love.

Notes

Introduction

1. Journal of Louisa May Alcott (hereafter cited as Alcott Journal), February 14, 1868, in Ednah D. Cheney, *Louisa May Alcott, Her Life, Letters, and Journals* (Boston: Roberts Brothers, 1890), p. 197; Louisa May Alcott, "Happy Women, No. III in a Series of Twelve Articles by Twelve Distinguished Women on Advice to Young Ladies," *New York Ledger* 24, no. 7 (April 11, 1868).

2. See, for example, Fred Weinstein and Gerald M. Platt, *The Wish to Be Free: Society, Psyche, and Value Change* (Berkeley: University of California Press, 1969); Lawrence Stone, *The Family, Sex and Marriage in England 1500–1800* (New York: Harper & Row, 1977); Randolph Trumbach, *The Rise of the Egalitarian Family: Aristocratic Relations in Eighteenth-Century England* (New York: Academic Press, 1978); Philip Greven, *Four Generations: Population, Land, and Family in Colonial Andover, Massachusetts* (Ithaca, N.Y.: Cornell University Press, 1970); Greven, *The Protestant Temperament: Patterns of Child-Rearing, Religious Experience, and the Self in Early America* (New York: New American Library, 1977); Edward Shorter, *The Making of the Modern Family* (New York: Basic Books, 1975); Daniel Scott Smith, "Parental Power and Marriage Patterns: An Analysis of Historical Trends in Hingham, Massachusetts," *Journal of Marriage and the Family* 35 (August 1973): 419–28.

3. Mary L. Shanley, "The History of the Family in Modern England—Review Essay," *Signs, Journal of Women in Culture and Society* 4, no. 4 (Summer 1979): 740–51.

4. Mary Beth Norton, *Liberty's Daughters: The Revolutionary Experience of American Women, 1750–1800* (Boston: Little, Brown, 1980); Linda Kerber, *Women of the Republic: Intellect and Ideology in Revolutionary America* (Chapel Hill: University of North Carolina Press, 1980).

5. Accurate census data for the eighteenth and early nineteenth centuries is hard to come by. In addition, marital status was not recorded by U.S. census takers until 1850. Estimates of age of marriage and numbers of unmarried are found largely in studies of select communities or population groups. See Daniel Scott Smith, "Family Limitation, Sexual Control, and Domestic Feminism in Victorian America," in Mary Hartman and Lois W. Banner, eds., *Clio's Consciousness Raised: New Perspectives on the History of Women* (New York: Harper Torchbooks, 1974), p. 120; Robert V. Wells, "Quaker Marriage Patterns in a Colonial Perspective," *William and Mary Quarterly* 29 (1972): 426–27; Wells, "Family History," *Journal of Social History* 9 (1975): 11–12; Philip S. Benjamin, *The Philadelphia Quakers in the Industrial Age, 1865–1920* (Philadelphia: Temple University Press, 1976), p. 236; Yasukichi Yasuba, "Birth Rates

of the White Population in the United States, 1800–1860. An Economic Study," *Johns Hopkins University Studies in Historical and Political Science* 79, no. 2 (1961): 109, 111, 114; Conrad and Irene Taeuber, *The Changing Population of the United States* (New York: John Wiley & Sons, 1958), p. 150.

6. For discussion, see Ruth B. Dixon, "The Social and Demographic Determinants of Marital Postponement and Celibacy: A Comparative Study" (Ph.D. diss., University of California, Berkeley, 1970).

7. Frances Gray of Boston, for example, spent most of her life educating and supporting her thirteen younger brothers and sisters when their mother died and their father deserted them. Patty Rogers of Exeter, New Hampshire, nursed a disabled and sickly father and cared for an alcoholic and mentally deranged brother. Her older sister and brother seemed to feel that this was her responsibility because they had families of their own. See the diaries of Frances Gray in the Massachusetts Historical Society and of Martha Rogers in the American Antiquarian Society.

8. Elizabeth Woolson and Louisa M. Alcott both undertook a variety of occupations in order to support themselves and contribute to their family coffers. See Woolson's papers in the Manchester Historical Association and Alcott's in the Houghton Library.

9. Rachel Stearns, for example, had often been told by her mother that she would never marry. Just why she believed this remains a mystery, but perhaps it had to do with Stearns's intense and unyielding personality. Mary A. Dodge may have been confirmed in her spinsterhood by her self-consciousness about an eye blinded in a childhood accident. Nancy C. Johnson believed that an amputated foot excluded her from the marriage market. Hannah Adams spoke of her "natural singularity" and sought seclusion. She was sensitive to her poor health, "infirm mind," and social awkwardness. See: the diaries of Rachel Stearns in the Schlesinger Library; Harriet A. Dodge, *Gail Hamilton's Life in Letters* (Boston: Lee and Shepard, 1901); information on Nancy C. Johnson in the David Johnson Papers, Connecticut Historical Society; *A Memoir of Miss Hannah Adams* (Boston: Gray & Bowen, 1832), pp. 6–7.

10. For discussion, see D'Ann Campbell, "Women's Life in Utopia: The Shaker Experiment in Sexual Equality Reappraised—1810–1860," *New England Quarterly* 51, no. 1 (March 1978): 23–38.

11. Nancy Cott, *The Bonds of Womanhood: "Woman's Sphere" in New England, 1780–1835* (New Haven: Yale University Press, 1977), pp. 76–80; Anthony F. C. Wallace, *Rockdale: The Growth of an American Village in the Early Industrial Revolution* (New York: Alfred A. Knopf, 1978), pp. 24–32.

12. For a discussion of such motives in the life of Sarah M. Grimké, see Gerda Lerner, *The Grimké Sisters from South Carolina, Pioneers for Women's Rights and Abolitionism* (New York: Schocken Books, 1971).

13. Daniel Scott Smith, "Family Limitation," p. 121; Yashuba, "Birth Rates," table IV-5, p. 109. In both cases, figures apply to all women in the U.S.A., not solely those native-born, Protestant, middle-class, white women who form the subjects of this study and among whom the percentages were much higher.

14. Anne F. Scott, "Women's Perspective on the Patriarchy in the 1850's," *Journal of American History* 61(June 1974): 52–64; Catherine Clinton, *The Plantation Mistress: Woman's World in the Old South* (New York: Pantheon Books, 1972); and Anne F.

Scott, *The Southern Lady: From Pedestal to Politics 1830–1930* (Chicago: University of Chicago Press, 1970). Some Southern women engaged in protests, either public or private, against slavery, and in this found their own independence strengthened—not unlike their Northern abolitionist sisters. Spinster Mary Telfair, for example, wrote her single friend Mary Few that, "I have abandoned the old fashion of having a waiting maid, the first step towards a reform. Alexander [her brother] seems to think I will be too independent for a Lady, but I already experience the salutary effects of running up and downstairs and waiting upon myself." Quoted in Clinton, *Plantation Mistress*, p. 12. Certainly the experience of the Grimké sisters was similar. See Lerner, *Grimké Sisters.*

15. Peter R. Uhlenberg, "A Study of Cohort Life Cycles: Cohorts of Native Born Massachusetts Women, 1830–1920," *Population Studies* 23 (1969): 420.

16. Susan P. King, "Old Maidism versus Marriage," in *Busy Moments of An Idle Woman* (New York: D. Appleton & Co., 1854), pp. 215–54. My thanks to Susan Koppleman for this reference. See her edited collection of nineteenth-century short stories, *Old Maids All*, forthcoming from Pandora Press, Routledge & Kegan Paul, London.

17. Marcia Guttentag and Paul F. Secord, *Too Many Women? The Sex Ratio Question* (Beverly Hills, Calif.: Sage Publications, 1983), p. 135. Guttentag and Secord give a combined sex ratio for the white South (represented by Virginia, North Carolina, South Carolina, Maryland, and Georgia) as 99.5 in 1850. They compare this to a sex ratio of 96 for New England (Massachusetts, Rhode Island, Connecticut, and New Hampshire). The 1850 census gives figures of 94 for Massachusetts and 97.5 for New Hampshire, with men slightly outnumbering women in Vermont, New York, Connecticut, and Maine. Seventh Census, U.S. 1850 (Washington, D.C., 1863), p. lxxxvi.

18. See Clinton, *Plantation Mistress*, pp. 85–86, for a discussion of the unmarried woman in the prewar South.

19. "The Responsibility of Women to Society," paper read at Association for the Advancement of Women, Annual Congress, New York, 1887, quoted in Anne F. Scott, *The Southern Lady*, p. 131; Paul S. Boyer, "Laura Clay," in Edward T. James, Janet W. James, and Paul S. Boyer, eds., *Notable American Women, 1607–1950* (Cambridge, Mass.: Belknap Press, 1971), 1:346–48.

20. Clare de Graffenreid, "What Do Working Girls Owe to One Another?" *Discussions of the Convention of Association of Working Girls' Societies* (New York, 1890), quoted in Scott, *The Southern Lady*, p. 131; Lala C. Steelman, "Clare de Graffenried," in *Notable American Women*, 1:452–54; Elizabeth Grimball to Meta Morris Grimball, December 8, 1866, Grimball Papers, University of South Carolina, quoted in Scott, p. 130.

21. James W. Patton, "Eliza Frances Andrews," in *Notable American Women*, 1:45–46. Other such Southern spinsters might include: Kate Cumming of Alabama (1828–1909), Julia Tutwiler of Alabama (1841–1916), or Celeste Parish of Virginia (1853–1918).

22. Polly Welts Kaufman, *Women Teachers on the Frontier* (New Haven: Yale University Press, 1984), p. 39. My thanks to Kaufman for the female occupational figures for Comanche, Iowa, as well. Although little studied, information on religious sisterhoods in the West may be found in Susan Peterson, "Religious Communities of Women in the West: The Presentation Sister's Adaptation to the Northern Plains Frontier,"

Journal of the West 21 (April 1982): 65–70; Lucile McDonald, "Mother Joseph," in Western Writers of America, *The Women Who Made the West* (New York: Doubleday & Co., 1980), pp. 120–29; Sister M. Madeleva, "Mother Angela Gillespie," in *Notable American Women*, 2:34–35. On Virginia City, see Marion S. Goldman, *Gold Diggers and Silver Miners. Prostitution and Social Life on the Comstock Lode* (Ann Arbor: University of Michigan Press, 1981), pp. 26–27. It is perhaps interesting to note that when twenty public schoolteaching positions were posted in Virginia City in 1877, 120 unmarried women applied (there were 20 such women listed as teachers in the 1875 occupational breakdown but 109 adult dependent daughters who might well have sought such work). Ibid., p. 29.

23. Olive Johnson White, "Experience of Pioneer Days," MS, Nellie Throop Magee Papers, Nebraska Historical Society.

24. My thanks to Katharine Harris for these figures from her Ph.D. dissertation, "Women and Families on Northeastern Colorado Homesteads, 1873–1920," in progress at the University of Colorado, Boulder. They are compiled from land-office tract book records listing the land entries for Logan and Washington counties in Colorado. The figures parallel those found by Sheryll Patterson-Black for Lamar, Colorado, and Douglas, Wyoming. Between 1891 and 1907, she found an increase from 4.8 to 18.2 percent in the numbers of women who filed land patents. Of these, 42.4 percent of women proved up, as compared to 37 percent of men. Sheryll Patterson-Black, "Women Homesteaders on the Great Plains Frontier," *Frontiers, A Journal of Women Studies* 1, no. 2 (Spring 1976): 68.

25. Edith Kohl, *Land of the Burnt Thigh* (New York: Funk and Wagnalls, 1938), pp. 175–76.

26. Mrs. D. W. Griswold, "Pioneering in Sioux County," in A. B. Wood, ed., *Pioneer Tales of the North Platte Valley and Nebraska Panhandle* (Gering, Neb.: Courier Press, 1938), pp. 188–89. Sheryll Patterson-Black describes the case of the four Chrisman sisters, who filed on adjoining 160-acre plots in central Nebraska. See Patterson-Black, "Women Homesteaders," p. 69.

27. Paul Corey, "Bachelor Bess: My Sister," *South Dakota Historical Collections* 37 (1975): 5.

28. Lynette Wert, "The Lady Stakes a Claim," *Persimmon Hill* 6, no. 2 (1976): 18–23; Patterson-Black, "Women Homesteaders," p. 77.

29. A subject of considerable contemporary scholarship, much work has pictured women on the frontier as being the reluctant, sometimes coerced, participants in a venture largely initiated by and for men. See John M. Faragher, *Women and Men on the Overland Trail* (New Haven: Yale University Press, 1979); Julie Roy Jeffrey, *Frontier Women: The Transmississippi West, 1840–1880* (New York: Hill and Wang, 1979); Joan Jensen, *With These Hands: Women Working on the Land* (New York: The Feminist Press and McGraw-Hill Book Co., 1981); Lillian Schlissel, *Women's Diaries of the Westward Journey* (New York: Schocken Books, 1982); Christine Stansell, "Women on the Great Plains, 1865–1890," *Women's Studies* 4 (1976): 87–98. Contrary interpretations are made by Glenda Riley, *Frontierswomen: The Iowa Experience* (Ames: Iowa State University Press, 1981); Sandra L. Myres, *Westering Women and the Frontier Experience, 1800–1915* (Albuquerque: University of New Mexico Press, 1982); and Sheryll Patterson-Black, *Western Women in History and Literature* (Crawford, Neb.: Cottonwood Press, 1978).

30. Nancy Chodorow, *The Reproduction of Mothering: Psychoanalysis and the Sociology of Gender* (Berkeley: University of California Press, 1978); Jean Baker Miller, ed., *Psychoanalysis and Women* (Harmondsworth: Penguin Books, 1973); Carol Gilligan, *In a Different Voice: Psychological Theory and Women's Development* (Cambridge, Mass.: Harvard University Press, 1982).

Chapter 1

1. Martha Saxton, *Louisa May: A Modern Biography of Louisa May Alcott* (Boston: Houghton Mifflin, 1977), p. 325.
2. Louisa May Alcott, "Advice to Young Ladies: Being a Series of Twelve Articles, by Twelve Distinguished Women. No. III.—Happy Women," *New York Ledger* 24 (April 11, 1868): 7.
3. See Mary Ryan, *Womanhood in America* (New York: New Viewpoints Press, 1980), chap. 3; Nancy Cott, *The Root of Bitterness: Documents of the Social History of American Women* (New York: E. P. Dutton, 1972), pp. 11–14; Barbara Welter, "The Cult of True Womanhood, 1820–1860," *The American Quarterly* 18 (1966): 151–74.
4. Barbara Berg, *The Remembered Gate: Origins of American Feminism* (New York: Oxford University Press, 1978), p. 91.
5. Charles Burdett, *Blonde and Brunette, or the Gothamite Arcady* (New York: D. Appleton & Co., 1858), p. 179.
6. Lyle Koehler, *A Search for Power: The "Weaker Sex" in Seventeenth-Century New England* (Urbana: University of Illinois Press, 1980), p. 44. The acquisition of real property was severely limited. Although Salem township did briefly establish "maids lotts" for the unmarried, local residents feared the precedent. "Town Records of Salem, 1634–1695," 9: 28, Essex Institute, quoted in Koehler, p. 67.
7. Lawrence Stone, *The Family, Sex and Marriage in England 1500–1800* (New York: Harper & Row, 1977), p. 22; Koehler, *Search for Power*, p. 73.
8. Koehler, *Search for Power*, p. 44; the *Oxford English Dictionary*, which lists as obsolete the term *thornback* for old maid, provides the information that the young of this British sea skate were called *maids* or *maiden skates*.
9. John Dunton, *Letters Written from New England, A.D. 1686*, ed. William H. Whitmore, Publications of the Prince Society 4 (1867):99, quoted in Koehler, *Search for Power*, p. 44.
10. Changes in the meaning of the word *spinster* reflect these changes in attitudes. The *Oxford English Dictionary* notes that *spinster* shifted during the seventeenth century from its original meaning of female spinner (a task which held some status and which everyone was required to do whether woman, girl, or boy) to become the legal term for unmarried woman. Gradually, spinning was done in small manufactures and became a task primarily performed by unmarried, adolescent girls, intended to occupy idle hands. Just as homespun became less and less popular over the course of the eighteenth century (until the patriotic fervor of the revolutionary war), so the word *spinster* came increasingly to have negative connotations. Both were deemed second-rate goods.
11. William Hayley, *A Philosophical, Historical, and Moral Essay on Old Maids by a Friend to the Sisterhood* (London: T. Cadell, 1793), 1:125; "The Maiden Aunt," *The Atheneum*,

or the Spirit of the English Magazines 6, no. 12 (March 15, 1827): 471. This literature was, to a large extent, modeled on British satire.

12. Mary Beth Norton, *Liberty's Daughters: The Revolutionary Experience of American Women, 1750–1800* (Boston: Little, Brown, 1980), pp. 229–32.

13. "Lines, Written by a Lady, who was questioned respecting her inclination to marry," *Massachusetts Magazine* 6 (September 1794): 566.

14. Gail Hamilton (a.k.a. Mary Abigail Dodge), *A New Atmosphere* (Boston: Ticknor & Fields, 1865), pp. 231–32.

15. Daniel Wise, *The Young Lady's Counsellor: or, Outlines and Illustrations of the Sphere, the Duties and the Dangers of Young Women* (New York: Carlton & Phillips, 1852), pp. 239–40.

16. Lucy Larcom, "A Loyal Woman's No," *The Poetical Works of Lucy Larcom* (Boston: Houghton, Mifflin, 1884), p. 98.

17. Sarah Hanschurst to Sally Forbes, 1762, Library of Congress, quoted in Norton, *Liberty's Daughters*, p. 41; Rebecca Dickinson's Diary, in Daniel W. Wells and Reuben F. Wells, *A History of Hatfield, Massachusetts, 1660–1910* (Springfield, 1910), p. 206.

18. Anne Emlen [Mifflin], "Some Account of My Religious Progress," Historical Society of Pennsylvania. Susan B. Anthony said the same thing some forty-six years later when discussing "the future state" with a group of friends. Diary of Susan B. Anthony, February 3, 1839, Schlesinger Library. Nancy Rawson to Eunice Packard, September 30, 1793, New York Historical Society, quoted in Norton, pp. 240–41.

19. Betsy Mayhew to Pamela Sedgwick, June 25, 1792; Sedgwick to Mayhew, August 10, 1788, Massachusetts Historical Society; Gertrude Meredith to [Gertrude Parker?], 1806; Elizabeth Skinner to Gertrude Parker, July 9, 1803; E[lizabeth] P[arker] to Susan [Parker], December 14, [n.d.], Historical Society of Pennsylvania, quoted in Norton, p. 241.

20. Wise, *Young Lady's Counsellor*, pp. 233–34.

21. Eliza S. Bowne, *A Girl's Life Eighty Years Ago, Selections from the Letters of Eliza Southgate Bowne* (New York: Charles Scribner's Sons, 1887), p. 38; Eliza Chaplin to Laura Lovell, July 28 and August 28, 1820, Essex Institute.

22. Rebecca Gratz to Maria Gist Gratz, December 18, 1832, in David Philipson, *Letters of Rebecca Gratz* (Philadelphia: Jewish Publication Society of America, 1929), p. 165; Clementina Smith to Sophia duPont, March 23, 1841, Eleutherian Mills Historical Library; Samantha S. Vail to Susan B. Anthony, March 30, 1845, Schlesinger Library; Mary Barton to Clara Barton, April 20, 1855, Sophia Smith Collection, Smith College.

23. Robert Samuel Fletcher, *A History of Oberlin College from Its Foundations through the Civil War* (Oberlin: Oberlin College, 1943). Some may view such a debate as unremarkable, given the college's image as a radical institution—an image largely based on the antislavery activity of its students and its policy of opening the doors of higher education to women. However, Oberlin College did not encourage its female students to criticize their sex role or their marital vocation. Women participated in a separate curriculum and trained for their future roles as married women by doing the sewing, washing, cleaning, and cooking for the male students.

24. Among those who did were John Clowes, *The Golden Wedding Ring* (Boston: John B.

Allen, 1832), pp. 20–21; Timothy S. Arthur, *Married and Single; or, Marriage and Celibacy Contrasted in a Series of Domestic Pictures* (New York: Harper and Brothers, 1845), p. 140; George W. Burnap, *Lectures on the Sphere and Duties of Woman and Other Subjects* (Baltimore: John Murphy, 1841), p. 68.

25. Hamilton, *New Atmosphere*, pp. 205–06.
26. "The Happy Bride," *The Ladies Wreath and Parlor Annual* (New York: Burdick & Scovill, n.d.), p. 285; Alice Cary, *Married, not Mated; or, How They Lived at Woodside and Throckmorton Hall* (New York: Derby & Jackson, 1856).
27. Catharine M. Sedgwick, *Married or Single?* (New York: Harper & Brothers, 1857), 2: 284; Mrs. A. J. Graves, *Girlhood and Womanhood; or, Sketches of my Schoolmates* (Boston: J. H. Carter & Co., & Benjamin B. Mussey, 1844), p. 215; Mrs. Louisa C. Tuthill, *The Young Lady's Home* (Boston: William J. Reynolds & Co., 1847), p. 218; "An Old Maid," *Ladies' Magazine and Literary Gazette* 3, no. 7 (July 1830): 294.
28. Susan W. Jewett, "An Old Maid's Reflections on Woman's Rights," *The Ladies Repository* 14 (April 1854): 161. Mary Kelley's analysis of sentimental domestic fiction confirms the complexity of women's attitudes toward marriage during this period. Despite the idealization of the Cult of Domesticity, such literature also contained a protest against the limitations and evils of married life. Mary Kelley, "The Sentimentalists: Promise and Betrayal in the Home," *Signs, A Journal of Women in Culture and Society* 4, no. 3 (Spring 1979): 434–46.
29. Charles Brockton Brown, ed., "Is Marriage or Celibacy Most Eligible? Or, is the Matron or the Old Maid the Best Member of Society?" *The Literary Magazine and American Register* 2 (September 1804): 469; Benedict, the Married Man, "On the Undeserved Stigma Conferred on Single Ladies by the Title of Old Maid," *The Atheneum, or The Spirit of the English Magazines* 1 (September 1, 1817): 803; Mrs. Elizabeth Lanfear, *Letters to Young Ladies on their Entrance into the World* (London: J. Robins & Co., 1824), p. 52; Jason Whitman, *The Young Lady's Aid to Usefulness and Happiness* (Portland, Me.: S. H. Colesworthy, 1845), p. 257; Charles Butler, Esq., *The American Lady* (Philadelphia: Hogan & Thompson, 1839), p. 200; Artemus B. Muzzey, *The Young Maiden* (Boston: William Crosby & Co., 1840), p. 185.
30. See, for example, Lanfear, *Letters* pp. 50–51; J. A. Turner, "Link Not Thy Life and Fate to His," *Peterson's Magazine*, 35, no. 4 (April 1859): 285; John A. James, *The Family Monitor, or A Help to Domestic Happiness* (Boston: Crocker & Brewster, 1833), p. 56; Whitman, *Young Lady's Aid*, pp. 255–56; Butler, *American Lady*, pp. 189–90; Burnap, *Lectures*, pp. 66–67; Burdett, *Blonde and Brunette*, p. 288.
31. Hamilton, *New Atmosphere*, p. 231.
32. The phrase *single blessedness* was coined by William Shakespeare in *A Midsummer Night's Dream* (I.i.78). Young Hermia, having refused to marry her father's choice, is taken before the duke of Athens for judgment. She asks what will be her fate if she continues to object, and is told that she can enter a nunnery or die. Says the Duke:

> Thrice blessèd they that master so their blood,
> To undergo such maiden pilgrimage;
> But earthlier happy is the rose distill'd
> than that which withering on the virgin thorn
> Grows, lives, and dies in single blessedness.

Just as Shakespeare underwent something of a revival in the early nineteenth century, so too did the phrase *single blessedness*. For examples of its usage in public and private expression, see: Benedict, "On the Undeserved Stigma," p. 801; "Old Bachelors," *Ladies Literary Cabinet* 6, no. 9 (1822): 67; "Single Blessedness," *Ladies Literary Cabinet* 6, no. 9 (1822): 72; Clowes, *Wedding Ring*, p. 30; "Get Married," *The Universalist and Ladies Repository* 4 (September 1835): 150; Tuthill, *Young Lady's Home*, p. 332; Muzzey, *Young Maiden*, p. 139; Graves, *Girlhood and Womanhood*, p. 215; Arthur, *Married and Single*, p. 59; William E. Burton, "Leap Year; or, Woman's Privilege," *Godey's Lady's Book* 43 (July 1851): 45; *"Single Blessedness," or, Single Ladies and Gentlemen, against the Slanders of the Pulpit, the Press, and the Lecture Room* (New York: C. S. Francis and Co., 1852); Susan P. King, "Old Maidism versus Marriage," *Busy Moments of An Idle Woman* (New York: D. Appleton & Co., 1854), p. 233; Burdett, *Blonde and Brunette*, p. 179; Mary A. Livermore, *What Shall We Do with Our Daughters? Superfluous Women and Other Lectures* (Boston: Lee & Shepard, 1883), p. 152. In personal documents, see: Eliza Chaplin to Laura Lovell, July 28, 1820, Essex Institute; Clementina Smith to Sophia duPont, n.d. [W9-25282] and July 22, 1836, Eleutherian Mills Historical Library; Aaron M. McLean to Susan B. Anthony, August 5, 1839, Schlesinger Library; Mary A. Dodge, "A Short Sermon by a Lay Priestess," Notebook 1, June 30, 1849, Essex Institute; Catharine M. Sedgwick to Rev. Dewey, December 10, 1864, in Mary E. Dewey, ed., *Life and Letters of Catharine M. Sedgwick* (New York: Harper & Brothers, 1871), pp. 407–08.

33. Perfectionism was an important social force as well as a moral philosophy in the 1830s. It had nothing to do with the current meaning of *perfectionist*, as someone enmeshed in minutiae. Rather, the word referred to the idea that individuals, groups, even nations might make themselves morally blameless through a sudden, conscious act of will. For discussion of the idea and those who espoused it, and for its implications for antebellum reform, see Laurence Veysey, ed., *The Perfectionists: Radical Social Thought in the North, 1815–1860* (New York: John Wiley & Sons, 1973). See also, David B. Davis, ed., *Ante-Bellum Reform* (New York: Harper & Row, 1967).

34. Max Weber, in *The Protestant Ethic and the Spirit of Capitalism*, indicates that the emphasis in Protestant theology on individual salvation undermined the separate authority of social associations of all kinds. Its impact on the marital institution is suggested by the fact that female singlehood was exceptionally high (40 percent) among women in that most radically individualistic sect, the Quakers. See Philip S. Benjamin, *The Philadelphia Quakers in the Industrial Age, 1865–1920* (Philadelphia: Temple University Press, 1976), p. 236.

35. Nancy Cott, *The Bonds of Womanhood: "Woman's Sphere" in New England, 1780–1835* (New Haven: Yale University Press, 1977), p. 86. For discussion, see Cott, p. 140, and Joseph F. Kett, *Rights of Passage, Adolescence in America, 1790 to the Present* (New York: Basic Books, 1977), p. 76.

36. *"Single Blessedness,"* pp. 249–50.

37. Mrs. Joseph H. Hanaford, "The True Object of Life; or the Wishes Fulfilled," *The Family Circle and Parlor Annual* 13 (1852): 30. Said William Alger: "The assertion, then, that the distinctive office of woman is to be the helpmeet of man, does not imply that she ought to be legally or morally any more subservient to him than he to her; for the supreme duty of woman, as of every other human being, is, through the

perfecting of her own nature as a child of God, to fulfill her personal destiny in the universe." William R. Alger, *The Friendships of Women* (Boston: Roberts Brothers, 1868), pp. 1–2.

38. Dinah Mulock Craik, *A Woman's Thoughts about Women* (New York: John Bradburn, 1866), pp. 18–19; Anna Jameson, *Sisters of Charity and the Communion of Labour, Two Lectures on the Social Employment of Women* (London: Longman, Brown, Green, Longmans, & Roberts, 1859), p. 12.

39. Mulock, *A Woman's Thoughts*, pp. 62–63.

40. Muzzey, *Young Maiden*, p. 25.

41. "Dignity," *Ladies' Magazine and Literary Gazette* 5, no. 7 (July 1832): 311.

42. Journal of Lucy Larcom, January 16, 1882, quoted in Daniel D. Addison, *Lucy Larcom: Life, Letters and Diary* (Boston: Houghton Mifflin & Co., 1894), p. 214; Journal of Elizabeth Blackwell, 1845, quoted in Elizabeth Blackwell, *Pioneer Work in Opening the Medical Profession to Women* (New York: Schocken Book Reprint, 1977), pp. 31–32; George Tolman, *Mary Moody Emerson* (Cambridge, Mass.: Edward W. Forbes, 1929), p. 6; Graves, *Girlhood and Womanhood*, pp. 212, 215.

43. Nancy Cott, "Passionlessness: An Interpretation of Victorian Sexual Ideology, 1790–1850," *Signs, A Journal of Women in Culture and Society* 4, no. 2 (Winter, 1978): 219–36.

44. Mrs. C. Lee Hentz, "Aunt Mercy," *Godey's Lady's Book* 24 (January 1842): 41–54, 127–34.

45. Sedgwick, *Married or Single?* 2: 258; Harriet Beecher Stowe, *The Minister's Wooing* (Ridgewood, N.J.: Gregg Press Reprint, 1968), p. 312.

46. Among the early popular pieces on the subject was "The Hygienic Relations of Celibacy," *The Nation* 5 (October 31, 1867): 357–58.

47. Clowes, *Wedding Ring*, pp. 22–23; *"Single Blessedness,"* pp. 169, 182–83; "Hygienic Relations," p. 357. Perhaps so—the poet John Greenleaf Whittier, who lived with his unmarried sister Elizabeth, once told his cousin that "while he agreed with Paul that those who marry do well, he agreed with him also that those who do not marry do better." Cornelia Hancock wrote to her mother that although she was glad that her Aunt Eliza had married because she so wanted to, and that she was "willing any one should marry who wishes," still, for herself, she determined to "remain as Paul thought best." Albert Mordell, *Quaker Militant: John Greenleaf Whittier* (Boston: Houghton Mifflin, 1933), pp. 245–46; Cornelia Hancock to Rachel Hancock, April 1866, Friends Historical Library.

48. The issue of "redundant women" and the possibility of forming Protestant convents in which these women might serve were officially taken up by several prominent British organizations in 1862: the Convocation of Canterbury, the Social Science Congress, and the Church Congress at Oxford. For more on this idea in England, see Michael Hill, *The Religious Order* (London: Hienemann Educational Books, 1973); John M. Ludlow, *Woman's Work in the Church* (London: A. Strahn, 1866); Jameson, *Sisters of Charity*; F. Warre Cornish, *A History of the English Church in the Nineteenth Century* (London: MacMillan & Co., 1910). For discussion of institutionalization in the American press, see Brown, "Marriage or Celibacy," p. 471; Benedict, "On the Undeserved Stigma," p. 804; Margaret Coxe, *The Young Lady's Companion* (Columbus, Ohio: J. N. Whiting, 1839), p. 252; Catharine E. Beecher, *An Address to the Protestant Clergy of the United States* (New York: Harper & Brothers, 1846).

49. Catharine M. Sedgwick to Rev. Dewey, December 10, 1864, in Dewey, *Life and Letters*, pp. 407–08.

50. Beecher, *Address*, p. 33. See also Mary S. Gilpin to Sophia duPont, November 29, 1845, Eleutherian Mills Historical Library. This is a personal perspective on the frustrations of one woman in comparing the lack of institutional support which she received from the Episcopal church with that of a Catholic friend. Wrote Gilpin, "You will perceive the confident tone with which she speaks of the *church's* support for she thinks of her own—but alas! I feel that my efforts have had no such sustaining power, nor have individual members thereof manifested much that could make *me* think they would uphold me for the sake of our common Master." For years, Gilpin tried to engage the church's official support of her various educational projects.

51. Berg, *Remembered Gate*, p. 91; "Old Maids," *Ladies' Literary Cabinet* 21 (1822): 167; Julia Delafaye-Brehier, "The Two Sisters," *The Ladies Scrapbook* (Hartford: S. Andrus & Son, 1846), p. 58.

52. Hayley, *Essay*; "The Maiden Aunt," *The Atheneum* 6 (March 15, 1827): 469–73; Arthur, *Married and Single*; Mary Pease, "The Storm," *Godey's Lady's Book* 42 (June 1851): 341–44; Nathaniel Hawthorne, *The House of the Seven Gables* (New York: Dell, 1960).

53. "The Old Maid of the Family—A Sketch of Human Life," *The Atheneum* 3 (January 1, 1830): 276–80.

54. For other stories in the popular press that designated the maiden aunt as a wise counselor, family advisor, child-care worker, or domestic assistant, see: Letitia in Mary Howitt, "Single Sisters," *The Keepsake* (1845), pp. 62–71; Aunt Hetty in Effie Evergreen, "Ella Mason; or, the Romance of a Second Marriage," *Godey's Lady's Book* 42 (June 1851): 355–60; Miss Selwyn in Mary Devenant, "Emma Westfall," *Godey's Lady's Book* 26 (February 1843): 73–79; Aunt Mary in Harriet Beecher Stowe, "Eliza. From My Aunt Mary's Bureau," *Godey's Lady's Book* 20 (January 1840): 24–26; Anne Colyton in Mrs. Abdy, "The Jeweller's Daughter," *The Amaranth* (1855), pp. 49–53; Aunt Jemima in "Sketches of American Character: The Poor Scholar," *Ladies' Magazine* 1, no. 6 (June 1828): 245–66; Mary Vernon in Anna, "The Christmas Dinner," *Lady's Wreath and Parlor Annual* 9 (ca. 1853): 99–105; Aunt Penelope Ellerton in Mrs. S. T. Martyn, "Ida Clifford," *The Ladies Wreath* (1849–50), pp. 133–44, 176–87, 215–25; Aunt Penelope in Mrs. Emeline Plumer, "The Neglected Wife," *The Family Circle and Parlor Annual* 13 (1852): 103–10, 136–43.

55. Sarah C. Edgarton, "The Old Maid. A Sketch," *The Universalist and Ladies Repository* 6 (May 1838): 469. The image is strikingly similar to that envisioned in 1802 by Mary Moody Emerson as her ideal: "Were the genius of the Xian religion painted, her form would be full of majesty, her mien solemn, her aspect benign, and strongly impressed with joy and hope, her eyes raised to Heaven with tears for Zion and rays of glory descending to illuminate the earth at her intreaties!" See the George Tolman transcriptions of Mary Moody Emerson's Almanacks (hereafter cited as Emerson Almanack), November 8, 1804 (7131, p. 4), Houghton Library.

56. Edgarton, "The Old Maid," p. 470. For other examples of the sister of charity in women's literature, see Clemence Isaure in "Clemence Isaure," *The Amaranth* (1852), pp. 197–216; Lucy Latimer in Mary C. Vaughan, "Fruits of Sorrow; or an Old Maid's Story," *The Lady's Wreath and Parlor Annual* (ca. 1858), pp. 389–95; Susan de Witt in

Everallin, "Recollections—No. III; Susan de Witt," *Ladies Magazine* 2, no. 7 (July 1829): 320–25; Helen Clapp in "Flirtation," *Ladies Magazine* 1, no. 8 (August 1828): 361–68; Martha Gilmore in Everallin, "Early Friendships: No. III; The Confidant," *Ladies Magazine* 3, no. 9 (September 1830): 394–98; Aunt Mercy in Hentz, "Aunt Mercy," pp. 41–54, 127–34; Miss Atherton in "An Old Maid."

57. Issues of character occasionally overcame those of role. Take, for example, the story of Lucy Burton, a story entitled "Moral Courage." Lucy rejected marriage in order to provide for her mother and three siblings after the death of her father. She entered the trade of milliner so that they might all live together rather than be scattered among relatives and employers who might take them on as individual charity cases. By the end of the story, Lucy had taken over the milliner's shop in which she apprenticed. The author emphasizes that Lucy was a true woman, although "an active, energetic woman of business." After all, Lucy Burton had undertaken a difficult but womanly task (that is, family care) and performed it with great moral courage and femininity. "Lucy Burton had not stepped out of her sphere in the prosecution of her scheme. There was nothing coarse or bustling in her activity." Alice B. Neal, "Moral Courage," *Godey's Lady's Book* 42 (May 1851): 316–19, 367–72.

58. Robert V. Wells, "Quaker Marriage Patterns in a Colonial Perspective," *William and Mary Quarterly* 29 (1972): 426–27; Wells, "Family History," *Journal of Social History* 9 (1975): 11–12; Benjamin, *Philadelphia Quakers*, p. 236; Daniel Scott Smith, "Parental Power and Marriage Patterns: An Analysis of Historical Trends in Hingham, Massachusetts," *Journal of Marriage and the Family* 35 (August 1973): 425; Peter Uhlenberg, "A Study of Cohort Life Cycles; Cohorts of Native Born Massachusetts Women, 1830–1920," *Population Studies* 23 (1969): 410–11; Mary Ryan, *Cradle of the Middle Class: The Family in Oneida County, New York, 1790–1865* (Cambridge: Cambridge University Press, 1981), p. 223; Daniel Scott Smith, "Family Limitation, Sexual Control, and Domestic Feminism in Victorian America," in Lois Banner and Mary Hartman, *Clio's Consciousness Raised: New Perspectives on the History of Women* (New York: Harper Torchbooks, 1974), p. 120.

Chapter 2

1. "Why Is Single Life Becoming More General?" *The Nation* 6 (March 5, 1868): 190–91.

2. J. Potter, "The Growth of Population in America, 1700–1860," in D. V. Glass and D. E. C. Eversley, eds., *Population in History* (London: Edward Arnold, 1965), pp. 684–85; Daniel Scott Smith, "Family Limitation, Sexual Control, and Domestic Feminism in Victorian America," in Mary Hartman and Lois W. Banner, eds., *Clio's Consciousness Raised* (New York: Harper Torchbook, 1974), p. 121; Daniel Scott Smith, "Parental Power and Marriage Patterns: An Analysis of Historical Trends in Hingham, Massachusets," *Journal of Marriage and the Family* 35 (August 1973): 425; Lyle Koeler, *A Search for Power: The "Weaker Sex" in Seventeenth-Century New England* (Urbana: University of Illinois Press, 1980), p. 349.

3. Elisha W. Keyes, "Early Days in Jefferson County," *Collections of the State Historical Society of Wisconsin* 11 (1888): 196, quoted in James E. Davis, *Frontier America, 1800–1840. A Comparative Demographic Analysis of the Frontier Process* (Glendale, Wisc.: Arthur H. Clark Co., 1977), pp. 57–58.

4. A recent book attributes to the sex ratio considerable social significance. The authors suggest that low sex ratios—that is, greater numbers of women than men in the population—lead to increasing singlehood, sexual libertarianism, the economic and political independence of women, the acceleration of feminism, and the devaluation of marriage. I have found the sex ratio to be a very limited measurement, providing only an outside limit on the number of pairs statistically possible in a given population. It has only modest value in predicting social behavior and even less with regard to specific individuals. In addition, I find that a higher evaluation of both marriage and singlehood went hand-in-hand in this period. Female political and economic independence was limited, although growing, and female sexuality constrained, particularly among unmarried women. See Marcia Guttentag and Paul F. Secord, *Too Many Women? The Sex Ratio Question* (Beverly Hills, Calif.: Sage Publications, Inc., 1983).

5. Statistics were determined from population figures given in the Joint Special Committee of the House and Senate of the Massachusetts General Court, *Report as Relates to "The Emigration of Young Women to the West,"* Senate Document 156, March 29, 1865. See also, Peter Uhlenberg, "A Study of Cohort Life Cycles: Cohorts of Native Born Massachusetts Women, 1830–1920," *Population Studies* 23 (1969): 420.

6. Middlesex County, for example, boasted 85,463 women and 79,810 men—or an "excess" of 5,653 women. Essex had 69,971 women and 65,581 men, or 4,390 extra women. In Norfolk, Bristol, and Hampden, the statistics were: 43,047 to 40,412, or 2,635 more women than men; 38,651 women to 36,575 men or 2,076 more women than men; and 22,932 women to 21,826 men, or 1,106 more women than men. By contrast, Franklin County had a population of 14,541 women and 14,499 men, or only 42 more women than men; and Dukes County had 1,982 women to 2,213 men, or an excess of 231 men. Massachusetts Senate Document 156, p. 34.

7. Joseph F. Kett, *Rites of Passage: Adolescence in America 1790 to the Present* (New York: Basic Books, 1977), p. 96.

8. Of the 15 percent who did not, some (about 3–5 percent of the mill population) remained in the mills. Others left to undertake different occupations within or outside of the home. Thomas Dublin, *Women at Work: The Transformation of Work and Community in Lowell, Massachusetts 1826–1860* (New York: Columbia University Press, 1979), p. 264.

9. Thomas P. Monahan, *The Pattern of Age at Marriage in the United States* (Philadelphia: Stephenson-Brothers, 1951), 1:82.

10. Mary Ryan, *Cradle of the Middle Class: The Family in Oneida County, New York, 1790–1865* (Cambridge: Cambridge University Press, 1980), pp. 269, 274.

11. Ryan, *Cradle of the Middle Class;* Louise Tilly and Joan Scott, *Women, Work, and Family* (New York: Holt, Rinehart, Winston, 1978), p. 116; Dublin, *Women at Work,* pp. 35–37.

12. Nancy Cott, *The Bonds of Womanhood: "Woman's Sphere" in New England, 1780–1835* (New Haven: Yale University Press, 1977), chap. 1.

13. Dublin, *Women at Work,* pp. 31–32; Margaret Adams, *Single Blessedness* (Harmondsworth: Penguin Books, 1978), p. 35.

14. Cott, *Bonds of Womanhood,* pp. 30–35.

15. Massachusetts Senate Document 156, pp. 47–49.

16. Ryan, *Cradle of the Middle Class*, pp. 172–73.

17. Mary B. Woolson to Elizabeth Woolson, January 13, 1833; Elizabeth Woolson to [?], January 25, 1856, Manchester Historical Association.

18. Journal of Louisa May Alcott, November 1855, in Ednah D. Cheney, *Louisa May Alcott: Her Life, Letters, and Journals* (Boston: Roberts Brothers, 1890), p. 83.

19. Alcott Journal, January 1868, in Cheney, *Alcott*, p. 193. See also ibid., 1853, in Cheney, p. 69; ibid., April 1855, in Cheney, p. 80.

20. Louisa May Alcott to Anna Alcott, 1854, in Cheney, *Alcott*, p. 71. See also Alcott Journal, April 1859, in Cheney, p. 104; ibid., January 1864, in Cheney, p. 155; ibid., August 1866, in Cheney, p. 184; Louisa May Alcott to Anna Alcott, November 1858, in Cheney, p. 107.

21. Louisa May Alcott to Bronson Alcott, November 29, 1856, in Cheney, *Alcott*, p. 89.

22. Harriot Hunt, *Glances and Glimpses* (Boston: J. P. Jewett & Co., 1856), pp. 54–55.

23. Mary Beth Norton, *Liberty's Daughters: The Revolutionary Experience of American Women, 1750–1800* (Boston: Little, Brown, 1980), pp. 229–31; Michael Hindus and Daniel Scott Smith, "Pre-Marital Pregnancy in America, 1640–1971," *Journal of Interdisciplinary History* 5 (1975): 538, 540.

24. Smith, "Parental Power and Marriage Patterns," pp. 424–26.

25. Ruth Bronson Dixon, "The Social and Demographic Determinants of Marital Postponement and Celibacy: A Comparative Study" (Ph.D. diss., University of California, Berkeley, 1970).

26. H. R. Lanx et al., "Pre-Industrial Patterns in Colonial Family in America: A Content Analysis of Colonial Magazines," *American Sociological Review* 33 (1968): 230–35, 238.

27. Cott, *Bonds of Womanhood*, p. 77.

28. Eliza Bowne, *A Girl's Life Eighty Years Ago, Selections from the Letters of Eliza Southgate Bowne* (New York: Charles Scribner's Sons, 1887), p. 38.

29. Artemus B. Muzzey, *The Young Maiden* (Boston: William Crosby & Co., 1840), p. 193; John A. James, *The Family Monitor, or A Help to Domestic Happiness* (Boston: Crocker & Brewster, 1833), p. 57; Charles Butler, Esq., *The American Lady* (Philadelphia: Hogan & Thompson, 1839), p. 197.

30. J. A. Turner, "Link Not Thy Life and Fate to His," *Peterson's Magazine* 35, no. 4 (April 1859): 285. See also Jason Whitman, *The Young Lady's Aid, to Usefulness and Happiness* (Portland, Me., S. H. Colesworthy, 1838), pp. 281–82.

31. Rev. Daniel Wise, *The Young Lady's Counsellor; or, Outlines and Illustrations of the Sphere, the Duties and the Dangers of Young Women* (New York: Carlton & Phillips, 1852), pp. 243–45. See also John Clowes, *The Golden Wedding Ring; or Observations on the Institution of Marriage* (Boston: John Allen, 1832), pp. 18–19; Muzzey, *Young Maiden*, pp. 192–94.

32. Muzzey, *Young Maiden*, pp. 193–94.

33. Ibid., pp. 137–38; *"Single Blessedness," or, Single Ladies and Gentlemen, Against the Slanders of the Pulpit, the Press, and the Lecture-Room* (New York: C. S. Francis & Co., 1852), pp. 256–57; "Why Is Single Life Becoming More General?" pp. 190–91.

34. Diary of Catharine M. Sedgwick, May 24, 1834, Massachusetts Historical Society; Elizabeth Blackwell, *Pioneer Work in Opening the Medical Profession to Women* (New York: Schocken Books, 1977), p. 23; Cornelia Hancock to Rachel Hancock, October

15, 1866, Friends Historical Library. See also Diary of Emily Howland, April 12, 1880, Friends Historical Library; Mary A. Dodge to Judge French, January 1864, in Harriet A. Dodge, ed., *Gail Hamilton's Life in Letters* (Boston: Lee and Shepard, 1901), 1: 367.

35. Phoebe Cary, "Do You Blame Her?" in Mary Clemner Ames, *A Memorial of Alice and Phoebe Cary, with Some of Their Later Poems* (New York: Hurd & Houghton, 1874), pp. 337–38.

36. On "marital trauma," see Cott, *Bonds of Womanhood,* pp. 74–83; and Carroll Smith-Rosenberg, "The Female World of Love and Ritual: Relations between Women in Nineteenth-Century America," *Signs: Journal of Women in Culture & Society* 1 (1975): 22.

37. Diary of Catharine M. Sedgwick, October 12, 1836, Massachusetts Historical Society; Diary of Susan B. Anthony, July 10, 1839, Schlesinger Library.

38. Mary S. Gilpin to Sophia duPont, February 25, 1829, Eleutherian Mills Historical Library. For a discussion of the decline of parental authority and family name changes, see Daniel Scott Smith, "Child-Naming Patterns and Family Structure Change: Hingham, Massachusetts 1640–1880," paper prepared for Clark University Conference on the Family and Social Structure, April 27–29, 1972.

39. Katherine L. Herbig, "Friends for Freedom: The Lives and Careers of Sallie Holley and Caroline Putnam" (Ph.D. diss., Claremont Graduate School, 1977), p. 13.

40. For discussion of colonial practices, see Koehler, *Search for Power.*

41. The relative contributions of married and single women to antebellum reform and social organizations have not been studied. Mary Ryan's work on Utica suggests that married women belonged to such organizations in large numbers. See Ryan, "A Woman's Awakening: Evangelical Religion and the Families of Utica, New York, 1800–1840," *American Quarterly* 30, no. 5 (Winter 1978): 602–23. Impressions gathered from my own research into the antislavery movement suggest, however, that much of the day-to-day work was undertaken by spinsters. Elizabeth Neall Gay, Maria Weston Chapman, and Lucy Stone Blackwell all recognized that their work in the movement was limited by child-rearing and housekeeping responsibilities. See Elizabeth Neall Gay to Sarah Pugh, June 29, 1878, Columbia University; Maria W. Chapman to Mary A. Estlin, December 12, 1852, Boston Public Library.

42. George W. Burnap, *Lectures on the Sphere and Duties of Woman and Other Subjects* (Baltimore: John Murphy, 1841), pp. 125–26; Margaret Coxe, *The Young Lady's Companion* (Columbus, Ohio: J. N. Whiting, 1839), pp. 255–56.

43. Dinah Mulock Craik, *A Woman's Thoughts about Women* (New York: John Bradburn, 1866), p. 42.

44. Cott, *Bonds of Womanhood,* chap. 5, p. 168; Smith-Rosenberg, "Female World"; Lillian Faderman, *Surpassing the Love of Men: Romantic Friendship and Love between Women from the Renaissance to the Present* (New York: William Morrow & Co., 1981); Diary of Maria Mitchell, December 5, 1854, in Phebe Mitchell Kendall, *Maria Mitchell: Life, Letters, and Journals* (Boston: Lee and Shepard, 1896), p. 34.

45. Journal of Lucy Larcom, September 8, 1861, in Daniel D. Addison, *Lucy Larcom: Life, Letters, and Diary* (Boston: Houghton, Mifflin, 1844), p. 104.

46. Journal, May 15, 1861, in Addison, *Lucy Larcom,* p. 92.

47. Graceanna Lewis to Mary Townsend, January 26, 1845, collection of Mrs. Charles

Macaulay (hereafter known as Macaulay Collection); Carrie A. Rowland to Emily Howland, August 7, 1852, Cornell University Library microfilm.

48. There is considerable scholarly debate on this subject. A short list providing various perspectives would include: Blanche W. Cook, "Female Support Networks and Political Activism: Lillian Wald, Crystal Eastman, Emma Goldman," Chrysalis 3 (1977): 43–61; Cook, " 'Women Alone Stir My Imagination': Lesbianism and the Cultural Tradition," Signs: A Journal of Women in Culture and Society 4, no. 4 (Summer 1979): 718–39; Smith-Rosenberg, "Female World"; William R. Taylor and Christopher Lasch, "Two 'Kindred Spirits': Sorority and Family in New England, 1839–1846," New England Quarterly 36, no. 1 (March 1963): 23–41; Lesbian history issue of Frontiers, A Journal of Women Studies 4 (Fall 1979): 3; Lillian Faderman, "Female Same-Sex Relationships in Novels by Longfellow, Holmes, and James," New England Quarterly 60, no. 3 (September 1978): 309–32.

49. Graceanna Lewis to Mary Townsend, January 26, 1845, Macaulay Collection; Sarah Pugh to Mary Anne Estlin, August 26, 1853, Dr. Williams's Library.

50. Margaret Fuller, Woman in the Nineteenth Century (New York: W. W. Norton, 1971 reprint), p. 23; Mary Grew to Isabel Howland, April 27, 1892, Sophia Smith Collection, Smith Library. Grew also said, "I am of those who believe that there are ties of friendship strong as the conjugal one, where love is as deep, as earnest, as true" (Mary Grew to Helen B. Garrison, July 23, 1846, Boston Public Library). For contemporary male opinions, see John Chadwick: "But one can hardly think of Mary Grew at all without thinking of her friends, Sarah Pugh and Margaret Burleigh, especially the latter, devoted to her with that affection passing the love of men which many of the anti-slavery women manifested towards each other; in the affection of Caroline Putnam for Sallie Holley finding one of its loveliest illustrations." John White Chadwick, A Life for Liberty: Anti-Slavery and Other Letters of Sallie Holley (New York: G. P. Putnam's Sons, 1899); and William R. Alger, The Friendships of Women (Boston, Roberts Brothers, 1868) for similar sentiments. For current scholarship, see Nancy Cott, "Passionlessness: An Interpretation of Victorian Sexual Ideology, 1790–1850," Signs: A Journal of Women in Culture and Society 4, no. 2 (Winter 1978): 219–36.

51. Ryan, Cradle of the Middle Class, p. 223.

52. A Memoir of Miss Hannah Adams (Boston: Gray & Bowen, 1832), p. 69; Journal of Emily Blackwell, January 14, 1853, Schlesinger Library.

53. Kathryn K. Sklar, Catharine Beecher: A Study in American Domesticity (New York: W. W. Norton, 1976), p. 139. See also, Alice Cary to James T. Fields, n.d., Henry E. Huntington Library.

54. Mary A. Dodge to Judge French, January 17, 1866, in Dodge, Gail Hamilton's Life, 1:535; Lucy Larcom to Franklin Carter, July 18, 1881, in Addison, Lucy Larcom, p. 206.

55. Whitman, Young Lady's Aid, p. 255; Wise, Young Lady's Counsellor, p. 140; Muzzey, Young Maiden, pp. 185–86; Gail Hamilton, A New Atmosphere (Boston: Ticknor and Fields, 1865), p. 21. For similar attitudes, see Alice Cary, Married, Not Mated; or, How they lived at Woodside and Throckmorton Hall (New York: Derby & Jackson, 1856), p. 41; and Three Sisters (London: Clowes & Sons, 1856), pp. 16–17.

56. Diary of Lucy Chase, February 4, 1853, American Antiquarian Society.

57. Louisa May Alcott to Anna Alcott, n.d., in Cheney, Alcott, p. 169.

Chapter 3

1. Harriet Beecher Stowe, "Eliza. From My Aunt Mary's Bureau," *Godey's Lady's Book* 20 (January 1840): 24.
2. Diary of Catharine M. Sedgwick, May 18, 1828, in Mary E. Dewey, ed., *Life and Letters of Catharine M. Sedgwick* (New York: Harper & Brothers, 1871), p. 198.
3. For examples of rejected suitors, see Lucy Larcom to Esther Homiston, February 28, 1859, Massachusetts Historical Society; Catharine M. Sedgwick to Frances S. Watson, March 28, 1919, in Dewey, *Life and Letters*, pp. 208–09; Mary A. Dodge to George Wood, August 11, 1866, in Harriet A. Dodge, ed., *Gail Hamilton's Life in Letters* (Boston: Lee & Shepard, 1901), 1: 563; Catherine Birney, *The Grimké Sisters: Sarah and Angelina Grimké: The First Women Advocates of Abolition and Women's Rights* (Boston: Lee and Shepard, 1885), p. 19; Anne W. Weston to Deborah Weston, October 4, 1836, Boston Public Library; Mary Clemner Ames, *A Memorial of Alice and Phoebe Cary, with Some of Their Later Poems* (New York: Hurd & Houghton, 1874), p. 202; Helen Wright, *Sweeper in the Sky: The Life of Maria Mitchell, First Woman Astronomer in America* (New York: Macmillan Co., 1949), pp. 67–68; Henrietta S. Jaquette, *South after Gettysburg, Letters of Cornelia Hancock* (Philadelphia: University of Pennsylvania Press, 1937), p. x.
4. Katherine L. Herbig, "Friends for Freedom: The Lives and Careers of Sallie Holley and Caroline Putnam" (Ph.D. diss., Claremont Graduate School, 1977), p. 56.
5. See Elizabeth Baker to Emily Howland, May 14, 1854; Richard [?] to Emily Howland, November 26, 1854; Sallie Holley to Caroline F. Putnam, June 30, 1865; Caroline F. Putnam to Emily Howland, May 30, 1865; Anna Searing to Emily Howland, 1863, Cornell University; and Emily Howland to Anna Searing and Emma Brown, July 24, 1865, Friends Historical Library.
6. Diary of Emily Howland, May 10, 1877; also December 8, 1877, May 24, 1878, April 29, 1880, and April 5, 1902, Friends Historical Library.
7. Diary of Sarah Grimké, September 16, 1830, and September 1832, Clements Library.
8. Gerda Lerner, *The Grimké Sisters from South Carolina* (New York: Schocken Books, 1971), pp. 62–65.
9. Charles Burdett, *Blonde and Brunette, or the Gothamite Arcady* (New York: D. Appleton & Co., 1858), pp. 178–79; Catharine M. Sedgwick, *Married or Single?* (New York: Harper & Brothers, 1857), 1:29.
10. John A. James, *The Family Monitor, or A Help to Domestic Happiness* (Boston: Crocker & Brewster, 1833), p. 57.
11. Mrs. Elizabeth Lanfear, *Letters to Young Ladies on their Entrance into the World* (London: J. Robins & Co., 1824), p. 53. Other powerful metaphors such as a "death potion" or a "hazardous voyage" were also common and cannot have eased the minds of potential brides.
12. George Burnap, *Lectures on the Sphere and Duties of Woman and Other Subjects* (Baltimore: John Murphy, 1841), pp. 66–67.
13. Indeed, the experience of their mothers proved an important factor in these women's perceptions of marriage and its limitations. What was new for them, which their mothers did not have, was a sense that there might be alternative life-styles. See Rebecca Gratz to Ann B. Gratz, May 27, 1847, in David Philipson, *Letters of Rebecca Gratz* (Philadelphia: Jewish Publication Society of America, 1929), p. 348; Catharine

M. Sedgwick to Kate S. Minot, November 28, 1847, Massachusetts Historical Society; Diary of Lucy Chase, fragment dated November 16, American Antiquarian Society; Journal of Sarah Stoughton, April 21, 1869, American Antiquarian Society; Emily Howland to Caroline F. Putnam, September 26, 1869, Friends Historical Society. See also Diary of Susan B. Anthony, April 26, 1838, and letter dated August 18, 1839, Schlesinger Library; Lucy Larcom, "Leafy," MS, Essex Institute.

14. Charles Butler, Esq., *The American Lady* (Philadelphia: Hogan & Thompson, 1839), pp. 189–90.

15. "What happy creatures Old Maids are," *The Emerald* 1, no. 5 (December 1, 1810): 59.

16. Artemus B. Muzzey, *The Young Maiden* (Boston: William Crosby & Co., 1840), p. 164; T. L. Nichols, M.D. and Mrs. Mary S. Gove Nichols, *Marriage: Its History, Character, and Results; Its Sanctities, and Its Profanities; Its Science and Its Facts* (New York: T. L. Nichols, 1854), p. 92; "*Single Blessedness*" *or, Single Ladies and Gentlemen, against the Slanders of the Pulpit, the Press and the Lecture-Room* (New York: C. S. Francis & Co., 1852), p. 91.

17. Elinor Rice Hays, *Those Extraordinary Blackwells* (New York: Harcourt, Brace & World, 1967), p. 5; Journal of Emily Blackwell, February 18, 1852, Schlesinger Library; Catharine M. Sedgwick to Robert Sedgwick, October 8, 1817, Massachusetts Historical Society; Elizabeth Tappin to Elizabeth Douglas, July 10, 1842, quoted in Blanche G. Hersh, *The Slavery of Sex: Feminist-Abolitionists in America* (Urbana: University of Illinois Press, 1978), p. 42.

18. Nancy Cott, *The Bonds of Womanhood: "Woman's Sphere" in New England, 1780–1835* (New Haven: Yale University Press, 1977), p. 78.

19. Elizabeth Payson to Anna S. Prentiss, April 24, 1843, in G. L. Prentiss, ed., *The Life and Letters of Elizabeth Prentiss* (London: Hodden and Stoughton, 1897), pp. 79–80.

20. Mary A. Dodge to George Wood, April 29, 1867, in Dodge, *Gail Hamilton's Life,* 1: 586; Susan B. Anthony to Lydia Mott, 1859, quoted in Ida H. Harper, *Life and Work of Susan B. Anthony* (Indianapolis: Hollenbeck Press, 1898), 1: 171.

21. Elizabeth Blackwell to Barbara Bodichon, May 25, 1860, quoted in Hays, *Extraordinary Blackwells,* p. 155; Hersh, *Slavery of Sex,* p. 112; Carrie A. Rowland to Emily Howland, August 7, 1852, Cornell University.

22. Fred Weinstein and Gerald M. Platt, *The Wish to Be Free: Society, Psyche, and Value Change* (Berkeley: University of California Press, 1969), introduction. For discussion of how these philosophers included and neglected women, see Linda K. Kerber, *Women of the Republic: Intellect and Ideology in Revolutionary America* (Chapel Hill: University of North Carolina Press, 1980), chap. 1. See also Lawrence Stone, *The Family, Sex and Marriage in England 1500–1800* (New York: Harper & Row, 1977), chap. 6.

23. Kathryn K. Sklar, *Catharine Beecher: A Study in American Domesticity* (New Haven: Yale University Press, 1973), for discussion.

24. Muzzey, *Young Maiden,* p. 165.

25. Journal of Lucy Beckley, 1819, quoted in Cott, *Bonds of Womanhood,* p. 77; Herbig, "Friends for Freedom," p. 57; Nancy Flint to Mercy Flint Morris, n.d., quoted in Cott, *Bonds of Womanhood,* p. 55; Lucy Larcom to Mrs. I. W. Baker, June 9, 1846, quoted in Daniel D. Addison, *Lucy Larcom: Life, Letters, and Diary* (Boston: Houghton, Mifflin, 1894), pp. 34–35.

26. Letter to Emily Howland, April 23, 1858, Cornell University; Elizabeth Neall Gay to

Sarah Pugh, June 29, 1878, Columbia University; Maria W. Chapman to Mary A. Estlin, December 12, 1852, Boston Public Library.

27. Diary of Maria Mitchell, February 15, 1853, quoted in Phebe M. Kendall, *Maria Mitchell, Life, Letters, and Journals* (Boston: Lee & Shepard, 1896), pp. 25–26.

28. Gail Hamilton, *A New Atmosphere* (Boston: Ticknor & Fields, 1865), pp. 104–05.

29. See Ames, *Memorial*, p. 19; Catharine M. Sedgwick, "Notebook of Memories of Her Life" (1853), p. 136, Massachusetts Historical Society; Dewey, *Life and Letters*, p. 29; Henry Blackwell to Lucy Stone, July 12, 1854, and Lucy Stone to Henry Blackwell, quoted in Hersh, *Slavery of Sex*, p. 90; Harriot K. Hunt, *Glances and Glimpses* (Boston: J. P. Jewett & Co., 1856), pp. 6, 7, 9, 22.

30. Hunt, *Glances and Glimpses*, p. 181; Emily to Elizabeth Blackwell, June 4, 1902, Schlesinger Library; Benjamin to Emily Howland, n.d., Cornell University; Susan B. Anthony to Lucy R. Anthony, March 7, 1849, Schlesinger Library.

31. D'Ann Campbell, "Women's Life in Utopia: The Shaker Experiment in Sexual Equality Reappraised—1810–1860," *New England Quarterly* 51, no. 1 (March 1978): 28–29.

32. Charles Nordhoff, *The Communistic Societies of the United States; from Personal Visit and Observation: Including Detailed Accounts of the Economists, Zoarites, Shakers, the Amana, Oneida, Bethel, Aurora, Icarian, and Other Existing Societies, Their Religious Creeds, Social Practices, Numbers, Industries, and Present Condition* (New York: Hillary House, 1875), pp. 251–53.

33. Nordoff, *Communistic Societies*, pp. 253–55.

34. Hunt, *Glances and Glimpses*, pp. 233–34.

35. Hersh, *Slavery of Sex*, p. 210. For a contemporary example of Perfectionist thought, see Henry C. Wright, *Marriage and Parentage: or the Reproductive Element in Man, as a means to his Elevation and Happiness* (Boston: Bela March, 1854). For scholarly discussion of the range of nineteenth-century sexual attitudes, see John and Robin Haller, *The Physician and Sexuality in Victorian America* (Urbana: University of Illinois Press, 1974); G. J. Barker-Benfield, *The Horrors of the Half-Known Life, Male Attitudes toward Women and Sexuality in Nineteenth-Century America* (New York: Harper Colophon Books, 1976).

36. Emerson, Almanack, January 30, 1807 (7133, p. 5); April 21–23, 1807 (7133, p. 11), Houghton Library. For discussion, see Phyllis Cole, "The Advantage of Loneliness: Mary Moody Emerson's Almanacks, 1802–1855," in *Emerson Retrospect: Prospect and Retrospect* (Cambridge, Mass.: Harvard University Press, 1982), p. 15.

37. Lucy Larcom, "Sea and Shore," MS, Essex Institute.

38. A small group of "sex radicals" and certain utopian communities like the Oneida community advocated that sex be released from the social constraints of monogamous marriage. Mary S. Gove Nichols wrote about the liberation of sex from marriage as a form of both growth and autonomy. In her autobiographical novel, the heroine leaves her husband, who later accuses her of adultery: "Alas! there was no power in me to enable me to be faithful to myself, by being what he considered unfaithful to him, and no place in the world for such fidelity. If I had left a man who was loathsome to me, because I loved another, ever so noble or worthy of my love, no roof of friendship would have sheltered me, no heart would have dared excuse me. I might protest against falsehood and abuse; I might assert my faith in spiritual union, as I did; and

what I might do, that I did, not from calculation, but from instinct, the instinct of growth and development." Mary S. Gove Nichols, *Mary Lyndon, or, Revelations of a Life* (New York: Stringer & Townsend, 1855), pp. 162–63. Women such as the utopian society members or Nichols had greater sexual freedom, perhaps, than more traditional women, whether married or single. See also Hal D. Sears, *The Sex Radicals: Free Love in High Victorian America* (Lawrence: Regents Press of Kansas, 1977).

39. Graceanna Lewis to Esther Lewis, January 20, 1843, Macaulay Collection; Anne W. Weston to Deborah Weston, December 21, 1836, Boston Public Library.

40. Louisa May Alcott, *Diana and Persis* (New York: Arno Press, 1978), pp. 56, 61.

41. Ibid., p. 90.

42. Harriet Hosmer to William Crow, August 1854, in Cornelia Carr, *Harriet Hosmer: Letters and Memories* (London: Moffatt, Yard, 1913), p. 35.

43. Thomas H. Johnson, *The Poems of Emily Dickinson* (Cambridge, Mass.: Harvard University Press, 1955), no. 732. For discussion, see Sandra M. Gilbert and Susan Gubar, *The Madwoman in the Attic: The Woman Writer and the Nineteenth-Century Literary Imagination* (New Haven: Yale University Press, 1979), pp. 588–89. As important a statement perhaps appears in a letter from Emily to Susan Gilbert in 1852: "How dull our lives must seem to the bride and the plighted maiden, whose days are fed with gold . . . but to the *wife*, Susie . . . our lives perhaps seem dearer than all others in the world; you have seen flowers at morning, satisfied with the dew, and these same sweet flowers at noon with their heads bowed in anguish before the mighty sun; think you these thirsty blossoms will *now* need nought but—*dew?* No, they will cry for sunlight, and pine for the burning noon, though it scorches them, scathes them; they have got through with peace—they know that the man of noon is *mightier* than the morning and their life is henceforth to him. Oh Susie . . . it does so rend me . . . the thought of it when it comes, that I tremble lest at sometime I, too, am yielded up." Thomas H. Johnson, *The Letters of Emily Dickinson* (Cambridge, Mass.: Belknap Press, 1958), 1: 209–10.

44. Rebecca W. Hawes, "Maria Mitchell," report prepared for Ramapo Valley Chapter of the Daughters of the American Revolution, Ridgewood, N.J., October 1911, American Philosophical Society; Martha Wright to Elizabeth Cady Stanton, July 5, 1860, Sophia Smith Collection, Smith Library; Elizabeth Blackwell to Barbara Bodichon, September 7, 1864, quoted in Hays, *Extraordinary Blackwells*, p. 155.

45. Judith C. Breault, *The World of Emily Howland: Odyssey of a Humanitarian* (Millbrae, Calif.: Les Femmes, 1976), pp. 28–29.

46. Gail Hamilton, *Woman's Worth and Worthlessness* (New York: Harper & Brothers, 1872), p. 270.

47. Wright, *Sweeper in the Sky*, p. 234; Sedgwick, *Married or Single?*, p. vi.

48. Lucy Larcom, MS fragment, n.d., Essex Institute.

49. Catharine M. Sedgwick to Rev. Dr. Channing, August 24, 1837, in Dewey, *Life and Letters*, p. 271; Mary A. Dodge to Henry James, April 18, 1864, in Dodge, *Gail Hamilton's Life*, 1: 397.

50. Journal of Rachel W. Stearns, January 7, 1837, Schlesinger Library: Lucy Larcom, MS fragment, n.d., Essex Institute.

51. Lucy Larcom to John Durand, October 29, 1860, in Addison, *Lucy Larcom*, p. 66.

52. Sedgwick to Channing, in Dewey, *Life and Letters*, p. 271.

53. Mrs. N. Thorning Munroe, "The Sisters: or, Woman's Ambition," *The Universalist and Ladies' Repository* 9 (September 1840): 129–30. See also Timothy S. Arthur, *Married and Single; or, Marriage and Celibacy Contrasted in a Series of Domestic Pictures* (New York: Harper & Brothers, 1845); and Muzzey, *Young Maiden*, pp. 98–99.

54. Mary A. Dodge to Henry James, April 18, 1864, Dodge, *Gail Hamilton's Life*, 1: 398–99.

55. Elizabeth Blackwell to Hannah Blackwell, February 25, 1849, in Elizabeth Blackwell, *Pioneer Work in Opening the Medical Profession to Women* (New York: Schocken Books Reprint, 1977), p. 93.

56. Lucy Larcom, "The Unwedded," in *The Poetical Works of Lucy Larcom* (Boston: Houghton, Mifflin, 1884), pp. 26–27. It is interesting to note that the first short story published by a black in America reflected similar values and concerns. "The Two Offers" was written by the black poet, lecturer, and author Frances Ellen Watkins Harper (1825–1911) and was published in the *Anglo-African Magazine* of September/October 1859. The story revolves around two female cousins. Laura Lagrange, the daughter of rich and indulgent parents, marries a vain, philandering, selfish, charming rake. He soon neglects her and their child. Janette Alston is forced to work to support herself and her sickly mother. She eventually succeeds as a writer. Alston remains unmarried, despite a passionate youthful romance. She turns from her cousin's deathbed, determined to give her life to the antislavery movement. At story's end, she finds that "she had learned one of life's most precious lessons: that true happiness consists not so much in the fruition of our wishes as in the regulation of desires and the full development and right culture of our whole natures." My thanks to Susan Koppleman for bringing this story to my attention.

57. Anna Dickinson, unpublished speech on marriage and work, 1870, Library of Congress; William Leach, *True Love and Perfect Union* (New York: Basic Books, 1980), p. 159; *The Liberator*, June 13, 1860.

58. Elizabeth Blackwell to Barbara Bodichon, May 25, 1860, in Hays, *Extraordinary Blackwells*, p. 155.

Chapter 4

1. Susan B. Anthony to Daniel and Lucy R. Anthony, February 7, 1849, Schlesinger Library; Journal of Emily Blackwell, July 16, 1853, Schlesinger Library. Many women actually acted out such fantasies in the nineteenth century. See Jonathan Katz, *Gay American History: Lesbians and Gay Men in the U.S.A.: A Documentary* (New York: Avon Books, 1978), chap. 3; on freedom and independence as a motivation for women to dress like men, see Lillian Faderman, *Surpassing the Love of Men: Romantic Friendship and Love between Women from the Renaissance to the Present* (New York: William Morrow, 1981), pp. 48, 51, 52, 54, 59, and 61.

2. Ida H. Harper, *The Life and Work of Susan B. Anthony* (Indianapolis: Hollenbeck Press, 1898), 1:169; Helen Wright, *Sweeper in the Sky: The Life of Maria Mitchell, First Woman Astronomer in America* (New York: Macmillan, 1949), p. 162.

3. Journal of Sarah Stoughton, August 9 and August 27, 1870, American Antiquarian Society. See also Harriot Hunt, *Glances and Glimpses* (Boston: J. P. Jewett & Co., 1856), pp. 54–55.

4. Gail Hamilton, A New Atmosphere (Boston: Ticknor & Fields, 1865), p. 41.

5. Ibid., p. 41.

6. Laura Towne, July 5, 1875, in Rupert S. Holland, ed., Letters and Diary of Laura M. Towne (Cambridge, Mass., 1912), pp. 242–43; Diary of Emily Howland, 1871, Cornell University.

7. Mary Clemner Ames, A Memorial of Alice and Phoebe Cary, with Some of Their Later Poems (New York: Hurd & Houghton, 1874), p. 19; Janice Goldsmith Pulsifer, "Alice and Phoebe Cary, Whittier's Sweet Singers of the West," Essex Institute Historical Collections 109, no. 1 (January 1973): 13.

8. Ames, p. 19.

9. Mary A. Dodge to George Wood, May 18, 1864, in Harriet A. Dodge, Gail Hamilton's Life in Letters (Boston: Lee & Shepard, 1901), 1:409; Lucy Larcom to Franklin Carter, July 18, 1881, in Daniel D. Addison, Lucy Larcom, Life, Letters, and Diary (Boston: Houghton, Mifflin, 1894), p. 206.

10. Journal of Rachel Stearns, November 19, 1835, Schlesinger Library.

11. Cornelia Hancock to Ellen Child, February 1864, in Henrietta S. Jaquette, South after Gettysburg, Letters of Cornelia Hancock (Philadelphia: University of Pennsylvania Press, 1937), p. 46.

12. Diary of Catharine M. Sedgwick, May 18, 1828, Massachusetts Historical Society; Hunt, Glances and Glimpses, p. 214. My interpretation of Sedgwick's meaning differs somewhat from that of Nancy Cott. Cott believes that single women felt a sense of dependence and of inferiority because they were alienated from the home, in which women enacted their most important sex role as wives and mothers. I would contend that the power of a home to which Sedgwick referred was the authority of head-of-household and the capacity to define and control one's own environment. Single women were not alienated from traditional sex roles in the early nineteenth century. They adopted children in large numbers and all too often fulfilled the myriad domestic duties required of women, whether wives or daughters. They did long, however, for greater independence for themselves and for some release from domestic responsibility.

13. Eunice Callender to Sarah Ripley Stearns, April 8, 1828, Schlesinger Library; A Memoir of Miss Hannah Adams, Written by Herself, with Additional Notices by a Friend (Boston: Gray & Bowen, 1832), p. 58.

14. Susan B. Anthony, "The Homes of Single Women," MS, Library of Congress. Harriot Hunt also believed that there was "a necessity from the very nature of woman, for a home" (Hunt, Glances and Glimpses, p. 160). See also Graceanna Lewis to Rachel L. Fussell, March 26, 1878, Macaulay Collection.

15. "Prospectus," quoted in Edward Hitchcock, The Power of Christian Benevolence, Illustrated in the Life and Labors of Mary Lyon (Northampton, Mass.: Hopkins, Bridgman, 1852), p. 166.

16. Diary of Elizabeth Smith, December 5, 1850, American Antiquarian Society; Lucy Larcom to Jean Ingelow, December 15, 1867, in Addison, Lucy Larcom, p. 165.

17. Emerson Almanack, June 22, 1851 (7151, p. 12), Houghton Library; Hunt, Glances and Glimpses, p. 160.

18. Lucy Larcom to Philena Fobes, June 21, 1892, Essex Institute. See also Lucy Larcom to Esther Homiston, January 15, 1859, Massachusetts Historical Society.

19. Alcott Journal, 1845, March 1846, October 1872, in Ednah D. Cheney, Louisa May

Alcott, Her Life, Letters, and Journals (Boston: Roberts Brothers, 1890), pp. 45, 47, 267.

20. Emily Howland to Hannah Howland, May 15, 1866, Friends Historical Library.

21. Hunt, *Glances and Glimpses*, p. 214.

22. Anthony, "Homes of Single Women"; Lucy Larcom to Philena Fobes, February 16, 1858, Essex Institute.

23. Emily Howland to Belle, January 28, 1867, Friends Historical Society; Addison, *Lucy Larcom*, pp. 155–56.

24. Catharine M. Sedgwick to Frances S. Watson, March 9, 1831, in Mary E. Dewey, ed., *Life and Letters of Catharine M. Sedgwick* (New York: Harper & Brothers, 1871), p. 216; Phebe M. Kendall, *Maria Mitchell: Life, Letters, and Journals* (Boston: Lee & Shepard, 1896), p. 25. Among the many women who lived together for significant periods of time were Emily Blackwell and Elizabeth Cushier, Caroline F. Putnam and Sallie Holley, Laura Towne and Ellen Murray, Mary Grew and Margaret Jones Burleigh. Mary Anthony made a home for her sister Susan, as Lavinia Dickinson did for Emily. The three Lewis sisters of Media, Pennsylvania, the four Mott sisters of Albany, New York, and the five Smith Sisters of Glastonbury, Connecticut, all shared lives and homes. For discussion of a communal retirement home, see Mary Reed to Emily Howland, July 18, 1860, and Sallie Holley to Emily Howland, July 30, 1863, Cornell University.

25. Catharine E. Beecher and Harriet Beecher Stowe, *The American Woman's Home* (New York: J. B. Ford & Co., 1873), p. 204; Hunt, *Glances and Glimpses*, p. 132; Anthony, "Homes of Single Women."

26. Hunt, *Glances and Glimpses*, p. 160; Anthony, "Homes of Single Women."

27. Catharine E. Beecher, *Miss Beecher's Housekeeper and Healthkeeper* (New York: Harper & Brothers, 1856), p. 465. For discussion, see Kathryn K. Sklar, *Catharine Beecher: A Study in American Domesticity* (New York: W. W. Norton, 1976), p. 167.

28. Anthony, "Homes of Single Women."

29. *A Memoir of Miss Hannah Adams*, p. 4; Sarah M. Grimké, "Education of Women," Clements Library; Caroline F. Putnam to Sallie Holley, October 1, 1852, Cornell University.

30. See Emily Dickinson's remark to Joseph Lyman about her blindness: "Some years ago I had a woe, the only one that ever made me tremble. It was a shutting out of all the dearest ones of time, the strongest friends of the soul—BOOKS." Quoted in Richard B. Sewall, *The Life of Emily Dickinson* (New York: Farrar, Straus, & Giroux, 1974), p. 668. See also, Lucy Larcom to John G. Whittier, January 1, 1855, Essex Institute.

31. Caroline F. Putnam to Sallie Holley, May 22, 1853, Cornell University; Ellen M. O'Connor, ed., *Myrtilla Miner, A Memoir* (Boston: Houghton, Mifflin, & Co., 1885), p. 10; Pulsifer, "Alice and Phoebe Cary," pp. 12–13; Ames, *Memorial*, p. 19.

32. For discussions of women's education during the turn-of-the-century period, see Mary Beth Norton, *Liberty's Daughters: The Revolutionary Experience of American Women, 1750–1800* (Boston: Little, Brown, 1980), chap. 9; Linda K. Kerber, *Women of the Republic, Intellect & Ideology in Revolutionary America* (Chapel Hill: University of North Carolina Press, 1980), chaps. 7, 8; and Nancy Cott, *The Bonds of Womanhood: "Woman's Sphere" in New England, 1780–1835* (New Haven: Yale University Press, 1977), chap. 3.

33. Gerda Lerner, *The Grimké Sisters from South Carolina* (New York: Schocken Books, 1971), p. 17.

34. *A Memoir of Miss Hannah Adams*, pp. 8–9; Journal of Emily Blackwell, August 1851, Schlesinger Library; Sallie Holley to Caroline F. Putnam, May 21, 1853, in John White Chadwick, *A Life for Liberty: Anti-Slavery and Other Letters of Sallie Holley* (New York: G. P. Putnam's Sons, 1899), p. 124.

35. O'Connor, *Myrtilla Miner*, p. 10; Wright, *Sweeper in the Sky*, pp. 36–37; George Tolman, *Mary Moody Emerson* (Cambridge, Mass.: Edward W. Forbes, 1929), p. 9; Emerson Almanack (7153, p. 11), Houghton Library.

36. Lucretia Mott to Richard and Hannah Webb, May 14, 1849, Boston Public Library; Mary Reed to Emily Howland, December 18, 1859, and July 25, 1864, Cornell University.

37. Cornelia Hancock to Ellen Child, February 19, 1868, Friends Historical Library; Diary of Sarah M. Grimké, 1827, Clements Library: Lerner, *Grimké Sisters*, pp. 59–60; Wright, *Sweeper in the Sky*, p. 232; Sarah M. Grimké to Theodore Weld, September 20, 1837, in Gilbert Barnes and Dwight Dumond, eds., *Letters of Theodore Dwight Weld, Angelina Grimké Weld, and Sara Grimké, 1822–1844* (New York: D. Appleton-Century Co., 1934), 1: 449.

38. Emerson Almanack, June 21, 1827 (7136, p. 6), Houghton Library. Although she does not begin with her conversion, there is a point when she rededicates herself and her record: "Never was a date issued from the hand of royalty more important than the above. It is related to days and ages beyond this sphere. It is the record of virtue—the beginning of a portion of the history of a soul—struggling with weakness & ignorance & opposite appetites to the pure state of Heaven! God of infinite power & love, aid the being before thee to honor thee & herself in this little history." Emerson Almanack, December 26, 1806 (7133, p. 1) Houghton Library; Journal of Rachel W. Stearns, January 1, 1837, April 15, 1837, and September 12, 1835, Schlesinger Library. See also Frances E. Gray: "Self-examination, daily practised, is all important for the welfare of the soul, there are, however, but few peoples who will bring themselves to it." Diary of Frances E. Gray, May 24, 1830, Massachusetts Historical Society.

39. Kenneth Lockridge, *Literacy in Colonial New England* (New York: W. W. Norton, 1974), pp. 38, 13; William Matthew, *American Diaries: An Annotated Bibliography of American Diaries Written Prior to the Year 1861* (Boston: J. S. Canner, 1959), pp. 7, 10. For discussion, see Lyle Koehler, *A Search for Power: The "Weaker Sex" in Seventeenth-Century New England* (Urbana: University of Illinois Press, 1980), p. 54.

40. For diaries which present almost solely a record of religious devotions, see the Diary of Elizabeth Smith, 1773–1855, and the Diary of Sarah Lee, 1834, 1843, 1844, and 1848, American Antiquarian Society. See also Norton, *Liberty's Daughters*, p. 126.

41. Emerson Almanack, July 27, n.d. (7152, p. 1); October 22, 1840 (7147, p. a.); March 12, n.d. (7152, p. 4), Houghton Library; Alcott Journal, November 29, 1843, in Cheney, *Alcott*, p. 38; Emily Howland, "Moods of the Mind," February 10, 1861, Cornell University; Journal of Lucy Larcom, September 17, 1860, in Addison, *Lucy Larcom*, pp. 74–75. Sarah Stoughton's diary provided her with both a mode of self-examination and a structure for the long painful days during which she lay ill and dying. See Diary of Sarah Stoughton, January 10, 1871, American Antiquarian Society.

42. Maria Mitchell, "But a Woman," 1874, American Philosophical Society.

43. Diary of Maria Mitchell, September 10, 1855, in Kendall, *Maria Mitchell*, p. 42; Harriet Martineau, *Society in America* (Paris, 1842), 2:158–59. For an example of the weight of such opinion bearing down upon an individual, see the biography of Mary S. Gilpin in chapter 9, above.
44. Dodge, *Gail Hamilton's Life*, 2:801; Abigail W. May to Eleanor G. May, September 14, 1864, Schlesinger Library.
45. Alice Cary, November 24, 1868, in Ames, *Memorial*, p. 92.
46. *The Auburn Citizen*, July 1, 1892, Friends Historical Library.
47. Lucy Larcom to Philena Fobes, January 25, 1862, Essex Institute; Journal of Lucy Larcom, June 14, 1861, and June 23, 1861, in Addison, *Lucy Larcom*, pp. 94–95; Journal of Lucy Larcom, December 22, 1861, in Addison, p. 116; Journal of Lucy Larcom, June 22, 1862, in Addison, pp. 142–43; Lucy Larcom to John G. Whittier, February 22, 1855, Wheaton College; Lucy Larcom to John G. Whittier, February 4, 1887, in Addison, pp. 234–36.

Chapter 5

1. Mary Clemner Ames, *Eirene; or a Woman's Right* (New York: 1871), p. 201.
2. Susan Conrad, *Perish the Thought: Intellectual Women in Romantic America, 1830–1860* (Secaucus, N.J.: Citadel Press, 1978).
3. Frances Willard, *Glimpses of Fifty Years, 1839–1889* (Chicago: Women's Christian Temperance Union, 1889), p. 72.
4. Emily Howland, November 19, 1848, Friends Historical Library; Willard, *Glimpses of Fifty Years*, p. 70; Alice Stone Blackwell, "Dr. Emily," Schlesinger Library. The fact that age could bring home gender differences to women was new to the mid-nineteenth century. This sense of gender deprivation had not existed in the less age-graded eighteenth century, when men did not receive the vote at age twenty-one but when they married and acquired property.
5. Jane Maris to Esther J. Trimble, July 3, 1859; Graceanna Lewis to Esther A. Fussell, May 17, 1842, Macaulay Collection; Emily Howland, Birthday MS, November 20, 1852, Friends Historical Library. See also, Journal of Emily Blackwell, October 30, 1850, Schlesinger Library.
6. Quoted in Lyle Koehler, *A Search for Power: The "Weaker Sex" in Seventeenth-Century New England* (Urbana: University of Illinois Press, 1980), p. 44.
7. Eunice Callender to Sarah Ripley, January 26, 1808, Schlesinger Library.
8. Jane Maris to Esther J. Trimble, July 3, 1859, Macaulay Collection; Journal of Emily Blackwell, October 30, 1850, Schlesinger Library; Diary of Emily Howland, November 20, 1852, Friends Historical Library.
9. So, too, the death of her mother and the desertion of her father (who left her with thirteen siblings to care for) inspired Frances E. Gray to convert—first to the evangelical Baptists, then the Episcopalians, then back again to the Baptists. Diary of Frances E. Gray, October 17, 1831, June 27, 1832, November 1832, September 1834, Massachusetts Historical Society.
10. Kathryn K. Sklar, *Catharine Beecher: A Study in American Domesticity* (New York: W. W. Norton, 1976), p. 31.
11. Nancy Cott, *The Bonds of Womanhood: "Woman's Sphere" in New England, 1780–*

1835 (New Haven: Yale University Press, 1977), p. 140. Kett agrees about the potentially assertive impulse within the conversion experience. He found that in some individuals the level of religious anxiety was so raised during the conversion crisis that relief came only when the person decided to cast aside his or her previous life and follow the call to Christian activism. Joseph F. Kett, *Rites of Passage: Adolescence in America, 1790 to the Present* (New York: Basic Books, 1977), p. 76.

12. Diary of Elizabeth Smith, December 5, 1852, American Antiquarian Society.

13. R. Pierce Beaver, "Pioneer Single Women Missionaries," *Occasional Bulletin*, Missionary Research Library, 4 (September 30, 1953): 12. See also individual biographies such as Daniel T. Fiske, *The Cross and the Crown; or Faith Working by Love: as Exemplified in the Life of Fidelia Fiske* (Boston: Congregational Sabbath School and Publishing Society, 1868). Women in the antislavery and moral reform movements also left their homes as a result of conversion. See, for example, the life of Sarah Pugh, antislavery activist and Quaker. *Memorial of Sarah Pugh: A Tribute of Respect from Her Cousin* (Philadelphia: J. B. Lippincott Co., 1888).

14. For example, Lucy Richards, who dedicated herself to the Indians of upstate New York. *Memoirs of the Late Miss Lucy Richards, of Paris, Oneida, New York.* (New York: G. Lane & P. P. Sandford for the Methodist Episcopal Church, 1842).

15. American Board of Commissioners for Foreign Missions, *Annual Report*, 1828, p. 63.

16. Fiske, *The Cross and the Crown*, p. 63.

17. Ibid., pp. 95–96.

18. Ibid., p. 295.

19. Ibid, p. 361.

20. Mary P. Ryan, "A Women's Awakening: Evangelical Religion and the Families of Utica, New York, 1800–1840," *American Quarterly* 30, no. 5 (Winter 1978): 604

21. Journal of Rachel W. Stearns, October 15, 1834, Schlesinger Library.

22. Ibid., October 15, 1834.

23. Ibid., December 5, 1834.

24. Ibid., October 4, 1834.

25. Ibid., November 19 and 20, 1834.

26. Ibid., January 1 and 7, 1834.

27. Ibid., November 20, 1834.

28. Her journal ends with this information, and her fate is unknown.

29. Willard, *Glimpses of Fifty Years*, p. 124.

30. Ibid., pp. 124–25.

31. *The Auburn Citizen*, July 1, 1892, Friends Historical Library.

32. Diary of Emily Howland, November 19, 1847; November 19, 1848; November 19, 1856, Friends Historical Library.

33. Carrie A. Rowland to Emily Howland, December 23, 1852, Cornell University.

34. Rowland to Howland, December 23, 1852.

35. S. White to Emily Howland, January 11, 1857, Cornell University.

36. S. White to Emily Howland, September 6, 1857, Cornell University; Rachel Talcott to Emily Howland, April 25, 1858, Cornell University.

37. Rebecca to Emily Howland, September 10, 1857, Cornell University.

38. Rebecca to Emily, September 10, 1857.

39. Louisa May Alcott expressed her determination to practice nursing in terms of the

experiences it would open to her and the outlet it would provide. In her diary for November 1862, she wrote: "Thirty years old. Decided to go to Washington as nurse if I could find a place. Help needed, and I love nursing, and *must* let out my pent-up energy in some new way. . . . I want new experiences, and am sure to get 'em if I go. So I've sent in my name, and bide my time writing tales, to leave all snug behind me." Although Alcott nursed for only six weeks before becoming so ill that she had to return home, the book she wrote about her experiences, *Hospital Sketches*, propelled her on her way as a popular and well-paid author. See Ednah D. Cheney, *Louisa May Alcott, Her Life, Letters, and Journals* (Boston: Roberts Brothers, 1890), p. 140.

40. Henrietta S. Jaquette, *South after Gettysburg, Letters of Cornelia Hancock* (Philadelphia: University of Pennsylvania Press, 1937), p. 5.

41. Cornelia Hancock to Rachel Hancock, July 26, 1863, in Jaquette, *South After Gettysburg*, pp. 14–15.

42. Jaquette, pp. 14–15.

43. Cornelia Hancock to Rachel Hancock, April 12, 1864, in Jaquette, pp. 81–82; Cornelia Hancock to Ellen Child, July 8, 1863, in Jaquette, pp. 10–11.

44. Cornelia Hancock to Rachel Hancock, n.d., in Jaquette, pp. 86–87; Cornelia Hancock to Ellen Child, May 31, 1864, in Jaquette, pp. 96–97.

45. Cornelia Hancock to Rachel Hancock, August 14, 1863, in Jaquette, p. 18; also Cornelia Hancock to Ellen Child, August 6, 1863, in Jaquette, p. 15.

46. Cornelia Hancock to Rachel Hancock, February 27, 1866, Friends Historical Library.

47. Cornelia Hancock to Sarah Child, January 4, 1864, in Jaquette, p. 37.

48. Richard B. Sewall, *The Life of Emily Dickinson* (New York: Farrar, Straus and Giroux, 1974), p. 394; Emily Dickinson to Jane Humphrey, in Thomas Johnson, *The Letters of Emily Dickinson* (Cambridge: Belknap Press, 1958), 1:196–97. I have relied on Sewall's interpretation of Dickinson's developing sense of calling, finding it more persuasive than other Dickinson biographies and more in line with what I have found in the lives of other creative spinsters.

49. Sewall, *Life of Emily Dickinson*, pp. 133–34; Emily Dickinson to Frances Norcross, in Johnson, *Letters*, 2:397.

50. Sewall, *Life*, p. 426; Emily Dickinson to Abiah Root, May 7 and May 17, 1850, in Johnson, *Letters*, 1:99.

51. Sewall, *Life*, p. 392; Emily Dickinson to Jane Humphrey, January 23, 1850, in Johnson, *Letters*, 1:81–85.

52. Sewall, *Life*, p. 393; Emily Dickinson to Jane Humphrey, January 23, 1850, in Johnson, *Letters*, 1:81–85.

53. Sewall, *Life*, p. 118; Emily Dickinson to William A. Dickinson, March 27, 1853, in Johnson, *Letters*, 1:235.

54. Sewall, *Life*, pp. 394, 398, 423; Emily Dickinson to Jane Humphrey, in Johnson, *Letters*, 1:196–97; Emily Dickinson to Abiah Root, in Johnson, 1: 81–85; Emily Dickinson to Joseph Lyman, in Richard Sewall, *Lyman Letters: New Light on Emily Dickinson and Her Family* (Amherst: University of Massachusetts Press, 1965), p. 78.

55. Thomas H. Johnson, *The Poems of Emily Dickinson* (Cambridge, Mass.: Harvard University Press, 1955), no. 195.

56. Ibid., no. 569; Sewall, *Life*, pp. 487–88.

57. Ibid., no. 270; Sewall, *Life*, p. 506.

58. Ibid., no. 508; Sewall, *Life,* p. 505.
59. Ibid., no. 789; Sewall, *Life,* p. 507.
60. Suzanne Juhasz, *Naked and Fiery Forms, Modern American Poetry by Women: A New Tradition* (New York: Harper Colophon Books, 1976), chap. 1.
61. Louisa May Alcott, *Diana and Persis,* ed. Sarah Elbert (New York: Arno Press, 1978), p. 56.
62. Ibid., p. 63.
63. Such self-doubt could be seen in women with a variety of intellectual and artistic callings. Lucy Larcom, for example, wrote: "I have written for newspapers this winter. My ideas of the *Atlantic* are too high for me often to offer it anything my thoughts let slip. My standard is so far beyond my performance, that I am very glad to let them glide away unnoticed, and unnamed, on the path of the weekly tide wave of print" (Daniel D. Addison, *Lucy Larcom: Life, Letters, and Diary* [Boston: Houghton, Mifflin, 1844], p. 153). Maria Mitchell wrote similarly in her diary on October 17, 1854: "I have just gone over my comet computations again, and it is humiliating to perceive how very little more I know than I did seven years ago when I first did this kind of work. To be sure, I have only once in the time computed a parabolic orbit; but it seems to me that I know no more in general. I think I am a little better thinker, that I take things less upon trust, but at the same time I trust myself much less. The world of learning is so broad, and the human soul is so limited in power! We reach forth and strain every nerve, but we seize only a bit of the curtain that hides the infinite from us." See Phebe M. Kendall, *Maria Mitchell: Life, Letters, and Journals* (Boston: Lee & Shepard, 1896), pp. 33–34. For similar comments, see Abigail W. May, Journal, September 11, 1865, Schlesinger Library; Graceanna Lewis to Maria Mitchell, July 18, 1881, American Philosophical Society; Susan B. Anthony to Elizabeth C. Stanton, June 5, 1856, Library of Congress.
64. David Reisman, *The Lonely Crowd: A Study of Changing American Character* (New Haven: Yale University Press, 1950), p. 303.
65. Emerson Almanack, 1817 (7168, pp. 4–5), Houghton Library.
66. For discussion, see Sandra M. Gilbert and Susan Gubar, *The Madwoman in the Attic: The Woman Writer and the Nineteenth-Century Literary Imagination* (New Haven: Yale University Press, 1979), pp. 590–91.

Chapter 6

1. Rachel Hancock to Cornelia Hancock, February 1, 1866, Friends Historical Library.
2. Cornelia Hancock to Rachel Hancock, May 9, 1871, Friends Historical Library.
3. Diary of Susan B. Anthony, 2:40, Schlesinger Library.
4. Susan B. Anthony to Lucy Reed Anthony, October 15, 1848, Schlesinger Library.
5. Louisa May Alcott to the Lukens sisters, February 21, 1885, Boston Public Library.
6. Caroline F. Putnam to Sallie Holley, October 1, 1852, Cornell University. There is a fascinating letter from Graceanna Lewis to her mother, in which she tries to weigh the various duties that she feels. She was in York, Pa., teaching school—an economically and morally satisfactory position. But there had been an accident and an illness at home, and Graceanna felt that she might be needed there. In her unease, she talked it through with her mother: "In the first place the school is now fairly under way under

our management, and uncle thinks were I to leave it could not be carried to satisfaction—he says they might as well give up the affair now. In the next, the occupation suits my taste, I do not feel it too much exertion either for mind or body—and again I have become interested in the scholars and having taken them along thus far I would rather continue as far as I can with them,—again I feel as if I am doing some more good both in a moral and pecuniary point of view—than when at home. There is a *struggle* between these reasons and my feelings. You know I love my home and friends—and did I think my assistance were needed there it would make me unhappy even tho' doing the best in my power here." Graceanna Lewis to Esther Lewis, June 19, 1842, Macaulay Collection.

7. Guilelma Breed to Emily Howland, April 2, 1860, Cornell University.

8. For Sarah Pugh's growth in her Bristol activity, see her letters to Richard Dana Webb, publisher of the *Anti-Slavery Advocate*, August 27, 1852, and December 4, 1852, Boston Public Library. At first Pugh proposed tentatively that she felt a duty to relieve Mary A. Estlin from some of her work and hoped that she would "in some degree" be able to do so. Within four months she had taken over the Estlin correspondence and assured Webb that he need not bother the sickly Estlins with small details about their newspaper, as she could make arrangements to meet all deadlines. For comments on Pugh's effectiveness as antislavery editor and organizer in Bristol, see Lucia Mitchell to Maria W. Chapman, September 25, 1852; Emma Mitchell to Anne W. Weston, November 3, 1852; and Mary A. Estlin to Maria W. Chapman, January 10, 1853, Boston Public Library.

9. Sarah Pugh to Mary A. Estlin, April 11, 1854, Dr. Williams's Library.

10. *Memorial of Sarah Pugh: A Tribute of Respect from Her Cousin* (Philadelphia: J. B. Lippincott Co., 1888), pp. 97–98.

11. The "woman question" concerned itself with whether women would or would not be allowed to participate in the World Convention and in antislavery societies on an equal basis with men—that is, with the full privileges of membership, including speaking in meetings, voting, serving on committees, and holding office. The issue had been one of several which caused the American Anti-Slavery Society to divide into two separate national organizations in 1839 and 1840. When the Garrisonian abolitionists elected women to represent them at the World Convention, the more conservative British and American delegates at first reissued the invitation for male delegates only, and then, when the women arrived anyway, refused to accept their credentials and allow them to be seated. This action only served to focus attention on the women and the issue of equal participation, which the British women had not raised. For discussion, see Aileen Kraditor, *Means and Ends in American Abolitionism: Garrison and His Critics on Strategy and Tactics, 1834–1850* (New York: Vintage Books, 1967). Elizabeth Cady Stanton, then a young woman attending the convention with her husband, said that it was the actions of the women there which first caused her to think about women's rights and inspired her to convene the Seneca Falls Convention.

12. The conference was equally important for other women. See Mary Grew's diary of the trip, in the Schlesinger Library.

13. There are several letters in the Friends Historical Library from former students describing the various Kimber sisters and their roles in the school. See the S. C. Haines and Howard M. Jenkins collections.

14. Lucretia Mott to Richard and Hannah Webb, March 23, 1846, Boston Public Library.
15. Sarah Pugh to Mary A. Estlin, November 13, 1854, Dr. Williams's Library.
16. Mary A. Dodge to George Wood, August 11, 1866, in Harriet A. Dodge, *Gail Hamilton's Life in Letters* (Boston: Lee & Shepard, 1901), 1:563.
17. Daniel T. Fiske, *The Cross and the Crown; or Faith Working by Love: as Exemplified in the Life of Fidelia Fiske* (Boston: Congregational Sabbath School and Publishing Society, 1868), p. 119; Diary of Laura M. Towne, April 17, 1862, in Rupert S. Holland, ed., *Letters and Diary of Laura M. Towne, Written from the Sea Islands of South Carolina 1862–1884* (Cambridge, Mass., 1912), p. 8.
18. Benjamin Howland to Emily Howland, April 29, 1858, Cornell University.
19. Gail Hamilton, *A New Atmosphere* (Boston: Ticknor & Fields, 1865), pp. 41–43, 45.
20. See Kathryn K. Sklar, *Catharine Beecher: A Study in American Domesticity* (New York: W. W. Norton, 1978) for discussion.
21. Martha Saxton, *Louisa May* (Boston: Houghton Mifflin, 1977), p. 275.
22. Ibid, p. 276.
23. Louisa May Alcott to Abigail M. Alcott, January 1, 1865, quoted in Saxton, p. 281.
24. Laura Stebbins to Emily Howland, August 5, 1867, Friends Historical Library.
25. Stebbins to Howland, August 5, 1867.
26. Diary of Patty Rogers, February 25, March 4, and March 28, 1785, American Antiquarian Society.
27. Rogers, May 5, May 7, July 23, July 27, October 1, November 4, and November 10, 1785.
28. Sarah Pugh to Mary A. Estlin, November 13, 1853, Dr. Williams's Library.
29. A[bigail] K[imber], August 18, 1853, MS fragment, Dr. Williams's Library.
30. Ida H. Harper, *The Life and Work of Susan B. Anthony* (Indianapolis: Hollenbeck Press, 1898), 1:218.
31. Mary Grew to Sidney H. Gay, April 10, 1848, Columbia University.
32. *Memorial of Sarah Pugh*, pp. 97–98.
33. Carrie A. Rowland to Emily Howland, 1859, Cornell University.
34. Benjamin Howland to Emily Howland, June 5, 1857, Friends Historical Library.
35. Emily Howland to Hannah Howland, July 29, 1857, Cornell University.
36. Theophilus Parsons, *Memoir of Emily Elizabeth Parsons* (Boston: Little, Brown, 1880), pp. 44–45.
37. Ibid., pp. 45–46.
38. Ibid., p. 50.
39. Fiske, *Cross and the Crown*, p. 54.
40. Ibid., pp. 57–58.
41. "Miss Lyon was often heard to say in subsequent years, 'I little knew how much that prayer-meeting would cost me.' " Ibid., p. 55.
42. Sarah Chase to Anthony Chase, April 20, 1861, American Antiquarian Society.
43. Anthony Chase to Sarah Chase, April 28, 1861, American Antiquarian Society.
44. Eliza Chase to Sarah Chase, April 1861, American Antiquarian Society.
45. Emily Howland to Slocum Howland, May 7, 1863, Cornell University.
46. Hannah Howland to Emily Howland, June 2, 1858, Cornell University.
47. The memoir is full of letters and diary comments on the subject. See, for example, pp. 63, 108–09, 114, 119, 192, 247–49, 256–57, 269–70, and 347.

48. Emily Dickinson to Susan Gilbert, February 6, 1852, and June 1852, in Thomas H. Johnson, *Emily Dickinson, Selected Letters* (Cambridge, Mass.: Belknap Press, 1971), pp. 77, 88–89.

49. There is considerable scholarly debate about the nature of Emily Dickinson's muse—and its gender. See Joanne Feit Diehl, " 'Come Slowly—Eden': An Exploration of Women Poets and Their Muse," *Signs: Journal of Women in Culture and Society* 3, no. 3 (Spring 1978): 572–87; Lillian Faderman's response to Diehl, in *Signs* 4, no. 1 (Autumn 1978): 188–91; Louise Bernikow's response, pp. 191–95; Adrienne Rich, "Vesuvius at Home: The Power of Emily Dickinson," *Parnassus* 5 (1976): 49–74.

50. Adalaide Morris, "Two Sisters Have I: Emily, Vinnie, and Susan Dickinson," *The Massachusetts Review*, forthcoming. My thanks to Morris for showing me the prepublication manuscript.

51. See, for example, Alcott's Journal for February 1861, on writing, and for May 1865, on her response to critical reviews.

52. Alcott did have such figures in her fiction, and not only in the unpublished *Diana and Persis*. She wrote, for example, about the relationship of two women, Christie and Rachel, in which Rachel's presence gave Christie purpose and happiness. Although the two were divided for a time by marriage, in the end they lived together. See Alcott, *Work: A Story of Experience* (New York: Schocken Books Reprint, 1977).

53. See Elizabeth P. Peabody to Maria Chase, April 28, 1822, Smith College; Sallie Holley and Caroline F. Putnam to Emily Howland, January 1, 1858, Cornell University; Lucy Larcom to Philena Fobes, February 6, 1858, Essex Institute.

54. Mary Reed to Emily Howland, May 22, 1858; Carrie A. Rowland to Emily Howland, November 22, 1857; Phebe M. Coffin to Emily Howland, June 10, 1858, Cornell University.

55. Elizabeth P. Peabody to Maria Chase, October 4, 1823, Smith College; *A Memoir of Miss Hannah Adams, Written by Herself with Additional Notices by a Friend* (Boston: Gray & Bowen, 1832), p. 7; Diary of Frances E. Gray, September 13, 1834, Massachusetts Historical Society; Eliza Nelson to Laura Lovell, April 8, 1866, Essex Institute.

56. Elizabeth P. Peabody to Maria Chase, 1822, Smith College.

57. Lillian Faderman, *Surpassing the Love of Men: Romantic Friendship and Love between Women from the Renaissance to the Present* (New York: William Morrow, 1981), pp. 226–27; Susan Conrad, *Perish the Thought: Intellectual Women in Romantic America, 1830–1860* (Secaucus, N.J.: Citadel Press, 1978), pp. 57–65.

58. Faderman, *Surpassing the Love of Men*, pp. 226–27.

Chapter 7

1. Carroll Smith-Rosenberg, "The Female World of Love and Ritual: Relations between Women in Nineteenth-Century America," *Signs: Journal of Women in Culture and Society* 1, no. 1 (Autumn 1975): 1–30; Mary Beth Norton, *Liberty's Daughters: The Revolutionary Experience of American Women, 1750–1800* (Boston: Little, Brown, 1980), pp. 102–05; Mary P. Ryan, *Cradle of the Middle Class: The Family in Oneida County, New York, 1790–1865* (Cambridge: Cambridge University Press, 1981), pp. 191–98.

2. See Wilson C. McWilliams, *The Idea of Fraternity in America* (Los Angeles: University of California Press, 1973); Nancy Cott, *The Bonds of Womanhood: "Woman's Sphere" in New England, 1790–1835* (New Haven: Yale University Press, 1977).

3. Alexander Swift, for example, married first Susan and then Elmina Cary, who was fifteen years younger than her sister. See "Some Passages in the Life of an Old Maid," *Garland* (1830), pp. 56–87, for a fictional account of a man who courted two sisters. Clinton points out the large numbers of widowers among the Southern planter class who practiced this custom. See Catherine Clinton, *The Plantation Mistress: Woman's World in the Old South* (New York: Pantheon Books, 1982), pp. 78–79.

4. Daniel T. Fiske, *The Cross and the Crown; or Faith Working by Love: as Exemplified in the Life of Fidelia Fiske* (Boston: Congregational Sabbath School and Publishing Society, 1868), p. 376; diary of Elizabeth Smith, December 31, 1843, American Antiquarian Society.

5. Carrie A. Rowland to Emily Howland, 1859, Cornell University.

6. Eunice Callender to Sarah Ripley Stearns, August 13, 1814, Schlesinger Library.

7. Although the feeling of loss involved in a sister's death seems understandable, the grief engendered by a sister's marriage may seem more elusive to the modern mind. The idea was fostered by antebellum didactic literature. *The American Magazine* of 1835 advised that "Marriage is to a woman at once the happiest and saddest event of her life; it is the promise of future bliss raised on the death of all her present enjoyment" ("Marriage," *The American Magazine of Useful and Entertaining Knowledge* [1835], p. 350). *The Atheneum* acknowledged that, as a woman looked around her, "She beholds few . . . who cherish . . . that object who relied solely on them for happiness, in whose smiles they alone live, and for whom they have perhaps left all the ties of consanguinity and all the endearing affections of school-day esteem. She sees all this and she dreads to sacrifice a life of comparative contentment for a short spring of love, embittered with a remaining season of barren duty." Benedict, the Married Man, "On the Undeserved Stigma Conferred on Single Ladies by the Title of Old Maid," *The Atheneum, or The Spirit of the English Magazines* 1, no. 2 (September 1, 1817): 803.

8. *A Memoir of Miss Hannah Adams. Written by Herself, with Additional Notices by a Friend* (Boston: Gray & Bowen, 1832), pp. 7–8.

9. *Memoir*, p. 8. The effect is heightened by the *Notices* written by Hannah Farnham Sawyer Lee and appended to the *Memoir*. In these, Lee wrote: "But the friendship of these two sisters was such as 'strangers intermeddle not with.' The death of this sister seemed to be the dissolution of a tie, like that which occasioned the exclamation of David in his beautiful lamentation over Jonathan. 'Thy love to me was wonderful, passing the love of women.' " *Memoir*, p. 60.

10. Ibid., pp. 57, 58.

11. Alice Cary also wrote love poetry to the memory of her sister, Elmina Cary Swift. The poems were published as a *Lover's Diary* in 1868 and were negatively reviewed by male literary critics, who found such illusions overly sentimental and alien.

12. *Memoir*, p. 18.

13. Ibid., p. 59.

14. Adams had a second and younger sister who remained unnamed in her diary. She said in her memoirs that she was moved to publish her story in order that the royalties might provide a legacy for this sister. Clearly, however, the relationship did not carry

the same emotional weight as her love for Elizabeth, and her relationship with this sister did not replace that with Elizabeth. The love "surpassing that of men" was selective and did not automatically occur between siblings. Ibid., p. 89.

15. Mary E. Dewey, ed., *Life and Letters of Catharine M. Sedgwick* (New York: Harper & Brothers, 1871), p. 69.

16. Alcott Journal, May 1858 and May 1860, in Cheney, *Louisa May Alcott, Her Life, Letters, and Journal* (Boston: Roberts Brothers, 1890), pp. 98, 121.

17. Harriot Hunt, *Glances and Glimpses* (Boston: J. P. Jewett & Co., 1856), pp. 165–66.

18. Ibid., p. 214.

19. Edmund Quincy to Richard D. Webb, January 29, 1843, Boston Public Library.

20. Anne W. Weston to Deborah Weston, October 4, 1836, Boston Public Library. Another "proposal" of marriage illustrates the way in which spinsterhood could be utilized as a weapon against a woman when she took unpopular and public political positions. Anne W. Weston's antislavery activity had aroused the ire of slaveholders. One believed that he had the antidote for her unfeminine political activity and her love of blacks—he would mate her with one of his slaves: "Dear Madam, I am informed that you are very desirous to obtain a Husband and I understand you have taken quite a liking to the dark color and would prefer one of the real African breed. You must be very fond of sweet things and fine flavour. I admire your fine taste. I have a very bull Niger of the real African breed and I think he would suit your taste and if you will come out to Louisville in Old Kentuck you may marry him if you think you would be a good breeder for they will be worth five or six hundred Dollars a piece." John S. Jacob to Anne W. Weston, March 25, 1839, Boston Public Library.

21. There is evidence to suggest a romantic attachment between Anne W. Weston and British abolitionist George Thompson. See Lee Chambers-Schiller, "The Cab: A Trans-Atlantic Community, Aspects of Nineteenth-Century Reform" (Ph.D. diss., University of Michigan, 1977).

22. Edmund Quincy to Richard D. Webb, November 24, 1857, and June 11, 1852, Boston Public Library.

23. Anne W. Weston to Deborah Weston, November 19, 1836, and December 6, 1836; Deborah Weston to Maria W. Chapman, April 13, 1837; Anne W. Weston to Deborah Weston, October 17, 1837, Boston Public Library.

24. Anne W. Weston to Anne B. Weston, May 30, 1836; Deborah Weston to Anne W. Weston, November 19, 1837, Boston Public Library.

25. Deborah Weston to Anne W. Weston, November 13, 1836. See also, Anne W. Weston to Joseph B. Estlin, October 27, 1850, Boston Public Library.

26. Deborah Weston to Caroline Weston, March 21, 1839; Deborah Weston to Lucia Weston, n.d. (vol. 5., n. 74). See also Deborah Weston to Anne W. Weston, 1836 (vol. 8, n. 4); Anne W. Weston to Deborah Weston, February 13, 1837; Anne W. Weston to Mary A. Estlin, July 19, 1852; Caroline Weston, diary fragment, n.d. (vol. 6, n. 9), Boston Public Library.

27. Nancy Chodorow, *The Reproduction of Mothering: Psychoanalysis and the Sociology of Gender* (Berkeley: University of California, 1978); Ryan, *Cradle of the Middle Class*, p. 194.

28. Mary S. Gilpin to Sophia duPont, October 27, 1845; February 18, 1846, Eleutherian Mills Historical Library.

29. An example of such a relationship is that of Catharine Seely and Deborah Roberts. Seely, born in 1799, fell ill at the age of fifteen and remained virtually bed-ridden until her death at thirty-nine. For the last fourteen years of her life she was attended by her cousin, Deborah Roberts. Seely believed that her illness was inflicted on her so that she might bear up in righteousness, a model of Christian submission to her friends and family. And Roberts considered her devotion to Seely as part of God's plan to make Seely's life an example. Neither could conceive of life without Seely's illness or Roberts's ministrations. Wrote Seely, "We have been united in such a way that I think even death will not long separate us." Roberts agreed: "I can truly say no pains or privations that I have endured for her have had the least tendency to dissolve the tender ties of affection by which we have been so long united. I cannot wish to hold her from the Savior, who is altogether worthy, nor to detain her amidst the pains and conflicts of this probationary state, but nothing short of this could cause me to willingly resign her." There was no change in Seely's condition until Roberts contracted typhus. Then Seely suddenly died, apparently unable to face the prospect of losing her friend. Roberts, too, gave up the struggle: "it is not because I regret that she is at rest [that I cry], but to think of the loss I shall sustain if I recover; I have no desire, however to be raised up again, but that the Lord's will may be done." She died five days after Seely, at the age of thirty-seven. By framing the context of their relationship in terms of illness rather than work, and passive endurance rather than activism, the women's readings and discussions about the meaning of life and the nature of salvation produced more complacency than inner growth. Theirs was a static definition of life. Thus their mutual dependence served only to fetter them and never to foster autonomy. The result was literally fatal to both. See *Memoir of Catharine Seely, Late of Darien, Connecticut* (New York: Collins, Brother & Co., 1843), pp. 69, 105, 138.

30. Diary of Deborah Weston, February 22 (?), Boston Public Library. See, too, Anne W. Weston to Mary A. Estlin, March 25, 1851, and April 6, 1851; Anne W. Weston to Deborah Weston, October 17, 1837, Boston Public Library.

31. Caroline Weston to Deborah Weston, November 23 (?), Boston Public Library. See also, Anne W. Weston to Mary Weston, October 29, 1842; Anne W. Weston to Deborah Weston, September 8, 1836, Boston Public Library.

32. Anne W. Weston to Mary Weston, May 6, 1839, Boston Public Library.

33. Harriet Martineau to Crabbe Robinson, July 6, 1850, quoted in Robert K. Webb, *Harriet Martineau: A Radical Victorian* (New York: Columbia University Press, 1960), p. 25. For a similar perspective, see Mary A. Estlin to Caroline Weston, October 15, 1855, Dr. Williams's Library.

34. Richard D. Webb to Elizabeth Pease, March 28, 1849; Richard D. Webb to Edmund Quincy, August 11, 1851, Boston Public Library.

35. Edmund Quincy to Richard D. Webb, January 13, 1853, Boston Public Library.

36. "Much Afraid" was a character in John Bunyan's seventeenth-century parable, *Pilgrim's Progress*.

37. Sarah Pugh to Mary A. Estlin, December 18, 1853, Boston Public Library.

38. Anne W. Weston to Mary A. Estlin, January 14, 1851, and March 25, 1851, Boston Public Library.

39. Edmund Quincy to Richard D. Webb, June 10, 1869, Boston Public Library.

40. Anne W. Weston to Deborah Weston, n.d. (vol. 3, n. 51; vol. 3, n. 39), Boston Public Library. See also Anne W. and Lucia Weston to Deborah and Emma F. Weston, n.d. (vol. 3, n. 10), Boston Public Library. Anne W. Weston to Mary A. Estlin, October 17, 1865, Boston Public Library.

41. Deborah Weston to Maria W. Chapman, March 4, 1840, Boston Public Library.

42. Two sisters were considerably younger than the others. Lucia was consumptive. She never had much vitality or stamina. After years as an invalid, she died in Italy in 1861 at the age of forty. Emma, the youngest, had Maria's beauty but lacked her forceful-ness. The family decided that Emma should marry. They invested in "finishing" her in Europe, where she might garner a certain style and widen her opportunities to meet a suitably wealthy and titled husband. In 1852 she made a stunning debut in London society. Neither Lucia nor Emma participated in politics. Their places in the family constellation were nevertheless important. Lucia's role as family invalid prevented Anne from giving way to her nervous temperament: Anne's headaches, anxieties, and ills received kindly sympathy but paled beside Lucia's real physical deterioration. In fact, Anne rallied to serve as family nurse when Deborah attended Lucia. Emma's social success was a source of vicarious pride in her sisters, who had felt isolated from proper Boston society because of their liberal politics and activism. Emma's marriage represented womanly success to a world that deemed her sisters unwomanly.

43. Edmund Quincy to Richard D. Webb, November 22, 1863, Boston Public Library.

44. Anne W. Weston to Mary A. Estlin, February 25, 1855, Boston Public Library.

45. On the way home from Philadelphia, Maria collapsed in feverish delirium. Although she recovered, she never again took the antislavery platform in public. Chambers-Schiller, "The Cab," pp. 121–22.

46. Deborah Weston to Mary Weston, September 17, 1836; Caroline Weston to Deborah Weston, October 12, 1836, and n.d. (vol. 5, n. 22); Anne W. Weston to Deborah Weston, January 9, 1837, Boston Public Library.

47. Anna S. Blackwell, "Dr. Emily Blackwell," Schlesinger Library.

48. Journal of Emily Blackwell, August 20, 1850, and November 23, 1851, Schlesinger Library.

49. Elizabeth Blackwell to Emily Blackwell, November 20, 1850, quoted in Elizabeth Blackwell, *Pioneer Work in Opening the Medical Profession to Women* (New York: Schocken Books Reprint, 1977), p. 172.

50. Journal of Emily Blackwell, August 18, 1850, and August 25, 1850, Schlesinger Library.

51. Ibid., November 26, 1850.

52. Ibid., December 29, 1850.

53. Ibid., May 29, 1851.

54. Ibid., August 31, 1853.

55. Ibid., January 6, 1852.

56. Ibid., January 22, 1852.

57. Ibid., March 23, 1852.

58. Ibid., July 24, 1852.

59. Ibid., October 12, 1851.

60. Ibid., June 9, 1853.

61. Ibid., December 19, 1852; October 8, 1835.

62. Ibid., February 17, 1854.

63. Alice S. Blackwell, "Dr. Emily," p. 4.

64. Elinor R. Hays, *Those Extraordinary Blackwells* (New York: Harcourt, Brace & World, 1967), p. 138.

65. Journal of Emily Blackwell, 1858.

66. Emily Blackwell to Barbara Bodichon, April 25, 1860, Schlesinger Library.

67. Hays, *Extraordinary Blackwells*, p. 165.

68. Ibid., p. 166.

69. Emily Blackwell to Elizabeth Blackwell, April 2, 1908, Schlesinger Library.

70. Hays, *Extraordinary Blackwells*, p. 298.

71. Ibid., p. 187.

72. Rhoda died in November and Lucy on December 10, 1833. The deaths were presaged by a collective family vision of Rhoda and Lucy sinking into the ground in full daylight. Thereafter, Lucy's ghost was often "seen" by various members of the family, usually before another family death. Mary Clemner Ames, *A Memorial of Alice and Phoebe Cary, with Some of Their Later Poems* (New York: Hurd & Houghton, 1874), p. 17.

73. Ibid., p. 203–04.

74. Phoebe apparently exerted her independence in some things. In 1852 Alice reported that their "close sympathy has been broken by religious difference." Alice Cary to William D. Gallagher, February 11, 1852, quoted in Janice G. Pulsifer, "Alice and Phoebe Cary, Whittier's Sweet Singers of the West," *Essex Institute Historical Collections* 109, no. 1 (January 1973): 32.

75. Ames, *Memorial*, p. 214.

76. Ibid., pp. 207–08; 75–76.

77. There were many examples of sisters who died close to one another in time. The Carys died five months apart. But "a week after Hannah [Brown of Boston]'s departure, her sister Elizabeth followed her. Their lives had been blended for many years,—excessive grief beclouded her reason and she passed away" (Hunt, *Glances and Glimpses*, p. 40). Mary Townsend died in June 1851; her younger sister Hannah Townsend died a few days later, and the two were buried side by side (Edwin Fussell to Graceanna Lewis, July 11, 1851, and July 25, 1851, Macaulay Collection). For that matter, Emily Blackwell died of enterocolitis in September, 1910, just three months after Elizabeth (who never recovered from falling down a flight of stairs).

78. Phoebe Cary to John G. Whittier, March 31, 1871, Essex Institute.

79. "Reminiscences of Eliza Perkins Cabot," Schlesinger Library, quoted in Cott, *Bonds of Womanhood*, pp. 78–79.

80. Gerda Lerner, *The Grimké Sisters from South Carolina: Pioneers for Woman's Rights and Abolition* (New York: Schocken Books, 1967), pp. 144–45.

81. Marion Harland, "The Passing of the Home Daughter," *The Independent* 71, no. 3267 (July 13, 1911): 88–91.

82. Journal of Maria Mitchell, December 5, 1854, American Philosophical Society.

83. Howland Papers, series 2, box 1C, Friends Historical Library.

84. Louise Bernikow, *Among Women* (New York: Harmony Books, 1980), p. 143.

85. Caroline F. Putnam to Sallie Holley, October 1, 1852, Cornell University.

86. Caroline F. Putnam to Sallie Holley, May 15, 1853, Cornell University.

87. Caroline F. Putnam to Sallie Holley, May 22, 1853, Cornell University; Sallie Holley to Abigail K. Foster, April 5, 1854, American Antiquarian Society.
88. For detailed information about the lives of these two women, see Katherine L. Herbig, "Friends for Freedom: The Lives and Careers of Sallie Holley and Caroline Putnam" (Ph.D. diss., Claremont Graduate School, 1977).
89. Caroline F. Putnam to Abigail K. Foster, November 8, 1857, American Antiquarian Society.
90. Sallie Holley to Abigail K. Foster, March 1, 1855, American Antiquarian Society.
91. Sallie Holley to Abigail K. Foster, May 13, 1857, American Antiquarian Society; Sallie Holley to Caroline F. Putnam, November 9, 1867, Friends Historical Library.
92. Sallie Holley to Caroline F. Putnam, November 18, 1861, in John W. Chadwick, *A Life for Liberty: Anti-Slavery and Other Letters of Sallie Holley* (New York: G. P. Putnam's Sons, 1899), pp. 186–87.
93. Caroline F. Putnam to Emily Howland, March 29, 1858, Cornell University.
94. Caroline F. Putnam to Emily Howland, January 1, 1858, Cornell University.
95. Sallie Holley to Caroline F. Putnam, October 6, 1867, in Chadwick, p. 203.
96. Caroline F. Putnam to Emily Howland, March 29, 1858, Cornell University.
97. Caroline F. Putnam to Sallie Holley, November 1868, *The National Anti-Slavery Standard*, February 13, 1869.
98. Emily Howland to Hannah Howland, November 13, 1873, Friends Historical Library; Caroline F. Putnam to Samuel J. May, January 27, 1893, Massachusetts Historical Society.
99. Sallie Holley to Caroline F. Putnam, January 12, 1892, in Chadwick, *Life for Liberty*, pp. 281–82; also Sallie Holley to Maria Porter, December 5, 1892, in ibid., pp. 298–99.
100. Caroline F. Putnam to Samuel J. May, December 18, 1884, and January 27, 1893, Massachusetts Historical Society.
101. Bernikow, *Among Women*, p. 143.

Chapter 8

1. Anthony F. C. Wallace, *Rockdale: The Growth of an American Village in the Early Industrial Revolution* (New York: Alfred A. Knopf, 1978), p. 109.
2. Clementina Smith to Sophia duPont, March 25, [1837]; n.d. (W9-25282); March 28, 1840, Eleutherian Mills Historical Library.
3. Mary E. Dewey, ed., *Life and Letters of Catharine M. Sedgwick* (New York: Harper and Brothers, 1871), p. 247; Ednah D. Cheney, *Memoirs of Lucretia Crocker and Abby W. May* (Boston: Massachusetts School Suffrage Association, 1893), p. 46; Sarah Pugh to Elizabeth Pease, January 20, 1846, Mary Grew to Helen B. Garrison, November 10, 1846, Sarah Pugh to Richard and Hannah Webb, April 25, 1847, Mary Grew to Helen B. Garrison, September 17, 1851, Mary Grew to Helen B. Garrison, August 19, 1850, Sarah Pugh to Mary A. Estlin, August 10, 1861, Boston Public Library; Margaret J. Burleigh to Emily Howland, August 26, 1857, and August 6, 1858, Cornell University; Sarah Pugh to Mary A. Estlin, March 25, 1856, and June 22, 1860, Dr. Williams's Library; Abigail W. May, journal extracts, October 1, 1849, August 10–September 7, 1864, May 2, 1873, Schlesinger Library; Sallie Holley to

Caroline F. Putnam, September 7, 1861, September 29, 1861, October 24, 1861, in John W. Chadwick, *A Life for Liberty: Anti-Slavery and Other Letters of Sallie Holley* (New York: G. P. Putnam's Sons, 1899), pp. 181, 183, 185; Kathryn K. Sklar, *Catharine Beecher: A Study in American Domesticity* (New York: W. W. Norton, 1976), pp. 184–87; Anne W. Weston to Mary A. Estlin, January 14, 1851, and March 25, 1851, Boston Public Library.

4. Barbara Berg, *The Remembered Gate: Origins of American Feminism* (New York: Oxford University Press, 1978), p. 120; Carroll Smith-Rosenberg, "The Hysterical Woman: Sex Roles and Role Conflict in Nineteenth-Century America," *Social Research* 39 (Winter 1972): 652–78; Robert S. Seidenberg, "The Trauma of Eventlessness," in Jean Baker Miller, ed., *Psychoanalysis and Women* (Harmondsworth: Penguin Books, 1973), pp. 350–62.

5. Richard Cloward and Frances F. Pivan, "Hidden Protest: The Channeling of Female Innovation and Resistance," *Signs: A Journal of Women in Culture and Society* 4, no. 4 (Summer 1979): 651–69.

6. *Memorial of Sarah Pugh: A Tribute of Respect from Her Cousin* (Philadelphia: J. B. Lippincott Co., 1888), p. 35.

7. Theophilus Parsons, *Memoir of Emily Elizabeth Parsons* (Boston: Little, Brown, 1880), pp. 44–45; Cornelia Hancock to Ellen Child, July 8, 1863, in Henrietta S. Jaquette, *South after Gettysburg: Letters of Cornelia Hancock* (Philadelphia: University of Pennsylvania Press, 1937), pp. 10–11; Daniel T. Fiske, *The Cross and the Crown; or Faith Working by Love: as Exemplified in the Life of Fidelia Fiske* (Boston: Congregational Sabbath School and Publishing Society, 1868), p. 63.

8. Carrie A. Rowland to Emily Howland, February 10, 1854, Cornell University.

9. Diary of Emily Howland, May 16, 1877, Friends Historical Library.

10. Ibid., December 11, 1877, Friends Historical Library; extract from diary, April 25, 1883, Cornell University.

11. Margaret Jones Burleigh to Emily Howland, March 28, 1872, Friends Historical Library.

12. Margaret Jones Burleigh to Emily Howland, June 1, 1856, Cornell University.

13. Cornelia Hancock to Emily Howland, August 10, 1865, Cornell University.

14. Hancock to Howland, August 10, 1865.

15. For discussion, see Lucy Larcom to Mrs. Pratt, January 15, 1863; Lucy Larcom to the editors of the *Traveller*, November 3, 1881; Lucy Larcom to the editor of the *Christmas Traveller*, November 25, 1884; Lucy Larcom to Susie [Ward], April 30, 1890, Essex Institute.

16. *Our Young Folks at Home.* See Lucy Larcom to Harriet B. Stowe, November 20, 1868, Essex Institute. Lucy Larcom to Mrs. Pratt, January 15, 1863, Essex Institute.

17. At some point in the mid-1880s, Whittier arranged for a $100 annual pension to be sent anonymously to Larcom from a Philadelphia Quaker home. Although she did not want to accept the money, he urged her not to "waste thy remaining strength in rebellion." She did not know that he had arranged this or the various annual subscriptions sent by publisher George W. Childs (see Daniel D. Addison, *Lucy Larcom: Life, Letters, and Diary* [Boston: Houghton, Mifflin, 1894], pp. 233–36). On his death, Whittier left her the copyrights for the books they had compiled together. Larcom then discovered that he had been a well-to-do man and for the first time expressed

bitterness about their arrangement. She wrote: "I am glad I did not ever know that he was rich. He used to want to pay my bills when we were at West Ossippe, etc., but I declined, for I supposed he was almost as poor as myself, though I know of late years his books have paid well. I am very glad he left me the copyright of the books I compiled with him; and indeed it was only right, as I worked so hard on them. The *Songs of Three Centuries* nearly cost me my health; the publisher's 'rished' it so. I was good for nothing for three or four years after, as far as writing went. But he never knew" (Addison, *Lucy Larcom*, p. 279). See also Lucy Larcom to Miss Eaton, October 4, 1877, Essex Institute.

18. Lucy Larcom to John G. Whittier, February 22, 1855, Wheaton College Archives, in Grace F. Shepard, "Letters of Lucy Larcom to the Whittiers," *The New England Quarterly* 3, no. 3 (1930): 501–02.

19. Shepard, *Letters*, p. 502.

20. Lucy Larcom to Philena Fobes, February 4 and November 7, 1856, and January 25, 1862, Essex Institute. She still felt that way years later. In 1880 she again told Fobes, "I never though it was my *calling* to teach." Lucy Larcom to Philena Fobes, December 29, 1880, Essex Institute.

21. Lucy Larcom to Philena Fobes, May 8, 1858, Essex Institute. See also Lucy Larcom to Philena Fobes, December 18, 1884, Essex Institute; Journal of Lucy Larcom, February 21, 1862, and March 11, 1862, in Addison, *Lucy Larcom*, pp. 127, 130–31.

22. Sallie Holley to Caroline F. Putnam, September 30, 1852, and March 24, 1854, Chadwick, *Life for Liberty*, pp. 95, 140.

23. Sallie Holley to Caroline F. Putnam, September 7, 1861; September 29, 1861; October 24, 1861, in Chadwick, *Life for Liberty*, pp. 181, 183, 185.

24. William E. Barton, *The Life of Clara Barton, Founder of the American Red Cross* (Boston: Houghton Mifflin Co., 1922), 2:4–5.

25. Ibid., pp. 86–88.

26. Sarah Pugh to Mary A. Estlin, August 10, 1861, Dr. Williams's Library. See also Sarah Pugh to Mary A. Estlin, June 22, 1860, Dr. Williams's Library.

27. Maria Mitchell, "Address to the Congress of Women," 1865, American Philosophical Society.

28. Her study was inspired by Mary Townsend's work, *Life in the Insect World: or, Conversations upon Insects between an Aunt and Her Nieces*, published in 1844. Graceanna had wished for "a study kindred to hers" and began to study the birds that visited the family farm. She wanted to catalogue and describe them in a companion volume to Townsend's. See Phebe Hanaford, *Daughters of America; or, Women of the Century* (Augusta, Ga., 1876), p. 261.

29. Debra Warner, *Graceanna Lewis: Scientist and Humanitarian* (Washington, D.C.: Smithsonian Institution Press, 1979), pp. 83–84.

30. Warner, *Graceanna Lewis*, pp. 97–98. After her experience with the American Association for the Advancement of Science and the Academy for Natural Science, Lewis was understandably cautious about publicly presenting her research. In 1881, in response to a circular from the Association for the Advancement of Women's Committee on Science, she wrote: "I have two or three papers which I wish before long to lay before the Academy. They have been deferred for several years as I wished to think them out fully before venturing upon them." Graceanna Lewis to Maria Mitchell, July 18, 1881, American Philosophical Society.

31. Diary of Emily Howland, February 10, 1861, Friends Historical Library.
32. Mary Grew to Sidney H. Gay, April 10, 1848, Columbia University Library; Sallie Holley to Emily Howland, August 27, 1865, Cornell University; Catharine M. Sedgwick to Rev. Dr. Channing, August 24, 1837, in Dewey, *Life and Letters*, p. 271.
33. Diary of Catharine M. Sedgwick, May 18, 1828, in Dewey, pp. 197–98. She revealed the same sentiment in a short story, "Old Maids," dedicated to Harriet Martineau. The heroine tells a young friend the value of the single life, "that all beautiful and loveable young women do not of course get married—that charms and virtues may exist and find employment in single life—that a single woman, an old maid . . . may love and be loved if she has not a husband, and children of her own." She adds, "I would by no means persuade you or any woman to *prefer* single life. It is not the 'primrose path.' Nothing less than a spirit of meekness, of self renunciation, and of benevolence, can make a woman, who has once been first, happy in a subordinate and *second best* position. And this under ordinary circumstances is the highest place of a single woman." Catharine M. Sedgwick, "Old Maids," from *Tales and Sketches* (Philadelphia: Carey, Lea & Blanchard, 1835), pp. 101–02, 107.
34. Lucy Larcom to Esther Homiston, November 18, 1857, and June 1, 1858, Massachusetts Historical Society.
35. Lucy Larcom to Esther Homiston, June 1, 1858, and September 25, 1858, Massachusetts Historical Society.
36. Lucy Larcom to Esther Homiston, February 28, 1859, Massachusetts Historical Society.
37. Lucy Larcom to Esther Homiston, October 1859, Massachusetts Historical Society.
38. "The Hygienic Relations of Celibacy," *The Nation*, 5, no. 122 (October 31, 1867): 357–58; George H. Napheys, A.M., M.D., *The Physical Life of Women. Advice to Maiden, Wife, and Mother* (Philadelphia: George Maclean, 1870), p. 290.
39. Carroll Smith-Rosenberg, "From Puberty to Menopause: The Cycle of Femininity in Nineteenth-Century America," in Mary Hartman and Lois W. Banner, *Clio's Consciousness Raised* (New York: Harper & Row, 1974), pp. 30–33.
40. She also described herself as a tree that never bore fruit and a diseased Christmas rose. Judith C. Breault, *The World of Emily Howland: Odyssey of a Humanitarian* (Millbrae, Calif.: Les Femmes Press, 1976), p. 118.
41. Diary of Emily Howland, April 25, 1879, Friends Historical Society.
42. Journal of Rachel Stearns, January 26, 1837, Schlesinger Library.
43. Ibid., June 25 and September 17, 1837, Schlesinger Library.
44. Ibid., December 17, 1837, Schlesinger Library.

Chapter 9

1. Lucy Chase to "Friends," July 1, 1864, American Antiquarian Society; Lucy Larcom to Philena Fobes, May 8, 1858, Essex Institute; Journal of Lucy Larcom, October 5, 1861, in Daniel D. Addison, *Lucy Larcom: Life, Letters, & Diary* (Boston: Houghton Mifflin, 1894), p. 105.
2. Giraud Chester, *Embattled Maiden: The Life of Anna Dickinson* (New York: G. P. Putnam's Sons, 1951), p. 76; John W. Chadwick, *A Life for Liberty: Anti-Slavery and Other Letters of Sallie Holley* (New York: G. P. Putnam's Sons, 1899), p. 270; Mary A. Dodge to Hannah S. Dodge, March 31, 1860, in Harriet Augusta Dodge, *Gail Hamilton's Life in Letters* (Boston: Lee and Shepard, 1901), 1:280.

3. Louisa May Alcott, Moods (Boston: Loring, 1865).
4. Mary Reed to Emily Howland, November 13, 1859, Cornell University; Diary of Emily Howland, May 18, 1873, and November 26, 1879, Friends Historical Library. When Howland heard that even the famous, popular, and successful Civil War nurse Clara Barton was dissatisfied with her life, she wrote: "It must be so with us all. The more we strive, the more we realize our weaknesses and failures." Diary of Emily Howland, 1902, Cornell University; Diary of Sarah Pugh, October 6, 1850, Memorial of Sarah Pugh: A Tribute of Respect from Her Cousin (Philadelphia: J. B. Lippincott Co., 1888), p. 38.
5. Journal of Emily Blackwell, August 24, 1850, Schlesinger Library; Journal of Rachel W. Stearns, September 23, 1836.
6. Carrie A. Rowland to Emily Howland, February 19, 1859, Cornell University.
7. Diary of Susan B. Anthony, Schlesinger Library.
8. Sklar describes the way in which Beecher took up the cause of Delia Bacon, who was abandoned by her suitor, Alexander MacWhorter, a Yale theologian. Beecher brought a court case against MacWhorter for breach of promise and, furthermore, published a book about it. These activities humiliated Bacon, who gradually slipped into depression, was institutionalized for insanity, and then died. Sklar suggests that Beecher's pursuit of this case provided her with an opportunity to work out her own hostility toward male authority without having to delve consciously into her own motivation and feelings. Kathryn K. Sklar, Catharine Beecher: A Study in American Domesticity (New Haven: Yale University Press, 1973), pp. 187–92.
9. "Female Orators," The Mother's Magazine 6 (1838): 27.
10. Henry F. Harrington, "Female Education," Ladies Companion 9 (1838): 293; Ida H. Harper, The Life and Work of Susan B. Anthony (Indianapolis: Hollenbeck Press, 1898), p. 90. For a work of fiction that makes the same point, see the popular Timothy S. Arthur, Married and Single; or, Marriage and Celibacy Contrasted in a Series of Domestic Pictures (New York: Harper & Brothers, 1845), particularly pp. 105–07, for his portrayal of the intellectual hermaphrodite Flora Enfield.
11. Lillian Faderman, Surpassing the Love of Men: Romantic Friendship and Love between Women from the Renaissance to the Present (New York: William Morrow & Co., 1981), pp. 233–34; John and Robin Haller, The Physician and Sexuality in Victorian America (Urbana: University of Illinois Press, 1974), pp. 76–87.
12. The same was true of other women. Examples were Rachel Stearns, Myrtilla Miner, and Anna Dickinson. Like Gilpin, they were seen as difficult, aggressive, self-righteous, self-centered, and idiosyncratic. Dickinson was institutionalized for insanity in a highly publicized dispute with her family over her earnings as an orator and actress. Miner was removed from the administration of her school for black women and later collapsed of "brain fever" while traveling in the West, raising funds. Sterns collapsed when deprived of the administration of her Southern school for women.
13. Although only scattered demographic studies of antebellum asylum populations exist, such figures do suggest that late-eighteenth- and nineteenth-century institutions held an extraordinary number of single women. This proportion exceeded the percentage of the unmarried women in the population itself but, like it, grew over the course of the century. From 1780 to 1830, roughly 31 percent of the women institutionalized in the Pennsylvania Hospital Asylum in Philadelphia were single. From 1840 to 1880, this

proportion rose to 40–43 percent. Women made up roughly one-half of the patient population, although there were far more male admissions from 1780 to 1850 (70 percent). Unmarried men greatly outnumbered married men during the early period by 58 to 37 percent; the figures were 47 to 46 percent for the last half of the century. This disproportion in marital status of male and female patients continues today. Nancy Tomes regards the increasing admissions of women to asylums as evidence of a new social respectability for the asylum and its moral treatment program under the direction of Dr. Thomas S. Kirkbride. Similar figures, however, characterized the patient populations of state institutions in New York, where 41 percent of the female population from 1840 to 1890 were unmarried. Certainly one can assume that some in this population were unmarried *because* they were insane. In addition, I would suggest that the phenomenon had to do with narrowing ranges of acceptable behavior and growing restrictions on assertive and independent women over the course of the century. The Pennsylvania Hospital served a fairly well-to-do population in the second period. The New York State institutions served the indigent, poor, and foreign-born. See Ellen Dwyer, " 'The Weaker Vessel': The Law versus Social Realities in the Commitment of Women to Nineteenth-Century New York Asylums" (unpublished paper, Department of Forensic Studies, Indiana University, p. 10; Nancy Tomes, "The Persuasive Institution: Thomas Story Kirkbride and the Art of Asylum-Keeping, 1841–1883" (Ph.D. diss., University of Pennsylvania, 1978), pp. 47, 216, 220, and 238.

14. Thomas L. Karnes, *William Gilpin: Western Naturalist* (Austin: University of Texas Press, 1971), pp. 10–14.
15. Mary S. Gilpin to Sophia duPont, June 11, 1850, and June 2, 1851, Eleutherian Mills Historical Library.
16. Diary of Sophia duPont, November 28, 1832, Eleutherian Mills Historical Library.
17. Mary S. Gilpin to Sophia duPont, November 29, 1845.
18. Mary S. Gilpin to Sophia duPont, September 19, 1844.
19. Prospectus Iwanwick(?) Place School, Eleutherian Mills Historical Library.
20. Mary S. Gilpin to Sophia duPont, March 16, 1843.
21. Mary S. Gilpin to Sophia duPont, December 11, 1843.
22. Mary S. Gilpin to Sophia duPont, n.d. (W9-33714, W9-38722).
23. Mary S. Gilpin to Sophia duPont, March 15, 1844.
24. Ibid.
25. Mary S. Gilpin to Sophia duPont, n.d. (W9-25498).
26. The lack of female support in Gilpin's case underscores the significance of the rela-tionships and their value to women who experienced the love and care of sisters and friends.
27. Mary S. Gilpin to Sophia duPont, n.d. (W9-25498).
28. Mary S. Gilpin to Sophia duPont, December 11, 1843.
29. Ibid.
30. Mary S. Gilpin to Sophia duPont, n.d. (W9-25498).
31. Ibid.
32. Mary S. Gilpin to Sophia duPont, September 19, 1844.
33. Mary S. Gilpin to Sophia duPont, December 2, 1844, and May 11, 1845.
34. Mary S. Gilpin to Sophia duPont, May 26, 1845, and June 5, 1845.

35. Mary S. Gilpin to Sophia duPont, October 27, 1845; May 11, 1845.

36. Clementina Smith to Sophia duPont, November 4, 1845; Sophia duPont to Clementina Smith, November 14, 1845; Mary S. Gilpin to Sophia duPont, October 27, 1845.

37. Mary S. Gilpin to Sophia duPont, November 29, 1845.

38. Mary S. Gilpin to Sophia duPont, February 18, 1846; April 25, 1846.

39. Mary S. Gilpin to Sophia duPont, January 31, 1847; March 25, 1847.

40. Mary S. Gilpin to Sophia duPont, October 11, 1847.

41. Ibid.

42. Mary S. Gilpin to Sophia duPont, December 13, 1847.

43. Mary S. Gilpin to Sophia duPont, October 1848.

44. Mary S. Gilpin to Sophia duPont, May 13, 1851.

45. For a discussion of Sophia duPont's life and marriage, see Anthony F. C. Wallace, *Rockdale: The Growth of an American Village in the Early Industrial Revolution* (New York: Alfred A. Knopf, 1978).

46. Mary S. Gilpin to Sophia duPont, June 2, 1851.

47. Ibid.

48. Mary S. Gilpin to Sophia duPont, November 15, 1851.

49. Ibid.

50. Prospectus, Institution for the Superior Preparatory Training of Teachers, Governesses, Nursery Governesses, &c., March 20, 1852, Painter Library, Tyler Arboretum. My thanks to Mary Johnson for bringing this to my attention.

51. See Tomes for a description of the Kirkbride regimen.

52. Sophia duPont to Clementina Smith, October 10, 1857.

53. Newspaper clipping, n.d.; William Gilpin to Mary S. Gilpin, June 20, 1875, Colorado Historical Society.

54. Mary S. Gilpin to Sophia duPont, December 22, 1844.

55. William Gilpin to Mary S. Gilpin, June 20, 1875, Colorado Historical Society.

Chapter 10

1. Mary Clemner Ames, *A Memorial of Alice and Phoebe Cary, with Some of Their Later Poems* (New York: Hurd and Houghton, 1874), pp. 79–80; Harriot Hunt, *Glances and Glimpses* (Boston: J. P. Jewett & Co., 1856), p. 51; Mary A. Livermore, *What Shall We Do with Our Daughters? Superfluous Women and Other Lectures* (Boston: Lee & Shepard, 1883), p. 61.

2. "Why is Single Life Becoming More General?" *The Nation* 6, no. 140 (March 5, 1868): 190–91; Livermore, *Superfluous Women*.

3. Rev. John Todd, D.D., *Woman's Rights* (Boston: Lee & Shepard, 1867), p. 26.

4. Margaret G. Wilson, *The American Woman in Transition: The Urban Influence, 1870–1920* (Westport, Conn.: Greenwood Press, 1979), p. 16; Anne F. Scott, *The Southern Lady: From Pedestal to Politics 1830–1930* (Chicago: University of Chicago Press, 1970), p. 113.

5. Quoted in Rosalind Rosenberg, *Beyond Separate Spheres: Intellectual Roots of Modern Feminism* (New Haven: Yale University Press, 1982), p. 10. See also William Goodell, "The Dangers and the Duty of the Hour (the Faulty System of Female Education; the

Decay of Home Life and the Unwillingness of Our Women to Become Mothers),"
Transactions of Medical and Chirurgical Faculty 88 (Baltimore, 1881): 71–87.

6. Robert L. Dickinson and Lura Beam, *The Single Woman: A Medical Study in Sex Education* (Baltimore: Williams & Wilkins Co., 1934), p. 63.

7. Rosenberg, *Beyond Separate Spheres*, p. 11.

8. Carroll Smith-Rosenberg, "From Puberty to Menopause: The Cycle of Femininity in Nineteenth-Century America," in Lois Banner and Mary S. Hartman, *Clio's Consciousness Raised* (New York: Harper & Row, 1974), pp. 30–33; "The Hygienic Relations of Celibacy," *The Nation* 5, no. 122 (October 31, 1867): 357–58; George H. Napheys, *The Physical Life of Women: Advice to Maiden, Wife, and Mother* (Philadelphia: George Maclean, 1870), p. 290.

9. Napheys, *Physical Life of Women*, pp. 40–41. A same view was reflected in the fiction of the period. Corinne Boyle, for example, who had broken her engagement in order to care for her "idiot" twin sister Lucile, was described as "a butterfly [who] had folded its wings tightly and been fastened again into the chrysalis. Whims and habits—little 'old maidisms' learned in her straight and eventless existence—clung to her like barnacles to a becalmed ship." The author believes that, "The petty, oftentimes annoying, oftener ludicrous peculiarities that incrust the characters of so many single women, are not always the offspring of selfishness. They seem to me more like dead shoots that would have been noble, beneficent growth, had not circumstances stifled them in their birth." To make certain that the reader understood that Boyle's unattractive physiognomy and mannerisms were the result of her single life and not her character or genetic make-up, the author contrasts Miss Boyle with her married sister and declares: "Celibacy in man or woman is an offence against natural laws, and the offender bears the stamp for all time. Nobody could mistake our excellent aunt for anything but an elderly maiden of increasingly uncertain age," a woman handsome in her youth, once of vivacious and pleasing personality and demeanor. Marion Harland, "One Old Maid," *Godey's Lady's Book*, 82, no. 487 (January 1871): 73, 69.

10. On the changing definition of marriage, see: W. I. Thomas, "The Older and Newer Ideals of Marriage," *The American Magazine* 67, no. 6 (April 1909): 548–52; Elaine T. May, *Great Expectations: Marriage and Divorce in Post-Victorian America* (Chicago: University of Chicago Press, 1980); Robert L. Griswold, *Family and Divorce in California, 1850–1890: Victorian Illusions and Everyday Realities* (Albany: State University of New York Press, 1982).

11. In addition to the above, see G. J. Barker-Benfield, *The Horrors of the Half-Known Life: Male Attitudes Toward Female Sexuality in Nineteenth-Century America* (New York: Harper & Row, 1976). The aggressive assertion of virility and the manly virtues so prescribed by Theodore Roosevelt may have been one defense against this sense of male neediness. See Peter G. Filene, *Him/Herself: Sex Roles in Modern America* (New York: Harcourt, Brace, Jovanovich, 1975), chap. 2.

12. May, *Great Expectations*, p. 167. See also, Robert V. Wells, *Revolutions in Americans' Lives: A Demographic Perspective on the History of Americans, Their Families, and Their Society* (Westport, Conn.: Greenwood Press, 1982), chap. 6; Carl Degler, *At Odds: Women and the Family in America from the Revolution to the Present* (Oxford: Oxford University Press, 1980), chap. 7; William O'Neill, *Divorce in the Progressive Era* (New Haven: Yale University Press, 1967); Carol D. Wright, *A Report on Marriage and*

Divorce in the United States 1867–1886 (Washington, D.C.: Government Printing Office, 1889).

13. Rosenberg, *Beyond Separate Spheres*, pp. 22–23. On fertility control, see also: Degler, *At Odds*, chap. 8; Linda Gordon, *"Woman's Body, Woman's Right": A Social History of Birth Control in America* (New York: Viking, 1976); Wells, *Revolutions*, chap. 5.

14. On purity legislation, see David J. Pivar, *Purity Crusade—Sexual Morality and Social Control 1868–1900* (Westport, Conn.: Greenwood Press, 1973); Ruth Rosen, *The Lost Sisterhood: Prostitution in America, 1900–1918* (Baltimore: Johns Hopkins University Press, 1982), chaps. 1 and 2.

15. Quoted in Filene, *Him/Herself*, p. 44. See also Theodore Roosevelt, "The American Woman as Mother," *Ladies Home Journal*, July 1905, p. 3; Theodore Roosevelt, "The Successful Mother," *Ladies Home Journal*, June 1908, p. 11. My thanks to Anne Marie Pois for these references. See also, Theodore Roosevelt, "The Duties of American Citizenship," address to the Liberal Club of Buffalo, New York, in William H. Harbaugh, *The Writings of Theodore Roosevelt* (New York: Bobbs-Merrill, 1967), pp. 3–4; Lucas Malet, "The Threatened Re-subjection of Woman," *The Living Age* 245, no. 3180 (June 17, 1905): 705–15.

16. Wilson, *American Woman in Transition*, p. 119. The percentage of women in the labor force grew as well. In 1870, 14.7 percent of all females sixteen or older were employed; by 1920, the figure was 24 percent. The female labor force had increased by 63 percent. Wilson, p. 118.

17. Ibid., p. 118.

18. Marion Harland, "The Passing of the Home Daughter," *The Independent* 71, no. 3267 (July 13, 1911): 88–91; Carolyn Shipman, "The Anomalous Position of the Unmarried Woman," *The North American Review* 190, no. 3 (September 1909): 339.

19. Winifred D. Wandersee, *Women's Work and Family Values, 1920–1940* (Cambridge, Mass.: Harvard University Press, 1981), p. 89. See also Margery W. Davies, *Woman's Place Is at the Typewriter: Office Work and Office Workers, 1870–1930* (Philadelphia: Temple University Press, 1982).

20. Quoted in Wandersee, *Women's Work*, p. 101.

21. Ida M. Tarbell, *The Ways of Woman* (New York: Macmillan Co., 1916), pp. 3–18.

22. Ida M. Tarbell, *The Business of Being a Woman* (New York: Macmillan Co., 1912).

23. Degler, *At Odds*, p. 164.

24. Agnes Repplier, "The Spinster," *Harper's Bazar* 38, no. 2 (February 1904): 117, 119. My thanks to Susan Koppleman for this reference.

25. Anna Garlin Spencer, "The Day of the Spinster," in *Woman's Share in Social Culture* (Philadelphia: J. B. Lippincott Co., 1925), pp. 11–12, 105–06, 107.

26. See, for example, the discussion in Dickinson and Beam, *The Single Woman*, chap. 10.

27. Lillian Faderman, *Surpassing the Love of Men: Relations among Women from the Renaissance to the Present* (New York: William Morrow, 1981), pp. 239–49.

28. The meaning of *hermaphroditism* changed from that earlier in the century. Whereas previously it had been a metaphorical term stemming from Greek mythology, it became a medical diagnosis. Hermaphrodites were literally considered a third sex. See Nancy Sahli, "Smashing: Women's Relationships before the Fall," *Chrysalis* 8 (1979): 17–27.

29. Quoted in Faderman, *Surpassing the Love of Men*, p. 338.

30. Wilhelm Stekel, *Frigidity in Woman in Relation to Her Love Life* (New York: Liveright Publishing Co., 1926), 2:289.

31. Faderman, *Surpassing the Love of Men*, pp. 314–31.

32. Frances Donovan, *The Schoolma'am* (New York: Frederick A. Stokes, 1938), pp. 35–36.

33. Vida D. Scudder, *On Journey* (New York: E. P. Dutton & Co., 1937), pp. 212–14.

34. "Sex O'Clock in America," *Current Opinion* 55, no. 2 (August 1913): 113–14.

35. For discussion, see Mary Ryan, *Womanhood in America from Colonial Times to the Present* (New York: Franklin Watts, 1983), pp. 238–44.

36. On the sex life of various "working girls," see Frances Donovan, *The Woman Who Waits* (Boston: R. G. Badger, 1920); *The Saleslady* (Chicago: University of Chicago Press, 1929).

37. Quoted in Rosenberg, *Beyond Separate Spheres*, p. 200.

38. Dickinson and Beam, *The Single Woman*, p. 203.

39. Robert L. Dickinson, "Medical Reflections upon Some Life Histories," in Ira S. Wile, M.D., *The Sex Life of the Unmarried Adult* (New York: Garden City Publishing Co., 1934), pp. 199, 200, 210.

40. Ryan, *Womanhood*, p. 242.

41. Marcia Guttentag and Paul F. Secord, *Too Many Women? The Sex Ratio Question* (Beverly Hills, Calif.: Sage Publications, 1983), p. 15.

42. Christine J. Huber, *The Pennsylvania Academy and Its Women: An Exhibition Catalogue* (Philadelphia: Pennsylvania Academy of Fine Arts, 1974), pp. 19–20.

43. Leila Rupp, " 'Imagine My Surprise': Women's Relationships in Historical Perspective," *Frontiers: A Journal of Women Studies* 5, no. 3 (Fall 1980): 61–71; Patricia Palmieri, "In Adamless Eden: A Portrait of Academic Women at Wellesley College, 1875–1920" (Ed.D. diss., Harvard Graduate School of Education, 1980).

44. For suggestive reading, see Mary Ryan, "The Heterosexual Imperative," in *Womanhood in America*, pp. 238–44; Michel Foucault, *The History of Sexuality: An Introduction* (New York: Pantheon Books, 1979).

Conclusion

1. Margaret Fuller, *Woman in the Nineteenth Century* (New York: W. W. Norton Reprint, 1971), pp. 36, 38. Margaret Fuller was not a spinster in the same sense as other women in this study were. She married, sometime between 1847 and 1849 at roughly thirty-eight years' old, an Italian nobleman who shared her enthusiasm for the Italian revolution. It has been suggested that she had to leave America, with its rigid gender roles, in order to see marriage as an appealing life and to find a man who could nurture and love her while supporting her intellectual aspirations. See Paula Blanchard, *Margaret Fuller: from Transcendentalism to Revolution* (New York: Dell, 1979), pp. 274–76.

2. Susan B. Anthony, August 27, 1880, Schlesinger Library.

3. Lucy Larcom to Philena Fobes, January 10, 1853, Essex Institute; Lucy Larcom to Jean Ingelow, December 15, 1867, in Daniel D. Addison, *Lucy Larcom: Life, Letters, and Diary* (Boston: Houghton, Mifflin, 1894), p. 165.

4. Lucy Larcom to Philena Fobes, January 10, 1853, Essex Institute; Addison, *Lucy Larcom*, p. 31; Lucy Larcom to John G. Whittier, January 1, 1855, Essex Institute.

5. Addison, *Lucy Larcom,* p. 298.

6. Maria Mitchell, MS, American Philosophical Society.

7. Fuller, *Woman in the Nineteenth Century,* pp. 97, 98, 101.

8. Phoebe Cary, "A Woman's Conclusions," in Mary Clemner Ames, *A Memorial of Alice and Phoebe Cary, with Some of Their Later Poems* (New York: Hurd and Houghton, 1874), pp. 155–57.

9. Catharine Beecher, *Woman's Profession as Mother and Educator with Views in Opposition to Woman Suffrage* (Philadelphia: George Maclean, 1872), pp. 86–87; Emily Howland to Mary Grew, August 24, 1893, Friends Historical Library; Emily Howland to Caroline F. Putnam, July 29, 1906, Friends Historical Library.

10. Eliza Fell to William Darlington, November 12, 1854, New York Historical Society. See Sally Gregory Kohlstedt, "In from the Periphery: American Women in Science, 1830–1880," *Signs: A Journal of Women in Culture and Society* 4, no. 1 (Autumn 1978): 85.

11. See, for example, Lucy Larcom: "The talk among the nieces just now is of Margaret Meacom's engagement. The middle-aged girls seem to be absconding from the single ranks. I am rather glad of it, for I was always afraid my example was a bad one; though I cannot say I am sorry I have persevered, and that I expect I shall, to the end" (Lucy Larcom to Octavia L. Parkhurst, August 22, 1890, Essex Institute). Said Ellen Maitland: "If I thought there was any probability that young ladies would be tempted to declare against matrimony, I would not have confessed so freely how happy and contented I have always been in my single blessedness. But I know very well that not one among them will be disposed to follow my example, if she should meet a man whom she could love, particularly if *he* should happen to love *her.* So that I think there is no danger of my strengthening the ranks of the maiden sisterhood by my representations." Mrs. A. J. Graves, *Girlhood and Womanhood: Or, Sketches of My Schoolmates* (Boston: T. H. Carter & Co., and Benjamin B. Mussey, 1844), p. 215.

12. Fuller, *Woman in the Nineteenth Century,* p. 96.

13. Prospectus in Lewis papers, Macaulay Collection; *New York Ledger* 24, no. 7 (April 11, 1868).

14. Susan B. Anthony, "The Homes of Single Women," MS, Library of Congress; Catharine Beecher and Harriet Beecher Stowe, *The American Woman's Home* (New York: J. B. Ford & Co., 1873), p. 204

15. See William Leach, *True Love and Perfect Union: The Feminist Reform of Sex and Society* (New York: Basic Books, 1980), for discussion.

16. Judith C. Breault, *The World of Emily Howland: Odyssey of a Humanitarian* (Millbrae, Calif.: Les Femmes Press, 1976), p. 164.

Selected Bibliography

Manuscript Collections

American Antiquarian Society. Clara Barton Papers; Chase Family Papers; Cheever Family Papers; Foster Papers; Gale Papers; Lee Diaries; May Papers; Paine Family Papers; Rogers Family Papers; Seecomb Family Papers; Smith Papers; Stoughton Papers. Worcester, Massachusetts.

American Philosophical Society. Mitchell Papers (microfilm). Philadelphia, Pennsylvania.

George Arents Research Library. Holley-Putnam Correspondence. Syracuse, New York.

Boston Public Library. Antislavery Collection; Quincy-Webb Correspondence; Weston Papers. Boston, Massachusetts.

Clements Library. Grimké-Weld Papers. Ann Arbor, Michigan.

Columbia University Library. Gay Papers. New York, New York.

Connecticut Historical Society. Barrett Papers; Noyes Diaries; Smith Papers. Hartford, Connecticut.

Connecticut State Library. Elliot Diary; Smith Papers. Hartford, Connecticut.

Cornell University Library. Howland Papers. Ithaca, New York.

Eleutherian Mills Historical Society. duPont Collection. Wilmington, Delaware.

Essex Institute. Nathanial Bowditch Collection; Dodge Papers; Larcom Papers; Nelson Papers; Waters Family Papers; Whittier Papers. Salem, Massachusetts.

Friends Historical Library. Fussell Papers; Howland Papers (microfilm); Jenkins Papers; Haines Papers; Hancock Papers; Mott Papers; Palmer Papers. Swarthmore, Pennsylvania.

Houghton Library, Harvard University. Alcott Papers; Barton Papers; Blagden Collection; Dix Papers; Emerson Papers. Cambridge, Massachusetts.

Library of Congress. Anthony Papers; Blackwell Papers; Cushman Papers; Dickinson Papers. Washington, D.C.

Mrs. Charles R. Macaulay, private collection. Lewis/Fussell Papers. Media, Pennsylvania.

Manchester Historical Association. Woolsen Papers. Manchester, New Hampshire.

Massachusetts Historical Society. Adams Papers; Antislavery Collection; Gray Papers; Larcom Papers; Samuel J. May Collection; Sedgwick Collection. Boston, Massachusetts.

Pennsylvania Historical Society. Parker Papers. Philadelphia, Pennsylvania.

Arthur and Elizabeth Schlesinger Library on the History of Women in America, Radcliffe College. Adams Papers; Anthony Papers; Beecher Papers; Blackwell Papers; Callender Papers; Grew Diary; Hosmer Papers; May Papers; Stearns Papers. Cambridge, Massachusetts.

Sophia Smith Collection, Smith College Library. Barton Papers; Frank Carpenter Collection; Hale Family Papers; Hunt Family Papers; Garrison Papers; Mott Papers; Peabody Family Papers; Smith Papers. Northampton, Massachusetts.

Dr. Williams's Library. Estlin Papers. London.

Memoir, Autobiography, & Biography

Anonymous. *Memoir of Catharine Seely, Late of Darien, Connecticut.* New York: Collins, Brother & Co., 1843.

———. *Memoirs of the Late Miss Lucy Richards, of Paris, Oneida, New York. Written by herself. Edited by another hand. Revised by the editor.* New York: G. Lane & P. P. Sandford for the Methodist Episcopal Church, 1842.

———. *Memoirs of Lucretia Crocker and Abby W. May.* Boston: Prepared for private circulation at the request of the Massachusetts School Suffrage Association, 1893.

———. *Memorial of Sarah Pugh: A Tribute of Respect from Her Cousin.* Philadelphia: J. B. Lippincott Co., 1888.

Adams, Hannah. *A Memoir of Miss Hannah Adams.* Written by herself, with additional notices by a friend (Hannah Farnham Sawyer Lee). Boston: Gray & Bowen, 1832.

Addison, Daniel D. *Lucy Larcom: Life, Letters, & Diary.* Boston: Houghton, Mifflin & Co., 1894.

Ames, Mary C. *A Memorial of Alice and Phoebe Cary, with Some of Their Later Poems.* New York: Hurd and Houghton, 1874.

Atkinson, Caroline P. *Letters of Susan Hale.* Boston: Marshall Jones Co., 1918.

Barnes, Gilbert, and Dumond, Dwight, eds. *Letters of Theodore Dwight Weld, Angelina Grimké Weld, and Sarah Grimké, 1822–1844.* New York: D. Appelton-Century Co., 1934.

Barton, William E. *Life of Clara Barton, Founder of the American Red Cross.* Boston: Houghton Mifflin Co., 1922.

Bent, Mary W. *"Miss Lizzie," Portrait of a New England Teacher.* Boston: Mt. Vernon Press, 1937.

Biddle, Gertrude B., and Lowie, Sarah D., eds. *Notable Women of Pennsylvania.* Philadelphia: University of Pennsylvania Press, 1942.

Birney, Catherine. *The Grimké Sisters: Sarah and Angelina Grimké: The First Women Advocates of Abolition and Woman's Rights.* Boston: Lee and Shepard, 1885.

Blackwell, Elizabeth. *Pioneer Work in Opening the Medical Profession to Women.* Reprint. New York: Schocken Books, 1977.

Blanchard, Paula. *Margaret Fuller: From Transcendentalism to Revolution.* New York: Delta/Seymour Lawrence, 1978.

Bolton, Ethel S. *A History of the Stanwood Family in America.* Boston: Rockwell and Church Press, 1899.

Bowne, Eliza S. *A Girl's Life Eighty Years Ago: Selections from the Letters of Eliza Southgate Bowne.* New York: Charles Scribner's Sons, 1887.

Breault, Judith C. *The World of Emily Howland: Odyssey of a Humanitarian.* Millbrae, Calif.: Les Femmes Press, 1976.

Chadwick, John W. *A Life for Liberty: Anti-Slavery and Other Letters of Sallie Holley.* New York: G. P. Putnam's Sons, 1899.

Cheney, Ednah D. *Louisa May Alcott: Her Life, Letters, and Journals.* Boston: Roberts Brothers, 1890.

Chester, Giraud. *Embattled Maiden: The Life of Anna Dickinson.* New York: G. P. Putnam's Sons, 1951.

Cole, Phyllis. "The Advantage of Loneliness: Mary Moody Emerson's Almanacks, 1802–1855." In Joel Porte, ed., *Emerson and Retrospect: Prospect and Retrospect,* pp. 1–32. Cambridge, Mass.: Harvard University Press, 1982.

Dewey, Mary E. *Life and Letters of Catharine M. Sedgwick.* New York: Harper & Brothers, 1871.

Dodge, Harriet A. *Gail Hamilton's Life in Letters.* Boston: Lee & Shepard, 1901.

Dodge, Mary A. *Memorial of Mrs. Hannah Stanwood Dodge.* Cambridge, Mass.: Author, 1869.

Dodge, Joseph T. *Genealogy of the Dodge Family of Essex City, Massachusetts.* Madison, Wisconsin. Author, 1898.

Earhart, Mary. *Frances Willard: From Prayers to Politics.* Chicago: University of Chicago Press, 1944.

Fiske, Daniel T. *The Cross and the Crown; or, Faith Working by Love: As Exemplified in the Life of Fidelia Fiske.* Boston: Congregational Sabbath School & Publishing Co., 1868.

Fiske, Fidelia. *Recollections of Mary Lyon.* Boston: American Tract Society, 1866.

Fuller, Elizabeth. "Diary Kept by Elizabeth Fuller, Daughter of Rev. Timothy Fuller of Princeton." In Francis E. Blake, *History of the Town of Princeton, in the County of Worcester and Commonwealth of Massachusetts, 1759–1915,* 1: 302–23. Princeton: Published by the Town, 1915.

Graves, Mrs. A. J. *Girlhood and Womanhood: or, Sketches of my Schoolmates.* Boston: T. H. Carter & Co., and Benjamin B. Mussey, 1844.

Harper, Ida H. *Life and Work of Susan B. Anthony.* Indianapolis: Hollenbeck Press, 1898.

Haven, Henry P. *Memoir of Frances Manwaring Caulkins.* Boston: David Clapp & Son, 1869.

Hays, Elinor R. *Those Extraordinary Blackwells.* New York: Harcourt, Brace & World, 1967.

Hitchcock, Edward. *The Power of Christian Benevolence, Illustrated in the Life and Labors of Mary Lyon.* Northampton: Hopkins, Bridgman, 1852.

Holland, Rupert S. *Letters and Diary of Laura M. Towne: Written from the Sea Islands of South Carolina, 1862–1884.* Cambridge, Mass.: 1912.

Hunt, Harriot. *Glances and Glimpses.* Boston: J. P. Jewett & Co., 1856.

Jaquette, Henrietta S. *South after Gettysburg: Letters of Cornelia Hancock*. Philadelphia: University of Pennsylvania Press, 1937.

Johnson, Mary. "Antoinette Brevost, A Schoolmistress in Early Philadelphia." *Winterthur Portfolio, a Journal of American Culture* 15, no. 2 (Summer 1980): 151–68.

Johnson, Thomas H. *The Letters of Emily Dickinson*. Cambridge, Mass.: Belknap Press, 1958.

———. *The Poems of Emily Dickinson*. Cambridge, Mass.: Harvard University Press, 1955.

Kendall, Phebe M. *Maria Mitchell: Life, Letters, & Journals*. Boston: Lee & Shepard, 1896.

Kelley, Mary. "A Woman Alone: Catharine Maria Sedgwick's Spinsterhood in Nineteenth-Century America." *The New England Quarterly* 51, no. 2 (June 1978): 209–25.

Lansing, Marion. *Mary Lyon through Her Letters*. Boston: Books, Inc., 1937.

Leach, Joseph. *Bright Particular Star: Life and Times of Charlotte Cushman*. New Haven: Yale University Press, 1970.

Lerner, Gerda. *The Grimké Sisters from South Carolina: Pioneers for Women's Rights and Abolitionism*. New York: Schocken Books, 1971.

Marshall, Helen F. *Dorothea Dix, Forgotten Samaritan*. Chapel Hill: University of North Carolina, 1937.

Marcus, Jacob R. *The American Jewish Woman, 1654–1980*. New York: KTAV Publishing House, 1981.

Miller, Isabel. *Patience and Sarah*. New York: McGraw Hill, 1969.

Moon, Robert C. *The Morris Family of Philadelphia*. Philadelphia: R. C. Moon, 1898–1909.

O'Connor, Ellen M. *Myrtilla Miner, A Memoir*. Boston: Houghton, Mifflin & Co., 1885.

Parsons, Theophilus. *Memoir of Emily Elizabeth Parsons*. Boston: Little, Brown, & Co., 1880.

Philipson, David. *Letters of Rebecca Gratz*. Philadelphia: Jewish Publication Society of America, 1929.

Prentiss, G. L., ed. *The Life and Letters of Elizabeth Prentiss*. London: Hodden & Stoughton, 1897.

Pulsifer, Janice G. "Alice and Phoebe Cary, Whittier's Sweet Singers of the West." *Essex Institute Historical Collections* 109, no. 1 (January 1973): 9–59.

———. "Gail Hamilton, 1833–1896." *Essex Institute Historical Collections*. 104, no. 3 (July 1968): 165–216.

Saxton, Martha. *Louisa May*. New York: Houghton Mifflin Co., 1977.

Scudder, Vida D. *On Journey*. New York: E. P. Dutton, & Co., 1937.

Sewall, Richard B. *The Life of Emily Dickinson*. New York: Farrar, Straus, and Giroux, 1974.

———. *The Lyman Letters: New Light on Emily Dickinson and Her Family*. Amherst: University of Massachusetts Press, 1965.

Shepard, Grace F. *Letters of Lucy Larcom to the Whittiers*. Reprint from *The New England Quarterly* 3, no. 3 (1930): 501–18. Boston: Southworth Press, 1930.

Sharf, Frederic A. "Fidelia Bridges, 1834–1923, Painter of Birds and Flowers." *Essex Institute Historical Collections* 104, no. 3 (July 1968): 217–38.

Sklar, Kathryn K. *Catharine Beecher: A Study in American Domesticity.* New Haven: Yale University Press, 1973.

Stern, Madeline B. *Louisa May Alcott.* Norman: University of Oklahoma Press, 1950.

Stone, Ellen A. "Diary and Letters of Caira Robbins, 1794–1881." *Lexington Historical Society Proceedings,* no. 4 (1905–10): 61–81.

Swint, Henry P. *Dear Ones at Home.* Nashville: Vanderbilt University Press, 1966.

Tharp, Louise H. *The Peabody Sisters of Salem.* Boston: Little, Brown & Co., 1950.

Tolman, George. *Mary Moody Emerson.* Cambridge, Mass.: Edward W. Forbes, 1929.

Warner, Deborah J. *Graceanna Lewis: Scientist and Humanitarian.* Washington, D.C.: Smithsonian Institution Press, 1979.

Emma Willard and Her Pupils or Fifty Years of Troy Female Seminary, 1822–1872. New York: Mrs. Russell Sage, 1898.

Willard, Frances E. *Glimpses of Fifty Years, The Autobiography of an American Woman.* Chicago: H. J. Smith & Co., 1889.

Wright, Helen. *Sweeper in the Sky: The Life of Maria Mitchell, First Woman Astronomer in America.* New York: Macmillan Co., 1949.

Fiction and Prescriptive Literature

Anonymous. "Alleged Decline in Marriage." *Living Age* (June 15, 1899), pp. 198–200.

———. "The Best Woman in the World." *Lady's Wreath* 1, no. 4 (1847–48): 101–05.

———. "The Betrothal." *The Amaranth* (1854), pp. 72–99.

———. "The Blighted Heart." *The Universalist and Ladies' Repository* 4 (January 1836): 289–95.

———. "Character Note. The New Woman." *Cornhill Magazine* 23, no. 136 (October 1894): 365–68.

———. "The Christmas Dinner." *The Ladies Wreath and Parlor Annual* 9 (ca. 1853): 99–105.

———. "Clemence Isaure." *The Amaranth* (1852), pp. 197–216.

———. "Dignity." *Ladies' Magazine and Literary Gazette* 5, no. 7 (July 1832): 309–11.

———. "Female Influence." *The Nation* 5, no. 108 (July 1867): 73–74.

———. "Flirtation." *Ladies' Magazine* 1, no. 8 (August 1828): 361–68.

———. "Get Married." *The Universalist and Ladies' Repository* 4 (September 1835): 150.

———. "The Godfather." *Godey's Lady's Book* 21 (November 1840): 203–12.

———. "The Happy Bride." *The Ladies Wreath and Parlor Annual* (ca. 1857); pp. 283–90.

———. "The Hygienic Relations of Celibacy." *The Nation* 5, no. 122 (October 1867): 357–58.

———. "Letter from Spain, Religious Vows of Females." *The Atheneum, or the Spirit of the English Magazines* 11 (May 15, 1822): 155–60.

———. "The Maiden Aunt." *The Atheneum, or the Spirit of the English Magazines* 6, no. 12 (March 1827): 469–73.

———. "Marriage." *The American Magazine of Useful and Entertaining Knowledge* 1 (1835): 350.

———. "The Mistaken Milliner: A Tale of Ambition." *Godey's Lady's Book* 14 (May 1837): 224–26.

———. "The Moon." *Ladies' Magazine* 1, no. 4 (April 1828): 184–89.

———. "My Aunt's Story, or the Reward of Coquetry." *Godey's Lady's Book* 24 (April 1842): 192–96.

———. "The Mysterious Lady." *The Amaranth* (1854); pp. 20–29.

———. "Old Bachelors." *Ladies' Literary Cabinet* 5, no. 9 (January 1822): 67–68.

———. "An Old Maid." *Ladies' Magazine and Literary Gazette* 3, no. 7 (July 1830): 289–95.

———. "The Old Maid of the Family—A Sketch of Human Life." *The Atheneum, or the Spirit of the English Magazines* 3, no. 7 (January 1830): 276–80.

———. "Old Maids." *Ladies' Literary Cabinet* 5, no. 18 (March 1822): 141.

———. "Old Maids." *Ladies' Literary Cabinet* 5, no. 21 (March 1822): 167.

———. "Old Maids." *Ladies' Literary Cabinet* 6, no. 26 (December 1822): 204.

———. "Old Maids." *Godey's Lady's Book* 63 (1861): 227–28.

———. "The Revery of an Old Maid." *Littell's Living Age* 31: 411–14.

———. "The Rights of Married Women." *Godey's Lady's Book* 14 (May 1837): 212–14.

———. "Sex O'Clock in America." *Current Opinion* 55, no. 2 (August 1913): 113–14.

———. "Single Blessedness." *Ladies' Literary Cabinet* 6, no. 9 (July 1822): 72.

———. *"Single Blessedness," or Single Ladies and Gentlemen, against the Slanders of the Pulpit, the Press, and the Lecture-Room.* New York: C. S. Francis & Co., 1852.

———. "Sketches of American Character: Political Parties." *Ladies' Magazine* 2, no. 7 (July 1829): 299–307.

———. "Sketches of American Character: The Poor Scholar." *Ladies' Magazine* 1, no. 6 (June 1828): 245–66.

———. "Sketches of American Character: Walter Wilson." *Ladies' Magazine* 1, no. 1 (January 1828): 5–16.

———. "Some Passages in the Life of an Old Maid." *Garland* (1830), pp. 56–87.

———. "The Star of Evil Destiny." *The Amaranth* (1851); pp. 161–80.

———. "The Threatened Re-Subjection of Woman." *The Living Age* 245, no. 3180 (June 17, 1905): 705–15.

———. *The Three Sisters: A Sketch from Life.* London: W. Clowes & Sons, 1856.

———. "The Token." *Ladies Magazine* 1, no. 1 (January 1828): 29–30.

———. "What Happy Creatures Old Maids Are." *The Emerald* 1, no. 5 (December 1810): 59–60.

————. "When Shall Our Young Women Marry? A Compilation of Opinions." *Brooklyn Magazine* 4 (April 1886): 10–14.

————. "Why is Single Life Becoming More General?" *The Nation* 7, no. 140 (March 1868): 190–91.

Abdy, Mrs. "The Jeweller's Daughter." *The Amaranth* (1855), pp. 49–53.

Alcott, Louisa M. "Advice to Young Ladies: Being a Series of Twelve Articles, by Twelve Distinguished Women. No. III. Happy Women." *New York Ledger* 24, no. 7 (April 11, 1868).

————. *Diana and Persis*, ed. Sarah Elbert. New York: Arno Press, 1978.

————. *Work. A Story of Experience.* Reprint. New York: Schocken Books, 1977.

Alcott, William A. *The Moral Philosophy of Courtship and Marriage.* Boston: John P. Jewett & Co., 1857.

Alger, William R. *The Friendships of Women.* Boston: Roberts Brothers, 1868.

Allen, Lizzie. "Mary Lee." *The Ladies Wreath and Parlor Annual* (ca. 1858 or 1859), pp. 201–16.

Allen, Nathan. "Divorces in New England." *North American Review* (June 1880), pp. 547–64.

Arthur, Timothy S. *Married and Single; or, Marriage and Celibacy Contrasted in a Series of Domestic Pictures.* New York: Harper and Brothers, 1845.

————. "Sweethearts and Wives." *Godey's Lady's Book* 23 (December 1841): 264–69.

————. "Which is the Lady?" *Godey's Lady's Book* 24 (April 1842): 198–202.

Bachelor Maid. "Work for Women." *Independent* (June 25, 1912), pt. 1, pp. 182–86.

Benedict, the Married Man. "On the Undeserved Stigma Conferred on Single Ladies by the Title of Old Maid." *The Atheneum, or The Spirit of the English Magazines* 1, no. 2 (September 1817): 801–06.

Bradbury, Hannah. "Earning a Dollar." *The Ladies' Wreath and Parlor Annual* (ca. 1858), pp. 235–43.

Brontë, Charlotte. "Woman's Lot." *Godey's Lady's Book* 42 (March 1851): 193–94.

Brown, Charles B. "Is Marriage or Celibacy Most Eligible? Or, is the Matron or the Old Maid the Best Member of Society?" *The Literary Magazine and American Register* 2, no. 12 (September 1804): 468–70.

Brownson, Orestes A. "The Laboring Classes." *The Boston Quarterly Review* 3 (July 1840).

Bruce, Helen. "Poor Kitty Gray, or the Warning Vision." *The Ladies' Wreath and Parlor Annual* (ca. 1858), pp. 87–92.

Burdett, Charles. *Blonde and Brunette, or the Gothamite Arcady.* New York: D. Appelton & Co., 1858.

Burnap, George W. *Lectures on the Sphere and Duties of Woman and Other Subjects.* Baltimore: John Murphy, 1841.

Burton, William E. "Leap Year; or, Woman's Privilege." *Godey's Lady's Book* 29 (August 1844): 84–90.

Butler, Caroline H. "Affectation." *Godey's Lady's Book* 28 (June 1844): 265–70.

Butler, Charles. *The American Lady.* Philadelphia: Hogan and Thompson, 1839.

Calverton, V. F. *The Bankruptcy of Marriage.* New York: Macaulay Co., 1928.

Cary, Alice. *Married, Not Mated; or, How They Lived at Woodside and Throckmorton Hall.* New York: Derby & Jackson, 1856.

Chesebro, Caroline. "Miss Job." *Godey's Lady's Book* 43 (July 1851): 43–47.

Clowes, John. *The Golden Wedding Ring; or Observations on the Institution of Marriage.* Boston: John Allen, 1832.

Cobbe, Frances P. *Essays on the Pursuits of Women.* London: Emily Faithful, 1863.

Coxe, Margaret. *The Young Lady's Companion.* Columbus: J. N. Whiting, 1839.

Deforest, Virginia. "Our Keziah; or Self Control." *Godey's Lady's Book* 25 (November 1842): 205–09.

Craik, Dinah Mulock, *A Woman's Thoughts about Women.* New York: John Bradburn, 1866.

Delafaye-Brehier, Julia. "Two Sisters." *The Ladies Scrap Book.* Hartford, Conn.: S. Andrus & Son, 1846.

———. "Fifteen Years Difference." *Godey's Lady's Book* 15 (August 1837): 86–89.

Devanant, Mary. "The Cousins." *Godey's Lady's Book* 27 (July 1843): 19–27.

———. "Emma Westall." *Godey's Lady's Book* 26 (February 1843): 73–79.

———. "Harwood Hall." *Godey's Lady's Book* 43 (November 1851): 273–78.

Dickins, Mary Angela. "The Ever-Blessed Kettle." *New England Home Magazine* (January 1, 1899), pp. 7–12; (January 8, 1899), pp. 58–60.

Dickinson, Robert L., and Beam, Lura. *The Single Woman. A Medical Study in Sex Education.* Baltimore: Williams & Wilkins Co., 1934.

Dodge, Hannah A. *Chips, Fragments and Vestiges by Gail Hamilton.* Boston: Lee & Shepard, 1902.

Donovan, James W. *Don't Marry! Or Advice as to How, When & Who.* New York: J. S. Ogilvie, 1891.

Edgarton, S. C. "The Old Maid. A Sketch." *The Universalist and Ladies' Repository* 6 (May 1838): 469–70.

Eliot, Charles W. "The Normal American Woman." *Ladies Home Journal,* January 1908, p. 15.

Embury, Emma C. "The Awakened Heart." *Godey's Lady's Book* 28 (1844): 5–9.

Everallin. "Early Friendships: No. III; The Confidant." *Ladies' Magazine* 3, no. 9 (September 1830): 394–98.

———. "Early Friendships: No. IV; Jefferson Barney." *Ladies' Magazine* 3, no. 9 (September 1830): 445–48.

———. "Recollections: No. III; Susan De Witt." *Ladies' Magazine* 2, no. 7 (July 1829): 320–25.

Evergreen, Effie. "Ella Mason; or, the Romance of a Second Marriage." *Godey's Lady's Book* 42 (June 1851): 355–60.

Ferrero, Guglielmo. "The New Woman and the Old." *Hearst Magazine* (July 1912), pp. 70–77.

Fleming, Anna. "Aunt Sarah; or the Lady with the Mole on Her Nose." *Godey's Lady's Book* 27 (August 1843): 52–54.

Gibson, Mary W. Stanley. "The Iron Ring." *The Lady's Wreath and Parlor Annual* (ca. 1858), pp. 423–28.

Graves, Mrs. A. J. *Woman in America; Being an Examination into the Moral and Intellectual Condition of American Female Society.* New York: Harper & Brothers, 1841.

Hale, Matthew. *A Letter of Advice to His Grandchildren Matthew, Gabriel, Anne, Mary, and Frances Hale.* Boston: Wells and Lilly, 1817.

Hamilton, Cicely. *Just to Get Married.* New York: S. French, 1914.

———. *Marriage as a Trade.* New York: Moffat, Yard & Co., 1909.

Hamilton, Gail. *A Battle of the Books.* Cambridge: Riverside Press, 1870.

———. *A New Atmosphere.* Boston: Ticknor & Fields, 1865.

———. *An Object Lesson in Woman's Rights.* n.p., 1892.

———. *Woman's Worth and Worthlessness.* New York: Harper & Brothers, 1872.

———. *Woman's Wrongs: A Counter-Irritant.* Boston: Ticknor & Fields, 1868.

Hanaford, Mrs. Joseph H. "The True Object of Life; or the Wishes Fulfilled." *The Family Circle and Parlor Annual* 13 (1852): 23–31.

Harland, Marion. "One Old Maid." *Godey's Lady's Book* 82 (January 1871): 67–74.

———. "The Passing of the Home Daughter." *The Independent* 71, no. 3267 (July 13, 1911): 88–90.

Harper, Frances Ellen Watkins. "The Two Offers." *Anglo-African Magazine* (September/October 1859).

Hayley, William. *A Philosophical, Historical, and Moral Essay on Old Maids by a Friend to the Sisterhood.* London: T. Cadell, 1793.

Hentz, Mrs. C. Lee. "Aunt Mercy." *Godey's Lady's Book* 24 (January 1842): 41–54, 127–34.

Holland, S. "The Disappointed Manoever." *Godey's Lady's Book* 20 (March 1840): 124–30.

Hood, Edwin P. *Representative Women; Queens, Heroines, Peasants, Confessors, and Philanthropists.* London: Partridge & Oakey, 1853.

Hood, Red Riding. "Angelina's Fainted." *The Amaranth* (1852), pp. 46–56.

Howitt, Mary. "Single Sisters." *The Keepsake; A Christmas, New Year's, and Birthday Present for 1845* (1845), pp. 63–71.

Humphreys, Mary. "Women Bachelors in New York." *Scribner's* (November 1896), pp. 626–35.

Irving, Helen. "The Valentine Party." *The Lady's Wreath and Parlor Annual* (ca. 1853), pp. 129–38.

James, John A. *The Family Monitor, or A Help to Domestic Happiness.* Boston: Crocker & Brewster, 1833.

Jameson, Anna. *Sisters of Charity & The Communion of Labour. Two Lectures on the Social Employment of Women.* London: Longman, Brown, Green, Longmans, & Roberts, 1859.

Jewett, Susan W. "An Old Maid's Reflections on Woman's Rights." *The Ladies' Repository* 14, (April 1854): 161–64.

Jewsbury, Geraldine E. "The Story of Angelique." *The Amaranth* (1855), 102–28.

Johnson, J. *The Advantages and Disadvantages of the Marriage-State, As entered into with Religious or Irreligious Persons.* London: Robert Jackson, 1778.

King, Susan P. "Old Maidism versus Marriage." *Busy Moments of An Idle Woman* New York: D. Appelton & Co., 1854.

Lane, Haddie. "Modern Aristocrats." *Godey's Lady's Book* 43 (December 1851): 342–46.

Lanfear, Elizabeth. *Letters to Young Ladies on their Entrance into the World.* London: J. Robins & Co., 1824.

Larcom, Lucy. *The Poetical Works of Lucy Larcom.* Boston: Houghton Mifflin & Co., 1884.

Livermore, Mary A. *What Shall We Do with Our Daughters? Superfluous Women and Other Lectures.* Boston: Lee & Shepard, 1883.

Martyn, Mrs. S. T. "Ida Clifford." *The Ladies Wreath* (1849–50): 133–44, 176–87, 215–25.

Melville, Herman. "The Paradise of Bachelors and Tartarus of Maids." *Selected Tales and Poems.* New York: Rinehart & Co., 1950, p. 206–29.

Miles, Miss M. "Grace Tiwerton." *Godey's Lady's Book* 15 (July 1837): 38–41.

Munroe, Mrs. N. Thorning. "The Sisters: or, Woman's Ambition." *The Universalist and Ladies' Repository* 9 (September 1840): 128–37.

Muzzey, Artemus B. *The Young Maiden.* Boston: William Crosby & Co., 1840.

Neal, Alice B. "Moral Courage." *Godey's Lady's Book* 42 (May 1851): 316–19, 367–72.

Nichols, T. L., and Nichols, Mary S. Gove. *Marriage: Its History, Character, and Results; Its Sanctities, and Its Profanities; Its Science and Its Facts. Demonstrating Its Influence, as a Civilized Institution, on the Happiness of the Individual and the Progress of the Race.* New York: T. L. Nichols, 1854.

Pease, Mary S. "The Storm." *Godey's Lady's Book* 42 (June 1851): 341–44.

Phelps, E. J. "Divorce in the United States." *Forum* (December 1889), pp. 349–64.

Pidsley, Mrs. "Woman's Lot." *Peterson's Magazine* 35, no. 5 (May 1859): 380.

Pindar, Susan. "Aunt Mable's Love Story." *Graham's Magazine* 33 (1848): 107–10.

Plumer, Emeline P. "The Neglected Wife." *The Family Circle & Parlor Annual* 13 (1852): 103–10, 136–43.

Power, Miss. "The Postman's Knock." *The Amaranth* (1847), 111–36.

Rockwell, Rose. "Old Letters; or Aunt Amy's Reminiscence." *The Ladies' Wreath and Parlor Annual* (ca. 1858): 345–49.

Sangster, M. E. "Miss Ruth's Inheritance." *Advocate and Family Guardian* 38, no. 10 (May 16, 1872): 111–12.

Sedgwick, Catharine M. *Married or Single?* New York: Harper & Brothers, 1857.

———. "Old Maids." *Tales and Sketches by Catharine Maria Sedgwick.* Philadelphia: Carey, Lea, & Blanchard, 1835.

Shipman, Carolyn. "The Anomalous Position of the Unmarried Woman." *North American Review* 190, no. 3 (September 1909): 338–46.

Spencer, Mary G. "Day of the Spinster." *Woman's Share in Social Culture*, pp. 89–113. Reprint. Philadelphia: J. B. Lippincott Co., 1923.

Stekel, Wilhelm. *Disorders of the Instincts and the Emotions. The Parapathiac Disorders. Frigidity in Woman.* New York: Liveright Publishing Corp., 1926.

Stowe, Harriet E. Beecher. "Eliza. From My Aunt Mary's Bureau." *Godey's Lady's Book* 20 (January 1840): 24–26.

Stowe, Harriet B. *The Minister's Wooing.* Reprint. New Jersey: Gregg Press, 1968.

Strickland, Agnes. "Whitethorne Farm." *The Amaranth* (1847), 85–110.

Tarbell, Ida M. *The Business of Being a Woman.* New York: Macmillan Co., 1912.

————. *The Ways of Woman.* New York: Macmillan Co., 1916.

Todd, John. *Woman's Rights.* Boston: Lee & Shepard, 1867.

Thomas, W. I. "The Older and Newer Ideals of Marriage." *American Magazine* 67, no. 6 (April 1909): 548–52.

Trollope, Mrs. "Old Maids in France." *The American Magazine of Useful and Entertaining Knowledge* 2 (1839): 435–36.

Tuthill, Louisa C. *The Young Lady's Home.* Boston: William J. Reynolds & Co., 1847.

Turner, J. A. "Link Not Thy Life and Fate to His." *Peterson's Magazine* 35, no. 4 (April 1859): 285.

Vaughan, Mary C. "Duty. Ada Lester's Story." *The Lady's Wreath and Parlor Annual* (ca. 1857 or 1858), pp. 125–36.

————. "Fruits of Sorrow; or an Old Maid's Story." *The Lady's Wreath and Parlor Annual* (ca. 1858 or 1859), pp. 389–95.

Weems, M. L. *Hymen's Recruiting Sargeant: or the New Matrimonial Tat-too for the Old Bachelors.* Philadelphia: Weems, 1812.

Whitman, Jason. *The Young Lady's Aid, to Usefulness and Happiness.* Portland, Me.: S. H. Colesworthy, 1838.

White, T. W. "The Lyceum, No. II—Old Maids," *Southern Literary Messenger* 3, no. 8 (August 1837): 473–74.

Wilcox, Suzanne. "The Unrest of Modern Woman." *Independent* (June 8, 1909), pp. 62–66.

Wile, Ira S., ed. *The Sex Life of the Unmarried Adult. An Inquiry and Interpretation of Current Sex Practices.* New York: Vanguard Press, 1934.

Wise, Daniel. *The Young Lady's Counsellor; or, Outlines and Illustrations of the Sphere, the Duties and the Dangers of Young Women.* New York: Carlton & Phillips, 1852.

Wright, Henry C. *Marriage and Parentage: or The Reproductive Element in Man, as a means to his Elevation and Happiness.* Boston: Bela Marsh, 1854.

Current Scholarship

Adams, Herbert B. "Allotments of Land in Salem to Men, Women, and Maids." *Johns Hopkins University Studies in Historical and Political Science* 9–10 (1883).

Adams, Margaret. *Single Blessedness.* New York: Basic Books, 1976.

Arnold, Roxane, and Chandler, Olive, eds. *Feminine Singular: Triumphs and Tribulations of the Single Woman. An Anthology.* London: Femina Books, 1974.

Benjamin, Philip S. *The Philadelphia Quakers in the Industrial Age, 1865–1920.* Philadelphia: Temple University Press, 1976.

Berg, Barbara J. *The Remembered Gate: Origins of American Feminism. The Woman and the City, 1800–1860.* New York: Oxford University Press, 1978.

Bernard, Richard M., and Vinovskis, Maris. "The Female Teacher in Ante-Bellum Massachusetts." *Journal of Social History* 10 (1977): 332–45.

Bogue, Donald J. *The Population of the United States.* Glencoe, Ill.: The Free Press, 1959.

Boylan, Anne M. "Evangelical Womanhood in the Nineteenth Century: The Role of Women in Sunday Schools." *Feminist Studies* 4, no. 3 (October 1978): 62–80.

Bullough, Vern, and Voght, Martha. "Women, Menstruation and Nineteenth-Century Medicine." *Bulletin of the History of Medicine* 47 (1973): 66–82.

Campbell, D'Ann. "Women's Life in Utopia: The Shaker Experiment in Sexual Equality Reappraised—1810–1860." *The New England Quarterly* 51, no. 1 (March 1978): 23–38.

Cargan, Leonard, and Melko, Matthew. *Singles: Myths and Realities.* Beverly Hills, Calif.: Sage Publications, 1982.

Conrad, Susan. *Perish the Thought: Intellectual Women in Romantic America, 1830–1860.* Secaucus, N.J.: Citadel Press, 1978.

Cook, Blanche W. "Female Support Networks and Political Activism: Lillian Wald, Crystal Eastman, Emma Goldman." *Chrysalis* 1, no. 3 (October 1977): 43–61.

Cott, Nancy F. *The Bonds of Womanhood: "Woman's Sphere" in New England, 1780–1835.* New Haven: Yale University Press, 1977.

———. "Passionlessness: An Interpretation of Victorian Sexual Ideology, 1790–1850." *Signs: Journal of Women in Culture and Society* 4, no. 2 (Winter 1978): 219–36.

Davis, James E. *Frontier America, 1800–1840: A Comparative Demographic Analysis of the Frontier Process.* Glendale, Calif.: Arthur H. Clark Co., 1977.

Degler, Carl. *At Odds: Women and the Family in America from the Revolution to the Present.* Oxford: Oxford University Press, 1980.

Dickersin, Gail. "Notes on Nineteenth-Century Feminist Verse." *Feminist Studies* 4, no. 3 (October 1978): 115–26.

Dublin, Thomas. *Women at Work: The Transformation of Work and Community in Lowell, Massachusetts, 1826–1860.* New York: Columbia University Press, 1979.

Faderman, Lillian. "Female Same-Sex Relationships in Novels by Longfellow, Holmes, and James." *The New England Quarterly* 51, no. 3 (September 1978): 309–32.

———. *Surpassing the Love of Men: Romantic Friendship and Love between Women from the Renaissance to the Present.* New York: William Morrow & Co., 1981.

Ferder, Fran. *Called to Break Bread? A Psychological Investigation of 100 Women Who Feel Called to Priesthood in the Catholic Church.* Mt. Rainier, Md.: Quixote Center, 1978.

Foucault, Michel. *The History of Sexuality: An Introduction.* New York: Pantheon Books, 1979.

Friedman, Lawrence J. *Inventors of the Promised Land.* New York: Alfred A. Knopf, 1975.

Gilbert, Sandra M., and Gubar, Susan. *The Madwoman in the Attic: The Woman Writer and the Nineteenth-Century Literary Imagination.* New Haven: Yale University Press, 1979.

Glass, D. V., and Eversley, D. E. C. *Population in History: Essays in Historical Demography.* London: Edward Arnold Ltd., 1965.

Greven, Philip. *Four Generations: Population, Land, and Family in Colonial Andover, Massachusetts.* Ithaca: Cornell University Press, 1970.

————. *The Protestant Temperament: Patterns of Child-Rearing, Religious Experience, and the Self in Early America.* New York: New American Library, 1979.

Guttentag, Marcia, and Secord, Paul F. *Too Many Women? The Sex Ratio Question.* Beverly Hills, Calif.: Sage Publications, 1983.

Hajnal, J. "European Marriage Patterns in Perspective." In D. V. Glass and D. E. C. Eversley, *Population in History,* pp. 101–43. London: Edward Arnold Ltd., 1965.

Haller, John S., and Haller, Robin M. *The Physician and Sexuality in Victorian America.* Urbana: University of Illinois Press, 1974.

Havens, Elizabeth M. "Women, Work, and Wedlock: A Note on Female Marital Patterns in the United States." *American Journal of Sociology* 78, no. 4 (1973): 975–81.

Hersh, Blanche G. *The Slavery of Sex: Feminist-Abolitionists in America.* Urbana: University of Illinois Press, 1978.

Kerber, Linda K. *Women of the Republic: Intellect and Ideology in Revolutionary America.* Chapel Hill: University of North Carolina Press, 1980.

Kett, Joseph F. *Rites of Passage: Adolescence in America, 1790 to the Present.* New York: Basic Books, 1977.

Koehler, Lyle. *A Search for Power: The "Weaker Sex" in Seventeenth-Century New England.* Urbana: University of Illinois Press, 1980.

Lantz, Herman R.; Britton, Margaret; Schmitt, Raymond; and Snyder, Eloise. "Pre-Industrial Patterns in the Colonial Family in America: A Content Analysis of Colonial Magazines." *American Sociological Review* 33, nos. 3–4 (1968): 413–26.

Lasch, Christopher, and Taylor, William R. " 'Two Kindred Spirits': Sorority and Family in New England 1830–1845." *New England Quarterly* 36 (1963): 23–41.

Leach, William. *True Love and Perfect Union: The Feminist Reform of Sex and Society.* New York: Basic Books, 1980.

Modell, John; Furstenberg, Frank F.; and Strong, Douglas. "The Timing of Marriage in the Transition to Adulthood: Continuity and Change, 1860–1975." *American Journal of Sociology* 84 supplement (1978): 120–50.

Monahan, Thomas P. *The Pattern of Age at Marriage in the United States.* Philadelphia: Stephenson Brothers, 1951.

Nordhoff, Charles. *The Communistic Societies of the United States.* Reprint. New York: Dover Publications, 1966.

Norton, Mary B. *Liberty's Daughters: The Revolutionary Experience of American Women, 1750–1800.* Boston: Little, Brown, 1980.

Peterson, Nancy L. *Our Lives for Ourselves: Women Who Have Never Married.* New York: Putnam, 1981.

Potter, J. "The Growth of Population in America, 1700–1860." In D. V. Glass and D. E. C. Eversley, *Population in History,* pp. 631–88. London: Edward Arnold Ltd., 1965.

Rosenberg, Rosalind. *Beyond Separate Spheres: Intellectual Roots of Modern Feminism.* New Haven: Yale University Press, 1982.

Ryan, Mary P. *Cradle of the Middle Class: The Family in Oneida County, New York, 1790–1865.* Cambridge, Mass.: Cambridge University Press, 1981.

———. "A Woman's Awakening: Evangelical Religion and the Families of Utica, New York, 1800–1840." *American Quarterly* 30, no. 5 (Winter 1978): 602–23.

Scott, Anne F. "What, Then, is the American: This New Woman?" *Journal of American History* 65, no. 3 (December 1978): 679–703.

Sears, Hal D. *The Sex Radicals: Free Love in High Victorian America.* Lawrence: Regents Press of Kansas, 1977.

Smith, Daniel Scott. "Family Limitation, Sexual Control, and Domestic Feminism in Victorian America." In Hartman, Mary S., and Banner, Lois, eds. *Clio's Consciousness Raised: New Perspectives on the History of Women.* New York: Harper Torchbooks, 1974.

———. "Parental Power and Marriage Patterns: An Analysis of Historical Trends in Hingham, Massachusetts." *Journal of Marriage and the Family* 35 (August 1973): 419–28.

Smith, Daniel Scott, and Hindus, Michael. "Premarital Pregnancy in America 1640–1966." *Journal of Interdisciplinary History* 6 (1975): 537–71.

Smith-Rosenberg, Carroll. "The Female World of Love and Ritual: Relations between Women in Nineteenth-Century America." *Signs, Journal of Women in Culture and Society* 1, no. 1 (Autumn 1975): 1–29.

———. "The Hysterical Woman: Sex Roles and Role Conflict in Nineteenth-Century America," *Social Research* 39 (Winter 1972): 652–78.

———. "Puberty to Menopause: The Cycle of Femininity in Nineteenth-Century America." *Feminist Studies* 1 (1973): 58–72.

Smith-Rosenberg, Carroll, and Rosenberg, Charles. "The Female Animal: Medical and Biological Views of Woman and Her Role in Nineteenth-Century America." *Journal of American History* 60 (1973): 332–56.

Spreitzer, Elmer, and Riley, Lawrence E. "Factors Associated with Singlehood." *Journal of Marriage and the Family* 36, no. 3 (August 1974): 533–42.

Stone, Lawrence. *The Family, Sex and Marriage in England, 1500–1800.* New York: Harper & Row, 1977.

Taeuber, Conrad, and Taeuber, Irene B. *The Changing Population of the United States.* New York: John Wiley & Sons, 1958.

Uhlenberg, Peter R. "A Study of Cohort Life Cycles: Cohorts of Native Born Massachusetts Women, 1830–1920." *Population Studies* 23 (1969): 407–20.

Wallace, Anthony F. C. *Rockdale: The Growth of an American Village in the Early Industrial Revolution.* New York: Alfred A. Knopf, 1978.

Weinstein, Fred, and Platt, Gerald M. *The Wish to Be Free: Society, Psyche, and Value Change.* Berkeley: University of California Press, 1969.

Wells, Robert V. "Demographic Change and the Life Cycle of American Families." *Journal of Interdisciplinary History* 2, no. 12 (1972–73): 275–82.

———. "Family History and Demographic Transitions." *Journal of Social History* 9 (1975): 1–19.

————. "Family Size and Fertility Control in Eighteenth-Century America: A Study of Quaker Families." *Population Studies* 25 (1971): 73–82.

————. "Quaker Marriage Patterns in a Colonial Perspective." *William and Mary Quarterly* 29, no. 3 (1972): 415–42.

————. *Revolutions in Americans' Lives. A Demographic Perspective on the History of Americans, Their Families, and Their Society.* Westport, Conn.: Greenwood Press, 1982.

.Wilson, Margaret G. *The American Woman in Transition: The Urban Influence, 1870–1920.* Westport, Conn.: Greenwood Press, 1979.

Yasuba, Yasukichi. "Birth Rates of the White Population in the United States, 1800–1860." *The Johns Hopkins University Studies in Historical and Political Science* 79, no. 2 (1961): 7–198.

Unpublished Sources

Carlson, Jean M. F. "Current Attitudes toward Women and Men Who Never Marry." Ph. D. dissertation, University of Michigan, 1974.

Cudworth, Bessie M., and Jacobs, Miles R. "Emily Howland, 1827–1929: An Unforgettable Person." MS, Cornell University Library, ca. 1954.

Dixon, Ruth B. "The Social and Demographic Determinants of Marital Postponement and Celibacy: A Comparative Study." Ph. D. dissertation, University of California, Berkeley, 1970.

Dwyer, Ellen. " 'The Weaker Vessel': The Law Versus Social Realities in the Commitment of Women to Nineteenth-Century New York Asylums." Unpublished paper. Department of Forensic Studies, Indiana University. n.d.

Hawes, Rebecca W. "Maria Mitchell." Prepared for the Ramapo Valley chapter of the Daughters of the American Revolution, Ridgewood, New Jersey. Microfilm. American Philosophical Society, October 1911.

Herbig, Katherine L. "Friends for Freedom: The Lives and Careers of Sallie Holley and Caroline Putnam." Ph. D. dissertation, Claremont Graduate School, 1977.

Johns, Barbara A. "The Spinster in Five New England Regionalists." Ph. D. dissertation. University of Detroit, 1979.

Sahli, Nancy. "Elizabeth Blackwell, M.D. (1821–1910): A Biography." Ph.D. dissertation, University of Pennsylvania, 1974.

Tomes, Nancy, "The Persuasive Institution: Thomas Story Kirkbride and the Art of Asylum Keeping, 1841–1883." Ph. D. dissertation, University of Pennsylvania, 1978.

Wyman, Margaret. "Women in the American Realistic Novel, 1860–1893." Ph.D. dissertation. Radcliffe College, 1950.

Appendix
Selected List of Women Studied

		Birthplace	Vocation	Occupation
Rebecca Dickinson	1736–	Hatfield, Massachusetts		Seamstress
Hannah Adams	1755–1831	Medfield, Massachusetts	Philosophy and History	Author
Rebecca Noyes	1759–	Stonington, Connecticut		Lacemaker
Martha Rogers	1761–1840	Exeter, New Hampshire		
Elizabeth Smith	1773–1855	Worcester, Massachusetts		
Nancy Hinsdale	1775–1857	Pittsfield, Massachusetts	Education	Teacher
Mary Moody Emerson	1774–1863	Concord, Massachusetts	Moral Philosophy	
Elizabeth Fuller	1776–	Princeton, Massachusetts		
Samantha Barrett	178?–1830	New Hartford, Connecticut		
Caroline Plummer	1780–1854	Salem, Massachusetts	Philanthropy	
Rebecca Gratz	1781–1869	Philadelphia, Pennsylvania	Philanthropy	
Zeloda Barrett	1786–	New Hartford, Connecticut		
Eunice Callender	1786–	Boston, Massachusetts		
Eliza Leslie	1787–1858	Philadelphia, Pennsylvania	Writing	Publisher
Amanda Elliott	1787–1839	Guilford, Connecticut		
Elizabeth Sturgiss	1788–1873	Worcester, Massachusetts		
Catharine M. Sedgwick	1789–1867	Stockbridge, Massachusetts	Writing	Author
Antoinette Brevost	1789–1823	Pittsburgh, Pennsylvania	Education	Teacher
Lucy Richards	1792–1837	Oneida, New York	Religion	Missionary
Anne Hall	1792–1863	Pomfret, Connecticut	Art	
Sarah M. Grimké	1792–1873	Charleston, South Carolina	Reform	Teacher,
Antoinette Brown	1792–1823	Pittsburgh, Pennsylvania	Education	Teacher

Appendix

		Birthplace	Vocation	Occupation
Julia E. Smith	1792–1886	Glastonbury, Connecticut	Scholarship	Farmer
Mary Davenport May	1793–1869	Boston, Massachusetts		
Caira Robbins	1794–1881	Lexington, Massachusetts		
Frances M. Caulkins	1795–1869	New London, Connecticut	History	
Cynthia Farrar	1795–1862	Marlborough, New Hampshire	Religion	Missionary
Margaretta A. Peale	1795–1882	Philadelphia, Pennsylvania	Art	
Charlotte A. May	1795–1873	Boston, Massachusetts		
Sophia Smith	1796–1870	Hatfield, Massachusetts	Philanthropy	
Mary Lyon	1797–1849	Buckland, Massachusetts	Education	Teacher
Abby H. Smith	1797–1878	Glastonbury, Connecticut	Scholarship	Farmer
Lucinda Read	1797–	Greensboro, Vermont		
Catharine Seely	1799–1838	Darien, Connecticut		Teacher
Catharine E. Beecher	1800–78	New London, Connecticut	Education	Teacher
Sarah M. Peale	1800–95	Philadelphia, Pennsylvania	Art	
Sarah Pugh	1800–84	Philadelphia, Pennsylvania	Reform	Teacher
Deborah Roberts	1801–38	Darien, Connecticut		
Dorothea Dix	1802–86	Hampden, Maine	Reform	Nurse
Abigail Kimber	1804–71	Kimberton, Pennsylvania	Science	Teacher
Elizabeth P. Peabody	1804–94	Concord, Massachusetts	Education	Teacher
Harriot Hunt	1805–75	Boston, Massachusetts	Medicine	Physician
Phebe Smith	1807–32	Lithgow, New York		
Catharine Storer	1807–85	Portland, Maine		Teacher
Caroline Weston	1808–82	Weymouth, Massachusetts	Reform	Teacher
Mary S. Gilpin	1810–91	Brandywine Valley, Delaware	Education	Teacher
Mary Louise Burgin	1811–91	Allentown, New Hampshire	Education	Teacher
Frances E. Gray	1812–	Roxbury, Massachusetts		Teacher
Mary Young Bean	1812–91	Keene, New Hampshire		Teacher
Anne Warren Weston	1812–90	Weymouth, Massachusetts	Reform	Teacher
Rachel W. Stearns	1813–	Greenfield, Massachusetts	Moral Philosophy	Teacher
Elizabeth Wallace	1813–80	Troy, New York		Teacher
Anna Hart Manwaring	1813–1890	New London, Connecticut	Education	Teacher

		Birthplace	Vocation	Occupation
Mary Grew	1813–96	Philadelphia, Pennsylvania	Reform	Teacher
Clementina Smith	1814–84	Brandywine Valley, Delaware	Moral Philosophy	
Deborah Weston	1814–	Weymouth, Massachusetts		Teacher
Myrtilla Miner	1815–64	Brookfield, New York	Reform	Teacher
Fidelia Fiske	1816–64	Shelburne, Massachusetts	Religion	Missionary, Teacher
Anna Blackwell	1816–1900	Counterslip, England		Journalist
Ann Ayres	1816–96	New York, New York	Religion	Episcopal Sister
Charlotte Cushman	1816–76	Boston, Massachusetts		Actress
Sallie Holley	1817–93	Canandaigua, New York	Reform	Antislavery lecturer
Harriette A. Dellaye	1817–97	Plymouth, New York	Philanthropy	Teacher
Sarah Everett Hale	1817–51	Boston, Massachusetts		Author
Maria Mitchell	1818–89	Nantucket, Massachusetts	Science	Teacher
Marian Blackwell	1818–97	Bristol, England		
Harriet Smith	1818–1905	Brandywine Valley, Delaware	Moral Philosophy	
Mariann Lewis	1819–66	Media, Pennsylvania		
Laura Lovell	1819–69	Bridgewater, Massachusetts		Teacher
Mary Olive A. Hunt	1819–1908	Gilmanton, New Hampshire	Medicine	Physician
Lucretia P. Hale	1820–1900	Boston, Massachusetts	Writing	
Susan B. Anthony	1820–1906	Adams, Massachusetts	Reform	Teacher, Lecturer, Journalist
Alice Cary	1820–71	Cincinnati, Ohio	Poetry	Author
Elizabeth Blackwell	1821–1910	Bristol, England	Medicine	Physician
Graceanna Lewis	1821–1912	Media, Pennsylvania	Science	Teacher, Illustrator
Clara Barton	1821–1912	North Oxford, Massachusetts	Reform	Nurse
Lucia Weston	1822–61	Weymouth, Massachusetts		
Lucy Chase	1822–1909	Worcester, Massachusetts	Reform	Teacher
Mary Reed	1823–	Philadelphia, Pennsylvania	Education	Teacher
Phoebe Cary	1824–71	Cincinnati, Ohio	Poetry	
Lucy Larcom	1824–93	Beverly, Massachusetts	Poetry	Teacher
Elizabeth Lewis	1824–63	Media, Pennsylvania		
Emily E. Parsons	1824–80	Boston, Massachusetts	Social Work	Nurse

		Birthplace	Vocation	Occupation
Laura Towne	1825–1901	Philadelphia, Pennsylvania	Reform	Nurse
Caroline F. Putnam	1826–1917	Farmersville, New York	Reform	Teacher
Elizabeth C. Bridges	1826–56	Salem, Massachusetts		Teacher
Emily Blackwell	1826–1911	Bristol, England	Reform	Physician
Emily Howland	1827–1929	Sherwood, New York	Reform	Teacher,
Ellen Collins	1828–1912	New York, New York	Reform	Landlord
Sarah E. Blackwell	1828–1901	Bristol, England	Art	
Julia Colman	1828–1909	Northampton, Massachusetts	Reform	Temperance author
Lucretia Crocker	1829–86	Boston, Massachusetts	Reform	Teacher
Abigail Williams May	1829–88	Boston, Massachusetts	Reform	Teacher
Eliza E. Chase	1829–96	Worcester, Massachusetts	Reform	Teacher
Harriet Hosmer	1830–1908	Watertown, Massachusetts	Art	Sculptor
Sarah E. Doyle	1830–1922	Providence, Rhode Island	Club work	
Emily Dickinson	1830–86	Amherst, Massachusetts	Poetry	
Anna Hallowell	1831–1905	Philadelphia, Pennsylvania	Reform	
Mary Spear	1831–	Newton, Massachusetts		Teacher
Louisa M. Alcott	1832–88	Concord, Massachusetts	Writing	Seamstress, Governess, Author, Teacher
Abigail F. Spear	1833–1927	Newton, Massachusetts		
Susan Hale	1833–1910	Boston, Massachusetts	Art	
Mary Abigail Dodge	1833–96	Hamilton, Massachusetts	Writing	Teacher, Governess, Journalist
Lavinia Dickinson	1833–99	Amherst, Massachusetts		
Fidelia Bridges	1834–1923	Salem, Massachusetts	Artist	
Caroline Spear	183?–	Newton, Massachusetts		
Sarah E. Chase	1836–1915	Worcester, Massachusetts	Reform	Teacher
Sarah Fuller	1836–1927	Weston, Massachusetts	Education	Teacher of deaf
Cornelia Hancock	1840–1927	Hancock's Bridge, New Jersey	Reform	Social Worker, Hotel Keeper, Nurse
Frances E. Willard	1839–89	Churchville, New York	Temperance Reform	Teacher, Administrator
Anna Dickinson	1842–1932	Philadelphia, Pennsylvania	Reform	Actress, Orator
Elizabeth Spear	1842–1934	Newton, Massachusetts	Education	Teacher
Sarah J. Stoughton	1848–71	Jaffrey, New Hampshire	Writing	

Index